Errors in English
and
Ways to Correct Them

About the Author

Harry Shaw is well known as an editor, writer, lecturer, and teacher. For a number of years he was director of the Workshops in Composition at New York University and teacher of classes in advanced writing at Columbia, at both of which institutions he has done graduate work. He has worked with large groups of writers in the Washington Square Writing Center at NYU and has been a lecturer in writers' conferences at Indiana University and the University of Utah and lecturer in, and director of, the Writers' Conference in the Rocky Mountains sponsored by the University of Colorado. In 1969, Mr. Shaw was awarded the honorary degree of Doctor of Letters by Davidson College, his alma mater.

He has been managing editor and editorial director of *Look*, editor at Harper and Brothers, senior editor and vice-president of E. P. Dutton and Co., editor-in-chief of Henry Holt & Co., and director of publications for Barnes & Noble, Inc.; he is now an editor at W. W. Norton & Co., Inc. He has contributed widely to many popular and scholarly national magazines and is the author or co-author of a number of books in the fields of English composition and literature, among them *Spell It Right!* and *Punctuate It Right!*, Barnes & Noble publications.

Errors in English

and

Ways to Correct Them

Second Edition

Harry Shaw

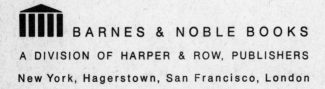

BARNES & NOBLE BOOKS

A DIVISION OF HARPER & ROW, PUBLISHERS

New York, Hagerstown, San Francisco, London

Table of Contents

Foreword

In our society few people fail to realize the importance of using good English. The late Will Rogers was never more humorous than when he remarked, "A lot of people who don't say *ain't*, ain't eatin'." Most of us, however, are properly concerned when others react unfavorably to mistakes we make in expressing ourselves. We understand that our use of language represents a significant form of our behavior.

By learning basic good usage we can concentrate on what we wish to communicate and stop worrying about detailed methods of doing so. Freed from restraint and anxiety, we can reveal our thoughts to others in the natural, easy way we should speak and write our language, but all too often do not.

This book will help you to improve your use of language by emphasis upon those common errors, and only those, which hinder communication and impede thought. Its concern with diction, sentence structure, spelling, punctuation, grammar, and pronunciation is directed not to the niceties of usage but to those frequent errors which cause trouble, chagrin, or embarrassment. It will serve not only as a home-study guide but also a reference book for office and home; it is detailed enough to solve most, or all, of the everyday problems which come up in your speaking and writing.

But if you do wish further information on any item in this book, or if what you find here stimulates your interest in additional study, many excellent volumes are readily available. For example, if you wish to pursue the study of English grammar in greater detail than it is represented here, secure a copy of *English Grammar* by George O. Curme. Or if you wish to perfect your ability to spell, try a full-length work on the subject such as *Spell It Right!* by the author of the book you are now reading.

For assistance in preparing this dictionary I am indebted to many people. Much that it contains is based upon problems which I have noted over the years in the usage and practices of fellow workers in various offices and in the writing and speaking of students whom I have had in class. I am indebted to many linguists and writers of other books in this field, but I wish especially to thank Professor George S. Wykoff, of Purdue University, and the late Paul Roberts of San Jose State College. Both were gifted teachers and shrewd and careful observers of language usage. Not only from prolonged talks with each have I profited, but from the writings of each I have taken material and adapted it for the purposes of this dictionary and guide. To both Professor Wykoff and Dr. Roberts I express hearty but totally inadequate thanks.

H.S.

Part I

Guide to Correct Usage

Words are but wise men's counters—they do but reckon by them; but they are the money of fools.

THOMAS HOBBES, *Leviathan*

To be sure, the English language is a changing and growing thing. All its users have, of course, a perceptible effect upon it. But in changing and growing it needs no contrived help from chitchat columnists or advertising writers or comic strip artists or television speakers. It will evolve nicely by itself. If anything, it requires protection from influences that try to push it too fast. There is need, not for those who would halt its progress altogether, but for those who can keep a gentle foot on the brake and a guiding hand on the steering wheel. . . .

THEODORE M. BERNSTEIN, *Watch Your Language*

Part I
Guide to Correct Usage

"I knew what I had in mind but I couldn't seem to get him to understand . . ." "I know what I mean but I can't seem to express it . . ." "It was a good, er—" "How can I say this to make you understand?"

These phrases sound familiar to all of us, don't they? Daily, even hourly, we have to express some thought which seems difficult to put into words. The problem is understandable: all our thinking is done in terms of concepts, words. Since we cannot help thinking almost constantly, we are forever using words in our thoughts or trying to select words to convey our ideas to other people. Thinking and diction (the choice and use of words) are inseparable.

When you enter into a conversation or write a letter or report, you *have* to have something to say and some purpose and interest in expressing that something, whatever it is. But in trying to find the words to convey what you have in mind you may often feel the inadequacy of your vocabulary. All of us have had the experience of not being able to find the right words to get across our meaning, of being misunderstood, of finding that we don't make ourselves clear. Thought and language are mutually dependent. That is, we cannot think without using words and, as Oliver Wendell Holmes once said, "A word is the skin of a living thought." Therefore, by choosing and using the most correct and effective words we possibly can, we express our ideas more clearly to others and simultaneously make our thinking clearer, more logical, more effective.

3

A person's choice and use of words tells as much about him or her as do manners, dress, and general deportment. Your choice of words is not wholly accidental. Listen to someone speak for a few moments, or read something which he has written, and you will learn much about the kind of person he is. Don't we often say of some acquaintance, "He talks like a lawyer," or an accountant, or businessman, or sailor? Some two thousand years ago, Publius wrote a maxim as true today as it was then: "Speech is a mirror of the soul; as a man speaks, so is he."

Because it is not easy to think clearly and precisely, it is difficult to achieve good diction. Each of us knows that our lack of mastery of words prevents our fully possessing hundreds of feelings and impressions which come to us from our thinking and observation. But although most of us promise to "do something" about our vocabularies, most of us are unwilling to make a real and concerted effort to do so.

Do not try to fool yourself: there is no simple, painless way to acquire and master a good vocabulary. Several books now on the market, some of them quite popular, promise easy short cuts to mastery, but these books are harmful and misleading. Occasionally referring to your dictionary will help a little, but not much. Sitting down to memorize words from your dictionary is almost worthless. The best and most direct attack upon the problem is to learn to use correctly and effectively the words which we already have in our potential vocabularies.

Authorities are agreed that each of us has three vocabularies. Our *active*, or *speaking*, vocabulary comes first. This comprises our most productive word stock, the words which we use daily in our speaking. This relatively small number of words we can learn to use with greater precision. Second, there is our *writing* vocabulary. This is also active in that we have frequent occasion to use its word supply in our writing; it contains some words which we do not constantly use in speech. In addition to these two active, or productive, vocabularies, each of us has a *potential*, or *recognition*, vocabulary. By means of this potential vocabulary, the largest of the three, we can understand speakers and can read and understand books, magazines, and newspapers. But in our reading and listening we encounter many words which we recognize and of which we have some understanding, possibly from the context, but which we would be unable to use in our own speaking and writing. Until we use such words, however—put them into circulation, that is—they are not really ours.

To get words from our potential into our active vocabularies requires consistent effort, but it is the best way to begin vocabulary improvement. Why? Because words in a recognition vocabulary are already in our consciousness; they are partly ours. Their values, although still vague to us, can be made exact and accurate. Furthermore, quite likely they are words which we shall *want* in our vocabularies. We have probably come across them time and again; they are not unusual and high-sounding words. They are words that have *use* value. Mastering them will help us to avoid the mistake of "swallowing the dictionary," a useless task which fails because it has no direct connection with our needs.

Although it is a first and important step, enlarging your vocabulary is but one part of the problem of diction. This problem resembles that of managing a store. The storekeeper has to keep replenishing his stock, but he also has to get rid of certain items which have proved unsatisfactory. He has to know what stock will be salable to what customers at what seasons of the year. He tries to keep in stock all the items for which there will be a demand, but frequently he has to place a "rush" order with a wholesaler for something not on his shelves or in his warehouse.

Similarly, we stock our word supplies as best we can. But we keep replenishing our stock; we cease using words and expressions when we find others that are more precise or more effective; we find that certain words will "do" on some one occasion but not on another; we constantly find that, no matter how large our vocabularies, we have to put in "rush" orders to dictionaries and wordbooks.

This is the three-way approach to diction: first, acquire a good stock of words; second, stop using certain words and expressions which do not measure up to accepted standards; third, select from your stock or from your dictionary those words—and only those words—which will most clearly, correctly, and forcefully express what you have in mind.

In this "Guide to Correct Usage," approximately 2,000 words and expressions are commented upon in terms of their correctness and suitability. Mastering the pages which follow immediately will not solve all your problems with diction but doing so will take you a giant step along the way.

WORD CHOICE

A, an. The choice between *a* and *an* depends on the initial sound of the word which follows. *An* should be used before a vowel sound, *a* before a word beginning with a consonant sound. See *Vowel* and *Consonant* in Part V. (*An* adult, *a* picture; *an* honor, *a* hopeful remark.)

Abandon, desert, forsake, leave, quit. *Abandon* implies leaving a person or thing as a final measure (to *abandon* one's home) or as a rejection of responsibility. (He *abandoned* his friend.) *Desert* emphasizes leaving in violation of one's obligation or oath. (The soldier *deserted* his post.) *Forsake* stresses giving up someone or something formerly held dear (to *forsake* one's only child). *Leave* means "to allow or cause to remain." (We shall *leave* some food on the table.) *Quit* means "to stop." (He *quit* smoking cigarettes.)

Ability, capacity. *Ability* means the power to do something, physical or mental (*ability* to speak in public). *Capacity* is the ability to hold, contain, or absorb (a room filled to *capacity*).

Abjure, adjure. *Abjure* means "to renounce"; *adjure* means "to entreat" or "to appeal." (He *abjured* all rights to citizenship. The minister *adjured* the congregation to be quiet.)

Abominably. See *Awful.*

About. This commonly used adverb has several meanings and shades of meaning, but all develop from the idea of "around," "on every side," "here and there" (look *about* you; travel *about*). *About* is colloquial when used in the sense of "almost" and "all but." In formal English, avoid such a statement as "We are *about* ready to leave."

Abridged. See *Unabridged.*

Absolutely. This word means "completely," "perfectly," "wholly." In addition to being greatly overused as an intensifier, it is wordy in such an expression as "*absolutely* complete." Never use *absolutely* or any other such modifier with words like *complete, perfect, unique,* etc. See *Unique.*

Accent, ascent, assent. *Accent* means emphasis in, or manner of, speaking (*accent* on the first syllable, an English *accent*); *ascent* means a rising, a going up (the *ascent* of Mount Hood); *assent* means consent or agreement. (Give your *assent* to my request.)

Accept, except. *Accept* means "to receive" or "to agree with"; *except* means "to omit" or "to exempt." (I will not *accept* your offer. The men were punished but Tom was *excepted*.)

Access, excess. *Access* mean "admittance" or "way of approach"; *excess* means "surpassing limits." (He has *access* to the room. This amount is in *excess* of the budget.)

Accidently. This is an illiteracy. (See *Illiteracies* in Part V.) The word should be *accidentally*.

Accompanied by, with. *By* is used in this construction unless there is an element of combining or supplementing. (The player was *accompanied by* a group of fans. John *accompanied* his remarks *with* a grin.)

According to, with. Idiomatic usage (see *Idiom* in Part V) calls for the use of *to*. (He took the medicine *according to* directions.)

Accord with, to. The idiomatic preposition is *with* in this construction. (I am in *accord with* your suggestion.)

Accuse of, with. Idiom (see *Idiom* in Part V) requires the use of *of* in this phrase. (He was *accused of* the crime.)

Acme, climax. *Acme* means "the highest point." (His recital was the *acme* of perfection.) *Climax* implies a scale of ascending values and is applied to the highest point in interest, force, intensity, etc. (The *climax* of the day's events was the display of fireworks.)

Acquire. See *Get*.

Acquitted of, from. The idiomatic preposition is *of*. (He was *acquitted of* the charge.)

Act, action. An *act* is a deed, a thing done. (This is an *act* of mercy.) *Action* is closely related in meaning to *act* but more exactly implies the doing of something, of being in motion or operation. (His *action* was courageous.)

Actual. See *Real*.

A.D., B.C. *Anno domini*, the year of the Lord, is represented by the letters A.D. "Before Christ" is abbreviated to B.C.

Ad. This is a colloquial abbreviation, much used, for *advertisement*. In formal writing, avoid such abbreviations as *ad*, *auto* for *automobile*, *phone* for *telephone*, *exam* for *examination*, etc.

Adapt, adept, adopt. To *adapt* is "to adjust" or "to make suitable." (He will *adapt* himself to his environment.) *Adept* means "skilled." (He is *adept* in shuffling cards.) To *adopt* is "to accept" or "to take as one's own." (We shall *adopt* your proposal. We *adopted* the little child.)

Addicted, devoted. The former has a bad, or unfavorable, sense of "given to a practice, or habit." *Devoted* has a favorable sense of being attached, or given over, to someone or something. (He is *addicted* to drugs. Sue was *devoted* to the theater.)

Adept. See *Adapt*.

Adjure. See *Abjure*.

Ad lib. This verb, meaning "to improvise," "to extemporize," is both overused and colloquial. It is derived from the Latin phrase *ad libitum* meaning "at pleasure" and is appropriately used in music to mean "freely." Avoid using *ad lib* to mean adding words and gestures not in the script or not intended to be said or otherwise expressed.

Admission, admittance. *Admission* means "allowing to enter." (He sought *admission* to the palace.) *Admittance* means "right of entry" or "being admitted." (*Admittance* is by invitation only.)

Admit, allow, concede, confess. *Admit* means "to permit to enter." (This ticket will *admit* two people.) *Allow* means "to let," "to permit." (*Allow* me to join you.) *Concede* means "to yield," "to acknowledge." (He *conceded* victory to his opponent.) *Confess* means "to acknowledge a fault, crime," etc., or "to declare one's faith in." (I *confess* the fault is mine. The minister *confessed* his faith in God.)

Admittance. See *Admission*.

Adopt. See *Adapt*.

Advance planning. This is a wordy phrase which should be avoided, in both speech and writing. A basic meaning of *plan* is "to foresee," "to devise ahead." Hence, *advance* is superfluous and should be omitted.

Adverse, averse. The former means "hostile," "opposed." (They held an *adverse* opinion of the plan.) *Averse* means "unwilling" or "reluctant." (The mother was *averse* to giving permission.)

Adverse to, against. The correct idiomatic expression is *adverse to*, not *adverse against*. (The doctor is *adverse to* our proposal.)

Advise. This word, meaning "to counsel," "to give advice to," is overused in business letters and other forms of communication for "tell," "inform." (I am pleased to *tell* you—not *advise*—that the order has been received.)

Adviser, advisor. Both spellings are correct. *Adviser* was formerly more common, but *advisor* is being increasingly used now—perhaps from analogy with *advisory*. Each means "one who advises."

Affect, effect. As a verb, *affect* means "to influence" or "to assume." (This book has *affected* my thinking.) *Effect* as a verb means "to cause" and as a noun means "result." (Your good work will *effect* an increase in your bonus. This play will have a good *effect* on youth.)

Affectation, affection, affecting. The first term means "insincerely displaying or pretending a quality or trait" and refers to artificial behavior. (He had an *affectation* of speech.) *Affection* is a mental state or disposition. (I regard all my friends with *affection*.) *Affecting* means "touching," "full of pathos." (The ragged children were an *affecting* sight.)

Affinity, infinity. These two words have a superficial resemblance but entirely different meanings. *Affinity* implies "close relationship or connection" and involves similarity of structure or some kind of resemblance. The idea of connection can be strong enough to involve *attraction* as when we say that two people have an *affinity* for each other or that small boys have an *affinity* for dirt. *Infinity* means "endless or unlimited space, time, distance, quantity, etc." (Rays of light originating in *infinity* are considered parallel.)

After all is said and done. An overused and weak expression; a cliché.

Aggravate. This word actually means "to intensify," "to increase something unpleasant," or "to make worse." Used colloquially, *aggravate* means "to annoy or provoke." (Standard usage: Sneezing *aggravated* his wound. The mosquito *annoyed*—not *aggravated*—me.)

Agree. This word is correctly used with different prepositions in various idiomatic expressions. (Standard usage: *agree to* a proposal; *agree on* a plan; *agree with* a person.)

Aim to prove, aim at proving. The former expression is idiomatically correct. (I *aim to prove* my point.) *Aim at proving* is often heard but is considered either colloquial or dialectal.

Ain't. This contraction is considered illiterate or dialectal and is cautioned against in standard English, both written and spoken. The word, which stands for *am not*, is often used even by educated people, but it has not been accepted in the sense that *isn't* (for *is not*), *aren't* (for *are not*), *weren't* (for *were not*), etc., have been.

Air, airs. The former means the mixture of gases which we all breathe, and the latter refers to "affected manners and graces." Each is a good word suitable in standard English. Avoid such slangy or colloquial phrases, however, as *give him the air* (to dismiss, reject), *take the air* (to go out or away), *up in the air* (angry, excited, upset), and *to put on airs*.

Aisle, isle. The former means a "passageway" or "corridor." (The bride walked slowly down the *aisle*.) *Isle* means "land surrounded by water." (Popolec is a deserted *isle*.)

Alibi. Used colloquially to mean "an excuse or any kind of defense," the word precisely and correctly should be used to imply "a plea or fact of having been elsewhere when an offense was committed." *Alibi* is often used in the loose sense mentioned above and is now a trite and jaded expression.

Alien, alienate, alienist. An *alien* is a foreign-born resident in a country who has not become a naturalized citizen and, generally, is a word used to mean a "foreigner" or "outsider." *Alienate* is a verb whose most common meaning is "to estrange," "to make unfriendly." (His rude behavior *alienated* all of his friends.) An *alienist* is a medical doctor, a psychiatrist who specializes in mental diseases; the term *alienist* is used principally in legal cases.

Allay, alley, alleys, allies, ally. *Allay* means "to rest" or "to relieve." (The drug will *allay* your pain.) *Alley* means a "narrow passage," and *alleys* is the plural. (This *alley* leads [These *alleys* lead] to the street.) *Allies* means "partners," "comrades," and *ally* is the singular. *Ally* is also a verb meaning "to join." (The *Allies* defeated their common enemy. England has sometimes been an *ally* of the United States. Don't *ally* yourself with that group.)

All in all. This is an idiomatic expression which is entirely correct but which has been used so often as to become a cliché. Avoid its overuse.

Allow. See *Admit*.

All ready. See *Already*.

All right, alright. The former expression is correct but has been overworked to mean "satisfactory" or "very well." *Alright* is analogous to *altogether* and *already* (both standard words), but itself is not yet an acceptable word in standard usage.

All the farther, all the faster, etc. These and similar expressions are considered nonstandard and objectionable when used to mean "as far as," "as fast as," etc. (This is *as far as*—not *all the farther*—I'm going.)

All together. See *Altogether*.

Allude, elude. The former means "to make reference to." (The speaker *alluded* to the warm weather.) *Elude* means "to escape," "to evade." (The criminal *eluded* the police for several days.)

Allusion, delusion, illusion. *Allusion* means "a reference to." (He made an *allusion* to Shakespeare.) A *delusion* is a belief which is contrary to fact or reality. (He is under the *delusion* that he is a war hero.) *Illusion* means "a deceptive appearance." (This is an optical *illusion*.)

All ways, always. The first means "without exception," the second "continually, forever." (He is fitted for the work in *all ways*. He will *always* be a generous person.) See *Generally always*.

Ally. See *Allay*.

Almost. See *Most*.

Alongside of. A colloquial expression. Omit the *of*. (The dinghy lay *alongside*—not *alongside of*—the steamer.)

Along these lines. A good expression which has become a cliché. Try to find a fresher phrase.

Aloud, out loud. The former is considered more nearly standard English. *Out loud* is thought to be both unidiomatic and colloquial.

Already, all ready. The former means "earlier," "previously." (When she arrived, her friend had *already* left.) *All ready* means "all are ready." (They will leave when they are *all ready*.)

Altar, alter. *Altar* is a noun which means "place of worship." (He knelt at the *altar*.) The second expression is a verb meaning "to change." (I intend to *alter* this dress.)

Alternate, alternative. *Alternate* means "occurring by turns, every other one." (We held shop meetings on *alternate* Thursdays.) An *alternative* is one of two ideas or things that are mutually exclusive. (I had no *alternative* but to go.) The plural of *alternative* is *alternatives*.

Altogether, all together. *Altogether* means "wholly," "completely." (He was not *altogether* pleased with his purchase.) *All together* means "all in company" or "everybody in one place." (The family was *all together* for Christmas.)

Alumnus, alumna. An *alumnus* is a male graduate; an *alumna* is a woman graduate. Respective plurals are *alumni* and *alumnae*. To refer to graduates of a school as *alum* or *alums* is colloquial or slangy.

A.M., a.m., P.M., p.m.   The first expression, spelled with either capitals or lowercase letters, means "before noon" (from the Latin *ante meridiem*). P.M. and *p.m.* mean "noon to midnight" (from the Latin *post meridiem*). Both are clear indicators of time. After them, do not use such expressions as "in the morning," etc. Figures, not words, are conventionally used. (We left at 9 a.m.) See *This morning*.

Amiable, amicable.   These words are closely related in meaning; they are derived from the same Latin word meaning "friendly." *Amiable* implies "sweetness of temper," "kindheartedness," "good-naturedly obliging." *Amicable* has somewhat similar meanings but stresses the idea of "at peace," "not disposed to quarrel." (Mr. Jacks is a kindly and *amiable* employer. All of my fellow employees are *amicable*.)

Among, between.   The former shows the relation of more than two objects; *between* refers to only two or to more than two when each object is considered in relation to others. (We distributed the candy *among* the six children. We distributed the candy *between* Jill and Gray. Understanding *between* nations is essential.)

Amoral.   See *Unmoral*.

Amount, number.   The former is used of things involving a unified mass—bulk, weight, or sums. (What is the *amount* of the bill?) *Number* is used of things which can be counted in individual units. (I have a *number* of hats and coats.)

And etc.   A redundant expression. *Etc.* (which see) is an abbreviation for Latin *et cetera*, meaning "and so forth." Omit the *and* in *and etc.*

And how!   A slang expression indicating strong feeling or approval. Avoid its use in standard English.

And/or.   Primarily a business and legal expression, *and/or* is objected to by purists and other especially fastidious users of English. It is somewhat vague and also has business connotations objectionable to some people. In formal English you should avoid using it. But it is a useful timesaver.

And which, and who. Correct sentence structure provides that these phrases should appear in clauses only if preceded by clauses which also contain *which* or *who*. (This is the first book *which* I bought *and which* I treasure—*not* This is the first book I bought *and which* . . .) See *"And which" construction*, in Part II, "Guide to Correct Sentence Structure."

Angel, angle. The first means "a celestial being"; the latter is "a geometric figure." (You are more devil than *angel*. The road turns at a sharp *angle*.) *Angle* is also overused as a colloquial substitute for "aspect" or "point of view."

Angry with, at. Idiomatically, one is angry *with*, not *at*, a person. (See *Mad*.) But you may be *angry about* an event or situation and *angry at* an animal or inanimate object.

Ante-, anti-. The first of these prefixes means "before" or "prior." The second means "against" or "opposite." (Wait in the *ante-room* for me. Do you have an *antidote* for this poison?) See *Ante-, anti-* in Part III, "Guide to Correct Spelling."

Anxious, eager. In precise use, *anxious* implies "anxiety," "worry," "uneasiness." (I am *anxious* about your health.) *Eager* means "keenly desirous," "wanting to." (I was *eager* to hear the news from home.)

Any. This useful word is colloquial when it is used to mean "at all." (He did not work *at all*—not *any*—this week.)

Anyway, anyways. *Anyway* means "in any case," "anyhow." (She was planning to go *anyway*.) *Anyways* has the same meaning as *anyway*, but it is considered either dialectal or colloquial when used to mean "in any case." (*Anyway*—not *anyways*—I want to go, too.)

Anywheres, nowheres, somewheres. These expressions are illiteracies. Omit the final *s* from each word: *anywhere, nowhere, somewhere*.

Apparent, evident. These words are closely related in meaning, but the former suggests the use of deductive reasoning. (It is *apparent* that Smith will win the election.) *Evident* implies the existence of external signs of some sort. (His disappointment was *evident*.)

Appraise, apprise. *Appraise* means "to judge" or "to estimate." (The auctioneer *appraised* the furniture.) *Apprise* means "to inform" or "to notify." (A newspaper account *apprised* me of the tragedy.)

Apprehend, comprehend. The former means "to seize," "to capture." (The sheriff will *apprehend* the forger.) *Comprehend* means "to understand." (I did not *comprehend* the lecturer's remarks.)

Apprise. See *Appraise*.

Apt, liable, likely. *Apt* suggests fitness or tendency. (She is *apt* in arithmetic.) *Liable* implies exposure to something burdensome or disadvantageous. (You are *liable* for damages.) *Likely* means "expected," "probable." (We are *likely* to have snow next month.) *Likely* is the most commonly used of the three terms. Distinction in meaning has broken down somewhat, but *apt* and *liable* used in the sense of "probable" are considered colloquial or dialectal.

Are, or, our. These three simple words are often confused. *Are* is a form of the verb "to be." (Where *are* you going?) *Or* is a conjunction suggesting an alternative. (Do you wish to go *or* stay?) *Our* is a form of the pronoun "we." (Where is *our* car?)

Aren't. This word is a contraction of *are not*. (We *aren't* going today.) *Are* is a plural form, so that *aren't* I is not a correct expression, since I is singular. Some affected speakers and writers tend to use *aren't* I in place of *ain't* I. Neither expression is recommended.

Arms of Morpheus. In Greek mythology, Morpheus was the god of dreams and son of the god of sleep. The first million people to write or say "in the arms of Morpheus" instead of "asleep" used an effective figure of speech, but the phrase is now worn out.

Around. This word is sometimes used colloquially for *about*. (There were *about*—not *around*—twenty people in the office.) See *Round*.

Arrant. See *Errand*.

Artistic temperament. This expression has been used so often and so inexactly that it has lost whatever force it originally had. Avoid all such overused expressions.

As. This is one of the most overworked words in the English language. It is a perfectly good word, but *since, because,* and *when* are more exact and effective conjunctions. (*Since*—not *As*—it was snowing, we decided to stay indoors.) *As* is also often misused in place of *that* or *whether.* (I doubt *that*—not *as*—I can go.) In negative comparisons, some writers prefer *so . . . as* to *as . . . as.* (He is not *so* heavy *as* his brother.) In general, use *as* sparingly; nearly always a more exact and effective word can be found.

Ascared. An illiteracy. The word is *scared. Ascared* is sometimes properly used in reporting dialectal speech, but not otherwise.

Ascent. See *Accent.*

As far as. See *All the farther.*

As good as, if not better than. A correctly phrased but awkward and mixed comparison. A statement will be more effective when "if not better" is put at the end. (*Awkward:* My work is *as good as, if not better than,* your work. *Improved:* My work is *as good as* yours, *if not better.*)

As if, like. In standard English, the subjunctive mood is used after *as if* and *as though.* (He talked *as if* [or *as though*] he *were* a rich man.) Clauses of comparison are introduced by *as* and *as if* in standard English. (He climbed the tree *as* a monkey would.) In colloquial English, *like* is often used in clauses of comparison and the use of *like* as a conjunction has greatly increased in the past few years: e.g., It looks *like* he would try harder. Standard English restricts *like* to its use as a preposition, with no verb following. (He looks *like* a monkey.) Be on guard when you have occasion to form a comparison; in formal English do not use *like* as a conjunction.

Ask a question. Such expressions as "I want to ask you a question" are common, but *ask a question* is really a wordy phrase. The word *question* means "query" and implies asking something. Omit either *ask* or *question.* (I want to *ask* you. I want to *question* you.)

As luck would have it. This phrase is trite. Try to find a fresher way to express your meaning. For example, you could say "by chance" or "by coincidence."

As per. An overworked business expression for "in accordance with" or "according to." Often the expression itself, as well as its less tired equivalents, is not needed at all.

As regards. A wordy and overworked expression for *concerning* or *about*. It is an example of jargon (see *Jargon* in Part V) and should be avoided. See *In regards to*.

Assay, essay. The former means "a test" or "to test." (The chemist started to *assay* the mineral.) *Essay* means "to attempt," "an attempt," or a literary effort. (Will you *essay* this difficult task? This is a delightfully written *essay*.)

Assent. See *Accent*.

Assure, ensure, insure. *Assure* means "to convince," "to guarantee." (I *assure* you of my good intentions.) *Ensure* and *insure* mean "to make certain" or "to guard against loss." (Please *insure* this package.) *Insure* is the preferred spelling.

At. This is a preposition with many meanings, among them "on," "in," "near." *At* is preferable to the preposition *to* in such expressions as "We ate dinner *at* home" and "He is *at* the office." The expression *at-home* is a compound, a noun meaning "an informal reception." (Mr. and Mrs. Stanley Houston are having an *at-home*—or will be *at home*—today.)

At about. This wordy phrase should be avoided in standard English. (The bus was scheduled to arrive *at*—not *at about*—sunset.)

At (a) loss for words. Another overworked expression. See *Triteness* in Part V.

At one fell swoop. This is a cliché. Avoid using it, since it will seem flat to many readers.

Attain. See *Get*.

Attend to, tend to. The former is more idiomatically acceptable in the sense of "waiting upon," "caring for." (Please *attend to* this at once.) *Tend to* has the more exact meaning of "leaning toward." (He *tends to* be critical of new ideas.)

Aught, ought, naught. *Aught* means "any little part," "in any respect." (You are right for *aught* I know.) *Ought* indicates duty, obligation. (Everyone *ought* to attend the meeting.) *Naught* means "nothing," "zero." (Our work availed *naught*.)

Aural. See *Oral*.

Auricle. See *Oracle*.

Authority about, authority on. The former is idiomatically incorrect. (Dr. Jones is an *authority on* Chaucer.)

Auto. See *Ad*.

Avenge, revenge. The former implies inflicting punishment for wrongs or oppressions. *Revenge* implies the infliction of punishment for an injury to one's self and connotes personal malice. (He swore to *avenge* himself upon the Russians. I sought *revenge* for the slanders spoken against me.)

Averse. See *Adverse*.

Avocation, vocation. The former suggests a hobby, something one does apart from regular work. One's *vocation* is one's calling, one's principal endeavor or source of livelihood. (My *vocation* is teaching school, but my *avocation* is gardening.)

Awake. See *Wake*.

Award, reward. *Award* implies a "decision" or "something given as a prize." *Reward* usually refers to something given in recompense for a good deed or for merit. (Jack received an *award* for his flower display. The fireman received a *reward* for saving the child's life.)

Away. This frequently used adverb has many meanings, all acceptable in standard English: "hence," "far," "aside," etc.; and as an adjective it means "absent," "gone," or "distant." *Away* is colloquial when used to mean "without delay," "immediately," as in "All right, sing *away*." See *Right away*.

Awful, awfully, abominably. These and such other expressions as *terrible*, *ghastly*, and *horrible* are loose, overworked intensives. If you need an intensive, use *very* (which see). A wise newspaper editor once told his staff to use *very* only rarely. "Write *damn* if you feel a *very* coming on. Then I'll knock it out," he said. See *Counter word* in Part V.

Awhile, a while. *Awhile* is an adverb meaning "for a time." *A while* has much the same meaning, but in this phrase *while* is a noun. (Wait *awhile* and I'll go with you. I cannot leave for *a while*.)

Back. See *Refer*.

Back down, etc. Like *back out*, which also has the meaning of "withdraw," *back down* is colloquial and should be avoided in standard English. Also colloquial are such expressions as *back talk*, meaning an impertinent or fresh reply, and to *back water*, meaning "to retract."

Backlog. An overused and colloquial term often employed in business and industry to mean a reserve of unfilled orders or, loosely, any sustaining reserve.

Bacon, bring home the. A colloquial and trite expression meaning "to earn a living," "to succeed," or "to win."

Bad, badly, ill. *Bad* is an adjective meaning "not good," "not as it should be." *Badly* is an adverb meaning "harmfully," "wickedly," "unpleasantly." *Ill* is both adjective and adverb and means "sick," "tending to cause harm or evil," or "in an ill manner," "wrongly." (She was very *ill*.) *Bad* and *badly* are often incorrectly used with the verb *feel*. ("I feel *bad* today"—not *badly*—unless you mean that your sense of touch is impaired.)

Badly. A colloquial expression for "very much." Avoid its use in this sense in formal writing and speaking.

Bag. This useful word with the general meaning of "container" or "receptacle" appears in several expressions not suitable in standard English: *bag and baggage* (entirely, completely, all one's possessions); *to have*, or *be, in the bag* (to have success assured); *left holding the bag* (left to suffer consequences or blame); *to bag* (to obtain or collect).

Balance, remainder. The latter term means "what is left over." *Balance* has many meanings, but its use as "remainder" is considered colloquial. (He ate the *remainder*—not *balance*—of the meal.)

Ball, bole, boll, bowl.   A *ball* is a round object. (Nancy threw the *ball*.) A *bole* is a tree trunk. (The *bole* of the maple was struck by lightning.) A *boll* is the pod of a plant. (He picked up a cotton *boll*.) A *bowl* is a receptacle; as a verb, *bowl* means "to roll." (This is a pewter *bowl*. He liked to *bowl* every evening.)

Barge in.   The use of this expression to mean "enter" or, with *into*, to mean "collide," is considered colloquial. *Barge in* or *into* is also called slang by some linguists and an illiteracy by others. By any name, it should be avoided in standard English.

Baring, barring, bearing.   *Baring* means "uncovering." (There he stood, *baring* his head to the wind.) *Barring* means "excepting." (All the apples were packed, *barring* the rotten ones.) *Bearing* means "carrying" or "enduring." (She is *bearing* up under her grief.)

Basic fundamentals.   This is a wordy phrase from which "fundamentals" should be dropped. *Basic* means "essential" or "fundamental."

Bathed in tears.   A trite, tired expression which should be avoided in standard English.

Bazaar, bizarre.   A *bazaar* is a market, fair, or shop. *Bizarre* means "odd" or "queer." (The church had a *bazaar* to raise money. Her fancy dress costume was *bizarre*.)

B.C.   See *A.D.*

Beach, beech.   A *beach* is a sandy shore, a strand. A *beech* is a kind of tree. (No *beech* grows on this *beach*.)

Bearing.   See *Baring.*

Be burned up.   This expression when used to refer to a fire is acceptable, but when it is used to mean "angry" or "upset," it is considered both slangy and colloquial.

Beech.   See *Beach.*

Beggars description.   This is a cliché, an expression once effective but now merely tiresome.

Being as. This is a colloquial or illiterate substitute for *since, because, inasmuch as,* etc. (*Since*—not *Being as*—I have some sugar, I'll lend you some.)

Be laid up. This expression is considered colloquial and not suitable for use in standard English. The same may be said for other expressions beginning with *be,* such as *be mixed up, be on one's toes, be on the go, be on the job, be sidetracked, be up against.* All such expressions are common in everyday speech but are frowned upon in formal writing.

Believe, feel. *To believe* implies "to think," "to judge," "to have convictions about." *Feel* suggests "emotions," "feeling," but not "reason." (I *believe* you have a sound attitude toward life and therefore I *feel* happy for you.)

Beside, besides. *Beside* is normally a preposition meaning "by the side of." *Besides* is an adverb meaning "moreover," and, infrequently, is a preposition meaning "except." (The old man sat *beside* the fireplace. I can't go because I have no money, and *besides,* I don't feel well.)

Be sure and. This expression is considered both colloquial and unidiomatic.(When you get there, *be sure to*—not *sure and*—write to me.)

Between. See *Among.*

Bewilder. See *Puzzle.*

Biannual, biennial. The former means "coming twice a year." (The directors have a *biannual* meeting in March and September.) *Biennial* means "happening every two years" or "lasting or living for two years." (When he was a member of the legislature he attended *biennial* meetings in 1956 and 1958.) A *biennial* is a plant which produces seeds and flowers the second year and then dies.

Bidding, biding. The former means "a command" or "a summons." (He came quickly at the President's *bidding.*) *Biding* means "waiting," "expecting." (The attorney was *biding* his time to enter a plea.)

Big shot. This expression is common, but it is considered both colloquial and slangy in standard English. *Big* is also considered to be slang or a colloquialism in such expressions as *big butter-and-egg man; to go over big; what's the big idea?; big deal.*

Billed. See *Build.*

Bird. This word appears in many shopworn expressions, such as *birds of a feather, a bird in hand is worth* . . . , *bird of ill omen,* and *eat like a bird. Bird* is colloquial or slangy when used to mean "an odd person" (Harold is a queer *bird*) and in the expression "to give someone *the bird*" (sound of disapproval or derision).

Bitter end. A trite and weary expression which should be avoided in standard English.

Bizarre. See *Bazaar.*

Blame me for it, blame it on me. Both of these expressions are in everyday use, but only the former is considered idiomatically correct and proper. *Blame it on me* is either dialectal or colloquial.

Bloc, block. A *bloc* is a group of people.(The members of the club formed a solid *bloc* in voting.) As a noun, *block* means "a solid," and as a verb it means "to impede." (This is a huge *block* of stone. He tried to *block* my campaign.)

Blond, blonde. The tendency to use *blond* as a noun in referring to men and *blonde* in referring to women has broken down somewhat. However, precise usage calls for retaining the feminine *e* ending of the French word.

Blowup. In the meaning of "an explosion," *blowup* is an acceptable word. In the sense of "an angry or hysterical outburst," it is considered colloquial or slangy.

Boar, Boer, boor, bore. A *boar* is a male hog. A *Boer* is a descendant of Dutch colonists in South Africa. *Boor* refers to a rude, awkward, or ill-mannered person. *Bore* means "to drill" or "to dig."

Bole, boll. See *Ball.*

Bone up. A slang expression meaning "to apply oneself diligently," "to study hard." Avoid in standard English usage.

Boor, bore. See *Boar*.

Born, borne, bourn (bourne.) *Born* means "given birth to," or "brought into the world." (Betty was *born* in 1952.) *Borne* means "carried" or "supported." (The coffin was *borne* by six friends of the deceased.) *Bourn,* also spelled *bourne*, means "a goal," "a limit," "a boundary." ("The undiscovered country from whose *bourne* no traveler returns.")

Borough, borrow, burro, burrow. A *borough* is a governmental unit. (You live in the *Borough* of Richmond.) *Borrow* means "to receive with the intention of returning." (He wants to *borrow* some money.) A *burro* is a donkey. (You lead the horse and I'll ride the *burro*.) As a noun, *burrow* means "a tunnel," "a hole"; as a verb, it means "to dig." (The mole made a *burrow* in the turf. *Burrow* deeper under the blankets.)

Bouillon. See *Bullion*.

Bourn, bourne. See *Born*.

Bowl. See *Ball*.

Brainy. This is a colloquialism when used to mean "intelligent," "mentally keen."

Brake, break. A *brake* is a device for stopping. *Break* means "to separate," "to destroy." (The *brake* on the truck was defective. Be careful; don't *break* the water glasses.) *Break* is colloquial in such expressions as *give someone a break, a bad break* (misfortune).

Brave as a lion. A cliché. Try to phrase a better figure of speech, one that is fresher and more vigorous.

Breadth, breath, breathe. *Breadth* refers to distance or width. A *breath* is "an exhalation of air." *To breathe* is "to take in (or exhale) air." (The river was one hundred yards in *breadth*. His *breath* was frozen in the cold air. *Breathe* deeply and you will feel better.)

Break. See *Brake*.

Breath, breathe. See *Breadth*.

Brewed, brood. The former means "fermented" or "steeped."

Brood refers to offspring. (Jackie *brewed* a brisk cup of tea. You have a large *brood* of children.)

Bridal, bridle. The former refers to a bride. *Bridle* means "headgear" for an animal. (We went to the *bridal* party. This horse objects to a *bridle*.)

Brilliant performance. This phrase has been so overused as to lose its brightness and effectiveness. Try to substitute a less trite expression.

Bring up. See *Raise*.

Britain, Briton. *Britain* (watch the spelling) is a place name. (He lives now in Great *Britain*.) *Briton* refers to a person. (He is proud to be a *Briton*.)

Broach, brooch. *To broach* is "to bring up." (Do not *broach* that subject.) *Brooch* refers to "a pin with clasp." (Janet wore an expensive *brooch*.)

Broke. This word has standard uses, but it is slang when used to mean "out of money." To *go broke* (become penniless) and *go for broke* (dare or risk everything) are also slang expressions.

Brooch. See *Broach*.

Brood. See *Brewed*.

Brown as a berry. This is a tired old phrase which no longer possesses force and appeal. Besides, many berries aren't brown.

Budding genius. A cliché. Not all young geniuses are "budding"; search for a fresher adjective.

Build, billed. *To build* is "to make," "to establish." *Billed* is a form of "to bill." (Let's *build* our home here. He was *billed* for fifty dollars.)

Bullion, bouillon. The latter is a broth, a kind of soup. *Bullion* means "ingots." (This dish was made with chicken *bouillon*. There's much gold *bullion* stored at Fort Knox.)

Bum. This word should always be avoided in standard English. It has several meanings as adjective, noun, and verb, all of them slangy or highly colloquial: "to lead an ideal life," "to sponge," "a drunken loafer," "a spree."

Bump.   In the sense of "collide" this is a standard word. When it is used to mean "displace from one's job or airline reservation" it is considered both slangy and colloquial. *Bump off* is a slang expression for "kill." In some sections of the United States, *bump into* is spelled "bunk into," a dialectal and highly colloquial expression.

Bunch.   This is a colloquialism for "a group of people," "crowd," or "set." (Our *set*—or *group* or *crowd* or *gang*—was closely knit at that time.)

Burn.   This word appears in several trite expressions, among them *to burn one's bridges, to burn the candle at both ends,* and *to burn one's self out. Burn* is slang when used to mean "electrocute," and *burn up* is slang in the sense of "to make or become angry."

Burro, burrow.   See *Borough.*

Bursted, bust, busted.   *Bursted* is an illiteracy (see *Illiteracies* in Part V). The principal parts (which see in Part V) of this verb are *burst—burst—burst.* Both *bust* and *busted* are slangy or dubiously colloquial when used for *burst.*

Busy as a bee.   A trite expression. Also, some bees are lazy—even as you and I.

By leaps and bounds.   A cliché. Use the phrase when referring to mountain goats; otherwise, try to find something fresher.

Cactus.   This word for a well-known prickly plant illustrates the problem of plurals in English. (See *Foreign plurals,* Part III, "Guide to Correct Spelling.") *Cactus* comes from a Greek word, and precise users of English usually spell the plural *cacti.* Gradually, however, the spelling *cactuses* is becoming more general. Some dictionaries indicate that both plural forms are acceptable.

Cake.   The expression *take the cake,* meaning "to excel" or "to win the prize," is slang. "Have your *cake* and eat it too" is a trite expression.

Calculate, reckon, guess.   These words are *localisms* (which see in Part V) for "think," "suppose," and "expect." Each of the words has standard and acceptable meanings, but in the senses indicated above they should always be avoided except in informal conversation.

Calendar, calender, colander. A *calendar* is a "table," a "register," to measure time. (This is an old *calendar* for 1960.) A *calender* is a machine with rollers. (The *calender* gave the cloth a shiny finish.) A *colander* is a pan with perforations (or "holes" to be simple). (Jo used a *colander* to wash the spinach.)

Call someone. Such expressions as *call on the carpet* and *call on the phone* are colloquial and should be restricted to informal conversation. *To call*, meaning "to scold," is considered slang.

Calvary, cavalry. *Calvary* is the name of a hill. *Cavalry* refers to troops on horseback. (Jesus was crucified on *Calvary*. J.E.B. Stuart was a *cavalry* leader.)

Can, may, might. *Can* suggests "ability," physical and mental. (He *can* make good progress if he tries hard enough.) *May* implies permission or sanction. (The office manager says that you *may* leave.) The distinction between *can* and *may* (ability *vs.* permission) is illustrated in this sentence: I doubt that you *can*, but you *may* try if you wish. *May* also expresses possibility and wish (desire): It *may* rain today (possibility); *may* you have a pleasant trip (wish, desire). *Might* is used after a governing verb in the past tense, *may* after a governing verb in the present tense: He *says* that you *may* go; he *said* that you *might* go.

Cannon, canon. A *cannon* is a large gun. (The artillerymen pulled the *cannon* into position.) A *canon* is a law or rule. (This is an important *canon* of the church.)

Cannot help, cannot help but. The first of these expressions is preferable in such statements as "I *cannot help* talking about . . ." The *but* should be omitted since its addition results in an illogical double negative: *cannot help* and *can but*.

Canon. See *Cannon*.

Can't hardly. Omit the contraction of *not*. (I *can* hardly hear you.) *Can't hardly* is an illogical *double negative* (which see in Part II, "Guide to Correct Sentence Structure").

Canvas, canvass. *Canvas* is a kind of cloth. *To canvass* is "to solicit" or "to request." (The *canvas* of the tent was covered with pine needles. He will *canvass* the block for donations.)

Capacity. See *Ability.*

Capital, capitol. The first of these words may be employed in all meanings except that of "a building." A *capitol* is an edifice, a building. (He raised new *capital* for the company. The sightseeing bus passed the state *capitol.*)

Captain of industry. A worn-out phrase. Many ranks of workers exist in industry, from privates to generals. Use a little imagination; don't use the first trite expression which occurs to you.

Carat, caret, carrot, karat. *Carat* refers to "weight." (The diamond weighed one *carat.*) A *caret* is a mark. (Use a *caret* to show the missing letter.) A *carrot* is a vegetable beloved by rabbits and some people. (A *carrot* may be edible if it is scraped.) *Karat* is a variant spelling of *carat.*

Card. This is a slang word when used to refer to a witty or eccentric person. (Joe certainly is a *card.*) *To put one's cards on the table* is a cliché.

Caret, carrot. See *Carat.*

Case. This word has many meanings. For its use in language, see Part V. As a counter word (which see in Part V) it has many vague meanings. *Case, phase, factor, instance, nature, thing,* etc., are prime examples of jargon (see Part V). *To case,* in the sense of "examine carefully," is slang. Don't use *case the joint* in standard English.

Casual, causal. The first of these words means "not planned," "incidental." *Causal* means "relating to cause and effect." (Janet paid me a *casual* visit. A *causal* factor in his decision was lack of money.)

Cavalry. See *Calvary.*

Ceiling, sealing. A *ceiling* is "an overhanging expanse." *Sealing* means "fastening" or "closing." (The library has a high *ceiling.* Few people try *sealing* letters with wax.)

Censer, censor, censure. A *censer* is an incense burner. *To censor* is "to examine." *To censure* is "to condemn" or "to find fault."

(He bought a lovely ornamented *censer*. The authorities *censor* all mail. The superintendent will strongly *censure* you for laziness.)

Center of attraction.   A trite expression. So is its counterpart, *cynosure of all eyes*. Good writers have found livelier ways of expressing this meaning. So can you.

Certain.   This word is overused and is unnecessary in such expressions as "this certain boy" and "that certain affair."

Charted, chartered.   *Charted* means "mapped." *Chartered* means "hired," "engaged." (He sailed the *charted* waters in a *chartered* yacht.)

Chased, chaste.   The former means "pursued" or "followed." *Chaste* means "pure," "unsullied." (Not all *chaste* girls are *chased* by boys.)

Check, check up, check with.   *Check* is an acceptable word with many standard uses. However, it has been used so often in such expressions as *check up on*, *check with*, and just plain *check* in the sense of "to corroborate" or "to agree" that it has become worn out. Let's give this cliché a long rest.

Checkered career.   Your life and mine have been varied and diversified. But can we find some better and less trite expression to describe them than this weary one? I think so.

Chip in.   In the sense of "to contribute" this expression is thought to be either slangy or colloquial.

Choose, chose.   The latter is the past tense of the verb *choose*. They differ in spelling, pronunciation, and tense. (I *chose* an apple for dessert yesterday and I shall *choose* one today.)

Choral, chorale.   See *Coral*.

Chord, cord.   A *chord* is a combination of musical tones. (The pianist played the opening *chords*.) A *cord* is a string or a rope. (Tie your packages with sturdy *cord*.)

Chose.   See *Choose*.

Cite, sight, site.   *Cite* means "to summon" or "to quote." (Please *cite* your authority.) *Sight* means "view," "vision." (The snow-capped mountain was a beautiful *sight*.) *Site* means "location." (This is a good *site* for the new building.)

Clear as crystal. Crystal *is* clear, and the first million times this expression was used it was effective and image-producing. But now it's a weary cliché. Other things are also clear. Why not use one of them in a figure of speech?

Climactic, climatic. *Climactic* pertains to *climax*, the final and most forceful one of a series of ideas or events. (The duel was the *climactic* scene of the drama.) *Climatic* pertains to *climate*, "weather conditions." (Edith likes *climatic* conditions in the Virgin Islands.)

Climax. See *Acme*.

Clinging vine. An apt expression to denote dependence or reliance upon. Unfortunately, the phrase has been so overworked as to lose its pristine vigor. Avoid this trite expression.

Close to nature. A cliché. Good writers have discovered other ways to describe this condition. So can we.

Clothes, cloths. The former means "body covering." (Anne bought her husband a new suit of *clothes*.) *Cloths* are "pieces of cloth." (Please put these wash *cloths* in the laundry.)

Coarse, course. The former means "unrefined" or "common." (This is a *coarse* piece of cloth. He is a *coarse* person.) *Course* has several meanings, all of them distinct from that of "unrefined." (He took the easy *course*.)

Colander. See *Calendar*.

Cold as ice. Formerly an effective expression and still an apt one but now a cliché. Many substances are colder than ice anyway in this age of chemical marvels. Slangy, colloquial, or trite are such expressions as *cold feet, to blow hot and cold, to cold-shoulder, throw cold water on*, and *cold comfort*. *Cold* is slang when used to mean "insensible" or "completely mastered."

Coma, comma. *Coma* suggests a "state of unconsciousness." (Dot was in a *coma* for three days before her death.) A *comma* is a mark of punctuation.

Come across, etc. This phrase is considered colloquial (suitable only for informal use) in the meaning of "to give, say, or do what is wanted." Other colloquial expressions involving the word *come* are *come and get it* (a summons to eat); *come around* (to concede or yield, to come to visit); *come back* (to return to a previous state, to retort); *come down on* (to scold, upbraid); *come in for* (to get, acquire); *come on* (get started); *come through* (to do or give what is wanted); *how come?* (how is that? why?).

Comma. See *Coma.*

Commentate. This word, perhaps by association with the often-used word *commentator*, is being increasingly used as a verb. Possibly some day it will make its way into dictionaries; until then use the shorter and more acceptable word *comment.*

Common, mutual. The former means "belonging to many or to all." *Mutual* means "reciprocal." (Airplanes are *common* carriers. Our respect and love were *mutual.*) Avoid the redundancy of such a statement as "He and I entered into a mutual agreement."

Compare, contrast. *Compare* is used to point out likenesses, similarities (used with the preposition *to*) and to examine two or more objects to find likenesses or differences (used with the preposition *with*). *Contrast* always points out differences. (The poet *compared* his lady *to* a dove. The teacher *compared* my report *with* Jane's and found no signs of copying. In *contrast to* your work, mine is poor.)

Complected. This abomination of a word may be considered an illiteracy or a dialectal expression. The standard word is "complexioned." (Janet was dark-*complexioned.*)

Complement, compliment. *Complement* implies something which completes. (This jewelry will *complement* your dress.) A *compliment* is flattery. (Beulah enjoyed the *compliment* paid to her.)

Complete. See *Absolutely.*

Comply to, with. The former expression is not idiomatically acceptable. The latter is. (Will you *comply with* my request?)

Comprehend. See *Apprehend.*

Comprehensible, comprehensive. The former means "intelligible," "understandable." (Ninki's action was not *comprehensible.*) *Comprehensive* means "inclusive," "including much." (This volume is a *comprehensive* account of the Battle of Waterloo.)

Concede. See *Admit.*

Conducive to, conducive with. The former expression is idiomatically more suitable than the latter. (Your apology was *conducive to* better feeling in the office.)

Confess. See *Admit.*

Confidant, confidante, confident. *Confidant* (feminine, *confidante*) means "one who is trusted," "a close friend." *Confident* means "assured," "certain." (David was a *confidant* of Eleanor. Eleanor was a *confidante* of David. The manager was *confident* of exceeding the quota.)

Conform in, to, with. *Conform in* is rarely used in idiomatic speech. Both *conform to* and *conform with* are. (Try to *conform with*—or *to*—your orders.)

Conscience, conscious. *Conscience* means "sense of right and wrong." (His *conscience* began to bother him.) *Conscious* means "awake," "able to feel and think." (Elizabeth was badly injured but still *conscious.*)

Conscientiousness, consciousness. The former means "uprightness" or "honesty." (The official was rewarded for his *conscientiousness.*) *Consciousness* is a noun meaning "awareness." (The driver died before regaining *consciousness.*)

Consist of, consist in. The former phrase is used to designate the parts of which something is made up or composed. (The team *consists of* five players.) *Consist in* is more often used to describe an idea or term. (Pessimism *consists in* always expecting the worst that could happen.)

Conspicuous by its absence. A trite expression to be avoided.

Consul, council, counsel. A *consul* is an official. (Robin visited the American *consul* in Naples.) *Council* means "an assembly," "a group." (This is a *council* of senior citizens.) *Counsel* is both noun and verb and means "advice" or "to advise." (The physician gave me expensive *counsel*. The manager will *counsel* fast action by the board of directors.)

Contact, contacted. Each of these words has perfectly proper uses, but as business terms they have been grossly overworked. Possible substitutes: *communicate with, call, call upon, telephone*, etc.

Contemptuous, contemptible. The former means "scornful" or "disdainful." *Contemptible* means "deserving to be scorned," "mean." (The boss was *contemptuous* of all my actions. Hitler was a thoroughly *contemptible* person.)

Contend. Idiomatic usage requires that we *contend against* an obstacle, *contend for* a principle, and *contend with* a person. (Postmen *contend against* rain and sleet. Jefferson *contended for* his ideas. You will have to *contend with* your enemies in the shipping room.)

Continual, continuous. In some uses these words are interchangeable. A subtle distinction is that *continual* implies "a close recurrence in time," in "rapid succession" and that *continuous* implies "without interruption." (The *continual* ringing of the telephone bothers me. The ticking of the clock was *continuous*.)

Continue on. This is a wordy phrase. *Continue* means "to endure," "to last." Hence, *on* is unnecessary to convey full meaning.

Continuous. See *Continual*.

Contrast. See *Compare*.

Convince, persuade. The former means "to overcome the doubts of." *Persuade* implies "influencing a person to an action or belief." (I am *convinced* that you are right and you have *persuaded* me to help you.) *Convince to* is not idiomatic. (Wrong: I *convinced* him *to* see the play. Right: I *persuaded* him *to* see the play. I *convinced* him *that* he should see the play.)

Cool customer. This is a slang phrase which should be avoided in standard English. Also colloquial or slangy are such expressions involving *cool* as *to lose a cool thousand, to cool one's heels.*

Co-operate together. *Co-operate* implies "working together," "combining efforts." Omit *together*.

Coral, corral, choral, chorale. *Coral* consists of "skeletons of marine animals." (The ship foundered on a *coral* reef.) A *corral* is a pen or enclosure. (This ranch needs a larger horse *corral*.) *Choral* and *chorale* are usually pronounced differently, but as nouns they have identical meanings: a simple hymn sung by choir and congregation. *Choral* is also an adjective.

Cord. See *Chord*.

Core, corps, corpse. *Core* means "center." (The *core* of an apple is not edible.) *Corps* refers to a group of people. (The recruits were assigned to the engineering *corps*.) A *corpse* is a dead body. (We carried the *corpse* to the local cemetery.)

Corporal, corporeal. The former means "bodily," "physically," or a low-ranking officer. (The *corporal* does not believe in *corporal* punishment for his squad.) *Corporeal* means "material" or "tangible." (Dee's father left no *corporeal* property to his family.)

Corps, corpse. See *Core*.

Corral. See *Coral*.

Correspond. Idiomatic usage requires that something *correspond to* something else and that one *correspond with* someone else. (This figure does not *correspond to* that one. Let's *correspond with* each other while you are away.)

Correspondent, corespondent. The latter applies to someone charged with a misdemeanor in marital affairs. (Jane was named as *corespondent* in Martha's divorce action.) *Correspondent* has several meanings, but all of them imply writing or commerce. (Nancy is a busy *correspondent*, mailing a dozen letters every week.)

Could of. An illiteracy. Possibly because of its sound it is sometimes written for *could have*. (The rusty nail *could have*—not *could of*—hurt you.) See *Would of*.

Council, counsel.   See *Consul*.

Couple, couple of.   These phrases are colloquial in the sense of "two," "a pair." (She gave me *two*—not *a couple of*—tickets.)

Course.   See *Coarse*.

Creak, creek.   *Creak* means "to make a sound." A *creek* is a small stream. (The bed will *creak* if you jump on it. The children waded in the *creek*.)

Credible, creditable, credulous.   *Credible* means "believable." (Your excuse is *credible*.) *Creditable* means "praiseworthy," "deserving approval." (Your sales record is *creditable*.) *Credulous* means "gullible," "easily convinced." (Where boys were involved, Helen was much too *credulous*.)

Creek.   See *Creak*.

Crews, cruise.   The former refers to seamen or any group of persons. (The captain discharged both *crews* of workmen.) A *cruise* is a voyage. (He is on a *cruise* in the Mediterranean.)

Cupful.   This word, meaning "as much as a cup will hold," is now spelled as one word containing one *l*. Idiomatically, we write "four cupfuls" rather than "four cups full," although either is correct. There is a slight difference in meaning or stress between the expressions "four cupfuls" and "four full cups."

Currant, current.   A *currant* is a small, seedless raisin. (This recipe requires a box of *currants*.) *Current* means "a stream," or "contemporary." (This river has a swift *current*. He tries to keep up with *current* affairs.)

Cute.   This is an overworked and somewhat vague word which generally expresses approval. Probably *charming, attractive, piquant, pleasing, vivacious*, or one of a dozen other adjectives would come nearer the meaning you have in mind.

Cymbal, symbol.   A *cymbal* is a musical instrument. *Symbol* means "sign" or "token." (The *cymbal* is made of brass. "Old Glory" is a *symbol* of the United States.)

Dairy, diary.   A *dairy* is a milk enterprise. A *diary* is a daily record. (The cows ambled from the field to the *dairy* building. Lee's *diary* is intimate and revealing.)

Dame Fortune. A trite expression to be avoided in standard English.

Data. This word was originally the plural of Latin *datum*. In colloquial English it is sometimes used with a singular verb, but it is considered plural in standard English. (*These data are* not reliable.) See *Foreign plurals*, Part III, "Guide to Correct Spelling," for a discussion of plurals such as *data, phenomena*, etc.

Date. When used to mean "a social appointment with the opposite sex," *date* is colloquial.

Dead, deadly. Each of these words is fully respectable but each appears in many expressions to be avoided in standard English. Trite, slangy, or colloquial are *dead to the world dead beat, dead certain, in deadly earnest, dead-pan, dead set, dead tired, deadly dull*.

Deal. This overworked business term is colloquial when used to mean "agreement," "arrangement," "plan."

Decease, disease. The former means "death"; the latter means "sickness." (This *disease* led to his *decease*.)

Decent, descent, dissent. *Decent* means "suitable" or "respectable." (Please wear a *decent* hat to the reception.) *Descent* is the "act of descending, coming or going down." (Our *descent* from the mountain was slow.) To *dissent* is "to differ" or "to disagree." (Justice Holmes will *dissent* from that opinion.)

Defendant. See *Plaintiff*.

Definite, definitive. The former means "clear," "explicit." (The shop foreman made a *definite* proposal.) *Definitive* means "decisive," "complete," "final." (This is a *definitive* plan for the campaign.)

Delusion. See *Allusion*.

Depend upon it. *Depend* is often used with *on* or *upon* in the meaning of "be dependent" or "rely." The idiom is standard English, all right, but the phrase in its second meaning has been worn threadbare with overuse.

Deprecate, depreciate. The former means "to express disapproval." (He *deprecated* our best efforts.) *Depreciate* means "to lower in value." (The stock dividend *depreciated* the par value of the security.)

Depths of despair. A cliché. Without descending to the depths, you needn't despair of finding a fresher way to express this concept.

Descent. See *Decent.*

Des'ert, desert', dessert'. These three words involve problems in spelling, pronunciation, and meaning. The first, with accent on the first syllable, means "barren ground." (The *desert* is one hundred miles wide.) *Desert* (with accent on the second syllable) means "to abandon" (which see). (Don't ever *desert* your true friends.) *Dessert* (note the double *s*) is "a sweet food." (Apple pie is his favorite *dessert.*)

Desire. See *Want.*

Desire of, to. *Desire to* is idiomatically correct. (I *desire to* accompany you.)

Desirous of, to. *Desirous of* is idiomatically correct. (Roberta was *desirous of* fame and fortune.)

Despite, in spite of. These terms have identical meanings. The latter is somewhat more usual in everyday speech, but the former is generally preferable, since one word does the work of three.

Dessert. See *Desert.*

Device, devise. The former is a noun meaning "a contrivance." The latter is a verb meaning "to make," "to invent." (The scientist *devised* an interesting *device.*)

Devoted. See *Addicted.*

Diary. See *Dairy.*

Die, dye, dying, dyeing. *To die* is "to cease to live" and *dying* is the participle. (The *dying* man did not want to *die.*) *To dye* is "to color"; the participle of this verb is *dyeing.* (The girl *dyeing* the dress with red *dye* is named Abigail.)

Differ. Idiom provides as follows: *differ with* a person; *from* something else; *about* or *over* a question. All clear?

Different from, than, to. *Different than* and *different to* are considered colloquial by some authorities, improper and incorrect by others. Even so, these idioms have long literary usage to support them and certainly they are widely used. No one ever objects on any grounds to *different from*. Use *different from* and be safe, never sorry.

Dining, dinning. The former means "eating," whereas the latter pertains to noise or uproar. They also differ in pronunciation and spelling. (A *dining* room; the sound *dinning* in my ears.)

Discomfit, discomfort. The former means "to frustrate," "to thwart." (Your plan will *discomfit* mine.) *Discomfort* means "uneasiness," "distress." (His broken finger caused him *discomfort*.)

Discover, invent. The former implies being "the first to find out about, see, or know about." *Invent* means "to make, devise, or fabricate." (Did Columbus really *discover* America? Did Edison really *invent* the phonograph?)

Discreet, discrete. *Discreet* means "judicious" or "thoughtful." (You must be *discreet* when talking to your employer.) *Discrete* means "separate," "distinct." (Your problem and mine are *discrete*.)

Disdain for, disdain of. Idiom decrees that we should have *disdain for* something, never *disdain of*.

Disease. See *Decease*.

Disinterested, uninterested. The former means "unbiased," "not influenced by personal reasons." *Uninterested* means "having no interest in," "not paying attention." (The minister's opinion was *disinterested*. I was completely *uninterested* in the play.) As a colloquialism, and somewhat inexact, too, *disinterested* is often used in the sense of "uninterested," "indifferent."

Disregardless. See *Irregardless*.

Disremember. An illiteracy. Never use this word in standard English.

Dissent. See *Decent*. Also, the proper idiomatic phrase is *dissent from*, not *dissent with*.

Divers, diverse. *Divers* means "several" or "sundry." (He suggested *divers* approaches to the problem.) *Diverse* means "different," "varied." (They have *diverse* attitudes toward life.)

Done, don't. The principal parts of this verb are *do—did—done.* *Done* is frequently used as the past tense of *do.* (We *did*—not *done*—our work early today.) *Don't* is often used incorrectly for *doesn't.* (It *doesn't*—not *don't*—make much difference to me.)

Doomed to disappointment. A trite expression.

Double cross. A slang expression for "betrayal." As both verb (*double-cross*) and noun, it should not be used in standard English.

Doubt if, whether. These phrases assume there is room for doubt. *Doubt if* is considered colloquial and less proper idiomatically than *doubt whether.* (I *doubt whether* he will repay the loan.)

Drank, drunk. Principal parts of the verb are *drink—drank—drunk.* (He *drank*—not *drunk*—a cup of tea. I have *drunk*—not *drank*—a glass of coffee.) *Drunk* is sometimes avoided when referring to an intoxicated person. We say that Jack is "under the influence" or that he has "indulged to excess." Or we use humorous slang and remark that "Jack got plastered." *Drunk* is a perfectly good word and should be used as needed.

Drastic action. A tired expression. Several synonyms or near-synonyms for *drastic* will be less trite.

Drop me a line. A colloquial and somewhat wordy expression for "write."

Drop off. Colloquial when used to mean "to fall asleep." *To have the drop on* someone is also slangy or colloquial.

Drug, drugged. Principal parts are *drag—dragged—dragged.* *Drug* and *drugged* are perfectly good words but are outright illiteracies when used as parts of the verb *drag.* (We *dragged*—not *drug* or *drugged*—him to his room.)

Drunk. See *Drank.*

Dual, duel. The former means "twofold." (The actor has a *dual* role in that play.) *Duel* means "combat" or "a fight." (The courtier challenged his rival to a *duel.*)

Due to. Some authorities label this phrase "colloquial" when it is used to mean "because of." Nevertheless, it is widely used in this sense by capable speakers and writers. Purists prefer such expressions as *owing to, caused by, on account of,* and *because of.* If you wish your English to be above all criticism, avoid using *due to* as a preposition. His illness was *caused by* (not *due to*) exposure. Most importantly, remember that *due to the fact that* is a wordy way of saying the short and simple word *since.* See *Fact that.*

Dull thud. Why do many things and objects fall with a "dull thud"? The phrase does imitate the sound (onomatopoeia), but there must be some further reason. Habit? Probably. Anyway, a worn-out expression.

Dye, dyeing, dying. See *Die.*

Each . . . are. *Each,* even if not followed by *one,* implies one. Any plural words used in modifying phrases do not change the number. (Each *is*—not *are* —expected to contribute *his* share. *Each one* of you *is* a fraud.)

Eager. See *Anxious.*

Earthy. See *Of the earth.*

Eat. This happy verb indicates an action to which all of us are devoted. However, the phrases *eat out* and *eat in* are considered informal, colloquial. So is the phrase *to eat one's heart out.* *Eats* as a noun substitute for *food* or *meals* is both colloquial and slangy.

Effect. See *Affect.*

Egg. Understandably, such a short and familiar word as *egg* is used in many expressions which are slangy, trite, or colloquial. In standard English avoid *a good egg* (an agreeable person); *lay an egg, throw eggs at, put all one's eggs in one basket, egghead* (an intellectual); *egg* (bomb, torpedo, hand grenade).

Either . . . or, neither . . . nor. The former means "one of two." *Neither* means "not one of two." *Or* is used with *either,* *nor* with *neither.* The use of *either . . . or* and *neither . . . nor,* co-ordinating more than two words, phrases, or clauses is sanctioned by some dictionaries but not by others. (*Either* of you *is* satisfactory for the role. *Neither* the boys *nor* the girls wished to dance.)

Elder, eldest, older, oldest. Each of these terms is a form of *old*. *Elder* and *older* have about the same meaning, as do *eldest* and *oldest*. However, *elder* and *eldest* are rarely used today and, when they are, apply to members of the same family, as in *elder brother*, *eldest child*, etc. Sometimes, too, they are used in such journalistic phrases as "*elder statesman*." In today's usage, both *elder* and *eldest* often sound archaic.

Elegy, eulogy. Each of these words pertains to "praise," but they differ in meaning as well as in spelling and pronunciation. An *elegy* is a poem of lament and praise for the dead. (His favorite poem was Gray's "Elegy in a Country Churchyard.") *Eulogy* pertains to "speech or writing in praise of a person, thing, or event." (The coach delivered a *eulogy* to the winning team.)

Elicit, illicit. The former is a verb meaning "to bring out," "to draw forth." (This request should *elicit* the data we need.) *Illicit* is an adjective meaning "unlawful," "improper." (Millie was accused of being an *illicit* trader in narcotics.)

Elude. See *Allude*.

Emigrate, immigrate. The former means "to leave"; the latter means "to enter." (Our foreman *emigrated* from Poland in 1938. Many people have tried to *immigrate* to this country in the last decade.) The corresponding nouns, *emigration* and *immigration*, are similarly distinguished in meaning.

Enamored about, of. The word *enamored*, meaning "captivated" or "charmed," is overworked by advertisers and schoolgirls. If you do wish to use it, be sure to employ the correct idiomatic phrase. One is *enamored of* something, not *enamored about* it.

Enclosed herewith. This wordy phrase appears often, especially in business letters. *Enclosed* is sufficient in itself since it implies "placed in" as of now. *Please find enclosed* is business jargon. Why not say, simply, "I am enclosing . . ."?

Ensure. See *Assure*.

Enthuse. This word is a formation from "enthusiasm." Most dictionaries label *enthuse* as colloquial, although it is shorter and more direct than preferred locutions such as *be enthusiastic about*, or *become enthusiastic over*. Even so, the word is greatly overused and somewhat "gushy"; do not use it in formal English.

Envelop, envelope. The verb *en vel'op* (accent on second syllable) means "to cover," "to wrap." (Fire will soon *envelop* the entire block.) *En'vel ope* (accent on first syllable) is a noun meaning "a covering." (Put a stamp on this *envelope*.)

Epic struggle. A stereotype, a cliché. *Epic* has many synonyms or near-synonyms (*heroic, grand, majestic, imposing*, etc.). You don't *have* to use this trite expression.

Epigram, epitaph, epithet. An *epigram* is a "witty, pointed statement." (One of Wilde's most famous *epigrams* is "There is no sin except stupidity.") An *epitaph* is an "inscription on a tomb" or a "tribute to a dead person." (What is the *epitaph* on that mausoleum?) An *epithet* is a "descriptive name." (The italicized words are an *epithet* in this sentence: The Army team is referred to as *Black Knights of the Hudson*.)

Equal to the occasion. A cliché. You can find a fresher way to express this idea if you are "equal to the occasion."

Equitable, equable. The former means "fair" or "just." *Equable* means "steady," "uniform." (The judge handed down an *equitable* decree. Our climate in June is *equable*.)

Errand, errant, arrant. An *errand* is a "trip" or "a task." (I'll run the *errand* for you.) *Errant* means "roving," "wandering." (I don't understand your *errant* behavior.) *Arrant* means "notorious." (The sailor proved to be an *arrant* coward.)

Essay. See *Assay*.

Etc. *Etc.* is an abbreviation of the Latin *et cetera* and means "and so forth." It looks somewhat out of place in formal writing. Furthermore, it cannot be pronounced in speech without sounding individual letters or giving the entire phrase. Sometimes we use *etc.* at the end of a list to suggest that much more could be added. But do we really have anything in mind? See *And etc.*

Eulogy. See *Elegy*.

Ever, every. The former means "always"; the latter means "without exception." (He is *ever* a generous man. *Every* house in this town is made of wood.) *Ever* is considered colloquial in such an expression as "Was she *ever* tired!" and in *ever so*, meaning "extremely." *Every* is colloquial in such expressions as *every so often* and *every which way*.

Evident. See *Apparent*.

Exactly identical. See *Identical to*.

Exalt, exult. *Exalt* means "to raise" or "to praise." (The minister exhorted us to *exalt* God.) *Exult* means "to rejoice." (The boxer *exulted* over the decision.)

Exam. See *Ad*. This is a colloquial abbreviation for "examination." It should be used sparingly, if at all, in standard English.

Except. See *Accept*.

Exceptionable, exceptional. The former means "objectionable." *Exceptional* means "out of the ordinary." (Your constant whining is *exceptionable*. Caruso's voice was *exceptional*.)

Excerpt. See *Extract*.

Excess. See *Access*.

Excuse. See *Pardon*.

Expect, suspect. *Expect* means "to look forward to," "to anticipate." (I shall *expect* you tomorrow.) *Suspect* means "to distrust" or "to expect to be bad." (I *suspect* that Dot was the culprit.) *Expect* is colloquial when used to mean "suppose" and "guess" and also in the form of *expecting* in the sense of "being pregnant."

Expurgated. See *Unabridged*.

Extant, extent. The former means "still existing." (This is his only manuscript *extant*.) *Extent* refers to size and length. (What is the *extent* of this ranch?)

Extra. This useful word is colloquial when used to mean "unusually" as in "This cake is *extra* good." Use *exceptionally, especially, unusually,* etc.

Extract, excerpt. These words are related in meaning. The former means "to pull out," "to obtain" as a verb, and as a noun means "something extracted." (Ten of his teeth were *extracted*. This is a bottle of vanilla *extract*.) *Excerpt* means "to select," "to take out" as a verb, and as a noun means "a passage selected or quoted." (Please *excerpt* your favorite line from this poem. This *excerpt* from Milton suggests his great learning.) See *Unabridged*.

Exult. See *Exalt*.

Eyes like stars. A tired expression; many things glitter or shine other than stars. The word *eye* appears in a number of expressions which are considered slangy, colloquial, or dialectal. In standard English avoid such expressions as *give a person the eye*, *in a pig's eye*, *my eye!*, *get an eyeful*, *eye opener* (for an alcoholic drink), *eyewash* (for nonsense or flattery) .

Facetious, factious, factitious, fictitious. *Facetious* means "lightly joking" and is usually used in a derogatory manner. (Settle down and don't be so coy and *facetious*.) *Factious* means "causing dissension, strife." (That group is a *factious* element in this office.) *Factitious* means "artificial." (Our greatest *factitious* need today is for more gadgets in the home.) *Fictitious* means "imaginary," "not real." (Edith gave an entirely *fictitious* account of her trip.)

Fact that, the fact remains that. These are roundabout, wordy substitutes for *that* and *the fact is*, respectively. See *Due to*.

Fain, feign. The former means "ready," "eager." The latter means "to invent," "to fabricate." (I would *fain* go with you. He *feigned* illness to avoid work.) *Fain* is rarely used, being considered somewhat archaic and poetic.

Faint, feint. To *faint* is "to lose consciousness." *Feint* means "to pretend" or "to deceive." (I feel as though I'm going to *faint*. The player *feinted* his opponent out of position.)

Fair sex. A trite expression for womankind.

Familiar landmark. A trite expression. In fact, the word *familiar* is so familiar that we tend to overuse it in such expressions as *familiar conversation*, *familiar sight*, and *old familiar faces*.

Farther, further. There words are interchangeable in meaning, but precise writers and speakers prefer *farther* to indicate space, a measurable distance. *Further* more exactly indicates "greater in degree, quantity, or time" and also means "moreover" and "in addition to." (We walked two miles *farther*. Let's talk about this *further*.)

Faze. This word, which means "to disturb" or "to agitate," is considered colloquial in this spelling by some authorities. More usual spellings are *feaze* and *feeze*.

Feature. As both verb and noun, *feature* is an overworked colloquialism in the sense of "emphasize" or "emphasis." *Feature* is slang in the expression *Can you feature that?* meaning, presumably, "Can you imagine that?"

Fed up. An expressive but slangy term meaning "to become disgusted, bored." Don't use it when you're trying to impress an intellectual.

Feel. This useful word appears in several expressions which are colloquial or dialectal. In standard English avoid using *feel of* (for *feel*), *feel like* (for *wish to, desire*), *feel up to* (for *feel capable of*). Also, see *Believe*.

Feign. See *Fain*.

Feint. See *Faint*.

Fellow. This is a word of many meanings. Its use to mean an "individual," "person," "man," "boy," etc., is colloquial. *Feller* and *fella* may be considered as slang expressions, as dialect, or as illiteracies. Take your pick of epithets.

Female. Fastidious usage restricts *female* to designations of sex in scientific contexts. If *female* is considered colloquial, and it is, then what word can we use to express "female human being of whatever age"? Correct usage can indeed be a nuisance at times.

Few and far between. A trite expression. You can phrase less overworked expressions for "paucity," "scarcity." That is, you can if you'll try.

Fewer, less. Both of these words imply a comparison with something larger in number or amount. *Fewer* applies only to number. (*Fewer* horses are seen on the streets these days.) *Less* is used in several ways: *less* material in the dress; *less* courage; *less* than a dollar. (The *less* money we have the *fewer* purchases we can make.)

Fiber (fibre) of his being. An unusually trite expression. Avoid it.

Fictitious. See *Facetious.*

Figuratively. This word means "metaphorically," "representing one thing in terms of another," "not literally." (*Figuratively* speaking, you acted like a mouse.) See *Literally.*

Figure. This word is colloquial when used to mean "think," "expect," "suppose," "believe." (I *believe*—not *figure*—him to be an honest man.)

Filthy lucre. Lucre means "money" or "riches." *Filthy lucre* is supposedly a humorous and somewhat derogatory way of referring to money. Overused, the phrase is now a cliché. Besides, some money is clean.

Fine. This is a much overused word in the general sense of approval. It is colloquial when used as an adverb: Mona sang *well* (not *fine* or *just fine*).

First began, first begun. *Begin* means "to originate," "to start." Omit *first* from these wordy expressions.

Firstly, secondly. These are acceptable words, but most skilled users of the language prefer *first* and *second* because they are just as accurate and are shorter.

First-rate, second-rate. These words suggesting rank or degree of excellence are vastly overused. *First-rate* is colloquial in the sense of "very good" or "excellent" or "very well."

Fix. This is a word of many meanings. In standard English it means "to make fast." As a verb, it is colloquial when used to mean "to arrange matters," "to get revenge on." As a noun, it is used colloquially for "difficulty," "predicament."

Flair, flare. The former means "talent" or "ability." To *flare* is "to blaze up." (She has a real *flair* for designing dresses. My anger would *flare* up every time Max spoke.)

Flaunt, flout. To *flaunt* means "to make a gaudy display of." *Flout* means "to mock" or "to scoff at." (Nan was determined to *flout* all conventions. Bill *flaunted* his inherited fortune all over the town.)

Flowed, flown. Often mistaken for each other, these two words are quite different. *Flowed* is the past participle of *flow*. (The river *flowed* to the sea.) *Flown* is the past participle of *fly*. (The birds have *flown*.)

Flower of the Old South. A cliché, as workworn and timeworn as "magnolias and moonlight."

Flunk. A colloquialism for "to fail" and "failure," this word should not appear in standard English as either verb or noun.

Folks. This word is colloquial when used to refer to "relatives" and "family." Both dialectal and colloquial is the expression *just folks*, meaning "simple and unassuming people." *Folksy* is a colloquial word for "sociable."

Fools rush in. Alexander Pope wrote, in his *Essay on Criticism*, "For fools rush in where angels fear to tread." The phrase, *fools rush in*, was so apt that it has been worn bare since the time of Pope. Search for a brighter way to express this concept. Shakespeare found one in *King Richard III*: "Wrens make prey where eagles dare not perch." Have a try yourself.

Footprints on the sands of time. Longfellow was the first to use this expression in his poem "A Psalm of Life." It was a good figure of speech then and for some time thereafter. But it's a fuzzy image now; let's put it aside.

Forbear, forebear. *Forbear* means "to refrain," "to desist from." (George could not *forbear* repeating the story.) *Forebear* applies to an ancestor, "one who came before." (Sybil's *forebears* immigrated to this country from Denmark.)

Forbid. A common and familiar word, *forbid* has several idiomatic constructions. (The ordinance *forbids* children's playing in the streets. He will *forbid* our going. I *forbid* you to leave.)

Force of circumstances. This is a phrase worn so smooth through overuse that it has lost its original effectiveness.

Forceful, forcible. The former means "effective," "vigorous." *Forcible* means "got or obtained by force, strength." (He made a *forceful* sales appeal. The thief made a *forcible* entry through the window.)

Forebear. See *Forbear*.

Forego, forgo. The prefix *for* which gives *forgo* its early meaning of "neglecting" and hence "relinquishing" is distinct from the *fore* of *forego*, which means "before." However, both spellings of this word when meaning "to abstain from," "to renounce," are acceptable.

Foreword, forward. A *foreword* is a "preface" or "introduction." *Forward* suggests "movement onward." (This book needs no *foreword*. The line moved *forward*.)

Forgo. See *Forego*.

Formally, formerly. The first term means "in a formal manner," "precisely," "ceremonially." The latter means "in the past." (The defendant bowed *formally* to the judge. Betty was *formerly* an employee of that company.)

Former, latter. *Former* and *latter* refer to a group of only two units. To refer to a group of more than two items, use *first* and *last* to indicate order.

Formerly. See *Formally*.

Forsake. See *Abandon*.

Fort, forte. *Fort* means an "enclosed place," a "fortified building." *Forte* means "special accomplishment or ability." (The Indians burned the settlers' *fort*. His *forte* is playing the violin.)

Forward. See *Foreword*.

Free from, of. The former of these phrases is idiomatically correct. *Free of* is considered either colloquial or dialectal.

Free gratis. *Gratis* means "without payment," "free." Use either *free* or *gratis*, not both.

Freeze, frieze.   *To freeze* is "to congeal with cold." (Please *freeze* this leg of lamb.) *Frieze* is an architectural term. (This temple has several notable *friezes*.)

Frightened at, by, of.   *Frightened by* and *frightened at* are idiomatically correct. *Frightened of* is either colloquial or dialectal.

From whence.   *Whence* means "from what place." Actually, then, *from whence* is wordy and *from* should be omitted. Because the phrase appears in the *Bible* and in the *Book of Common Prayer*, however, it is not likely to disappear from usage, despite the redundancy involved.

Funeral, funereal.   The word *funeral* is applied to "ceremonies at burial." *Funereal* is related but means "sad," "dismal." (His *funeral* was attended by scores of his friends. The *funereal* look on his face puzzled me.)

Funny.   This is a common and useful word but it is vastly overworked. Its use to mean "strange," "queer," "odd," "remarkable" is considered colloquial. Its primary meaning is "humorous" or "comical."

Further.   See *Farther*.

Gamble, gambol.   The former means "to wager," "to bet." (He *gambled* on horse races.) To *gambol* is to "skip about." (The tots were *gamboling* on the lawn.)

Generally always.   From this wordy expression you should eliminate one word or the other. In this phrase each word has about the same generalized meaning.

Genius, genus.   The former refers to great ability. (Bach was a man of *genius*.) *Genus* refers to class or kind. (What is the *genus* of this plant?)

Get, acquire, attain, obtain, procure.   These words are related in meaning, and distinguishing among them requires care and thought. *Get* is a rather general word which may or may not imply effort or initiative. *Acquire* suggests something added to something already possessed. *Attain* suggests "arriving at." *Obtain* implies the reaching of a goal or possession hoped for. *Procure* is also a general term and means "to get by any means whatever." (Don't *get* so pleased with yourself. I'll *acquire* more stock in that company. My father *attained* a ripe old age. He *obtained* the prize he sought. The soldiers will *procure* food for the refugees.) For additional comment on *get*, see *Got*.

Get one's dander up. This is a colloquial phrase, much overused in certain sections of the United States. Do you know what *dander* means? It's a colloquial word for "anger" or "temper."

Get the hang of something. A useful but colloquial expression. Actually, *get* is a vague word the use of which should be restricted in standard English. For example, such phrases as *get ahead of* (meaning "to surpass"), *get going, get off easy*, and *getup* (meaning "make-up") are also colloquial.

Gibe, jibe. The former means "to scorn," "to sneer at." (Please don't *gibe* at me.) *Jibe* has the same meaning as *gibe* but may also be used to refer to changing direction. (The boat *jibed* twice on the homeward run.)

Gild, guild. To *gild* something is to "overlay it with gold." A *guild* is an association or union. (The potter will *gild* this vase for you. Joe belonged to a *guild* of craftsmen.)

Gilt, guilt. The former means "gold on surface." (This cup has a border of *gilt*.) *Guilt* means "wrongdoing" or "crime." (He confessed his *guilt* to the magistrate.)

Goes without saying. A cliché.

Going on. This term is colloquial both in the meaning of "an event" (a fine *going on*) and in stating ages (six *going on* seven).

Golden locks, golden tresses. Trite expressions which should be left to TV commercials.

Good, well. The former is an adjective with many meanings (a *good* time, *good* advice, *good* Republican, *good* humor, etc.). *Well* functions as both adjective and adverb. As an adjective it means "in good health" and as an adverb it means "ably" or "efficiently." (I feel *well* once again. The sales force worked *well* in this campaign.)

Goodly number. A trite expression.

Go off halfcocked. This is a colloquial expression, to be avoided in formal writing and speaking. The word *go* is used in many other familiar expressions which are also considered colloquial: *plenty of get-up and go, a pretty go, to have a go, no go, to give a go-ahead.*

Gorilla, guerrilla. The former is a manlike ape. (The *gorilla* in this zoo is named Otto.) A *guerrilla* is an irregular soldier, a member of a predatory band. (General Marion's forces were often called *guerrillas.*) Note the spelling of *guerrilla*—two *r*'s and two *l*'s.

Got, gotten. The principal parts of *get* are *get—got—got* (or *gotten*). Both *got* and *gotten* are acceptable words; your choice will depend upon your speech habits or on the rhythm of the sentence you are writing or speaking. *Got* is colloquial when used to mean "must," "ought," "own," "possess," and many other terms. (I *ought*—not *got*—to go.) See *Get* and *Have got to.*

Gourmand, gourmet. These words have to do with eating, but they are different in meaning. A *gourmand* is a large eater. (Diamond Jim Brady was a *gourmand,* often eating for three hours at a time.) A *gourmet* is a fastidious eater, an epicure. (As a French chef, he considers himself a *gourmet.*)

Graduate. This word has several meanings, all of which are in some way related to marking in steps, measuring. Idiom decrees that one *graduate from*—not *graduate*—a school.

Grand. This word means "imposing," "magnificent," "noble," etc. It is overused as a vague counter word meaning "delightful" or "admirable." *Grand* is colloquial in such expressions as *look grand, a grand time, feel grand.*

Gratis. See *Free gratis.*

Green as grass. A cliché. Remember, too, that grass is often not green.

Green with envy. A trite expression.

Grip, gripe. The former refers to the "act of holding firmly." (John had a tight *grip* on the chair.) *Gripe* means "to pinch," "to distress." (Don't eat that; it will *gripe* you.) As a noun or verb meaning "complaint" or "to grumble," "complain," *gripe* is a slang term.

Grisly, gristly, grizzly.   *Grisly* means "horrible," "ghastly." (The scene of the wreck was *grisly*.) *Gristly* pertains to tough, elastic tissue. (This steak is *gristly*.) *Grizzly* means "grizzled," "gray." (The trapper's beard was *grizzly*.)

Guerrilla.   See *Gorilla*.

Guess.   See *Calculate*.

Guild.   See *Gild*.

Guilt.   See *Gilt*.

Guy.   This word has several meanings but we most often use it colloquially to refer to a man, boy, or individual generally. Some experts regard this use of the word as slang; it should be avoided in standard English. *To guy* someone is a slangy way to express the sense of teasing or joshing.

Gyp.   This word, which probably derives from *gypsy*, is a slang term which refers to a swindler, a cheat, and to cheating or swindling. It's expressive enough but hardly dignified or tasteful; omit from standard English.

Had.   The past tense of *have*, this word has many acceptable uses. *Had ought* is hardly a suitable synonym for *ought*, *should*, or *obliged*, however. (We *should*—not *had ought to*—leave now.) *Had better* and *had best* are acceptable idiomatic phrases meaning "ought to" and the like, but *hadn't ought* is a nonstandard and redundant form. Similarly, *had of* is not acceptable as a substitute for *had*. In short, be careful in using *had*: it can, and does, cause trouble.

Hail, hale.   The former means "to greet." (Harry *hailed* Lee as she approached.) *Hale* means "healthy," "vigorous." (His goal was to be *hale* in mind and body.)

Hair, hare.   The former is a threadlike outgrowth. A *hare* is a rabbit. (He has no *hair* on his head. The dog chased the *hare*.)

Hair-raising.   This phrase is colloquial when used to mean "terrifying," "horrifying." Other phrases involving the use of *hair* which are considered colloquial or slangy are *get in one's hair*, *let down one's hair*, and *hair of the dog that bit me*.

Hale. See *Hail*.

Hang, hung. The principal parts of *hang* are *hang—hung—hung*. However, when the word refers to the death penalty, the parts are *hang—hanged—hanged*. (The draperies are *hung*. The murderer was *hanged*.)

Happy pair. A cliché. *Happy* also appears in such to-be-avoided slang expressions as *slap-happy*, *flak-happy*, etc.

Hare. See *Hair*.

Have gone. See *Went*.

Have got to. A colloquial and redundant expression for "must," etc. See *Got*. (I *must*—not *have got to*—do my laundry today.) *Have* is a useful linking verb and appears in many expressions which we use constantly. In standard English we should avoid using such expressions as *have a check bounce*, *have cold feet*, *have a lot on the ball*, and *have it in for someone*. In these expressions, the *have* is only partly responsible for the colloquialism. But in the term *a have nation*, as contrasted with a *have-not* one, the *have* itself is responsible.

Head. This word of many meanings is colloquial in a variety of expressions. In formal speaking and writing you should avoid using such phrases as *to head for*, *heads up*, *out of one's head*, *to take a header*, and *heady* (smart).

Healthful, healthy. These words are often used interchangeably, but *healthful* precisely means "conducive to health"; *healthy* means "possessing health." In other words, places and foods are *healthful*, people and animals are *healthy*. (I wonder whether he is a *healthy* person because he lives in a *healthful* climate.)

Heap, heaps. *Heap* means a "mass," a "mound." Both *heap* and *heaps* are colloquial when used to mean "a great deal," "a large amount." (He owns much—not *a heap of* or *heaps of*—real estate.)

Hear, here. The former means "to become aware of sounds."

The latter means "in this place." (Did you *hear* me? I said to come *here*.)

Hear by the grapevine.   This is one of many expressions using the word *hear*. Most of them are suitable in standard English, but this one, as well as *hear tell* (for *hear* or *learn*), is considered colloquial.

Heart.   This word has several literal (denotative) meanings and many secondary (connotative) ones. Such phrases as *by heart, after my own heart, take to heart,* and dozens more are familiar to all of us. Most of them are idiomatically correct and suitable in formal English. However, nearly all of them have been used so often, by you and me and everyone else, that they have lost much of their appeal and force. Such phrases as *heartfelt thanks* and *heart's content* seem particularly trite.

Heated argument.   A cliché. Arguments which give off more warmth than light can otherwise be described.

Heaven's sake, for.   Some linguists consider this term colloquial, since it is heard much more than it is written. Standard or not, it is surely a trite expression. So, too, is *Good Heavens!*

Height.   This word, meaning "topmost point" or "highest limit," gives no trouble as to meaning but is often misspelled and mispronounced. Only colloquial pronunciation permits sounding the final *t* as *th*; the word ends with *t*, not *th*.

He-man.   A slang expression for a strong, virile man.

Hence.   See *Hither* and *Thence*.

Here.   See *Hear*.

Hide-out.   A colloquial term meaning "hiding place," "secret place."

Highbrow.   See *Lowbrow*.

Hit below the belt.   This term is both colloquial and trite. So, too, are *hit the hay, hit the ceiling,* and *hit the deck*.

Hither, thither, hence, thence, whence.   *Hither* and *thither* are antonyms (opposites) meaning "to or toward *this* place" and "to or toward *that* place." Neither is often used today except in the trite expression *hither and thither*. *Hence* has several meanings, the most frequent of which is "from this time." (A year *hence*, I'll meet you again.) Another meaning is "consequently" or "therefore." *Thence* means "from that time" or "from that place." (He arrived in Albany and *thence* proceeded to Boston.) For *whence*, see *From whence*. Also see *Thence*.

Hoard, horde.   A *hoard* is a "store of laid-up articles or items." (This is the squirrels' *hoard* of nuts.) *Horde* means "crowd." (A *horde* of picnickers descended upon the beach.)

Hold down.   The word *hold* appears in many familiar expressions which are fully acceptable even in formal English: *hold back*, *hold forth*, *hold out*, etc. But *hold up* in the sense of overcharging or robbery is colloquial and so is *hold down* in the sense of "keeping" a job.

Hole, whole.   A *hole* is a "cavity," an "opening." (The *hole* was five feet deep.) *Whole* means "intact" or "complete." (This is the *whole* story.)

Holy, holey, holly, wholly.   *Holy* means "sacred" or "consecrated." (This cathedral is a *holy* place.) *Holey* means "having a hole or holes." (My socks are *holey*.) *Holly* refers to small trees or shrubs with bright-red berries. (We decorated the room with *holly*.) *Wholly* means "completely" or "entirely." (She was *wholly* on your side.)

Holy bonds.   Such phrases as *holy bonds of wedlock* and *holy estate of matrimony* are trite. Such an expression as *holy terror* is considered slangy. *Holy* is a word to be revered, treated with great respect. Don't overuse it.

Home, homey.   Do not loosely use *home* for *house*. Do not omit the preposition in such an expression as *I am at home*. Most importantly, remember that *homey* is a colloquial word for *homelike*.

Hoping, hopping.   The former means "wanting" or "desiring." The latter means "leaping," "springing." (I'm *hoping* to catch the next train. Stop *hopping* about the room.)

Horde.   See *Hoard*.

Hot. This acceptable word appears in many expressions which are either slangy or colloquial. In formal English, don't use such expressions as *hot air* (for "empty talk"), *get hot* (for "act spiritedly"), *make it hot for, hot foot, hot rod, hot water* (for "trouble" or "difficulty"), *not so hot* (for "unsuitable").

How. Meaning "in what manner" and "by what means," *how* is acceptable in many familiar expressions. It is colloquial or slangy, however, in expressions such as *howdy, How come?,* and *How!* as a humorous imitation of an American Indian's greeting.

Human, humane. The word *human* refers to a person. Some especially careful or precise writers and speakers do not use the word alone to refer to man as man; they say or write "human being." However, the practice of using the word alone as a noun has a long and sound background. *Humane* means "tender," "merciful," "considerate." (His treatment of the prisoners was *humane.*)

Hunch. This word has acceptable meanings as both verb and noun. In the sense of "a premonition or feeling that something is going to happen," it is colloquial and should be avoided in standard English.

Hung. See *Hang.*

I, me. The former is the nominative case of the personal pronoun, the latter the objective (accusative) case. Since case of pronouns causes much trouble (see *Case* in Part V), be careful in using *I* and *me.* Watch especially a compound phrase after a verb or preposition. (This order applies only to you and *me*—not *I.* It is *I*—not *me*—who blamed you. He threw the challenge in the face of you and *me*—not *I.*)

Ibid. This is an abbreviation of Latin *ibidem,* meaning "in the same place." It is often used in footnotes in scholarly writing, usually capitalized but only because it normally comes first in a sentence or phrase. For other abbreviations frequently used or encountered in reading, see *I.e.*

Idea. This is a handy word often used vaguely or indiscriminately. (My *purpose*—not my *idea*—is to become a private secretary.)

Identical to, with. *Identical with* is idiomatically correct. Such phrases as *identically the same* and *identical same person* are unnecessarily wordy, since *identical* means "the very same." Also, omit "exactly" from the phrase *exactly identical.*

Idle, idol, idyl. *Idle* means "worthless," "useless," "pointless." (We engaged in *idle* talk.) An *idol* is an "image." (Don't make an *idol* of status in your community.) An *idyl* is a poem or short prose work describing a country scene. (I like Tennyson's "The Idylls of the King.")

I.e., e.g., viz., N.B., P.S. These and many other abbreviations commonly appear in writing. Although abbreviations are not recommended for formal writing, many of them are useful short cuts. For Latin *id est* (meaning "that is") we use the abbreviation *i.e. E.g.* is an abbreviation for Latin *exempli gratia,* meaning "for example." *Viz.* is the abbreviation of *videlicet,* meaning "namely." *N.B.,* or *NB,* stands for *nota bene,* meaning "note well." *P.S.,* or *p.s.,* is the abbreviation for "postscript"; *P.SS.,* or *p.ss.,* stands for "postscripts," from the Latin *postscripta.*

If, whether. In standard English, *if* is used to express conditions; *whether,* usually with *or,* is used in expressions of doubt and in indirect questions expressing conditions. (*If* it doesn't snow, we shall go [simple condition]. We have been wondering *whether* we would reach our sales quota [doubt]. I asked *whether* the doctor had arrived [indirect question].) In standard English, *if* is not used with *or.* (It does not matter *whether*—not *if*—you go or stay.) See also *Doubt if.*

If not better than. See *As good as.*

Ignorance is bliss. See *Where ignorance is bliss.*

Ill. See *Bad.*

Illicit. See *Elicit.*

Illusion. See *Allusion.*

Immigrate. See *Emigrate.*

Immoral. See *Unmoral.*

Impassable, impassible, impossible. *Impassable* means "not passable," "cannot be crossed or traveled over." (This road is *im-*

passable in winter.) *Impassible* means "incapable of suffering," "unfeeling." (His features were *impassible*—or *impassive*.) *Impossible* means "cannot be done or accomplished." (The office manager's suggestion is *impossible*.)

Impatient. Idiom decrees that we write or say *impatient for* something desired, *impatient with* someone else, *impatient of* restraint, and *impatient at* someone's conduct. Who ever said that the English language is simple?

Imply, infer. To *imply* is to suggest a meaning hinted at but not explicitly stated. (Do you *imply* that I am not telling the truth?) To *infer* is to draw a conclusion from statements, circumstances, or evidence. (After that remark, I *infer* that you no longer love me.)

Impossible. See *Impassible*.

Impostor, imposture. An *impostor* is a person who is a cheat or fraud. *Imposture* is the fraud or deception itself. (This *impostor* claims to be a jet pilot. There is a law against the *imposture* of selling watered stock.)

Impractical, impracticable. Distinctions in the meanings of these words have broken down somewhat, but the former means "theoretical" or "speculative." *Impracticable* means "not capable of being used," "unmanageable." (His suggestions are *impractical* and his blueprints are *impracticable*.) See *Unpractical*.

In, into. The former is used to indicate motion within relatively narrow or well-defined limits. (She walked up and down *in* her room for an hour.) *In* is also used when a place is not mentioned. (The airplane came *in* for a landing.) *Into* usually follows a verb indicating motion *to* a place. (When Marion strode *into* the room everyone fell silent.)

In accordance to, with. *In accordance with* is the preferred idiom. However, the phrase is wordy and trite.

In back of. This phrase is colloquial for "behind." However, *in the back of* and *in front of* are considered standard terms, although both are wordy. *Behind* and *before* are shorter and nearly always will suffice. (*Behind*—not *in back of*—the office was the storeroom. *Before*—or *in front of*—the house was a tree.)

Incidental, incidentally. The former is an adjective meaning "casual" or "associated." (*Incidental* costs amounted to one hundred dollars.) *Incidentally* is an adverb meaning "by chance," "accidentally." (You owe me some money and, *incidentally*, I am out of cash.)

Incite. See *Insight*.

Incredible, incredulous. A story or account or book is *incredible* (that is, "unbelievable"). A person is *incredulous* (that is, "unbelieving").

Indict, indite. The former means "to accuse" or "to charge with crime." (Bolo was *indicted* for manslaughter.) *Indite* means "to write," "to compose." (Lincoln *indited* a beautiful letter to the Widow Bixby.)

Individual. See *Party*.

Infer. See *Imply*.

Inferior than, to. The former is not standard idiom; the latter is. (This oil is *inferior to*—not *than*—that.)

Infinity. See *Affinity*.

Ingenious, ingenuous. *Ingenious* means "talented," "resourceful," or "tricky." (This is an *ingenious* computation device.) *Ingenuous* means "innocent," "frank," or "naïve." (Sally is an *ingenuous* little girl.)

In great profusion. A trite expression.

In line, on line. The first of these idiomatic terms is more widely used than the second throughout the United States. (Jim stood *in line* with the other boys.) However, *on line* may be used if doing so causes no confusion to your reader or listener. The word *line* appears in several expressions which are considered colloquial or dialectal: *come into line* (meaning "to correspond" or "agree"), *get a line on* (meaning "to find out about").

In regards to. Omit the *s* in *regards*. Better yet, substitute *concerning* or *about* for the entire phrase; one word is usually more effective than three. See *Regard*.

In search for, in search of. Both of these expressions are commonly used, but the latter is the preferred idiom.

Inside of, off of, outside of.   The *of* in each of these prepositional phrases is superfluous. (*Inside*—not *Inside of*—the barn, the horses are eating hay. The girl fell *off*—not *off of*—her tricycle. Will you travel *outside*—not *outside of*—the state?) When these phrases are not prepositional, the *of* should be included (the *outside of* the house, the *inside of* the tent).

Insight, incite.   *Insight* means "discernment," "penetrating mental vision." (He has a clear *insight* into our problem.) *Incite* means "to urge on," "to provoke." (The major *incited* his men to action.)

In spite of.   See *Despite*.

Insure.   See *Assure*

Interest, intrigue.   Each of these words has more than a dozen shades of meaning, but inexactness in their use usually involves employing *intrigue* when *interest* is the true meaning intended. "This story *intrigues* me" is not likely to express the meaning in mind, for *intrigue* means "to form an underhanded plot," "to use secret influence," "to carry on an illicit affair," etc. The primary meaning of *interest* is "to engage the attention of." *Intrigue* is a word whose overuse suggests an immature, gushy, "schoolgirl" style.

In the last analysis.   A tired old phrase.

In the spring a young man's fancy . . .   Tennyson wrote this first in "Locksley Hall," many years ago. It is now a cliché, and, furthermore, a coy and silly one at that. Older men—and women —fall in love just as young ones do. Nor is spring the only season in which this happens.

Into.   See *In*.

Intrigue.   See *Interest*.

Invalid.   When this word is pronounced with accent on the first syllable (*in'va lid*), it means a "sickly or infirm person." Pronounced as *in val'id* it means "of no force or cogency," "weak." (This contract was *invalid*.)

Invaluable.   See *Valuable*.

Invent.   See *Discover*.

Iron. This word appears in a number of expressions which are unusually trite: *Strike while the iron is hot, many irons in the fire, iron out* (for "smooth out" or "eliminate"). *Iron* is slang for "a small firearm" and is colloquial when used in the phrase *iron horse* to mean a locomotive or a bicycle or tricycle.

Irony. See *Sarcasm*.

Irregardless, disregardless. Each of these words is an illiteracy. That is, neither is a standard word and neither should be used under any circumstances, formal or informal. The prefixes *ir-* and *dis-* are both incorrect and superfluous in these constructions. Use *regardless*.

Is, was, were. These are all parts of the verb *to be*. It may help you to remember that *is* is singular in number, third person, present tense. (*He—*or *She* or *It—is* in the room.) *Was* in singular, first or third person, past tense. (*I—*or *He* or *She* or *It—was* in the room.) *Were* can be either singular or plural, second person in the singular and all three persons in the plural, and is in the past tense. (*You* [both singular and plural] *were* in the room. *We—*or *You* or *They—were* in the room.) The two most frequent errors in using *to be* are employing *was* for *were*, and vice versa, and using *is* in the first or second person instead of in the third, where it belongs. Study in Part V the terms used in the foregoing explanation.

Isle. See *Aisle*.

Is when, is where. These terms are frequently misused, especially in giving definitions. Grammatically, the fault may be described as using adverbial clauses in place of the noun clauses which are called for. "A subway *is where* you ride under the ground" can be improved to "A subway *is* (or *involves*) an electric railroad beneath the surface of the streets." "Walking *is when* you move about on foot" can be improved to "Walking *is the act of* (or *consists of*) moving about on foot."

It stands to reason. A cliché.

Its, it's, its'. This little three-letter combination causes more errors than any other grouping of letters in the English language. However, the distinctions among them are simple and easily learned. *Its* is the possessive form of *it*. (The dress has lost *its* shape.) *It's* is a contraction of *it is* and should never be used unless it means precisely this. (I think *it's* [it is] going to rain.) *Its'* is an illiterary; there is no such form or word in the language.

Jealous, zealous. The former means "resentful" or "envious"; idiom decrees that *jealous* should be followed by *of*, not *for*. (Nancy is *jealous of* Anne's beauty.) *Zealous* means "diligent," "devoted." (He was *zealous* in the duties of his office.)

Jibe. See *Gibe*.

Job. This word is frequently and inexactly used in the sense of "achievement." The chief objection to it is its overuse to cover many general and vague meanings. Furthermore, *job* is colloquial when used to mean "affair," and slang when applied to a robbery. In short, *job* is a useful word but should be employed carefully and sparingly. Consult your dictionary.

Karat. See *Carat*.

Key. See *Quay*.

Kick an idea around. *Kick* means "to give a blow or thrust" and "to drive" or "force." *To kick an idea around* is a slang phrase which apparently originated in advertising circles and has been tiresomely overused. *Kick off* or *kick the bucket* in the meaning of "to die" is also slang. *To kick* in the sense of "to complain," *a kick* in the sense of "a thrill, excitement," and *kick* meaning the effect of an alcoholic drink are all slang terms to be avoided in standard English. *Kickback*, meaning "response," is colloquial.

Kid. This word means "a young goat," in which sense it is rarely used. But *kid* in two other senses is one of the most ubiquitous words in the language. We use it to refer to a "child or young person" and we use *to kid* when we mean "to tease, banter, jest with." In both uses, the word is slangy and should not be employed in standard English.

Kind of a, sort of a. In these phrases the *a* is superfluous. Logically, the main word (which can be *kind*, *sort*, or *type*) should indicate a class, not one thing. (*What kind of*—not *what kind of a*—roast is this?) Although *kind of* and *sort of* are preferred in this construction, these same phrases may be used colloquially to mean "almost," "rather," "somewhat." (She was *rather*—not *kind of*—tired. Martha was *almost*—not *sort of*—reconciled to his leaving.)

Knock.   In the primary sense of "strike" and in several other meanings, *knock* is a legitimate word on any level of usage. We should avoid its use in such phrases and terms as *to knock* (criticize), *knock about* (colloquial for "to wander"), and *knock down* (colloquial in the sense of "to embezzle" or "to steal"). *Knock off*, meaning "to stop," as in "to knock off work," is ever more frequently heard, but it is still considered colloquial by most authorities.

Last but not least.   This is a favorite phrase of many people and has been for centuries. Both Edmund Spenser and Alexander Pope used about this wording and so did Shakespeare in *King Lear* and *Julius Caesar*. It's a good phrase but one "weary of well-doing." Why not give it a deserved rest?

Last straw.   A trite expression.

Later, latter.   The spelling of these words is often confused. They also have different meanings. *Later* refers to time. (He arrived at the office *later* than I did.) For *latter*, see *Former*.

Lay.   See *Lie*.

Lead, led.   These words show the confusion that our language suffers because of using different symbols to represent one sound. *Lead* (pronounced *lēd*) is the present tense of the verb and causes little or no difficulty. *Led* (pronounced like the metal) is the past tense and is often misspelled with *ea*. (*Lead* the blind man across the street. He *led* the blind man across the street yesterday.)

Lean, lien.   The former means "scant of flesh," "not fat." (This is a *lean* piece of meat.) *Lien* means "legal right." (Jack procured a *lien* on the property.)

Learn, teach.   Standard English requires a distinction in meaning between these words. (I'll *learn* the language if you will *teach* me.) *To learn someone something* is an illiteracy.

Least, lest. The former means "smallest," "slightest." The latter means "for fear that." (He did not give me the *least* trouble. Give me your picture *lest* I forget how you look.)

Leave, let. Both words are common in several idiomatic expressions implying permission, but *let* is standard whereas *leave* is not. (*Let*—not *leave*—me go with you.) Also see *Abandon*.

Led. See *Lead*.

Legible, readable. These terms are synonymous in the meaning of "capable of being deciphered or read with ease." *Readable* has the additional meaning of "interesting or easy to read." (Your handwriting is *legible*. This book is *readable*.)

Lend. See *Loan*.

Less. See *Fewer*.

Lessen, lesson. The former means "to become less," "to diminish." This medicine will *lessen* your pain.) A *lesson* is "something to be learned." (That should be a *lesson* to you.)

Lest. See *Least*.

Let. This word, with a primary meaning of "to allow," "permit," has many legitimate uses. Such phrases involving *let* as the following, however, are colloquial and should not be used in standard English: *let on* (in the sense of "pretend"); *let out* (as in "school let out"); *let up* (meaning "to cease"). *To let one's hair down* is both colloquial and trite. See also *Leave*.

Levee, levy. The former is an embankment. (The Mississippi River flowed over the *levee*.) *To levy* is "to impose" and *a levy* is an assessment. (The judge will *levy* a large fine. The *levy* was increased by ten per cent.)

Liable. See *Apt*.

Lie, lay, lye. The first of these words is the present tense (infinitive) of a verb meaning "to be in a recumbent or prostrate position." It also means a "falsehood." (Please *lie* down. Never tell a *lie*.) *Lay* has several meanings but it is most often used as the past tense of *lie*. (He *lay* down for a rest.) *Lye* is an alkaline substance. (Some soaps contain *lye*.)

Lien. See *Lean*.

Lifelong, livelong. The former means "for all one's life." (His *lifelong* desire was to see Tahiti.) *Livelong* means "whole," "entire." (We played baseball the *livelong* day.)

Lightening, lightning. The former means "making less heavy." The latter means "discharge of electricity." (Try *lightening* the load of wood on your wagon. *Lightning* was flashing in the summer skies.)

Like. See *As if*.

Likely. See *Apt*.

Limped into port. A cliché.

Line. This standard word has several nonstandard uses. It is considered slang in such expressions as *come into line* (meaning both "agree" and "behave properly"); *get a line on*; *he gave*, or *fed*, *her a line*. See *Along these lines*.

Lineament, liniment. *Lineament* refers to a feature or characteristic. (What is the most distinguished *lineament* of his face?) *Liniment* is a medicated liquid. (The *liniment* eased the pain in my arm.)

Liqueur, liquor. These words are related in meaning, but *liqueur* refers to a highly flavored alcoholic drink, whereas *liquor* is a distilled or spirituous beverage. (Rye was Joe's favorite *liquor*, but after dinner he drank a *liqueur* called chartreuse.)

Listen. This common word is often followed by a preposition. *Listen to* is standard idiomatic usage. (Listen *to*—not *at*—what I say.) To *listen in* on a conversation is an overused expression.

Literally. This word not only is overused but also is confused with *figuratively*. It is an antonym of the latter and really means "not imaginatively," "actually." See *Figuratively*.

Livelong. See *Lifelong*.

Loan, lend. Many careful writers and speakers use *loan* only as a noun (to make a *loan*) and *lend* as a verb (to *lend* money). Because of constant and widespread usage, *loan* is now considered a legitimate verb to be avoided only in formal English.

Locate. This is a standard word but is considered colloquial when used in the meaning of "take up residence" and "remember." (He *settled in*—not *located in*—Denver. Finally I *remembered*—not *located*—what you had told me.)

Long-felt want. A trite phrase.

Looking for all the world like. A weary phrase.

Loose, lose, loss. *Loose* means "not fastened tightly." (This is a *loose* connection.) *Lose* means "to suffer the loss of." (Don't *lose* your hard-earned money.) *Loss* means "a defeat," "a reverse." (The coach blamed me for the *loss* of the game.)

Lots of, a lot of, a whole lot. These terms are colloquial for "many," "much," "a great deal." The chief objection is that each is a vague, general expression.

Lousy. This word actually means "infested with lice." It is constantly used as a slang expression, however, to mean "dirty," "disgusting," "contemptible," "poor," "inferior," and "well supplied with" (*lousy* with money). Use it in only the most informal of informal conversations. You can startle or impress your friends by using *pediculous.*

Lowbrow, highbrow. These terms are being used so increasingly in both writing and speaking that presumably they will, in time, be accepted as standard usage. Their status now is that of either slang or colloquialisms, depending upon the authority consulted. For a while, at least, do not use them in formal writing and speaking. Need they be defined? For anyone who doesn't know, *lowbrow* refers to a person lacking, or considered to lack, cultivated and intellectual tastes. Naturally, *highbrow* is applied to those who do have such attainments. Both terms are frequently used in a derisive or derogatory manner.

Lucre. See *Filthy lucre.*

Luxuriant, luxurious. The former term refers to abundant growth; *luxurious* pertains to luxury. (The foliage was *luxuriant.* The motel accommodations were *luxurious.*)

Lye. See *lie.*

Mad. This short and useful word has many acceptable meanings such as "insane," "frantic," and "frenzied." Most authorities consider *mad* to be colloquial when it is used to mean "angry" or "furious." (I was *angry at*, or *furious with*—not *mad at*—him.)

Madam, madame. These words are interchangeable, although the former is customarily applied to women both married and unmarried, whereas *madame* is restricted by some (including French-speaking people) to married women. The plural form is *madams* or *mesdames*; the abbreviation most frequently heard is *ma'am*. Probably it would be well to think twice before referring to a woman as "a madam."

Mad as a wet hen. A trite expression. Anger can be characterized in many other ways.

Make. This is a useful word with many meanings. However, it is used in several phrases which are considered colloquial or slangy: *make it* (to do or achieve something), *make like* (to impersonate or imitate), *make over* (to be demonstrative), *make with* (to use, or to do something with), and *on the make* (trying to succeed socially, financially, or with a lover).

Mantle of snow. A cliché.

Marshal, martial. A *marshal* is an officer; *martial* means "warlike." (He was arrested by the *marshal*. The county was placed under *martial* law.) The word *marital* is sometimes confused with *martial*. *Marital* refers to marriage, connubial affairs. True, some *marital* episodes are *martial*, but is that what is meant when *i* is transposed?

Martyr, victim. The former means "a person tortured or killed because of his beliefs." A *martyr* is certainly a *victim*, but the latter is someone injured or killed as a result of causes over which he may or may not have had some control (*victims* of war; *victims* of automobile accidents).

Masterly, masterful. The former means "having the skill or knowledge of a master." (His concert was *masterly*.) *Masterful* means "powerful," "domineering." (George Washington must have been a *masterful* man.)

May. See *Can*.

Maybe, may be. The former means "perhaps." (*Maybe* you will finish your work early today.) *May be* (two words) is used to express possibility. (It *may be* going to rain today.)

McCoy, the real. This term is supposedly derived from advertisements of prize fights stating that a celebrated boxer named McCoy would actually appear and not an inferior fighter with the same name. Whatever its origin, the phrase is both a cliché and slang.

Me. See *I*.

Medal, meddle, metal, mettle. *Medal* means "commemorative design." (The fireman received a *medal* for bravery.) To *meddle* is "to interfere." (Oscar will *meddle* in your affairs.) *Metal* means "crystalline substance." (Gold, silver, and copper are *metals*.) *Mettle* means "disposition," "temper." (This task will try your *mettle*.)

Meets the eye. This phrase, usually given as *more than meets the eye*, is trite. So is *more than meets the ear*, which was first used by John Milton in "Il Penseroso."

Memorandum. This word of Latin origin which means "short note" or "record of events" has two plurals, both acceptable in standard English: *memoranda, memorandums*. See *Foreign plurals* in Part III, "Guide to Correct Spelling."

Metal. See *Medal*.

Method in his madness. Polonius, speaking of Hamlet's strange conversation, said: "Though this be madness, yet there is method in't." Several million people have echoed Polonius. Let's try another phrase.

Mettle. See *Medal*.

Might. See *Can*.

Might of. This is an illiteracy. (If you had asked, I *might have* —not *might of*—accompanied you.) See *Would of*.

Mighty. This word means "strong" or "powerful." When it is used to mean "very" or "extremely," it is considered a colloquial-

ism. (Tom was a *very*—not *mighty*—handsome boy.) But see
Very.

Miner, minor. A *miner* extracts minerals; a *minor* is a person
below legal age.

Moat, mote. A *moat* is a trench or large ditch. (The *moat* around
the castle was filled with water.) A *mote* is "a particle," "a
speck." (There is a *mote* of dust in his left eye.)

Monarch of all I survey. This is one of the two most famous lines
ever written by William Cowper. He died in 1800; the phrase
should have done the same long years ago. Try something
fresher. See *None the worse for wear*.

Monopoly for, of, on. Each of these phrases is used, but only
monopoly of is sanctioned as correct idiomatic usage.

Moors, moors, mores. *Moors* are Mohammedans. (Many *Moors*
live in North Africa.) Open land is referred to as *moors*. *Mores*
is a term applied to customs and folkways.

Moral, morale. The former has a meaning of "good," "proper."
(Frances' *moral* code was high.) *Morale* refers to a condition,
state of being, or attitude. (The *morale* in this factory is excellent.)

More in sorrow than in anger. Hundreds of Shakespeare's expressions were and are so effective that they have become clichés.
This one, as you may have guessed, is from *Hamlet*.

Mores. See *Moors*.

Morning. See *This morning*.

Most, almost. *Most* is the superlative of *many* and *much* and
means "greatest in amount, quality, or degree." *Almost* means
"very nearly," "all but." *Most* is colloquial when used for *almost*.
(He has *almost*—not *most*—finished his work.)

Mote. See *Moat*.

Mother Nature. Nature may indeed be the mother of us all, but
to say so is to employ a cliché.

Motif, motive. The former applies to a theme, a subject. (What
is the *motif* of that selection?) *Motive* means "incentive," "goal

or object of one's actions." (What was your *motive* in insulting the sales manager?) The prepositions *of* and *for* may also follow *motive* (the *motive of* the manager, the *motive for* this action).

Motley crew.   *Motley* means "heterogeneous," "of many different elements." A *crew* is a "group of people." Many groups of people, including your friends and mine, may indeed be motley, but the phrase itself is old and tired.

Muchly.   This is an illiteracy. That is, despite the fact that you may often hear the word, it really doesn't exist—not in standard English. Use *much* instead.

Must.   As a noun, this word is no longer considered slang by most authorities, but it is tiresomely overused to mean something essential or necessary, as in "This play is a *must*."

Mutual.   See *Common*.

Myriad lights.   The word *myriad* is an effective and even lovely way to express "an indefinitely large number," but it has been coupled with *lights* so much that the phrase has become trite.

Naught.   See *Aught*.

Naval, navel.   The word *naval* pertains to ships or shipping. (England was a great *naval* power.) *Navel* means "a pit," "a depression." (These are *navel* oranges from Florida. He was wounded in the stomach near his *navel*.)

N.B.   See *I.e.*

Needs no introduction.   The first ten thousand toastmasters to use this phrase were not accused of being trite. All later ones using this cliché should change the record.

Neither . . . nor.   See *Either . . . or*.

Nest.   This perfectly good word appears in several overused and trite expressions, among them to *feather one's nest* and *nest egg* (money reserve).

Nice.   This is a word with many meanings, including "agreeable," "pleasant," "attractive," and "delightful." Its overuse indicates the need for more specific substitutes.

Nipped in the bud. Sir John Suckling (1609–1642) started this phrase on its busy life. It is now quite stale.

None the worse for wear. William Cowper (1731–1800) coined this phrase, which was once fresh and vigorous but is now hackneyed. See *Monarch of all I survey*.

No place, nowhere. The former is a perfectly sound phrase ("There's *no place* like home"), but in standard English it cannot be a synonym for *nowhere*. (She could find her compact *nowhere*—not *no place*.) Be certain to spell *nowhere* correctly; *nowheres* is as dialectal as *no place*.

Not by a long shot. This phrase seems effective, but it is trite and is considered slangy by most authorities. The word *shot* appears in other expressions which are either colloquial or slangy and should not be used in standard English: *a long shot* (a bet against heavy odds); *have a shot at* (to try, attempt); *shot*, meaning a "drink of liquor," "something to bet on," or "worn out" (our chances were *shot*); and *shotgun wedding* (a forced marriage). See *Big shot*.

No thinking man. A cliché.

Notorious, noteworthy, notable, noted. *Notorious* means "infamous" (known for unsavory reasons). (Jack was a *notorious* liar.) Both *noteworthy* and *notable* mean "remarkable," "worthy of note." (The commencement exercises were *noteworthy*—or *notable*.) *Noted* means "famous," "well known." (Einstein was a *noted* physicist.)

Nowheres. See *Anywheres* and *No place*.

Number. See *Amount*. *Number* is slangy or colloquial in such expressions as *to get one's number, a smart number, one's number is up*.

O, oh. The former is usually part of a vocative (direct address), is normally capitalized, and is rarely followed by any mark of punctuation. *Oh* is an interjection, may be followed by a comma or exclamation point, and follows the usual rules for capitalization. (O George! You don't really mean that. Yet, *oh*, what love we had for him! *Oh*, what a day!)

Oblivious of, to. The former phrase is idiomatically standard; *oblivious to* is somewhat colloquial.

Observance, observation. The former refers to keeping or carrying out a duty, rule, or custom. *Observation* is a taking notice, a noting of facts. (The mayor insisted upon *observance* of all national holidays. The police placed the suspect under close *observation*.)

Obtain. See *Get.*

Occident. See *Orient.*

Oculist, ophthalmologist, optometrist, optician. The distinction between and among these terms is important to those who are one or the other and to people who have eye trouble. *Oculists* and *ophthalmologists* are holders of the Doctor of Medicine degree who specialize in diseases and disorders of the eye; the latter term is somewhat more esteemed—*ophthalmologists* frequently charge more than *oculists.* An *optometrist* does not hold an M.D. degree and deals primarily with the range and power of vision. An *optician* is a person who makes and sells eyeglasses and other optical instruments.

Of. *Of* is an exceedingly common word with a variety of standard uses. However, it is not a substitute for *have* after auxiliary verbs in such expressions as *could of, would of, might of, should of,* etc. (You *should have*—not *should of*—arrived earlier.)

Off of. See *Inside of.*

Official, officious, officer. *Official* pertains to holding an office or position of authority. (He was an *official* in the Treasury Department.) *Officer* resembles *official* but specifically means "anyone elected or appointed to a position in business, government, etc." (He is an *officer* who performs his duty religiously.) *Officious* means "meddlesome," "offering unwanted or unnecessary advice." (His manner toward all tourists was *officious*.)

Of the earth, earthy. A cliché. The phrase occurs in the King James translation of the *Bible, First Corinthians,* Chapter 15: verse 47. It is such a memorable phrase that it has been used almost to death, even by people who don't fully understand what it means. The *Revised Standard Version* gives the saying as "The first man was from the earth, a man of dust."

O.K.   This everyday term, which may be written with or without periods, is colloquial or business English for "all right," "correct," "approved." It is occasionally spelled *okay, okeh.* The terms *oke* and *okeydoke* are slang. For the debatable origin of *O.K.*, see any standard dictionary.

Older, oldest.   See *Elder, eldest.*

Once-over.   A slang term meaning "a swiftly appraising glance," or what boys and girls, men and women, quite often give each other.

On line.   See *In line.*

On the dot.   This phrase, meaning "at the exact time," is colloquial.

On the level.   This is a slang term meaning "honest(ly)" or "fair(ly)." To do one's *level best* is a colloquial method of expressing "the best one can do."

On the move.   This method of expressing "movement about from place to place" is both colloquial and trite. To *get a move on* is a slang expression for "hurry," "go faster."

On the part of.   This is a clumsy and wordy phrase which is equivalent to the short and simple *by.* (That was a generous gesture *by*—not *on the part of*—the neighbors.)

Ophthalmologist, optician, optometrist.   See *Oculist.*

Or.   See *Are.*

Oracle, auricle.   An *oracle* is "a place or medium for consulting the gods." (The Greek citizen visited the *oracle* of Diana.) *Auricle* is an anatomical term. (The *auricle* of his right ear is damaged).

Oral, aural, verbal.   *Oral* means "spoken." (The order was *oral*, not written.) *Aural* means "received through the ear," or "the sense of hearing." (After the concussion, Jane's *aural* sense was below normal.) *Verbal* means "of, in, or by means of words." In such a sentence as "Our contract was *verbal,*" it means "unwritten." *Oral* and *verbal* are thus often confused in everyday use.

Ordinance, ordnance. The former is a "rule" or "regulation." (There is an *ordinance* against smoking inside stores.) *Ordnance* means "military weapons." (Major Jackson teaches a course in *ordnance* at the military college.)

Orient, Occident. The former term refers to the East, Asia, the Far East. The adjective is *oriental,* "referring to the East." *Occident* suggests the countries west of Asia, specifically Europe and the entire Western Hemisphere. The adjective is *occidental* (*Occidental*) as opposed to *oriental* (*Oriental*).

Oscillate, osculate. The former means "to swing" or "to vibrate." (The pendulum of the clock *oscillates* without sound.) *Osculate* means "to kiss." (When did Romeo *osculate* Juliet?)

Ought. See *Aught.*

Our. See *Are.*

Out. This useful adverb has many meanings and many standard uses. However, it appears in several phrases which are substandard. Avoid using the following: *out of our way, all out* (meaning "completely"), *on the outs* (meaning "on unfriendly terms"), *out from under* (meaning "away from difficulty or danger"), *outsmart* (meaning "to outwit"). See *Pass out.*

Out loud. See *Aloud.*

Outside of. See *Inside of.*

Outstanding. An overworked *counter word,* which see in Part V.

Over with. This term is colloquial in the sense of "finished with," "done," "completed." (I am *finished with*—not *over with*—the medical examination.)

Paid, payed. *Paid* is the past tense and past participle of the verb *pay.* (He *paid* all his bills promptly.) *Payed* is used only in the sense of to *pay* out a cable or line. (He *payed* out the anchor line slowly.)

Pail, pale. A *pail* is "a bucket or other container." *Pale* means "of whitish appearance." (We drank an entire *pail* of milk. Wanda turned *pale* with fear.)

Pain, pane. The former means "suffering," "distress." (The victim writhed in *pain*.) *Pane* means a "plate of glass." (He replaced the broken *pane*.)

Pair, pare. *Pair* means "two of a kind." *Pare* means "to cut," "to trim." (This is a beautiful *pair* of horses. We had to *pare* a bushel of potatoes.)

Pal. This word is colloquial usage for "comrade," "intimate friend." To *pal around* with someone is also colloquial and hardly suitable in standard English.

Palate, palette, pallet. *Palate* refers to the roof of the mouth. (This dish was pleasing to her *palate*.) A *palette* is a board for painters. (The *palette* was smeared with many colors.) *Pallet* means a small makeshift bed. (The little boy had to sleep on a *pallet* that night.)

Pale. See *Pail*.

Pane. See *Pain*.

Paramount issue. It is true that some issues are *paramount* (supreme, chief), but the phrase mentioned has been used so often as to lose its effectiveness. Try something less trite.

Pardon, excuse. These words are closely related, but *pardon me* is sometimes considered more elegant and dignified than *excuse me*. Actually, small slips or blunders or accidents are *excused*, and more considerable faults (and even crimes) are *pardoned*. *Excuse* has an additional meaning of "giving or requesting permission to leave."

Pare. See *Pair*.

Partial, partially, partly. *Partial* is an adjective with two distinct meanings. The first meaning is that of "biased," "prejudiced," "showing favoritism" in such a phrase as "to be *partial* to." The other meaning of *partial* is "not complete or total," and in this meaning it is a synonym of *partly*. Usually, you should prefer *partly* to *partially*, unless the meaning is that of "limited degree."

(His *partial* knowledge of the subject was due *partly* to his youth.) *Partially* is an adverb with the same two meanings as *partial*. *Partiality* is a noun meaning "fondness for" or "tendency to favor unfairly."

Party, person, individual. Except in telephonic and legal language, *party* implies a group and should not be used to refer to one person except in a slang or colloquial sense. *Individual* refers to a single, particular person. As nouns, *individual* and *person* are synonymous. As an adjective, *individual* means "single," "separate," and is therefore unnecessary and repetitious when used to modify *person* or when "each" has been used. Both *individual person* and *each individual member* are wordy.

Passed, past. The former is the past tense of the verb *to pass*; the latter is the past participle. (The car *passed* us at sixty miles an hour. Your troubles are now *past*.) *Pass* is not only a verb; it is also a noun. In one or the other of these two categories, it appears in many expressions which are either colloquial or slangy, among them: *a pretty pass, make a pass at, pass out* (which see), *pass up*, and *pass the buck*.

Pass out. In the sense of "to faint" or "to become unconscious" *pass out* is a useful term but, as slang, should not appear in standard English.

Payed. See *Paid*.

Peace, piece. The former means "freedom from disturbance"; the latter refers to a portion. (*Peace* is the world's greatest need. Have another *piece* of pie.) See *Piece*.

Pedal, peddle. The former is a lever. (One *pedal* of the bicycle fell off.) To *peddle* is to sell at retail, to hawk. (Jack *peddled* vegetables from a cart.)

Pendant, pendent. The former is an ornament, a hanging object. (She fastened a gold *pendant* on her blouse.) *Pendent* means "suspended," "hanging." (The *pendent* tapestry was richly designed.)

Pending merger. A trite expression.

Pep, peppy. The first is a slang expression as both noun and verb.

The second term, an adjective, is fully as slangy. Use some such standard word as *energy*, *briskness*, *spirit*, or *vigor*.

Percent, per cent. This word (from Latin *per centum*, "by the hundred") may be spelled as either one or two words. *Percent* is colloquial when used as a substitute for *percentage* (the noun). *Percentage* is colloquial when used in the meaning of "profit" or "advantage," as in "What's the *percentage* in hard work?"

Perfect. See *Absolutely*.

Perpetrate, perpetuate. The former means "to do or perform something," "to be guilty of," "to commit." *Perpetuate* means "to preserve from oblivion," "to cause to continue to be remembered." (Joe *perpetrated* the crime in blind anger. This statue will *perpetuate* our memory of heroes.)

Perplex. See *Puzzle*.

Persecute, prosecute. The former means "to oppress," "to harass." (In the Soviet Union many helpless people are *persecuted*.) *Prosecute* means "to bring proceedings, usually legal." (The district attorney *prosecuted* all the charges vigorously.)

Personage, person. A *personage* is a distinguished or notable person. (We were addressed by no less a *personage* than the Secretary of State.) For *person*, see *Party*.

Personal, personnel. The former means "private," "individual." (The employer granted me a *personal* interview.) *Personal* is a much overused word. Perhaps because we wish to belong, to show a close relationship with something, we say or write such sentences as "He is a *personal* friend of mine." Shouldn't the *personal* be omitted? How many friends does each of us have who are not personal? *Personnel* means "a body of persons," usually a group employed in any work, establishment, enterprise, or service. (The *personnel* of this firm was carefully chosen.)

Persuade. See *Convince*.

Phone. See *Ad*. Also, *phone up* should never be used for "telephone."

Phony. As both adjective and noun, this word is slang. As a quick and easy substitute for "not genuine," "fake," *phony* is so often used that, presumably, it will in time be acceptable in standard English. Until then, no.

Physic, physical, psychic, psychical, physique. *Physic* is a term applied to a laxative or cathartic. (The doctor prescribed a *physic* for his patient.) *Physical* pertains to material or natural things or forces, as contrasted with mental, moral, and spiritual matters. (The force of gravity is a *physical* fact.) *Psychic* and *psychical* are synonyms; each pertains to the psyche, or mind. Each refers to matters beyond natural or known physical processes. (His awareness of our problem is so remarkable that it must be considered *psychic*.) *Physique* refers to the structure, constitution, form, and appearance of the body. (This athlete has a right to be proud of his *physique*.)

Picturesque scene. A cliché.

Piece. This common word is often used colloquially or dialectally to mean "a short distance" or "a little way." (I'll walk you a *piece* when you leave.) In the sense of "reprimand," "unfavorable opinion," *a piece of one's mind* is colloquial.

Pistil, pistol. The former is a seed-bearing organ. (This is the *pistil* of a flowering plant.) A *pistol* is a small firearm. (Don't point your *pistol* at me, please.) The phrase *hot as a pistol* is expressive enough, but all authorities consider it slangy.

Plain, plane. The former has several meanings; one of the most used is "simple" or "not complex." (He made a *plain* statement.) *Plane* refers to a flat surface. It also mean "social status or level." (You and I are on the same social *plane*.)

Plaintiff, defendant. A *plaintiff* is a complainant, one who brings a suit in a court of law. (Marcia was the *plaintiff* in this action.) A *defendant*, as opposed to a *plaintiff*, is a defending party, a person sued or accused. (As *plaintiff*, you brought the action and, as *defendant*, I shall oppose you.)

Plane. See *Plain*.

Plan on going, plan to go. Both of these expressions are in everyday use, but the former is considered colloquial and idiomatically not so sound as *plan to go*.

Pleasing prospect. A trite expression.

Plenty. This word is colloquial when used to mean "very," "fully." (The weather is very—not *plenty*—cold today.)

Plot thickens, the. A cliché.

Plus. The most common meaning of this word is "added to." It is, however, not a synonym for "and" and "with." Unacceptable in standard English is such a phrase as "My companion and I, *plus* two workers from a nearby office, . . ."

P.M., p.m. See A.M.

Poorly. When this word is used to mean "in poor health" it is colloquial. (I feel bad—not *poorly*—today.)

Portion, potion. The former refers to a part, piece, or quantity. (Have another *portion* of cake.) A *potion* is a drink, especially of poison or medicine. (Socrates drank the deadly *potion*.)

Powers that be. In the *Bible* (Romans 13:1) is the saying "The powers that be are ordained of God." Few will quarrel with this statement, but no one can deny that the phrase has been worked overly long and hard.

Practicable, practical. See *Impractical*.

Practice, practise. The former is the preferred spelling, but the latter is not incorrect. Meanings are numerous but the most usual one refers to "habitual or customary performance." (He made a *practice* of drinking ten glasses of water every day.)

Pray, prey. The former means "to entreat," "to beseech." *Prey* means, as a verb, to "seek for and seize, as an animal does," or "to exert a harmful or baleful influence." (These worshipers will *pray* for your health. These worries *preyed* upon his mind.)

Precede, preceding, proceed, proceeding, precedence, procedure. *Precede* means "to go or come before." (Please *precede* me into the hall.) *Preceding* means "previous." (The *preceding* program was transcribed.) *Proceed* means "to go forward or onward." (Let's *proceed* with our conversation.) *Proceeding* in its form as a verb means "going forward." (They are *proceeding* with their work.) As a noun, *proceeding* means "an action or course of action" and usually appears in the plural form. (The *proceedings* this evening were inexcusable. The district attorney started *proceedings* against the hit-and-run driver.) *Precedence* is a noun meaning "the act or fact of preceding." (This story has *precedence* over all others.) *Procedure* means "conduct or mode of action." (His *procedure* was carefully planned.)

Prefer (one) over, (another), prefer to. The latter of these expressions is idiomatically correct. (She *prefers* John *to* Henry.)

Prescribe, proscribe. The former means "to direct," "to order." *Proscribe* means "to banish," "to outlaw." (What did the nurse *prescribe* for your cough? Playing the radio after midnight is *proscribed*.)

Pretend like, that. *Pretend* means "to create an imaginary characteristic or to play a part." (He *pretended* to be a gangster.) *Pretend like* is considered either dialectal or illiterate. (He *pretended* that—not *like*—he was sick.) Or write "He feigned illness" or "He pretended to be ill."

Pretty. This counter word is greatly overused, nearly always inexactly and vaguely. Its use as a synonym for "rather" or "somewhat" is colloquial. (I did rather—not *pretty*—well with the sales presentation.)

Prey. See *Pray*.

Principal, principle. The former means "a sum of money" or "a chief person." As an adjective, *principal* means "main" or "chief." *Principle* is always a noun meaning "a governing rule or truth," "a doctrine." (The *principal* of that school was a man of *principle*.)

Prior than, prior to. Both terms are in common use but only the latter has the sanction of accepted idiom.

Proceed, proceeding, procedure. See *Precede*.

Procure. See *Get*.

Promising future. A cliché.

Prophecy, prophesy. The former is a noun meaning "prediction." *Prophesy* is a verb meaning "to foretell." (Was your *prophecy* about the election correct? From the very first returns, he could *prophesy* the outcome of the election.)

Propose, purpose. *Propose* is a verb meaning "to plan" or "to set forth." (We *propose* that you leave early today.) *Purpose* as a noun commonly means "intention" or "aim." (Is that your real *purpose?*)

Proposition. A colloquial and much overused word for "affair," "offer," "project," "undertaking," "proposal," etc.

Proscribe. See *Prescribe*.

Prosecute. See *Persecute*.

Proud possessor. A trite expression.

Proved, proven. As the past participle of "prove," *proved* is much more often used than *proven*. Both are correct in standard English, but *proved* is preferable because it is more readily understood and is always accepted. See *Test out*, below.

Provided, provided that, providing. *Provided* and *providing* are in standard use as conjunctions with the meaning of "if," "on condition," "it being understood," etc. Both *providing* and *provided* are often followed by *that*, although the addition is unnecessary. (I shall join the club, *provided*, or *providing*, I am asked.)

P.S. See *I.e.*

Psychic, psychical. See *Physic*.

Psychological moment, the. A trite expression.

Psychology, psychiatry. The former is a broader and more inclusive term than the latter. *Psychology* refers to "the science of mental states, processes, and human and animal nature." *Psychiatry* is "the practice or science of treating mental diseases." (The *psychology* of the driver is different from that of the man on foot. In order to practice *psychiatry* you must first be a doctor of medicine.)

Purpose. See *Propose*.

Put. This little word has a large number of colloquial and slangy uses. Avoid in standard English the use of such expressions as *stay put* (meaning "fixed"), *put across* (meaning "to carry out successfully"), *put it on* (meaning "to exaggerate"), *put it there* ("shake hands"), *put over* ("to accomplish"), *put up* ("to incite to action"), *put out* ("upset" or "disturbed").

Puzzle, perplex, bewilder. *Puzzle* is an overused word for which a more exact term can usually be found. *Puzzle* implies a baffling or confusing problem or situation which is difficult to understand or solve. When an element of worry or uncertainty is added, as it usually is, a more exact word is *perplex*. *Bewilder* is a stronger, more emphatic word than either *puzzle* or *perplex*; it implies such utter confusion that the mind is staggered beyond coherent thought. Avoid overusing *puzzle*; it is a rather loose and generalized word.

Quay, key. The former is a wharf; the latter is an instrument for unlocking or locking. (The fish were swimming near the *quay*. Where is the *key* to the house?)

Quiet, quit, quite. *Quiet* means "still" or "calm." (It was a *quiet* meeting.) *Quit* means "to stop," "to desist" (see *Abandon*). (Did you *quit* working?) *Quite* means "positively," "entirely." (I am *quite* certain there is a burglar in the house.)

Quite a. This phrase is colloquial when used to mean "more than." In standard English avoid using such phrases as "quite a few," "quite a bit," and "quite a lot."

Quitter, quits. *Quitter* is a colloquial term for one who gives up easily, without really trying. *To call it quits* is a trite expression.

Rabbit, rarebit. A *rabbit* is a rodent of the hare family. In standard English there is no such word as *rarebit*. It frequently appears in the phrase *Welsh rarebit* (a dish of melted cheese on toast) but only because of faulty etymology; the correct phrase is *Welsh rabbit*. However, *rare* and *bit* can be correctly used as two words. (That was a *rare bit* of humor.)

Rain, reign, rein. *Rain* is precipitation. (We had three inches of *rain* yesterday.) *Reign* means "rule" or "to rule." (This event occurred during the *reign* of Queen Elizabeth I.) A *rein* is a check or curb. (Bill tried to *rein* in the mare.)

Raise, raze, rise.   *Raise* means "to elevate," "to lift." (Please *raise* your eyes and look at me.) *Raze* means "to tear down." (The wreckers will *raze* this building.) *Rise* means "to get up." (When the chairman enters, everyone should *rise*.) Strictly, the word *raise* is never a noun; therefore it is colloquial to refer to a *raise* in wages. The word, in standard English, should be *rise*, but *raise* is admittedly far more common. When referring to bringing up children, *rear*, *raise*, and *bring up* may all be used. *Rear* is preferred in this connection, although *bring up* is also standard; *raise* is colloquial. To *raise Cain, raise the roof, raise a rumpus*, and *raise the devil*, are all slang. To *get a rise out of* someone or something is also slang.

Rang, wrung.   *Rang* is the past tense of the verb *ring*, meaning "to give forth a sound." (He *rang* the bell for ten minutes.) *Wrung* is a part of the verb *wring*, "to press or squeeze." (She *wrung* out the clothes before hanging them on the line.)

Rarebit.   See *Rabbit*.

Raze.   See *Raise*.

Readable.   See *Legible*.

Real.   In the sense of "really" or "very," *real* is an impropriety. (Are you *really*, or *very*, certain of your figures?—not *real* certain.)

Real, actual.   These words are closely related in meaning, but they may be subtly distinguished. *Real* places emphasis upon objective or material existence. In *actual*, emphasis is placed upon coming into a sphere of action or fact. (Is this *real* or only my imagination? Is this an *actual* assignment or only something to distract me?) The antonyms of *real* are *counterfeit, imaginary*, and *artificial*. The opposites of *actual* are *possible, theoretical*, and *virtual*.

Really and truly.   This is a trite expression and also a wordy one. *Really* and *truly* are related in meaning; one or the other is sufficient.

Rear.   See *Raise*.

Reason is because.   This construction has a long history of usage behind it, and it is found in the writing and speaking of many people, literary and otherwise. Those who object insist that the expression is illogical—not that there aren't many other acceptable illogical idioms in English. Since we do not say "The cause is because . . . ," why say "The reason is because . . ."? Logically we should give, not the *cause for the reason*, but the reason or cause itself, phrased as a noun or noun clause. See page 146.

Illogical: The *reason* for my absence *is because* of illness.
The *reason* why I went *was because* I had no work that afternoon.

Logical: The *reason* for my absence *is sickness*.
The *reason* I went *was that* I had no work that afternoon.

Reason why. This is a redundant expression. Omit *why* and, in most constructions, also omit *reason*. "The *reason why* I like this job is the salary I get" can be improved by writing "I like this job because of the salary."

Rebound, redound. The former means "to spring back." (At the good news his spirits will *rebound*.) *Redound* means "to have a a result or effect." (Your generosity will *redound* to your credit.)

Receipt, recipe. Both words mean "a formula," or "directions for making or preparing something." Fastidious users of the language prefer *recipe*, but in this meaning the terms are interchangeable. *Receipt* also means "a written acknowledgment of something received." It is considered badly overworked business jargon in such an expression as "We are *in receipt of* . . ."

Reckon. See *Calculate*.

Red as a rose. Coleridge wrote "Red as a rose is she" many years ago in "The Ancient Mariner." Countless thousands have imitated Coleridge. Why not be different?

Redound. See *Rebound*.

Reek, wreak. *Reek* means "vapor or fume," and as a verb means "to give off a strong, unpleasant smell." (A *reek* of kerosene permeated the room.) *Wreak* means "to give vent to." (Do not *wreak* your anger on us.)

Re-enforce, reinforce. Each of these words means "to strengthen." *Reinforce* is the preferred spelling because it is a bit more simple and its pronunciation is instantly clear. *Re-enforce* may also be spelled *reënforce.*

Refer, refer back. *Refer* means "to direct attention" or "to make reference"; therefore, *back* is superfluous. (Please *refer*—not *refer back*—again to my statement.) The same kind of faulty diction is evident in *repeat again* and *return back.*

Referee. See *Umpire.*

Regard, regards. The former is used with *as* to mean "consider" or "think." (I *regard* her *as* my best friend.) *In regard to* and *with regard to* are idiomatically sound, but both phrases are wordy and jargonic. In these same phrases, *regards* is nonstandard. Restrict your use of *regards* to the plural form of *regard* (noun). See *As regards* and *In regards to.*

Reign. See *Rain.*

Reign supreme. A trite expression.

Rein. See *Rain.*

Reinforce. See *Re-enforce.*

Remainder. See *Balance.*

Repeat again. See *Refer.*

Respectfully, respectively. The former means "in a respectful manner." (My full report is *respectfully* submitted.) *Respectively* means "severally," or "in specified order." (Farewell, *au revoir,* and *auf Wiedersehen* are ways of saying "good-bye" in, *respectively,* English, French, and German.)

Return back. See *Refer.*

Revenge. See *Avenge.*

Reverend, reverent. The former is a title for clergymen. (The *Reverend* Stanley Houston is our minister.) *Reverent* means "characterized by respect or sacredness." (The minister spoke of the deceased in *reverent* tones.)

Reward. See *Award.*

Rewarded by, for, with. Idiomatic usage decrees that one is *rewarded by* a person, *for* something done, and *with* a gift.

Right, rite, wright, write. *Right* has several meanings, the most common of which are "direction opposite to left" and "correct." (Turn *right* and you will be headed in the *right* direction.) A *rite* is a ceremony. (The *rite* of burial is always solemn.) *Wright* means "a creator" or "worker." (Mr. Jones was an excellent wheel*wright*.) *To write* is "to form characters, letters, etc." (Please *write* to your mother soon.)

Right away, rights, righto. *Right* is colloquial in these expressions and in *right off* and *right then*. Use, instead, such expressions as *immediately, at once,* or *promptly. Right* is dialectal when used to mean "very." (I had a *very*—not *right*—good trip.) *Rights* is colloquial in the expression *put something to rights. Right off the bat* is a slang expression. *Righto* is a British colloquialism.

Ring. See *Wring.*

Riot of color. A cliché.

Rise. See *Raise.*

Rite. See *Right.*

Round, around. In formally precise English, *around* is used to mean "along the circumference," "here and there," or "in every direction." *Round* means "in a circular motion" or "in a reverse motion." As an adjective in such expressions as *an all-round athlete, round* is informal and colloquial. So is *all-around* in the same meaning. In the sense of "to gather" or "to collect," *to round up* is colloquial. See *Around.*

Rout, route. These words are often mispronounced and are frequently mistaken for each other. *Rout* has several meanings, the most common of which is "to put to disorderly flight." (We will *rout* all our enemies.) *Route* means "a road," "a way." (What *route* should we follow to reach Denver?)

Run. This very common word has many acceptable uses and meanings. However, the following expressions are not standard and should be avoided: *to run after* (to seek the company of), *to run in* (to arrest), *run-around* (evasive excuse), *run-in* (a quarrel or fight), *run* (smuggle).

Sadder but wiser. This trite old phrase is probably a corruption of Coleridge's "A sadder and a wiser man/He rose the morrow morn." We can't improve on Coleridge; but we can strengthen our own expression considerably by avoiding such clichés.

Sad to relate. A trite expression.

Said, same, such. As an adjective, *said* is used in legal writing but is considered to be jargon in standard English. Unless you're a lawyer (or a lawyer's secretary) avoid such expressions as *said party*, *said person*, and *said proposal*. *Same* as a pronoun is also characteristic of legal and business use. Lawyers may insist upon its retention, but businessmen in general and you in particular should avoid such expressions as "check enclosed in payment for *same*." *Such* may be an adjective, an adverb, and a pronoun—all with standard uses. It is considered colloquial, however, when used in place of a demonstrative. (I could not tolerate *that*—not *such*.) *Such* is also colloquial when used as an intensive. (She is *a very*—not *such a*—sweet person.)

Sang, sung. *Sang* is the past tense of *sing*; *sung* is the past participle. (She *sang* for me yesterday. She has *sung* every day this week.)

Sank, sunk. Preferred principal parts of the verb *to sink* are *sink —sank—sunk*. *Sank* is always the past tense of *sink*, whereas *sunk* is the past participle and an alternative form, although not recommended, of the past tense. (The ship *sank* slowly. The pond has *sunk* four inches since yesterday.) The often used expression *to sink in* (to be understood slowly) is colloquial and should be avoided in standard English.

Sarcasm, irony. *Sarcasm* is "the making of taunting, sneering, cutting, or caustic remarks." *Irony* is "a method of expression in which the intended meaning of the words used is the opposite of their usual sense." The respective adjectives are *sarcastic* and *ironical* or *ironic*. (The office manager used *sarcasm* to make us work harder. He was employing *irony* when he said to every tardy person, "Oh, you're early today.")

Satire, satyr. The former means "ridicule" or "contempt." (That night she wrote a *satire* on office parties.) A *satyr* is either a "woodland deity" or a "lecherous man." (Pinero once wrote: "From forty to fifty a man is at heart either a stoic or a *satyr*.")

Saw. See *Seen*.

Say. See *State*.

Scarce, scare. The former means "not plentiful." (Berries are *scarce* this season.) *Scare* means "to startle" or "to frighten." (Don't try to *scare* me with that story.)

Sealing. See *Ceiling*.

Sea of faces. Both Sir Walter Scott and Daniel Webster referred to "a sea of faces." The expression is—or was—effective. It now seems weary from overuse.

Secondly. See *Firstly*.

Second-rate. See *First-rate*.

Seen, saw. The principal parts of *to see* are *see—saw—seen*. *Seen* is improperly used as the past tense; *saw* is incorrect as the past participle. (I *saw*—not *seen*—you yesterday. I *have seen*—not *have saw*—you every day this week.)

Seething mass of humanity. A cliché.

Self-made man. This is an effective expression for which no one has yet found a pungent substitute. Unfortunately, the original phrase is now trite.

Sell like hot cakes. This phrase, meaning "to be sold rapidly and in large quantities," is considered slang by some experts, a colloquialism by others. Whatever the restrictive label, avoid using it in standard English. *Sell* also appears in the colloquial expressions *sell oneself* (to convince another of one's worth), *sell out* (to betray), and *sell* (a trick or hoax).

Sensitive about, to. One can be *sensitive about* something (such as one's appearance) but one can be only *sensitive to* a stimulus. (Her fingers were *sensitive to* the feel of silk.

Sensual, sensuous. The former refers to gratification of the more gross bodily pleasures or appetites. *Sensuous* suggests the appeal of that which is pleasing to the eye, ear, touch, etc. (In his abandon he indulged in every *sensual* excess he could imagine. He loved the *sensuous* music.)

Set. See *Sit.*

Set-up. In the sense of "an easy victory," this term is slang. More importantly, *set-up* is being used widely to refer to anything related to organization, conditions, or circumstances. (What's the new *set-up?*) The term is vague, at best. Try to find something less used and more exact.

Shall, will. The distinctions in the use of *shall* and *will* have broken down somewhat, but a few careful speakers and writers still observe them.

1. Use *shall* in the first person and *will* in the second and third persons to express *simple futurity.* (I *shall* go. You [or He] *will* go.)
2. For *emphasis,* to express *determination, command, intention, promise,* etc., use *will* in the first person and *shall* in the second and third persons. (I *will* speak, no matter what the result may be. You *shall* speak [meaning "You must speak"].)

Should, would. In general, use *should* and *would* according to the rules for *shall* and *will.* These tables may be helpful:

Should:
1. Obligation—I *should* read more than I do.
2. Expectation (a corollary of *obligation*)—They *should* be here by this time.
3. Condition—If he *should* speak, listen carefully.
4. Simple future (first person only)—I *should* like to go.
Would:
1. Habitual action—He *would* walk in the park every day.
2. Condition (*after* a conditional clause)—If the weather were good, he *would* walk in the park.
3. Determination—He *would* do it, no matter how much we protested.
4. Wish or desire—*Would* I had gone with you!
5. Simple future (second and third persons only)—He said that he *would* go.
   (If the governing verb is in the past tense, use *would* to ex-

press futurity, as above. If the governing verb is in the present tense, use *will*: He *says* that he *will* go.)

Should of. See *Of.*

Show, show up. *Show* is a highly useful word with many legitimate meanings. It is colloquial, however, when used as a synonym for "affair," "chance," or "opportunity." (His speaking career was a dreadful *spectacle*, or *undertaking*—not *show*.) *Show* is also military slang for a "battle" or "campaign." To *show up* in the sense of "to be superior to" or "to expose" is colloquial. (Many *showed* her *up*.) *Show up* is also not acceptable in standard English when used to mean "arrive." (He didn't *show up*.)

Shudder, shutter. The former means "to shake" or "to tremble." (The account of the accident made me *shudder*.) A *shutter* is a screen or cover. (The *shutters* on the house were painted green.)

Sigh of relief. A trite expression.

Sight. See *Cite.*

Sign up, sign up for, sign up with. Each of these phrases is widely used, but each is considered colloquial by most authorities. Avoid them in standard English.

Simple life, the. A cliché.

Sit, set. *Sit*, predominantly an intransitive verb, not requiring an object, has the meaning of "place oneself." *Set*, predominantly a transitive verb, requiring an object, means "to put" or "to place." (*Set* the book on the table and come *sit* here.) *Set* used for *sit* in the meanings shown is dialectal or an impropriety. However, both words have several special meanings. For example, *set* has an intransitive use, as in "The sun *sets* early tonight."

Site. See *Cite.*

Situation. This is an overused and rather vague word. Especially avoid using it in such statements as "This is a selling, not a buying, *situation*."

Size, size up. *Size* is colloquial when used to mean "the true state of affairs" as in "That's the *size* of it." *Size* is not generally accepted as a modifier in standard English. (This *size of*—not this *size*—dress.) When used to mean "make an estimate or judgment of," *size up* is colloquial.

Skeleton in the closet.   You and I have skeletons in our closets. So does everyone else. Everyone admits this, constantly; there is not a more trite expression in our language.

Slap.   As both noun and verb, *slap* is correctly used to convey the idea of a blow or smack. It appears, however, in several adjectival or adverbial expressions considered either slangy or trite: *slap-bang* (for "careless," "slapdash"), *slap-happy* (for "dazed" or "foolish"), and *slap* for "directly" or "abruptly" (Jack ran *slap* into the stream).

Sleep the sleep of the just.   This is an exceptionally trite expression. It is probably inexact, too; many unjust people may sleep as soundly as you do. Incidentally, *sleep* in the sense of "provide sleeping accommodations" is colloquial. (This cabin will accommodate—not *sleep*—six people.)

Snow-capped mountains.   A cliché.

So.   Avoid overuse of *so* as a conjunction; an excessive use of *so* is a mark of immaturity, of childishness. Use more exact connectives. If a clause shows purpose, use *so that*. (Martha went with Fred *so that* she could be sure to catch the bus.) Do not use *so* as a general substitute for *extremely*, *indeed*, or *very*. (He is *very*—not *so*—kind.) See *Very*. Also see page 139.

So . . . as.   See *As*.

Some.   This word is not acceptable in standard English to indicate general or vague approval. (It was an *exciting*—not *some*—spectacle.)

Somebody's else.   Incorrect. The sign of the possessive should appear on the last word, not the first (*somebody else's* hat).

Sometime, some time.   This expression should be one word in the sense of "on some occasion" or "some other time" and two words when used to mean "a period of time." (Please write to me *sometime*. Typing this report will require *some time*.)

Somewheres.   See *Anywheres*.

Sort of a. See *Kind of a*.

Soul of honor. An unusually trite expression.

Stair, stare. A *stair* is "a step." To *stare* is "to gaze fixedly," "to glare." (Climb the *stairs* slowly. Don't just *stare* at me; do something.)

Stake, steak. The former has several meanings, perhaps the most common of which is that of a "post," a "pole." (That martyr was burned at the *stake*.) A *steak* is a slice of meat. (We served a five-pound *steak* to our guests.)

Stall for time. In the sense of "delay" or "deceive," *stall* is colloquial. Avoid it in such expressions as "Stop *stalling* and come to the point," "Try to *stall off* your creditors," and "That's just a *stall* to confuse us."

Stang. This word is the no-longer recognized or accepted past tense and past participle of *to sting*. The principal parts are *sting—stung—stung*.

Stare. See *Stair*.

State, say. Each of these words means "to utter," "to set forth in words." *State* is somewhat more formal, specific, and definite than *say*; otherwise, they are synonymous. *Say-so* meaning "right of decision" or "unsupported statement" is colloquial. (On whose *authority*—not *say-so*—do you issue this order?)

Stationary, stationery. The former implies having a fixed or unmoving position. (This rock is *stationary*.) *Stationery* means "paper for writing." (This is new *stationery*.)

Statue, stature, statute. A *statue* is a sculptured likeness. (This is a *statue* of Robert E. Lee.) *Stature* refers to height or elevation. (This soldier is six feet in *stature*.) *Stature* is often used figuratively (a man of moral *stature*). A *statute* is a law. (This *statute* forbids betting on horse races.)

Steak. See *Stake*.

Steal, steel. The former means "to take without permission." (It is a sin to *steal*.) *Steel* is a metal. (This blade is made of *steel*.)

Stile, style. A *stile* is a step. (Don't vault the fence; use the *stile*.) *Style* means "manner or mode of expression." (The jacket was cut in modern *style*.)

Still remain. In such an expression as "I still remain here," *still* is unnecessary. The word *remain* means "to stay while others go away," "to go on being." Consequently, *still* is not needed as an intensifier.

Stimulant, stimulation, stimulus. A *stimulant* is anything that stimulates, increases activity. (This drug is a heart *stimulant*.) *Stimulation* is a noun meaning "being stimulated or activated." (She enjoyed the *stimulation* of a brisk walk.) A *stimulus* is something that arouses or incites to action, an incentive. (His hunger provided a *stimulus* for him to work rapidly.)

Straight, strait. The former means "uncurved." (The road runs *straight* for more than a mile.) A *strait* is a narrow passageway and also has the meaning of "restricted," "confined," "tight." ("*Strait* is the gate, and narrow is the way.")

Strong as a lion. A cliché.

Struggle for existence, the. A cliché.

Sturdy as an oak. A cliché.

Style. See *Stile*.

Such. See *Said*.

Suit, suite. Each of these words has several meanings. The most common meaning of the former is "clothing," as in "a *suit* of clothes." *Suite* may mean a set of rooms or furniture. (The manager engaged a *suite* of rooms at the hotel.)

Sung. See *Sang*.

Sunk. See *Sank*.

Superior than, to. Only *superior to* is idiomatically sound. (She felt *superior to*—not *than*—her fellow workers.)

Sure. This word is used as adjective or adverb, but it is colloquial in the sense of "surely," "certainly," "indeed." (He was *certainly* —not *sure*—angry with the policeman.) *Sure* is also colloquial in such expressions as *sure enough* (meaning both "certainly" and "real") and *sure-fire* (certain to be successful).

Sure thing, a. A slang expression.

Suspect. See *Expect.*

Suspicion. When used to mean "suspect," *suspicion* used as a verb is both colloquial and dialectal. (We *suspected*—not *suspicioned*—that you were lying.)

Swam. See *Swim.*

Swell. This word is not acceptable in standard English as a modifier. It is colloquial when used to mean "stylish," "fashionable," and is downright slang when used as a general term of approval meaning "excellent." (That was an *excellent*—not a *swell*—meal.) In the meaning of "conceited," *swelled head* is considered colloquial or slangy.

Swim, swam, swum. These three words are the principal parts of the verb *to swim.* In illiterate and dialectal speech, *swam* and *swum* are often misused, but they have entirely distinct functions in standard English. (I *swam* the lake today. I *have swum* the lake every day this week.)

Swing a deal. This expression is both trite and colloquial. Use it, if you must, in business conversations but not in standard English. Also, *swing* is colloquial when used to mean "an upward or downward change in the price of stocks or other business activity or commodity."

Swum. See *Swim.*

Symbol. See *Cymbal.*

Take. *Take* is a good, simple, useful word, but it appears in many expressions which are substandard. For example, *take and* is a colloquial and wordy expression. In the sentence, "He *took and* beat the horse unmercifully," *took and* should be omitted entirely. *Take* is colloquial or dialectal in *he took sick, she takes well* (she photographs well), *the day's take* (money or profit received), *to take someone for* (to cheat), *to take it* (to withstand difficulty, hardship), *take it lying down* (submit without protest), *take it on the chin* (undergo punishment, pain, etc.), *take it out of* (to tire, exhaust), *take it out on* (to make another suffer), *take on* (to show emotion such as sorrow, anger, etc.), *take-in* (trickery), *take-off* (an amusing or mocking imitation), *taking* (contagious), said of a disease.

Take it easy. This is a trite expression which is used *ad nauseam*. So, also, is *take my word for it*. And why should someone who is arrested always be *taken into custody?*

Tasteful, tasty. The former means "having or showing good taste, sense, or judgment." *Tasty* means "flavorful," "savory," "the quality of tasting good." (The reception was a *tasteful* affair and the food served at it was *tasty*.) *Tasteful* for *tasty* is in rare or archaic use; *tasty* for *tasteful* is colloquial.

Taught, taut. The former means "trained" or "instructed." (The campers were *taught* how to swim.) *Taut* means "tightly stretched" or "tense." (My nerves are *taut*.) See *Learn*.

Teach. See *Learn*.

Tend to. See *Attend to*.

Test out. This is a common expression but a wordy one. *Out* is unnecessary in this expression as well as in *prove out*, *process out*, *examine out*, and *project out*.

Than, then. These words are often confused in writing and sometimes in pronunciation. *Than* is a conjunction in clauses of comparison. (He worked better today *than* he did yesterday.) *Then* is an adverb of time. (We *then* went to a restaurant.)

That. This useful word is both a pronoun and a conjunction, but its use as an adverb is colloquial. (I was *so very*—not *that*—sick I could have died.) Also, do not overuse *that* as either conjunction or pronoun. Omit the second *that* in this sentence: We think *that* if you are ready *that* we should go.

That which. This phrase is somewhat old-fashioned and perhaps overly formal as a substitute for *what*. (He had no idea of *what* —not *that which*—he wanted to do.)

Their, there, they're. These simple and common words cause much difficulty, but they are easy to keep straight. *Their* is a possessive pronoun. (This is *their* house.) *There* means "in or at that place." (Were you *there* when she arrived?) *They're* is a contraction of *they are.* (We are disappointed because *they're* not coming.)

Then. See *Than.*

Thence, hence. The former means "from that time," "thence-forth" and "from that place," "therefrom." (We departed *thence* as soon as we could.) *Hence* means "after now," "from this time." (A year *hence* the whole affair will have been forgotten.) See *From whence* and *Hither.*

Theory. This is a perfectly good word, originally meaning "a mental viewing," "an idea or mental plan involving a systematic statement of principles." In popular usage it has come to mean a mere notion, guess, conjecture, or hypothesis. (My *theory* is that he's bluffing.) In this inexact and somewhat loose sense, *theory* is vastly overused; try to select a more exact and less trite term for your meaning.

There. See *Their.*

Thereby hangs a tale. This was a favorite phrase of Shakespeare; he used it in *The Merry Wives of Windsor, As You Like It, The Taming of the Shrew,* and *Othello.* Rabelais and Cervantes also used it. Let's let these giants have it and substitute something perhaps not so effective but far less trite.

Therefor, therefore. The former means "for this," "for that." (He bought a hat and paid cash *therefor.*) *Therefore* means "hence," "consequently." (I don't feel well and *therefore* should not go.)

These kind, those kind, these sort, those sort. *Kind* and *sort* are singular nouns; *these* and *those* are plural modifiers. Say and write *this kind, these kinds, this sort, those sorts.*

They. This pronoun, as well as *their, theirs,* and *them,* should have a definite antecedent: a plural noun or pronoun. Otherwise, these pronouns should not be used. Each of them, but especially *they,* is colloquial when used indefinitely. (*They* have good roads in Delaware.) The sentence is more effective when phrased "Delaware has good roads" or "Motorists in Delaware enjoy good roads," or something definite and precise.

They're. See *Their.*

Things are looking up. This phrase has two strikes against it. First, *things* is a vague, general, and somewhat meaningless word. Second, *looking up* is a colloquial term for "improving" or "getting better." Therefore, to use the combined phrase is to miss a third strike. Don't.

This here. A dialectal or illiterate expression. (I'm going to ride *this*—not *this here*—horse.)

This morning at . . . a.m. A wordy expression which should never be used, even in informal conversation. Both *morning* and *a.m.* refer to time and either one or the other is sufficient. The same comment applies to *This afternoon at . . . p.m.* See A.M.

Thither. See *Hither.*

Thorough, though, threw, through. *Thorough* means "complete." (He gave the typewriter a *thorough* cleaning.) *Though* means "notwithstanding," "although." (I don't agree with you, *though* you may be correct.) *Threw*, the past tense of *to throw*, means "hurled," "tossed." (The cowboy *threw* more wood on the fire.) *Through* means "from one end or side to the other." (Please walk *through* the town with me.)

Thunderous applause. A cliché.

Thusly. An illiteracy. Use *thus.*

Till, until, 'til. Each of these words means "up to the time of." *Till* and *'til* (a shortened form of *until*) have the same pronunciation and are more often used within a sentence than at the beginning. *Until* more often appears at the beginnings of sentences and is sometimes considered somewhat more formal than its two synonyms. All three terms are correct in standard English.

Time marches on. A trite expression. Time moves in many, many ways, literally hundreds of ways. Dare to be a little different in your phrasing.

Time of my life. A cliché.

Tired but happy. A cliché.

To, too, two. Correct use of these words is largely a matter of careful spelling. *To* is a preposition (*to* the store) and the sign of an infinitive (*to* work). *Too* is an adverb meaning "also" or "overabundance of." (We, *too*, are working, but Jack is *too* lazy *to* get up.) *Two* is the number after one (*two* of us.) (The *two* secretaries were *too* tired *to* go.)

Too. See *To.* Also, avoid overusing *too* either as an intensive or as a replacement for "very." "I'm just *too* happy for words" is indicative of what has been called "schoolgirl style."

Too full for utterance. A trite expression. Besides, isn't "utterance" a rather silly word, even if it does appear in the famous poem, "We are coming, Father Abraham, . . . with hearts too full for utterance . . ."?

Too funny for words. A cliché.

Tortuous, torturous. The former means "winding," "crooked." *Torturous* means "full of, or causing, torture (pain)." (The path of the stream is *tortuous*. The surgeon began a *torturous* examination of the patient's neck.)

Toward, towards. Each of these words means "in the direction of" or "facing." The former is generally preferred, partly because it is one letter shorter and is easier to pronounce. Both are correct in standard English.

Transpire. One meaning of *transpire* is "to leak out," "to become known." Consequently, *transpire* is now frequently used as a somewhat inexact equivalent of *happen* or *occur*. Normally, either *happen* or *occur* is likely to convey the meaning you have in mind more exactly than the somewhat learned and pompous *transpire*.

Treat of, on. The preferred idiom is *treat of*. Actually, "discuss" and "deal with" sound more natural and are just as explicit.

Try and, try to. The correct idiom is *try to*. However, *try and* is in everyday use and has been for a century. Standard English would have you write "*Try to*—not *try and*—finish your work early."

Turn. Only a few words in our language have more meanings than this one. Naturally, therefore, *turn* appears in many phrases which are considered substandard. In formal English avoid such expressions as these: *out of turn* (rashly, imprudently); *turn in* (to go to bed); *turn out* (to get out of bed); and such trite expressions as *One good turn deserves another*.

Two. See *To*.

Type. See *Kind of a*. Also, in standard English, *type* is a noun or verb, although it is often used somewhat colloquially as an adjective (*ranch-type house*). *Type* is not acceptable in standard English as a substitute for *type of*. We do not say "What kind insect?" or "What sort insect?" Why say "What type insect?" (This *type of* reading—not this *type* reading—appeals to me.)

Umpire, referee. Each of these terms is applied to a person to whom anything is referred for a decision or settlement (*referee* in bankruptcy). In sports, referees and umpires are officials charged with the regulation of a contest, ruling on plays, etc. Although the terms have the same general meaning, *referee* and *umpire* have different meanings in different sports; for example, we have a *referee* in boxing and basketball, an *umpire* in baseball, and both a *referee* and an *umpire* in football. If you are an athlete or a sportswriter, you know the difference. If you are neither, consult a sports authority; a dictionary will be of little help except as indicated here.

Unabridged, abridged, expurgated. *Unabridged* means "not reduced in compass or scope by condensing, omitting, etc."; that is, it means "full length" or "not cut." *Abridged*, conversely, implies reduction. Thus we speak of an *unabridged* dictionary when we refer to one that is large and definitive, including virtually everything that it could reasonably be expected to contain. An *abridged* dictionary is one which is considerably shorter but which still retains all, or nearly all, information considered essential. An *expurgated* book is one from which passages thought obscene or otherwise objectionable have been removed. *Expurgated* has a sense of "purging," of "cleansing." *Abridged* and *unabridged* imply "shortened" and "full length," without any connotation of moral, social, or ethical values.

Unequal for, to. The former phrase is not idiomatically standard, but *unequal to* is. (*His abilities were unequal to the task.*)

Uninterested.   See *Disinterested*.

Unique.   This word means "having no like or equal" and expresses absoluteness as do words such as *round*, *square*, etc. Logically, therefore, the word *unique* cannot be compared; something cannot be "more unique," "less unique," "more round," "less round," etc. If a qualifying word such as "nearly" is used, the illogicality is removed. "This is the *most unique* painting in the museum" is not standard, but "This is the *most nearly unique* painting . . ." is.

Unmindful about, of.   The former phrase is not idiomatically acceptable in standard English. (He was *unmindful of*—not *about* —his poor health.)

Unmoral, amoral, immoral.   *Unmoral* means "having no morality," "nonmoral," "unable to distinguish right from wrong." Thus we may say that an infant or a mentally disordered person is *unmoral*. *Amoral* means "not concerned with moral standards," "not to be judged by criteria or standards of morality." Morons and animals, for example, may be called *amoral*. *Immoral* means "wicked," "contrary to accepted principles of right and wrong" The acts of thieves, murderers, rapists, embezzlers, etc., may be called *immoral*.

Unpractical, impractical, impracticable.   The first two of these terms are interchangeable, although *impractical* is considered by some writers as being slightly more formal and refined. Each means "not practical," "lacking practical usefulness or wisdom." *Impracticable* means "not capable of being carried out, used, or managed." (The minister was a good man but thoroughly *impractical*. The manager considered my plan *impracticable*.) See *Impractical*.

Until.   See *Till*.

Up.   This useful little word appears in many verb-adverb combinations (*grow up, give up, take up, use up*, etc.) In many other phrases it adds nothing to the meaning of the verb; it is considered colloquial in such expressions as *choose up, divide up, finish up, increase up*, etc. *On the up and up* is slang. *Up against* (meaning "face to face with") is colloquial. *Up against it* (meaning "in difficulty") is colloquial. *Up on* (meaning "informed about") and *up to* (meaning "scheming" or "plotting") are colloquial. *Up-and-coming* and *up one's alley* are other phrases to be avoided in standard English. *Open up* is wordy in the sense of "give access to" and is colloquial when used to mean "speak freely."

Urban, urbane. The former is characteristic of a city. (The population of the county is largely *urban*.) *Urbane* means "smooth," "polished." (The diplomat's manner was *urbane*.)

Us. See *We*.

Used to, used to could. In the phrase *used to*, the *d* is often elided in speaking so that it sounds like *use to*. In writing, the *d* must be included. *Used to could* is an illiteracy; write *used to be able*.

Vain, vane, vein. *Vain* has several meanings, among them "worthless" and "empty." (His threat was *vain*.) A *vane* is a direction pointer. (The farmer bought a new weather *vane*.) A *vein* is, among other things, a blood vessel. (The blade severed a *vein*, not an artery.)

Valuable, invaluable. *Valuable* implies such worth or value as to bring a high price (a *valuable* painting). *Invaluable* suggests worth or value so great that it cannot be appraised in monetary terms (your *invaluable* assistance).

Vane. See *Vain*.

Varsity. This is a shortened form of *university*—the *varsity* football team, *varsity* debating team, etc. Some exceptionally formal writers and speakers consider the word colloquial, but it is in general and accepted use today on all levels.

Vein. See *Vain*.

Venal, venial. The former means "corruptible," "mercenary." (The *venal* sheriff was arrested for his misdemeanors.) *Venial* means "excusable," "pardonable." (The sin you have committed is *venial*, not mortal.)

Venture a suggestion. A cliché.

Verbal. See *Oral*.

Very. V*ery*, like *so, surely, too, extremely, indeed,* has been so overused that it has lost much of its value as an intensive. Use these words sparingly and thoughtfully; consider whether your meaning isn't just as emphatic without them: "You are (*very*) positive about the matter." V*ery* is used colloquially to qualify participles; formal use has adverbs like *much* or *greatly*.

Colloquial: I was *very disgusted* with myself.
Formal: I was *very much disgusted* with myself.

Colloquial: I am *very torn* between the desire to go and the desire to stay.
Formal: I am *greatly torn* between . . .

Vial, vile, viol. A *vial* is a small vessel. (I have a *vial* of perfume for you.) V*ile* means "repulsive," "offensive." (The motorist's language was *vile*.) A *viol* is a musical instrument.

Vice. See V*ise*.

Victim. See *Martyr*.

Video. This word referring to the transmission of television images is rapidly growing in popularity. Purists insist that it is still colloquial, but general usage has decreed otherwise. Go ahead and use the word—even *look at video*. But read a good book every now and then, too.

Vie against, with. The former phrase is not accepted in standard English; the second idiom is.

Viewpoint. It required many years for this useful, natural, and economical substitute for *point of view* to be accepted as standard English. It has won its standing.

Vile. See V*ial*.

Vise, vice. The former is a device for holding. (The carpenter has many uses for a *vise*.) V*ice* has more than one meaning, but the most common is that of "evil practice." (The mayor is opposed to *vice* in every form.)

Viz. See I*.e*.

Vocation. See A*vocation*.

Waist, waste. The *waist* is the middle section of the body. (His *waist* measures thirty-four inches.) *Waste*, as a verb, means "to employ uselessly," "to squander." (Don't *waste* your energy.)

Wait on. In the sense of "serve" this is an acceptable phrase. (I have to *wait on* the customers now.) In the sense of "await" or "wait for," the phrase is dialectal or colloquial. (Please hurry; I don't want to *wait for*—not *wait on*—you.)

Waive, wave. The former means "to relinquish," "to give up." (I shall *waive* all rights to a hearing.) As a noun, *wave* means a "ridge" or "swell." (The *wave* tossed our craft high.)

Wake. Our language has several verbs to express "waking from sleep" and "waking someone from sleep." *Awake—awaked* and *awake—awoke* are correct, of course, but somewhat formal. (I *awoke* him.) *Awaken—awakened—awakened* is even more formal than *awake*. (I *awakened* him.) More commonly used than either is *wake—waked* or *woke—waked* or *woke*. (I *woke* him.) *Waken—wakened—wakened* is less used than *wake—waked—waked*. (I *waked* him.) Most commonly used of all are *wake up—waked up* or *woke up*. (I *waked up*—or *woke up*—at dawn. She *waked up*—or *woke up*—her sister at dawn.)

Walk. This word appears in several expressions which are both colloquial and trite: *walk out* (to go on strike); *walk out on* (to leave or abandon); *walkover* (an easy victory); *walk-up* (an apartment house without an elevator or an apartment in such a building); *take a walk* (to desert or leave, used especially in referring to withdrawal from a political party, association, etc.).

Want, wish, desire. *Want*, when it specifically suggests a longing for something lacking or needed, is an informal but correct equivalent of *wish*. *Wish* is not so strong a term as *desire*, which stresses intensity or ardor of longing. (I *want* to go with you if I can. I *wish* I had a new suit. I *desire* to make a real success of my marriage.)

Want for, want in, want out. The *for* in *want for* is dialectal. (He *wants*—not *wants for*—to see the circus.) Neither *want in* nor *want out* is acceptable in standard English. (The dog *wants to get out*—not *wants out*.)

Was. See *Is.*

Waste. See W*aist*.

Wave. See W*aive*.

Way, ways. The former is colloquial when used to mean "away." (The mine stands *away*—not *way*—across the state.) The following phrases involving *way* are also colloquial: *in a bad way, to come my way* (success), *act the way he does*. W*ays* is a dialectal substitute for *way* in such an expression as *a long ways to the river*.

We, us. The former is a plural pronoun in the nominative case, the latter a plural pronoun in the objective (accusative) case. (W*e* talked together for an hour until the train came to take *us* to our homes.)

Weaker sex, the. A cliché and, furthermore, a phrase which expresses a comparison wholly without foundation.

Weather, whether. The former applies to "state of atmosphere." W*hether* is a conjunction implying alternatives. (Because of the *weather* we didn't know *whether* to go or stay.) See *Doubt if*.

Well. See *Good*.

Welsh rarebit. See *Rabbit*.

Wends his way. A cliché.

Went, have gone. The principal parts of *to go* are *go—went—gone*. W*ent*, the past tense, cannot be used in standard English with an auxiliary verb. (We *go* today; we *went* yesterday; we *have gone*—not *have went*—every day this week.)

Were. See *Is*.

Wheel of fortune. A trite expression which probably owes its popularity to Shakespeare. In *King Henry* V, Shakespeare wrote "Giddy Fortune's furious fickle wheel . . ." and in *King Lear* appears "Fortune, good night, smile once more; turn thy wheel."

When, as, and if. This expression appears often in business talk. It should not be much used in nonbusiness contexts. Similarly, both *when and if* and *if and when* are used when referring to matters or events which are uncertain. Each of these phrases has become stereotyped and should be used sparingly.

Whence. See *From whence* and *Hither*.

Where. This is a useful and much-used word but it should not be substituted for *that* in standard English. (We noted *that* —not *where*—the umpire made a mistake.)

Where angels fear to tread. See *Fools rush in*.

Where at. As two words, this phrase is redundant for *where*. In standard English avoid such a statement as "Janet did not know *where* she was *at*."

Where ignorance is bliss. We owe this one to Thomas Gray's "On a Distant Prospect of Eton College." It is one of the most vigorous clichés in the language.

Whereof, wherein, whereon. These adverbs are correct, all right, but to the modern ear they seem somewhat pedantic and awkward. It is correct to refer to "the room *wherein* he lay," but present-day usage would be better served by writing "the room *in which* he lay." *Of what* will substitute for *whereof* and *on what* (or *on which*) for *whereon*.

Whether. See *Doubt if*, *If*, and *Weather*.

While, wile. *While* is colloquial when used in the sense of "although" or "whereas." (You thought I was present, *whereas* —not *while*—I never came at all.) The word *wile*, sometimes confused with *while* in both spelling and pronunciation, means "trick" or "stratagem." (That was just one of her feminine *wiles*.)

Who, whom. The former is the nominative case, the latter the objective. When in doubt, try as a memory device the substituting of *he* for *who* and *him* for *whom*, since the proper use of *he* and *him* is more easily recognized. I wonder *who* (or *whom?*) I should invite. I should invite him. Therefore: I wonder *whom* I should invite.

Whole. See *Hole*.

Whole lot. See *Lots of*.

Wholly. See *Holy*.

Who's, whose. The former is a shortened form of *who is*.

(*Who's* ahead in the office pool?) *Whose* is the possessive case of *who*. (*Whose* toes did I step on?)

Wile. See *While*.

Will, would. See *Shall* and *Should*.

Wire. This word is considered colloquial when used as a substitute for *telegram* or *telegraph*.

Wise. *Wise* is an acceptable adjective but is nonstandard in such expressions as *a wise guy, get wise to, get wise, put wise to, wise up,* and *wisecrack*.

Wise. This suffix has many standard uses and appears in such fully acceptable words as *clockwise, sidewise,* etc. Unfortunately, it has been greatly overused in recent years and appears in scores of awkward and strained neologisms: *ideawise, travelwise, laundrywise,* etc.

Wish. See *Want*.

With bated breath. Shakespeare coined this by-now trite phrase in *The Merchant of Venice. Reduced, diminished, held in, lessened, contracted, narrowed, decreased, dwindled, curtailed, shortened, attenuated,* and *pared down* are only a few words which might serve in avoiding this cliché. But hang on to *breath;* that seems essential.

Without. This useful word is both an adverb and a preposition. (We can do *without, without* doubt.) But it is dialectal or illiterate when used for the conjunction *unless*. (I cannot go *unless*—not *without*—I receive my pay check.)

Wont, won't. The former means "accustomed," or "used." (He was *wont* to take a walk every day.) *Won't* is a contraction of "will not." (This child *won't* do what the nurse suggests.)

Words fail, etc. Such expressions as *Words fail me* and *Words fail to express* are clichés. So are such expressions as *good as one's word, word of mouth, to eat one's words, have a word with, in so many words, take the words out of one's mouth, word for word.*

Work like a Trojan, work like a horse. We really don't know how hard the Trojans worked and, furthermore, some horses are lazy. Anyway, the phrases are tired.

Works.   This word is slang when it appears in such expressions as *get the works, give one the works, shoot the works.*

Worse for wear, the.   A cliché.

Worst kind, worst sort, worst way.   These are slang terms for *very much, greatly, intensely,* etc.

Would.   See *Should.*

Would of, could of, might of.   These terms are all illiteracies probably resulting from attempts to represent what is pronounced. In rapid and informal speech, that is, *would have* has the sound of *would of.* In each phrase, *have* should replace *of.*

Wrapped in mystery.   A trite expression.

Wreak.   See *Reek.*

Wreathed in smiles.   A cliché.

Wright.   See *Right.*

Wring, ring.   The former means "to squeeze," "to press." A *ring* is, among other things, a band of metal. (Take off your *ring* and *wring* out your wet clothes.)

Write.   See *Right.*

Wrought havoc.   A trite expression.

Wrung.   See *Rang.*

Wry countenance.   A cliché. *Wry* means "twisted," "distorted," "perverse," "contorted," "kinked," "crooked," "misshapen," "buckled." Perhaps one of these adjectives will help you select a less worn phrase. If not, a good thesaurus will.

Yank.   This is a slang term for "Yankee" and especially for American soldiers in World Wars I and II. As a verb, *yank* is dialectal in New England and colloquial everywhere else for "to jerk." (A good dentist *extracts,* or *pulls,* teeth; he doesn't *yank* them *out.*)

Yawl.   See *Yowl.*

Yolk, yoke. A *yolk* is part of an egg. A *yoke* is a frame or bar. (The recipe suggests six small egg *yolks*. The oxen were wearing *yokes*.)

Yore, your, you're. *Yore* means "time long past." (Women wore dimity in days of *yore*.) *Your* means "belonging to, or done by, you." (Where are *your* manners?) *You're* is a shortened form of *you are*. (*You're* out of *your* alleged mind.)

You all. In the sense of "all of you," this phrase has a recognized and standard plural meaning. When used to refer to one person, it may be considered either dialectal or an illiteracy.

Your, you're. See *Yore*.

Yowl, yawl. The former means "howl" or "wail." (The hound gave a mournful *yowl*.) A *yawl* is a sailboat. (What is the difference between a *yawl* and a ketch?)

Zealous. See *Jealous*.

Part II

Guide to Correct Sentence Structure

It is my ambition to say in ten sentences what everyone else says in a whole book—what everyone else does *not* say in a whole book.

NIETZSCHE, *Skirmishes in a War with the Age*

By being so long in the lowest form I gained an immense advantage over the cleverer boys. . . . I got into my bones the essential structure of the ordinary British sentence— which is a noble thing.

SIR WINSTON CHURCHILL, *My Early Life*

. . . prose, words in their best order; poetry, the best words in their best order.

COLERIDGE, *Lectures on Shakespeare and Milton*

Guide to Correct Sentence Structure

A usable definition of a sentence is that it is "one or more words conveying to the reader a sense of complete meaning." The word (or group of words) normally, but not always, has a subject and predicate; the subject may be expressed or it may be understood and not expressed; either subject or predicate may be understood from the context.

Remember that the foregoing statements refer to *grammatical* completeness. In one sense we do not have a complete thought until we have read or written a series of sentences. A pronoun in one sentence may take its meaning from an antecedent in another. Such words as *thus, these, another,* and *again,* and such phrases as *for example* and *on the other hand* frequently show that the thought about to be presented in a new sentence is related to the thought in a preceding sentence or paragraph.

When we say, then, that a sentence conveys a "sense of complete meaning" to the reader, we do not imply that we can dispense with its context (the statements which precede or follow it). We mean only that we have a group of words so ordered as to be *grammatically* self-sufficient. For example, the statement, "He took command on July 3, 1775," is grammatically complete. It has a subject, the pronoun *he,* and it has a verb, *took* (took command). In this sense the entire statement is complete and must be begun with a capital letter and be followed by a period. So far as total meaning is concerned, however, we need other sentences to tell us that *he* refers to George Washington and that the command which he assumed was that of Continental Forces in the War of the American Revolution.

The study of grammar may be of little value in itself. To be able to say by rote "A sentence is a group of words containing a single, complete thought, or a group of very closely related thoughts" is valueless in writing or speaking grammatically correct sentences unless the terms of the definition are understood, unless comprehension of the functions of parts of speech, of various kinds of sentences, gives meaning to that definition. To learn the parts of speech, to distinguish simple, complex, and compound sentences —such additions to our knowledge represent wasted effort until we begin to relate them to the writing of real sentences, until we see such knowledge operating upon the sentences which we write or speak. We will then see why the study of grammar is of little value in itself, but we will see more than that—we will find ourselves writing sentences grammatically correct and will know *why* and *how* we do so.

To learn to phrase good sentences, basic units of thought, is a worthwhile achievement. It has been said that the simple declarative sentence is the greatest invention of the human intellect.

Actually, the problems of writing sentences may be classed under three heads: *correctness, clearness,* and *effectiveness.*

Correctness
    Period fault (sentence fragment)
    Comma fault (comma splice)
    Fused sentence
    Dependent clauses misused

These four types of mistakes represent probably the most flagrant blunders in sentence construction and are most strictly to be avoided. They represent a somewhat negative approach to sentence construction, but avoiding them will add clarity and effectiveness which otherwise would be lacking.

Clearness

Sentence unity	Dangling modifiers
Incompleteness	Reference of pronouns
Word order	Mixed constructions
Split constructions	Transition

These topics represent eight important principles of sentence clarity. If your sentences fail to communicate your thoughts with exactness, master these principles and try to employ them in your own writing. In sentences, clearness is probably an even more important essential than correctness; for if a sentence is understood, the primary purpose of writing, communication, is achieved. Remember what Thoreau once wrote: "A sentence should read as if its author, had he held a plough instead of a pen, could have drawn a furrow deep and straight to the end."

Effectiveness

Wordiness	Faulty subordination
Parallelism	Position and arrangement
Consistency (point of view)	Choppy sentences
False co-ordination	Variety

Effective sentences result from both correctness and clearness; therefore, the twenty topics listed here are not mutually exclusive. For example, sentence unity may be considered as much a problem of correctness as of clarity. For another illustration, inexact transition between sentences or within sentences is both incorrect and ineffective. It will help, however, to keep your attention focused on sentence *correctness*, sentence *clearness*, and sentence *effectiveness*.

These twenty main topics have been broken up into more than one hundred specific problems of sentence structure. By concentrating upon one particular error at a time you can quickly master the sentence flaw involved and avoid it in future speaking and writing.

PROBLEMS OF SENTENCE STRUCTURE

Accordion sentence.   This is a sentence which, like an accordion, is alternately pulled out and pressed together. It is caused by faulty subordination. See *Excessive subordination.*

Adverbial clause for noun clause.   Do not thoughtlessly use an adverbial clause as a noun clause.

Dependent clauses function as separate parts of speech (noun, adjective, adverb); to use one of them for another is considered as serious an error as to use one part of speech for another.

> *Ineffective:* I heard *where* the weather forecaster said cold weather was coming.
>
> The reason the automobile stopped was *because* it had run out of gasoline.

Substitute *that* for the italicized word in each sentence. See *Adverbial clause for noun or noun phrase.*

Adverbial clause for noun or noun phrase.   Do not use an adverbial clause in place of a noun or noun phrase.

When and *where* are the chief offenders in this type of incorrect subordination.

> *Wrong:* Plagiarism is *where* you take the word of another and pass it off as your own.
>
> Anemia is *when* the blood has certain deficiencies.

Substitute nouns with modifiers for the adverbial clauses.

> *Better:* Plagiarism is the act of taking . . .
>
> Anemia is a condition in which the blood . . .

See *Adverbial clause for noun clause.*

"And/or."   This expression is frequently used in business letters and business and legal communications generally. It means, of course, "either *and* or *or*, according to what is meant." The use of this term in sentences is objected to by precise writers, but it appears in two of the three leading "desk" dictionaries with no restrictive label and is obviously being used ever more often by even careful writers. It seems particularly useful when three alternatives exist. (These consist of both circumstances mentioned and either one of the two.) "He willed her his debts, his personal *and/or* real property." Your sentences should not sound like business or legal jargon, but this particular expression does not deserve all the scorn which some have heaped upon it.

"And which" construction.   *And, but, or,* and other co-ordinating conjunctions connect elements equal in rank. The most frequent violation of this rule is the *and which* construction. Do not use *and which, but which, and who, but who* unless there is a preceding "which clause" or "who clause."

> *Wrong:* This is a beautiful tennis court, *and which* you will enjoy playing on with your friends.
>
> He showed much energy at first, *but which* soon vanished.
>
> He is a man of intelligence, *and who* is an industrious worker.

The simplest method of correcting these three sentences is to omit the conjunctions (but remember the punctuation of restrictive and nonrestrictive clauses). Parallelism can also be attained by adding a "who clause" or "which clause": "He is a man who is intelligent and who is an industrious worker." Such revision, however correct, is usually wordy and ineffective, as it is here. The sentence may be rewritten: "The man is intelligent and industrious." See *False Co-ordination*.

Arrangement of words. See *Position and arrrangement of words*.

Awkwardness. The word *awkward* implies unfitness for smooth, easy functioning. It means "clumsy," "bungling," "ungainly," "ungraceful." In sentence structure, *awkwardness* is a rather vague word of disapproval. It may refer to unnatural word order, unnecessary or useless repetition, clumsy phrasing, or any of a dozen other flaws and imperfections. Its causes are many, its remedies just as numerous. Only thorough knowledge of sentence errors and sentence potentials can aid you in avoiding awkwardness. Doing so is important; study hard all the entries in this "Guide to Correct Sentence Structure."

Beginning, ending sentence. Do not begin or end a sentence with weak and relatively unimportant words or ideas.

Sentences should usually be built with the most important idea at the beginning or end, the places of stress, places where the attention of the reader is most keen. You should remember, however, that transitional words and phrases, although seemingly colorless, are really significant and frequently deserve beginning positions. See *Transitional devices*.

Prepositions and parenthetical expressions are usually not "pivotal," or important, words. Thus you should place them within the sentence, although you should avoid artificiality and awkwardness in so doing.

> *Ineffective:* He had no brush to paint the house *with*. (It is not incorrect to end a sentence with a preposition, but this sentence will be more effective if rearranged so that due emphasis is given the relatively important word *house*: He had no brush with which to paint the house.)

Ineffective: However, he will die, the physician says.

Better: The physician says, however, that he will die.

See *Climactic order* and *Variety.*

Beginning sentence with numeral.   Standard advice is never to begin a sentence with a numeral. This admonition seems largely a matter of typography or a printing convention. However, it is a good rule to follow since beginning with a numeral sometimes causes momentary confusion.

Beginning sentence with preposition.   Such a construction is not incorrect but is usually ineffective. See *Preposition, ending sentence.*

Beginning with same word.   To avoid monotony (see *Monotonous sentence structure*), do not begin a number of successive sentences with the same word or phrase.

Avoid especially overuse of the outworn beginnings *there is, there are, it is, this, the, he,* and *we.*

> *Awkward:* It is just the trip he had planned. It is just the day for the trip. It is the consummation of all his hopes.
>
> *Improved:* It is just the trip he had planned and just the day for the trip, a consummation of all his hopes.

Beginning with subject.   Normal word order in the English sentence is subject + verb + complement. (He eats luncheon here every day.) Except for special meaning or to secure emphasis, this basic word order is preferable. And yet the sentence just quoted could be written: "Every day he eats luncheon here" or "Here he eats luncheon every day" or "Luncheon he eats here every day" or even "Here every day luncheon he eats"—although this kind of inversion gets out of hand quickly.

Our slavish addiction to normal word order, however, can, and often does, result in monotonous sentence structure. For example, do not place the subject at the beginning of every sentence.

Occasionally change the usual word order of subject + verb + complement; deviation from this order will avoid monotony and, if correctly done, will attract desired attention.

Usual order:	I saw that play when I was in Indianap-
	olis.
Position changed:	That play I saw when I was in Indian-
	apolis.

Usual order:	Those who can sleep through a dull
	movie are fortunate.
Position changed:	Fortunate are those who can sleep
	through a dull movie.

Blended sentence. Such a construction consists of two complete sentences joined together with no mark of punctuation between them. See *Fused sentence.*

Blends, mixed or confusing. A *blend* is a mixture of varieties (a *blend* of coffee). In language, it involves the mixing together of two or more word elements to fashion a third. (The word *electrocute* is a blend of *electric* and *execute*.) However, many blends are neologisms (*smog* for *smoke* and *fog*) and other blends can be illogical or illiterate. See *Illogical, mixed blends* and *Mixed, illogical constructions.*

"But which" construction. See *"And which" construction.*

Capitalization. The convention of starting every sentence with a capital (upper-case) letter is followed by everyone. Everyone also knows to capitalize proper names when they appear in sentences. For other uses of capitals, see *Capital letters* in Part IV, "Guide to Correct Punctuation and Mechanics."

Choppy sentences. Do not chop up the thought of one unified sentence into a series of short, jerky sentences.

Unity, clearness, and effectiveness are all thwarted by a series of jerky, short sentences which logically belong in a single predication. Such a series is monotonous and does not permit variety of sentence structure; it also gives undue emphasis to relatively unimportant ideas. The separate ideas should be properly co-ordinated and subordinated and placed together in a longer, unified sentence.

Faulty:	He picked up the pocketbook. He saw that it con-
	tained a large sum of money. He naturally wanted
	to keep it.

Better: When he picked up the pocketbook, he saw that it contained a large sum of money which, naturally, he wanted to keep.

Faulty: It was dark. She was afraid to enter the room. She called her brother. He did not hear her. This terrified her more than ever.

Better: Because it was dark, she was afraid to enter the room. When she called her brother, he did not hear her, and thus she was more terrified than ever.

See *Excessive co-ordination.*

Class of pronouns. See *Shifts in class or person of pronouns.*

Clearness. One of the fundamental virtues of writing and speaking is *clearness,* but the term is not easy to discuss. Making your sentences clear involves such matters as *unity, completeness, co-ordination, word order, transitional devices,* and the like. Each of these terms is discussed in its appropriate place in this section and should be consulted. And yet writing sentences which are free from muddiness, haziness, and cloudiness; which are easily and distinctly understood; which are entirely logical; which have no ambiguity or obscurity—such style results less from avoiding mistakes than from qualities of mind and heart which cannot readily be described or learned. This brief comment may not be helpful, or even *clear* to you. Now do you understand the problem of explaining *clearness?*

Climactic order. Arrange ideas in the order of their importance so as to secure climax.

Climax is attained when ideas in a sentence are so arranged that each succeeding idea has greater force than its predecessor. Avoid arranging the elements of a sentence so that it "sags," or loses force at the end.

Unemphatic: In this wreck, some died horrible deaths; some received serious injuries, and a few were barely scratched.

Better: A few were barely scratched in this wreck; but some received serious injuries; and some died horrible deaths.

> *Unemphatic:* We were frightened by the noises: the crashing of the thunder, the pouring of the rain, and the steady blowing of the wind.
>
> *Better:* We were frightened by the noises: the steady blowing of the wind, the pouring of the rain, and the crashing of the thunder.

The effectiveness of a sentence depends not entirely on the *position* of any single word or idea but on the arrangement of the whole sentence. The *sense* of the sentence must always be considered; the statement must be correct and clear. Effectiveness cannot be gained by a thoughtless or artificial attempt to employ the suggestion mentioned here; it will help to increase effectiveness only if its use does not destroy correctness, clearness, and naturalness. See *Position and arrangement of words.*

Comma fault (comma splice).   Do not write two sentences with only a comma between them.

Sentences must be complete and they must be unified. If you write two independent statements as one sentence, you violate the principle of unity. A writer who does this reveals a deficiency of thought or that he does not know where one sentence ends and another begins.

The comma fault (also called comma splice) may be corrected by substituting a period for the comma. If the two ideas are related, however, the blunder may be corrected by using a comma and a conjunction; by using a semicolon; or by subordinating one of the two statements.

> *Wrong:* The trees are very tall, they were planted ten years ago.
>
> *Right:* The trees are very tall. They were planted ten years ago. (Period.)
>
> The trees are very tall, for they were planted ten years ago. (Comma and conjunction.)
>
> The trees are very tall; they were planted ten years ago. (Semicolon.)
>
> The trees are very tall because they were planted ten years ago. (Subordination.)

Comparison, double, incomplete, mixed.   See *Faulty comparison.*

Completeness. A sentence is *complete* when it lacks none of its parts; it is whole, entire, full. It contains a subject and predicate, both of them expressed or implied. It omits no words necessary to sense or structure. In short, it is perfect, rounded in its coverage. To achieve completeness in sentence structure without being wordy is far from simple. As a start toward achieving this goal, see *Incompleteness* and *Wordiness*.

Conciseness. *Concise* means "brief," "condensed." In sentence structure it implies that much is said in few words. Good writing results from a wealth of ideas and economy in words, not the reverse—a scarcity of thought and a flood of words. Even fairly well-constructed sentences can be improved by deleting non-essential or redundant words, using direct word patterns for roundabout ones, and economizing on modifiers.

Many words commonly used contribute little to the meaning or structure of sentences. Such "deadwood" expressions may be illustrated by the italicized words which follow:

> Redundant: *Despite the fact that* he had always thought his foreman *to be of the* blunt *type*, he finally realized him *to be a* kindly *man*.
>
> Concise: He had always thought his foreman blunt, but he finally realized he was kindly.

A sentence such as "My typing had the effect of making the boss regret the decision which had led him to hire me" can be shortened to "My typing made the boss regret hiring me"—a reduction from nineteen words to eight. See *Deadwood in sentences* and *Wordiness*.

Consistency in the sentence. This term means that the parts of a sentence are in agreement, are similar, and that they must remain so unless there is good reason for shifting them. You should be consistent (avoid shifts) in *tense, voice,* and *pronoun reference*. Consistency also applies to shifts in *number, subject,* and *figures of speech*. See, under *Shifts . . . ,* further discussion of each of these problems of sentence consistency.

Co-ordination. See *False co-ordination*.

Dangling elliptical phrases and clauses. See *Dangling modifier*.

Dangling modifier.   A modifier dangles when it cannot unmistakably be connected with the sentence element it modifies. Verbal
phrases and elliptical clauses are chief sources of trouble; their
correct position is dependent upon careful, logical thinking.
Such phrases and clauses are properly used only when the substantives to which they refer are expressed in the sentences and
when these phrases and clauses are placed so near the modified
substantives that there can be no ambiguity.

Some professional writers use modifiers with nothing to
modify. Through carelessness or ignorance, they overlook a useful distinction: between verbals designating specific physical
action where confusion may arise and verbals designating logical
relationships where the implied term modified can usually be
understood.

Infinitives and participles are not inflected for number or
person and hence must be connected logically and clearly with
the words they modify. Sentences containing dangling verbal
phrases may be corrected in one of three ways: (1) by expanding
the verbal phrase into a dependent clause; (2) by supplying the
substantive which the dangling construction modifies; (3) by
placing the construction so near the substantive that there is no
confusion.

Ineffective: To oil the carriage, the wheels must be removed.

When buying a ticket, the price should be considered.

Being very expensive, I did not buy the ticket.

Improved: When one oils a carriage, he must remove the
wheels. (The dangling infinitive phrase is
expanded into a dependent clause.)

When buying a ticket, one must consider the
price. (The gerund phrase is supplied with
the substantive, *one*, to which it refers.)

The ticket being very expensive, I did not buy
it. (The dangling participial phrase is placed
next to the substantive, *ticket*, which it
modifies.)

When a verbal is used to specify a general action, it is not considered a dangling modifier: "*In diving*, the feet should be kept together."

Such words as *considering, in regard to, according to*, etc., are used prepositionally, not as verbals. Thus: "*Considering* everything, the proposal was fair" is a correct sentence. But avoid such constructions as "Thinking it over, it seems reasonable."

Avoid dangling elliptical phrases and clauses.

An elliptical expression is one from which something has been omitted. An elliptical clause is one from which the subject or verb, or both, have been left out. Sentences containing dangling elliptical clauses can be corrected by (1) supplying the omitted subject or verb, or (2) changing the independent clause. Elliptical phrases can similarly be corrected.

Ineffective: Never race the engine *before thoroughly warmed up.*

While entering the house, the bell rang.

Improved: Never race the engine before it is thoroughly warmed up. (The dangling elliptical clause is corrected by supplying the necessary words, *it is.*)

While entering the house, he heard the bell ring. (The dangling elliptical phrase is corrected by changing the main clause.)

Dangling verbal phrase.   See *Dangling modifier.*

Deadwood in sentences.   The word *deadwood* is a convenient label for that type of wordiness in which a word or phrase adds nothing to the statement in which it occurs. We use hundreds of such expressions; for example, *the fact that* adds nothing to the single word *fact*. In the following sentence, the words in brackets can be removed entirely without changing essential meaning:

[There was] only one excuse [that] was [in every way] acceptable; [and that was] I was ill.

See *Conciseness* and *Wordiness.*

Dependent clauses misused.   If you recognize the clearness and emphasis which proper subordination contributes to sentences, you will be likely to use a large number of dependent clauses. But correct subordination is difficult and requires careful thinking. Errors in subordination sometimes cause lack of clarity and sometimes result in ineffectiveness.

The misuse of dependent clauses is a complicated matter which involves various errors. See, for example, *Adverbial clause for noun clause, Adverbial clause for noun or noun phrase, Noun clause as subject, complement, "Is when, is where,"* etc.

Double negative. This construction consists of the use of two negative words in the same statement: He *couldn't* find his friend *nowhere*. The double negative appears in correct French and, indeed, was used repeatedly by Shakespeare and Chaucer and many other great writers in English. Actually, a double negative can intensify and enforce a negative sense, but it is considered a vulgar or highly colloquial form of expression in current English usage. See *Illogical, mixed blends*.

Double reference. This fault occurs when there are two possible antecedents for a pronoun.

The antecedent of every pronoun must be clear and definite. Ambiguous reference can be corrected by (1) repeating the antecedent; (2) using a synonym for the antecedent; (3) changing the construction of the sentence.

> *Vague:* The manager told George that *he* would vote in the next election.
>
> He took the books from the boxes and placed *them* on the floor.
>
> *Better:* The manager told George that he intended to vote in the next election. (The double reference is corrected by changing the construction of the verb phrase.)
>
> *Clear, but awkward:* The manager told George that he (the manager) would vote in the next election. (The double reference is corrected by repeating the antecedent.)
>
> *Better:* He took the books from the boxes and placed the volumes on the floor. (The faulty reference is

corrected by using a synonym for the antecedent.)
He removed the books and placed the boxes on
the floor. (The faulty reference is corrected by
changing the construction of the sentence.)

Effectiveness in sentences. It is possible to write sentences which are clear and correct and yet not effective. Effectiveness is a somewhat vague and elusive quality which is dependent upon many sentence characteristics. In general, effective sentences are those which produce desired results; they are efficient; they impress the reader with a sense of suitable form and adequate content. The qualities contributing most to effectiveness in sentences are *conciseness, parallelism, consistency, variety of structure,* and *position and arrangement of words.* See each of these terms for specific discussion.

Elliptical sentence. Although not grammatically complete, an elliptical sentence implies a complete predication and does not violate the rule about sentence fragments (*period faults*). See *Fragmentary sentence,* below. The following italicized expressions are correct:

> "Did you buy it?"
> "*Yes.*"
> "*For how much?*"
> "*Five dollars.*"

See *Dangling modifier.*

Emphasis. The word *emphasis* suggests force or stress, but emphasis in sentence structure implies accurately conveying your ideas to your reader or hearer. It involves leading your reader to see your thoughts in the same relative importance in which you see them.

Emphatic sentence structure may be attained in several ways. *Position and arrangement of words* (which see) is one means. *Repetition for emphasis* and *repetition for sentence transition* are two others; consult both entries. In sentence structure, *emphasis* and *effectiveness* mean much the same thing. See *Effectiveness in sentences.*

Ending sentence. See *Beginning, ending sentence.*

Excessive co-ordination. The immature writer will phrase his sentences as a child speaks. That is, he will construct a series of independent clauses loosely held together by co-ordinating conjunctions. A child might say: "We went to the circus, and we saw all the freaks, and we drank pink lemonade, and we had a good time."

If you think carefully you can express your ideas in constructions which will show their varying importance. Subordinate minor ideas so that the important statement may be more emphatic.

Avoid excessive co-ordination, then, because it is childish and monotonous and reveals a lack of judgment. See *Choppy sentences* and *False co-ordination*.

Excessive subordination. Sentences which contain a series of overlapping subordinate clauses are ineffective. In such a series, each clause depends upon the preceding. Sentence elements should be linked together, but they should not be built like an accordion.

Ineffective: It was an inexpensive toy which had been made in Japan, which once had cheap labor.

 These are the children who feed to the squirrels the nuts which they buy on the corner that is near the park.

Each of these statements should be broken into two sentences. See *Subordination*.

False co-ordination. *Co-ordinate* means "of equal rank." An independent clause should be joined to an independent clause by a co-ordinating conjunction. Use the *correct* co-ordinating conjunction; do not use *and* if *but* is called for; if two statements belong together, do not incorrectly place them in separate sentences.

Inaccurate: He told me this and with his voice quivering.

 The nurse was a pleasant person and had had good training, but who was a failure.

 She wanted to go, and she did not have the proper clothes to wear.

 The automobile is a Chevrolet. It was made by General Motors.

Improved: He told me this, his voice quivering.

The nurse, a pleasant person, had had good training but was a failure.

She wanted to go but did not have proper clothes.

The automobile, a Chevrolet, was made by General Motors.

See *Excessive co-ordination, Overuse of "so," Seesaw sentences,* and *Stringy sentences.*

Faulty comparison.   Comparison is the change in the form of an adjective or adverb to show greater or smaller degrees of quantity, manner, or quality. The three degrees of comparison are positive, comparative, and superlative. Several errors in comparison are not only possible in sentence construction; they are all too frequent.

Use the comparative degree with two, the superlative with more than two. In informal usage we hear such a statement as "Navy's team is the *best*" when only two teams are being compared. Careful speakers and writers would use *better* in such a sentence.

Bring me the *better* of those knives. (Two knives concerned.)

Bring me the *best* of those knives. (Three or more knives concerned.)

Avoid including the subject compared if the subject is part of the object with which it is compared.

Wrong: She is older than any girl in her group.
Correct: She is older than any *other* girl in her group.

In informal and colloquial English the superlative is sometimes used when no particular comparison is intended: "You are *most* generous." Such a use of *most* is rare in standard writing.

Avoid the trap of the double comparative: "This test was *more harder* than the other." Such expressions are permissible only in informal usage.

All words necessary to a comparison should be included. See *Incompleteness.*

Faulty parallelism.   See *Parallelism.*

Faulty reference of pronouns.   The relation of a pronoun to its antecedent (the substantive to which it refers) should be clear and unmistakable. Place the reference word as close as possible to its antecedent so that no intervening words may cause confusion. A *relative* pronoun must be in the same sentence as its antecedent, but a *personal* or *demonstrative* pronoun may be placed some distance away, even in another sentence if there are no intervening substantives to cause confusion.

See *Double reference, Implied reference, Indefinite "it," Indefinite "they," Indefinite "you,"* and *Vague reference.*

Faulty subordination.   See *Subordination* and also *Excessive subordination, Subordinate form for co-ordinate idea,* and *Upside-down subordination.*

Figures of speech.   These are words used in a nonliteral way, that is, extended or changed in meaning as when we speak of a *heavy* cold or *bed of roses.* Well-chosen figures add much to the effectiveness of sentences. But see *Shifts in figures of speech.*

Fragmentary sentence.   Do not write a subordinate part of a sentence as if it were a complete predication (sentence). This error is also known as the *period fault* (which see).

The word *sentence* can mean "a stated opinion." Accordingly, any group of words may be called a sentence. But in grammar, a sentence is not a sentence unless it has a subject and a predicate, implied or expressed, even though the predicate be merely a verb.

"Sentences" are occasionally incomplete because the writer is unable to distinguish between a complete predication and a group of words incapable of standing alone and "making sense." A phrase or a dependent clause cannot be written as a complete sentence; to write and punctuate one of them as such constitutes a *period fault.* Verbal and appositive phrases and dependent clauses of all kinds must be included in the same sentence with the main clause.

> *Wrong:*   I had no money for a trip to Europe. *When suddenly I was left a fortune.* (Dependent clause.)
> I labored hours every night. *Finally giving up all my efforts.* (Participial phrase.)

> The bank was destroyed by those who needed it
> most. *The small depositors*. (Appositive phrase.)

Such fragmentary sentences may be corrected by rewriting or by joining the dependent clause or phrase to a preceding or following whole sentence.

> *Revised:* I had no money for a trip to Europe. Suddenly I
> was left a fortune.
> I labored hours every night but finally gave up all
> my efforts.
> The bank was destroyed by those who needed it
> most, the small depositors.

Note: There are, however, two kinds of incomplete sentences which are permissible. See *Elliptical sentence* and *Justifiable fragmentary sentence.*

Fused sentence. Do not write two sentences with no punctuation between them. Instead, supply a terminal mark of punctuation (period, question mark, or exclamation point).

A serious grammatical error and violation of the principle of unity is to write two grammatically complete sentences with no mark of punctuation between them. The "fused," or "blended," sentence error is an even more flagrant violation of correctness than the *comma fault,* for the writer of a comma fault shows that he senses the need for punctuation of some sort.

A sentence is a complete and independent predication and should always be followed by a full stop, that is, a terminal mark of punctuation.

> *Wrong:* The automobile ran smoothly the train was rough.
> The next day he departed for Atlanta this city is
> the capital of Georgia.

Judged by their grammatical form, each of those two "sentences" contains two independent statements. Each "sentence" may be written as two separate sentences or, if the writer feels that the statements are sufficiently related in thought, other punctuation may be used. The result might be a compound sentence with a semicolon separating the clauses and a terminal mark at the end:

Revised: The automobile ran smoothly. The train was rough.

The automobile ran smoothly; the train was rough.

The methods used to avoid the *fragmentary sentence* (which see) may be applied to many fused sentences. For example, you may subordinate one of the statements: The next day he departed for Atlanta, the capital of Georgia.

Idiomatic usage. The word *idiom* has several meanings. In sentence structure it may mean the regular forms of expression of a particular language. For example, French idiom requires adjectives to follow the nouns they modify; in English idiom they usually precede. Idiomatic usage suggests natural, normal wording rather than "correct" or "academic" language.

Idiom can also mean a group of words which differs from the usual construction of the language. Such expressions may be exceptional in some way but they are fully acceptable and require no apology. Your sentences should employ idiomatic expressions *in their acceptable form*, even though many idiomatic expressions make little actual sense: "catch a cold," "strike a deal," "all thumbs," "how do you do?"

Illogical, mixed blends. Unless we are careful, certain blends will creep into our thinking and writing. In a sentence such as "He had no automobile in which to ride in," we have faultily blended *in which to ride* and *to ride in*. In speaking, we might well say "Despite of what you think, I say you are wrong." Here we have blended *in spite of* and *despite*. Such constructions are as much a result of careless thinking as of grammatical ignorance. When we write "Irregardless of that, he decided to stay," we have illogically blended *regardless* and *irrespective*.

Perhaps the most common violation of logical phrasing is the double negative (two negatives in the same statement). Informal speech abounds with such expressions as "can't hardly," "can't scarcely," "haven't scarcely," and the like. In formal English, however, avoid them. Although double negatives have been allowable in the past, they are currently out of style and unacceptable. We are not likely to say or write "I didn't get no food," or "I didn't see nobody," but always be careful in using such "negative" words as *but, nor, only, hardly, scarcely,* and *except.*

> *Questionable:* I *can't help but* admire him.
>
> They have *not hardly enough* money for the trip.

Also, see *Blends, mixed or confusing, Double negative,* and *Mixed, illogical constructions.*

Illogical construction. See *Mixed, illogical constructions.*

Implied reference. This flaw in sentence structure occurs when the antecedent of a pronoun is not expressed and must be inferred from context. One of the most common forms of implied reference is the use of the pronouns *this, which, that,* etc., to refer to an entire preceding statement rather than to some substantive in that statement.

> *Vague:* His brother is a dentist. *This* is the profession he intends to enter.
>
> I like to travel in Switzerland. *They* are always pleasant to visitors.
>
> I cannot answer your letter *which* makes me very sad.

> *Improved:* His brother is a dentist. Dentistry is the profession he intends to enter.
>
> I like to travel in Switzerland. The Swiss are always pleasant to visitors.
>
> I cannot answer your letter, a fact which makes me very sad.
>
> *or*
>
> It makes me very sad to think that I cannot answer your letter.

Note: Faults in the reference of *this, which, that,* etc., may be corrected by (1) summing up the idea of the preceding statement in a noun which acts as the antecedent; (2) making the statements co-ordinate; (3) rephrasing the sentence.

Inaccurate co-ordination. See *False co-ordination.*

Inaccurate subordination. See *Subordination.*

Incompleteness. A sentence not only must contain a single thought, or a group of closely related ideas, but must also be *complete*: that is, it must be capable of standing alone and "making sense." Because of inaccurate thinking, many writers do not express their ideas so completely that the latter will be fully understandable units of thought. The fault is that the writer knows, or thinks he knows, what he has in mind, but does not take the trouble fully to convey his idea. Likewise, some "sentences" are incomplete because the writer does not know the grammatical essentials of a sentence. Sound thinking and a minimum understanding of the "grammar" of a sentence should enable you to avoid two serious kinds of sentence incompleteness: (1) the omission of *words* necessary for clear, full expression and (2) the omission of essential *ideas*.

Do not omit a necessary verb or auxiliary verb.

Informal usage sanctions the omission of words which should be expressed in formal writing and speaking. Even in formal writing, such a sentence as "He made such a speech as only a politician can [make]," is complete and correct without the bracketed *make*. The following sentences, however, involve more serious breaches of clarity:

> *Doubtful:*   The lawn is mowed and the hedges trimmed.
> *Improved:*   The lawn is mowed and the hedges *are* trimmed.

The verb *is mowed* is singular; although not expressed, *is* is understood to accompany *trimmed*. One cannot correctly write "The lawn *is* mowed and the hedges *is* trimmed" because *hedges*, a plural noun, requires a plural verb.

> *Doubtful:*   He always has and always will work hard.
> *Improved:*   He always has worked and always will work hard.

Do not omit a necessary article, pronoun, preposition, or conjunction.

"The president and chief executive received my plea." (This sentence means that one man is both president and chief executive.)

> *Doubtful:*   He built an automobile which could go ninety miles an hour and pleased many people.

Improved: He built an automobile which could go ninety
               miles an hour and *which* pleased many
               people.

Doubtful: I have interest and regard for your work.
Improved: I have interest *in* and regard for your work.

Doubtful: I am requesting that statement be made again.
Improved: I am requesting *that* that statement be made
               again.

Do not omit words necessary in a comparison.

Do not omit *as* or *than* in a double comparison; do not omit
the standard of comparison or one term of the comparison.

Doubtful: I study my manual harder than Fred.
Improved: I study my manual harder than Fred does.
               I study my manual harder than I study Fred.

Doubtful: He is as strong, if not stronger, than John.
Improved, but awkward: He is as strong *as*, if not stronger
               than, John.
Preferable: He is as strong as John, if not stronger.

Doubtful: He is so weak.
Improved: He is so weak that he cannot do any work.
               He is unusually weak.

Doubtful: This is the best cake.
Improved: This is the best cake I have ever eaten.

*Include every idea essential to the sense or proper structure
of the sentence.*

It is difficult to determine whether incompleteness in thought
causes incompleteness in structure, or vice versa. But you should
remember not to leave any sentence elements grammatically incomplete by starting with one construction and shifting to
another.

Not clear: An automobile, unless you take good care of
               it, you will soon have to have it repaired.
Improved: An automobile will soon have to be repaired
               unless good care is taken of it.

Not clear: With these men functioning as a team is the reason for our successful campaign.

Improved: With these men functioning as a team, we had a successful campaign.

or

Because these men functioned as a team we had a successful campaign.

Do not use punctuation to replace necessary words.

Sometimes a careless writer inserts a mark of punctuation, usually a comma, where a needed conjunction such as *that* or a relative pronoun should be used.

Incomplete: We asked, she consider being our candidate for discussion leader.

The man, I saw on the tower was a workman.

Improved: We asked *that* she consider being our candidate for discussion leader.

The man *whom* I saw on the tower was a workman.

See *Punctuation substituting for words.*

Incongruous ideas. See *Unity.*

Indefinite "it." *It*, as a third person singular pronoun, neuter, should usually have an appropriate antecedent. When *it* is used impersonally (*it* seems, *it* is possible, *it* is raining, etc.), another *it* should not be used in the same sentence referring to a definite antecedent.

Dubious: In this picture *it* showed some of the dark side of rural life.

Better: This picture showed some of the dark side of rural life.

Dubious: In this magazine article *it* states that not all wars are victories for the victors.

Better: This magazine article states that not all wars are victories for the victors.

Dubious: Bar Harbor is a beautiful summer resort; we liked *it* and *it* is possible that we shall go there again.

Better: We liked Bar Harbor as a summer resort, and *it* is possible that we shall go there again.

Dubious: Our roof needs patching, and when *it* rains *it* leaks badly.

Better: Our roof needs patching, and *it* leaks badly in rainy weather.

Indefinite "they." *They, their, theirs, them,* as plural forms of the third person personal pronoun, should have definite antecedents: plural nouns or pronouns. Otherwise, these pronouns should not be used.

Dubious: *They* have good roads in Texas.
Better: Texas has good roads.

Dubious: *They* say that Mexico is becoming very popular among tourists.
Better: Many people are saying that Mexico is becoming popular among tourists.

Dubious: We do our shopping in Chicago, for we like *their* large department stores.
Better: We do our shopping in Chicago, for we like that city's large department stores.

Indefinite "you." In informal and colloquial writing, an expression such as "*You* can see the importance of money" is permissible, even though *you* may refer to no particular person or group. In general, however, when using *you*, be sure that you mean the person or persons whom you are addressing. For example, the following is inappropriate in writing designed for reading by an adult: "When you become a Boy Scout, *you* learn many useful things." If you wish to refer to a number of people in general and to no one in particular, use indefinite pronouns like *one, anyone, a person.*

Dubious: In meetings you should do more speaking.
Preferable: In meetings the participants should do more speaking.
When a youngster becomes a Boy Scout, he learns many useful things.

Inexact transition.   Use transitional devices frequently, but correctly.

> *Inexact:*   He did not get the telegram in time as it was delivered late. (Substitute *because* or *since* for *as.*)
>
> I wanted to study architecture, and my fiancée urged me to stay with the family business. (Substitute *but* for *and.*)
>
> I did not pay the bill because I still have the money in my pocket. (Substitute *for* for *because.*)
>
> I was so tired until I could not work. (Substitute *that* for *until.*)
>
> George wished to go; *on the other hand*, his landlord also wanted him to go. (Substitute *and* or *fortunately* or *similarly* for *on the other hand.*)

See *Transitional devices.*

Infinitive, split.   This construction involves placing a word or group of words (usually an adverb or adverbial group) between the sign of the infinitive (the word *to*) and the infinitive itself. A *split infinitive* (which see) is not an indication of illiteracy, but it is usually unnecessary and ineffective.

Inverted sentence.   An inverted sentence is one in which the verb comes before the subject. In some constructions, such as a question (Why do you say that?), the inversion is entirely grammatical. Inverted sentences, if not overused, add interest, but inversion is largely a mannerism. *Time* magazine has employed the device so frequently that, in parodying *Time's* style, the late Wolcott Gibbs composed what is perhaps the best-known inverted sentence ever written: "Backward ran the sentences until reeled the mind."

"Is when," "is where," "is because."   The most common conjunction used to introduce a noun clause is *that*. Other such words are *whether, if, lest, when, where,* and *why.*

There is controversy about the use of *when, where,* and *because* in introducing noun clauses functioning as subjective complements. That is, should we say "is when," "is where," "is because"? No one would argue for such a crude sentence as "A good time *is when* you have plenty of money and an attractive date." Nevertheless, "the reason is because" occurs occasionally. Formal usage clearly insists upon "the reason is that." See *Adverbial clause for noun or noun phrase* and *"Reason is because."*

Jerky sentence. See *Choppy sentences.*

Justifiable fragmentary sentence. Skilled writers often use fragmentary sentences for stylistic effect. Strictly speaking, a group of words without a verb or one without a subject cannot be a sentence. Yet the following short passage contains six groups of words, each punctuated as a sentence; only the first, fourth, and fifth are grammatically in sentence form. The others are not real sentences but are used for stylistic effect:

"He walked as though he were dreaming. Dreaming? Hardly. He was more detached than that. He was hypnotized! Lost in another world."

Be certain that you *know* the difference between a sentence and a fragment before you start experimenting. See *Fragmentary sentence.*

Length and form. Vary the length and form of successive sentences.

Sentences which follow each other should not all be of the same approximate length. Twelve to twenty-five words is normal length. For variety, use an occasional sentence of three or four words, one of thirty or forty.

Likewise, sentences should not all be simple, or compound, or complex. Remember, sentences of the childish or immature person are likely to be predominantly simple or compound, whereas the work of the skilled writer will abound in subordination (complex sentences).

You should not consciously attempt to vary your sentences while you are composing the first draft of your report or letter. If you do so, you are likely to pay more attention to the structure of sentences than to the ideas you are trying to express. After the first draft is completed, however, you should carefully revise sentences which are monotonously similar in beginning, length, and form.

The person who wrote this paragraph was quite properly concerned with developing the thread of the narrative, but he neglected revision.

> We set out at dawn for the place where we were going to fish. We looked forward eagerly to a morning of real sport. The air was fresh and balmy. We reached the lake in about half an hour. First, we placed some moist earth in the cans in which we carried the bait. Then we set up our rods. Next we located a comfortable spot on the shore. At last we were ready to begin fishing.

See *Effectiveness in sentences* and *Variety*.

Loose sentence. This is a term applying to a group of words in which grammatical form and essential meaning are complete before the end is reached. Loose sentences abound in our speech and writing and are not incorrect. However, sentence effectiveness requires that they be not overused in the same passage. See *Periodic sentence* and *Variety*.

Misleading parallelism. Do not use the same structural form for sentence elements which are not of equal value. Avoid a series of elements which appear to modify the same element but do not.

> *Wrong:*   For your sake for fifty dollars I will help you.
>
> It is important that each of you should bring his own ammunition and that it should be good ammunition.
>
> They left immediately, and they had a good automobile.
>
> *Improved:*   For your sake I will help you to the extent of fifty dollars.
>
> It is important that each of you should bring his own ammunition, which should be in good condition.
>
> They left immediately in a good automobile.
>
> *or*
>
> They left immediately in an automobile in good condition.

See *Parallelism*.

Misplaced clauses and phrases. See *Position of modifiers.*

Misrelated modifier. This is another term for *dangling modifier* (which see). A *misrelated modifier* is a construction which from its position in a sentence cannot sensibly modify the word or word group it seems to. Dangling participles are notable offenders. So, too, are infinitive phrases and phrases in general used as adjectives and adverbs. Correctness and clearness in an English sentence depend more upon proper word order than upon any other single element.

Mixed, illogical constructions. You may expect your reader to give careful attention, but you cannot expect him to untangle involved and mixed constructions or to correct mistakes in logic. He may make necessary corrections as he reads, but his attention is unwillingly attracted to errors and away from the important communication of ideas. Therefore, if you wish to present thoughts clearly and effectively, do not leave a grammatical construction unfinished once you have begun it, and avoid mixed, illogical blends which occur in single words and in phrases. See *Illogical, mixed blends* and *Unfinished grammatical construction.*

Modifier. A modifier is a word or group of words which makes the meaning of other words more exact by limiting or restricting them. The modifiers of nouns and pronouns are adjectives, adjective clauses, adjective phrases, and participles. Modifiers of verbs, adjectives, and adverbs are adverbs, adverbial clauses, and adverbial phrases.

The position of modifiers in a sentence is important for clearness. See *Dangling modifier, Position of modifiers,* and *Word order.*

Monotonous sentence structure. Monotony in sentence structure implies using groups of words which are so uniform and unvaried in style and structure as to become wearisome and dull. Monotony may be caused by using a series of short, simple sentences, by a series of *seesaw sentences,* and in various other ways. See *Beginning with same word, Beginning with subject,* and *Variety.*

Noun clause as subject, complement. Use a noun clause, not a sentence, as the subject or complement of *is* and *was.*

Faulty: I had sprained my ankle was the reason I could not
go to the meeting.
His only fault is he has a bad temper.

Better: The reason I could not go to the meeting was that
I had sprained my ankle.
His only fault is that he has a bad temper.

Note that a quoted sentence may be used as a noun clause.

Correct: "Her little face is like a walnut shell" is a line from
an English poem.

Number, consistency in.   See *Shifts in number.*

Numeral, beginning sentence with.   The rule: *Don't.* See *Begining sentence with numeral.*

Omission of necessary words.   See *Incompleteness.*

Overuse of "so."   Even though *so* is correctly used as a conjunctive adverb with a semicolon preceding, and even though it is frequently used between independent clauses with only a comma before it, the chief objection to *so* in such constructions is simply *overuse.* In constructions like those below, *so* can often be replaced by *therefore, thus, accordingly,* and the like, or predication may be reduced. See page 90.

Ineffective: The bridge was out on Route 8, *so* we had to
make a long detour on Highway 20.
Improved: Since the bridge was out on Route 8, we had to
make a long detour on Highway 20.

In correcting the overuse of *so,* guard against a worse error, that of using another conjunctive adverb with a comma before it and thus writing an unjustifiable comma splice.

Wrong: The bridge was out on Route 8, therefore we had
to make a long detour on Highway 20.

Sometimes *so* is misused when the writer means *so that* or *in order that:*

Ineffective: Do people want the government to spend more
money *so* they can pay higher taxes?

> *Improved:*   Do people want the government to spend more money *in order that* they can pay higher taxes?

See *Excessive co-ordination.*

Parallelism.   Parallelism means "like constructions for like ideas." You will convey your precise meaning to your readers, surely and effectively, if you construct your sentences so that the reader can immediately see what ideas are of equal importance. Parallel construction for like ideas is indispensable to clear, grammatically correct, effective sentences. Parallel movement, correctly handled, is one means of attaining an emphatic, vigorous style.

The simplest form of parallelism involves two or more words in a series. Using more complex forms, the writer can make two or more phrases parallel, or two or more dependent clauses, or two or more independent clauses, or two or more sentences.

Words: Henry is *slow* but *thorough.*
        The American colors are *red, white,* and *blue.*

Phrases: Every afternoon my grandfather is at the barber shop *telling yarns about his youth* or *hearing the yarns that his cronies tell.*

Dependent clauses: I was desperate *when I arrived late in town* and *when I found there were no desirable rooms available.*

Independent clauses: Julius Caesar's most famous statement was this: *"I came, I saw, I conquered."*

Sentences: Alfred Lord Tennyson was the British poet who wrote lyrics in his early life and dramas in his closing years. Robert Browning was the British poet who wrote dramas in his early career and other forms of poetry in his later life.

As an effective test for true parallelism, draw lines under parallel elements. Then draw a corresponding number of lines in parallel form and write the underlined words on these parallel lines. Examples from the illustrations above:

Every afternoon my grandfather is at the barber shop
  telling yarns about his youth

  or

  hearing the yarns that his cronies tell.

Julius Caesar's most famous statement was this:
  I came,
  I saw,
  I conquered.

Sentence elements co-ordinate in rank should be parallel in structure. An infinitive should be followed by an infinitive of similar form, a phrase by a phrase, a clause by a clause, etc.

  Wrong: He liked to run and playing golf.
  Right: He liked to run and to play golf.

  Wrong: He bought a radio with seven tubes and having a
                beautiful mahogany finish. (. . . tubes and
                a . . .)
              He desired to make a lot of money and that he
                might earn a good reputation. (. . . and earn
                a good . . .)

Absolute parallelism is not always required. Although in the following the form is not parallel, the functions are:

  He talked *slowly* and *with a stammer*.
  I saw *John, Henry*, and *a man whom I have not met*.

See *Misleading parallelism* and *Partial parallelism*.

Partial parallelism. In using the formula A, B, and C, make certain that the three sentence elements are parallel in form. If they are not, a faulty and unemphatic series will result.

  Undesirable: The story is vivid, interesting, and has a simple
                    plot.
  Improved: The story is vivid, interesting, simple in plot.
                    or
                    The story is simple, interesting, and vivid.

See *Parallelism.*

Passive voice. Avoid excessive use of the passive voice.

The use of the passive voice often detracts from the effectiveness of a sentence. Many sentences require a passive verb, but, as a general rule, the active voice gives sentences force and strength.

> *Unemphatic:* The lecture *is scheduled to be given* by Commissioner Smith on Wednesday.
> *Better:* Commissioner Smith *will give* the lecture on Wednesday.

See *Voice.*

Period fault. This error consists of an unjustifiable sentence fragment, a group of words set apart from other words with which it logically belongs. It is called a *period fault* because it can be considered an error in punctuation. More normally it is thought of as an error in sentence construction. See *Fragmentary sentence.*

Periodic sentence. Use periodic sentences to secure emphasis.

A periodic sentence is so constructed that its full meaning is not apparent until the end. Such a sentence creates suspense; something is held back, and the reader continues in a state of expectation. You should avoid frequent use of periodic sentences because an awkward and artificial style will inevitably result. But their occasional use is fully justified by the effectiveness of the suspense they achieve. Note the following:

> Tired, hungry, bewildered, and sick at heart, the derelict stumbled into the warm and brightly lit restaurant. At first hesitantly, then eagerly, then fiercely, he seized and devoured a basketful of rolls.

> On men reprieved by its disdainful mercy, the immortal sea confers in its justice the full privilege of desired unrest.

> If you ask whether we can meet the Soviet challenge by concentrating on our private interests instead of on the public interest, by losing a great many of our best young brains in poor schools before they ever get to the college level, by not using our intelligent women when the Russians are using theirs, by not making a genuine effort to get our

best brains into the most effective jobs to serve the nation, why I'm bound to say that the answer is "no."

JAMES A. RESTON

See *Climactic order* and *Loose sentence*, above, and *Sentence, arrangement of content*, Part V.

Person of pronouns. Pronouns are classified in three persons:

First person—*I, me, my, our, we*, etc.
Second person—*you, your*
Third person—*he, she, it, they, them*, etc.

See *Shifts in class or person of pronouns*.

Phrase as sentence. See *Fragmentary sentence*.

Point of view. This phrase means the place from which, or manner in which, something is viewed or considered. It also refers to one's mental attitude or opinion. In sentence structure the phrase really means *consistency* (which see).

Position and arrangement of words. Effectiveness in sentence structure requires that words be so *chosen* and *arranged* that they have maximum impressiveness. Writers frequently attain correctness and clarity in their sentences, but only the more diligent or more gifted compose sentences which really "get across" decisively and emphatically.

Not all words or ideas in a sentence are of equal importance; consequently you must attempt to place elements of thought so that relatively unimportant items will remain in the background and important ones will achieve prominence. You can attain such effectiveness only by proper co-ordination and subordination. See *Beginning, ending sentence, Climactic order, Length and form, Periodic sentence, Repetition for emphasis,* and *Variety*.

Position of modifiers. Clear word order is essential in the English sentence.

1. Do not misplace such words as *only, not, even, hardly*, etc.
Modifiers should be so exactly placed in a sentence as to convey precisely the meaning intended. In such a sentence as "I *only* want ten dollars," *only* apparently modifies the verb *want*.

Actually, it probably is intended to modify *ten dollars*: "I want *only* ten dollars."

The former position of *only* is so normal in both speech and writing, however, as hardly to be misunderstood by anyone. But remember that the placing of *only* or of any other modifying expression can have a decided effect upon meaning:

> *Only* the foreman told me to complete the work before noon.
>
> The *only* foreman told me to complete the work before noon.
>
> The foreman *only* told me to complete the work before noon.
>
> The foreman told *only* me to complete the work before noon.
>
> The foreman told me *only* to complete the work before noon.
>
> The foreman told me to *only* complete [split infinitive] the work before noon.
>
> The foreman told me to complete *only* the work before noon.
>
> The foreman told me to complete the *only* work before noon.
>
> The foreman told me to complete the work *only* before noon.
>
> The foreman told me to complete the work before *only* noon.
>
> The foreman told me to complete the work before noon *only*.

He *hardly* has enough stamina for that. (*Hardly* here may be construed as modifying the verb *has*; actually it should modify the adjective *enough*.) To remove any possible doubt in the reader's mind, write: He has *hardly* enough stamina for that.

Vague: Any woman who sees this picture, *even the most unattractive*, will identify herself with the lovely heroine.

Improved: Any woman, *even the most unattractive*, who sees this picture will identify herself with the lovely heroine.

2. Do not misplace clauses and phrases.

> V*ague:*   I picked up the gloves and put them on my hands, *which I had bought in San Francisco.*
>
> *Improved:*   I picked up the gloves *which I had bought in San Francisco* and put them on my hands.

> V*ague:*   In his remarks he discussed everyday matters and people whom you and I know *as simply as a child.*
>
> *Improved:*   In his remarks he discussed, *as simply as a child,* everyday matters and people whom you and I know.

See W*ord order.*

Predication. In grammar, predication refers to a word or words which make a statement about the subject of a clause or of a sentence. That is, it is the "action" part of a sentence. For sentence predication, see *Reducing predication.*

Preposition, ending sentence with. It is *not* incorrect to end a sentence with a preposition, but doing so is often stylistically ineffective. See *Beginning, ending sentence.*

Prolix sentence. A prolix sentence is one which is wordy, verbose, long-winded. The word *prolix* implies such a tiresome elaboration of trivial details as to be dull. See *Unnecessary details.*

Pronoun. A pronoun is a word which represents (stands for) a person or thing without actually naming it. It comes from Latin *pro* plus *nomen: for* plus *name* or *noun.* Usually, the meaning of a pronoun is completed by reference to a noun which is called the *antecedent* of the pronoun. In the sentence "The sales manager complimented *them, the men* who had exceeded the quota," *the men* is the antecedent of *them.*

In sentence structure, proper reference of pronouns is important. See, especially, *Double reference, Faulty reference of pronouns, Implied reference, Shifts in class* or *person of pronouns,* and V*ague reference.*

Punctuation substituting for words. Occasionally, a mark of punctuation or mechanics can be used in place of a word but, except for the dash and apostrophe, such use is likely to cause confusion or misreading. Normally, a sentence in which a mark can replace a word is faulty to begin with and should be recast. See *Incompleteness*.

Rambling sentence. This one is easy: a rambling sentence *rambles*. It does so by introducing too many details. See *Unity* and *Unnecessary details*.

"Reason is because." In standard English, the construction beginning "The reason is . . ." is followed by a noun or a noun clause usually introduced by *that*. (See *Noun clause as subject, complement*.) Yet we often hear such a sentence as "I couldn't go; the *reason was because* I had to work." In spite of its form, the construction introduced by "reason was . . ." is a noun clause rather than an adverbial one. But such a use should appear only in colloquial speech. Standard writing requires "I couldn't go; the reason *was that* I had to work." See *Adverbial clause for noun clause* and *Reason is because* in Part I.

Reducing predication. This device for achieving effective sentences involves using fewer words to make a statement—deleting unnecessary words and letting one word serve for two or three or more. One synonym, for example, can replace several words without changing intended meaning. For clearness and effectiveness in sentence structure, follow these suggestions:

1. Combine two short sentences into one.

> *From:* I am a mechanic in a repair shop. I am specializing in carburetor adjustment.
>
> *To:* I am a garage mechanic, specializing in carburetor adjustment.

2. Reduce a compound sentence to a complex or simple sentence.

> *From:* Joe E. Brown for years has been an excellent comedian, and there isn't anyone who doesn't like Joe E. Brown.
>
> *To:* Everyone likes Joe E. Brown, who for years has been an excellent comedian.

3. Reduce a complex sentence to a simple sentence.

> *From:* Everyone likes Joe E. Brown, who for years has been an excellent comedian.
>
> *To:* Everyone likes Joe E. Brown, for years an excellent comedian.

4. Reduce clauses to phrases (see preceding example also).

> *From:* . . . a haze which resembled the color of smoke.
> *To:* . . , a haze the color of smoke.

5. Reduce clauses and phrases to single words.

> *From:* . . . shouting until I became frantic.
> *To:* . . . shouting frantically.
>
> *From:* . . . a haze the color of smoke.
> *To:* . . . a smoke-colored haze.

6. Reduce two or more words to one.

> *From:* . . . a member of a lodge.
> *To:* . . . a lodge member.
>
> *From:* . . . a foreman in the Department of Shipping.
> *To:* . . . a shipping foreman.
>
> *From:* . . . are going to attend.
> *To:* . . . will attend.

See *Conciseness* and *Deadwood in sentences.*

Reference. This word has many meanings, all of them having to do with "directing attention to" or "indicating," "pointing out." In grammar and sentence structure, its primary application is to pronouns. Since a pronoun refers to something without naming it, its meaning must be completed by another word, or group of words, known as an *antecedent.* See *Double reference, Faulty reference of pronouns, Implied reference,* and *Vague reference.*

Repetition for emphasis. Repeat important words to gain sentence emphasis.

Faulty repetition should be avoided, but the effectiveness of many sentences can be increased by repeating pivotal words.

Thus, the ideas are "driven home," clinched. Study the effect of repetition in the following:

> *Give! Give* money when you see that women and children are hungry. *Give* sympathy when you can cheer a beaten man. *Give* time to study conditions in your own community. *Give* your whole self in an attempt to change and better the life of all humanity.

Notice in the following passage from Matthew Arnold the expert use of repetition, not only of words and phrases, but also of ideas:

> The pursuit of perfection, then, is the pursuit of sweetness and light. He who works for sweetness and light works to make reason and the will of God prevail. He who works for machinery, he who works for hatred, works only for confusion. Culture looks beyond machinery, culture hates hatred; culture has one great passion, the passion for sweetness and light. It has one even yet greater!—the passion for making them prevail.

See *Useless repetition.*

Repetition for sentence transition. The most effective kind of repetition for sentence transitions is the use of pronouns referring to preceding nouns and pronouns. Synonyms are also effective. Occasionally, too, key or important words can be repeated in several sentences. (See *Repetition for emphasis.*)

Study the following sentences from the first two paragraphs of Thomas Henry Huxley's "The Method of Scientific Investigation." Note how the italicized words illustrate various devices for sentence transition.

> The method of scientific investigation is nothing but the expression of the necessary mode of working of the human mind. *It* is *simply* the mode at which all phenomena are reasoned about, rendered precise and exact . . .
>
> You will understand *this better, perhaps, if* I give *you* some familiar example. *You* have all heard it repeated, I dare say, that *men of science* work by means of *induction* and *deduction, and* that by the help of *these operations, they,* in a sort of sense, wring from nature certain *other*

things which are called natural laws and causes, and that out of *these*, by some cunning skill of *their* own, *they* build up hypotheses and theories. *And* it is imagined by many that the *operations* of the common mind can be *by* no means compared with *these processes, and* that *they* have to be acquired by a sort of special apprenticeship to the craft. To hear *all these* large words *you* would think that the *mind* of *a man of science* must be constituted differently from *that* of *his* fellow men; *but if you* will not be frightened by terms, *you* will discover that *you* are quite wrong, *and* that *all these* terrible apparatus are being used by *yourselves* every day and every hour of *your* lives.

See *Transitional devices*.

Repetition, useless. See *Useless repetition*.

Run-on sentence. A run-on sentence is one made up of a series of grammatically complete sentences written with loose connectives. See *Excessive co-ordination*.

Sagging sentence. A sagging sentence loses force as it proceeds and tapers off at the end. This flaw results primarily from improper word order. See *Climactic order*.

Seesaw sentences. This construction takes its name from the playground: a balanced plank used by children (and by some adults when others aren't looking). Seesaw sentences are compound sentences with two independent clauses of approximately equal length, whether or not joined by conjunctions. A succession of such sentences, rocking back and forth, is monotonous. Try *reducing predication* (which see) or otherwise subordinating one of the independent clauses.

Separation, needless. Because English is not a highly inflected language, it is especially important that closely related sentence elements (subject and verb, verb and object, preposition and object, etc.) be kept as closely together as possible. Occasionally, related elements must be separated to avoid misreading (see *Position of modifiers*) but needless separation is faulty. See *Split construction* and *Split infinitive*.

Shift in sentence structure. Parts of a sentence which bear the same relationship to the statement being made should have the same grammatical construction. See *Parallelism.*

Shifting from one form to another may cause confusion. An adjective should be paralleled by another adjective, active or passive voice should remain consistent within a sentence, etc. Shifts may, and do, occur in *subject, voice, tense, figures of speech, person* and *class* of pronouns, *number*, etc. Study carefully the entries below beginning *Shifts in . . .* Shifted constructions in sentences defeat clarity and are a sign of carelessness or ignorance.

Shifts in class or person of pronouns. This error in sentence structure involves a shift in pronoun reference and violates the general rule that pronouns and antecedents must agree in person. The most common occurrence of this fault is shifting from the third person to the second:

> If *one* tries hard enough, *you* will inevitably succeed. (*One* is an indefinite pronoun in the third person; *you* is a personal pronoun, second person.) The sentence should read "If *you* try hard enough, *you* . . ." or "If *one* tries hard enough, *he* . . ."

Shifts in figures of speech. A figure of speech is an expression using words in an unusual or nonliteral sense to give freshness or beauty to style. Well-phrased similes and metaphors, as well as other figures of speech, add clarity and effectiveness to writing. However, you should not shift suddenly from figurative language to literal speech, or vice versa. Especially in the use of simile and metaphor, you should sustain one figure of speech and not shift to another. Through shifting, we get such a "mixed" figure as this:

> When she lost her job, she got into a rut and felt all at sea. (Whoever *she* is has trouble, but we can't help her because we are laughing too hard at the weird description of her predicament.)

Shifts in number. A common error in the use of number is a shift from plural to singular, or singular to plural, or failure to make pronouns and antecedents agree in number.

If *men* really try *their* best *he is* bound to succeed.
(Change *he* to *they* and *is* to *are*.)

A small child can be a great joy, but *they require* much
care. (Change *they* to *he* or *she*; *require* to *requires*.)

Shifts in sentence structure. You should not begin a sentence
with one construction and then shift, for no discernible reason,
to another. You should not leave unfinished any sentence element. See *Incompleteness* and *Unfinished grammatical construction*.

Shifts in subject and voice. Is the subject of a given sentence
acting (active voice) or *being acted upon* (passive voice)? Sentences are always more effective if one voice is consistently used
throughout a passage. Consistency in voice also aids in avoiding
shifts from one subject to another in compound and complex
sentences.

The furnace burns little coal, and at the same time Jim
says it is easily cleaned. (Jim says the furnace . . .)

As you look across the street, tall trees can be seen.
(. . . street, you can see . . .)

Shifts in tense. Maintain one point of view in time unless there
is excellent reason for changing. Do not change the tense from
present to past or from past to present in narration.

Incorrect: George was walking slowly down the street when
suddenly an automobile turned the corner. It
dashes wildly down the avenue, careening and
twisting as if its driver is crazy. George jumped
behind a tree to protect himself. (Change
dashes to *dashed*, *is* to *were*.)

See *Consistency in the sentence*.

Short sentences. Brief sentences are undeniably easier to read
and to keep clear in meaning than longer ones. Short sentences
abound in newspaper and advertising writing and, when properly
constructed, are effective. Even so, you should avoid overuse of
this type of sentence. See *Length and form, Monotonous sentence structure*, and *Variety*.

"So" overused. See *Overuse of "so."*

Spliced sentence. See *Comma fault.*

Split construction. Because many English words show little if any change, it is important to keep logically related elements together. Because of inaccurate thinking, writers sometimes unnecessarily split constructions. Awkwardness and ambiguity result.

1. Do not aimlessly separate the parts of a verb phrase.

> *Awkward:*   This tree *has*, although you would not think so, *been* here for thirty years.
>
> *Improved:*   Although you would not think so, this tree *has been* here for thirty years.

> *Awkward:*   He *is*, despite many objections from his family, *going* to sea.
>
> *Improved:*   He *is going* to sea, despite . . .
>   *or*
>   Despite many objections from his family, he *is going* to sea.

2. Place co-ordinate sentence elements together.

> *Wrong:*   *Although he was a good tennis player,* he never was ranked among the first ten, *although he practiced daily.*
>
>   *With fair weather* we should have an enjoyable trip, *with good luck.*
>
>   (The italicized elements in each sentence above are co-ordinate and belong together.)

3. Avoid the unnecessary separation of subject and verb, object and verb, preposition and object, and other such closely related sentence elements.

On occasion, greater smoothness may be achieved by separation. But separation of closely related elements should be made for deliberate stylistic effect, never aimlessly. Remember, too, that informal speech and writing permit more freedom in splitting constructions than does formal writing. In the latter, you have opportunity to revise your sentences so that they will be unmistakably clear.

Faulty: He threw, in one sweeping and uncontrolled motion, both books and newspaper on the floor. (Verb and object.)

Improved: In one sweeping and uncontrolled motion he threw both books and newspaper on the floor.

Faulty: He walked into, although he was terrified, the house. (Preposition and object.)

Improved: Although he was terrified, he walked into . . .

Split infinitive. There is little reason for putting an adverb or phrase between an infinitive and its sign *to: to* + adverb + infinitive. Many good speakers and writers use and defend the split infinitive; consequently, it no longer is considered a major fault. However, clearness and naturalness should be the tests for its use.

There is a faulty split infinitive and a split construction which is not faulty, but desirable. In such a sentence as "He failed to *entirely* pay for it," *entirely* is correctly placed next to the verbal *pay*, which it modifies. To place it after *failed* or after *it* or after *pay* would result in a confusing or awkward construction. You should master the rule, however, before testing the exceptions. The following example illustrates questionable splitting:

Faulty: He ordered us *to as soon as possible leave.*
Improved: He ordered us *to leave* as soon as possible.

Squinting modifier. A modifier is said to be "squinting" when it may refer to either of two parts of a sentence.

The man who can do this *well* deserves your praise. (*Well* may modify either *can do* or *deserves.*)

One way to correct this ambiguity is to add *certainly* after *well*. Then, the adverb *well* will apply to *can do* and the second adverb, *certainly*, to *deserves*. Or the sentence may be recast.

The repairman who does his work quietly *from the point of view of the housewife* is praiseworthy. (The italicized words may refer to either the preceding or the following part of the sentence.)

To remove ambiguity here, place the italicized phrase at the beginning or end of the sentence. Doing either will remove the ambiguity but will result in a construction which probably should be recast. See *Position of modifiers* and *Word order*.

Stringy sentences. Do not overwork the compound sentence; avoid excessive use of coordinating conjunctions between independent clauses. Reduce predication; that is, change an independent into a dependent clause, a dependent clause into a phrase, a phrase into a single word. (See *Reducing predication* and *Excessive subordination*.)

> *Immature:* George bought a new automobile, and it had power brakes, and there was a radio.
> He took us for a short drive, and we stopped at a store, and we bought some candy.

> *Improved:* George bought a new automobile which had power brakes and a radio.
> He took us for a short ride during which we stopped at a store and bought candy.

Subordinate form for co-ordinate idea. Avoid the use of a subordinate form for a co-ordinate idea.

> *Inaccurate:* He was heavy and slow, *while* his wife was lithe and active.

To make this sentence more effective, delete the *while* or substitute a correct co-ordinating conjunction, *but*.

> *Ineffective:* Born in Canada in 1890, he became an American citizen in 1935.
> I called to her, *though she refused to answer.*

> *Improved:* He was born in Canada in 1890 and became an American citizen in 1935.
> I called to her, but she refused to answer.

Subordination. This word means the act of placing in a lower class or rank. Whenever we select one idea for emphasis in a sentence we automatically decide to subordinate other ideas in the same sentence. If we did not do so, our sentences would be written in "primer" style—as though we were children just learning to speak.

Careful, thoughtful writing contains much subordination. The good writer recognizes that not all ideas deserve equal rank and judiciously places them in constructions which correspond to their importance. His thoughts are more clearly communicated to readers, who can see what the relationship of sentence elements actually is.

You should avoid excessive and faulty co-ordination, but in doing so you are likely to make errors in subordination. *Reducing predication* (which see) requires care; you must be certain that you know exactly what you wish to express in order not to obscure shades of meaning.

Errors in subordination are discussed under *Excessive subordination*, *Subordinate form for co-ordinate idea*, and *Upside-down subordination.*

Tautological construction. This term refers to the needless repetition of an idea in a different word, phrase, or sentence. For example, "necessary essentials" is a tautological construction inasmuch as *necessary* and *essentials* express the same idea. See *Useless repetition.*

Telegraphic style. Writing can be understood even when important words are omitted. Otherwise, many important telegrams and cables would be misinterpreted. The following, however, is not good style in formal writing: "Letter received. Leaving tomorrow noon. Reserve room Barrett Hotel. Regards."

Tense. This word is derived from Latin *tempus*, meaning "time." In grammar and sentence structure, *tense* means the distinctive form of a verb for the expression of distinctions in time: present, past, future.

Many errors in tense usage can occur in sentence construction. The most common errors involve *sequence* of tenses and consistency in use. Proper sequence requires that when, for example, the verb of a main clause is in the present tense the verb in a subordinate clause must also be in this tense. (Sequence of tenses is fully discussed under this heading in the sections dealing with grammar.) Consistent use of tenses implies not shifting from one tense to another within the same passage. See *Consistency in the sentence* and *Shifts in tense.*

Transitional devices.   Individual sentences may be correct, clear, and effective, and yet be neither clear nor effective when put together in a paragraph. If the order of sentences within the paragraph is logical, then any lack of clarity probably is due to faulty *transition*. Transition means "passage from one place, state, or act to another." There are three kinds of transition, as applied to writing: within the sentence, between sentences, and between groups of sentences (paragraphs).

Our own processes of thought are so familiar to us that we tend to forget that our readers do not understand quite so readily and fully as we do the exact relations of our ideas. Schopenhauer once remarked that thought follows the law of gravity in that it moves more easily from head to paper than from paper to head. The writer's thoughts not only must progress logically; they must be marked so plainly that the reader can easily grasp both them and their interrelations. Only thus can effective communication be achieved.

Make transitions clear by frequent and correct use of transitional words and phrases.

Transitional devices are not needed within or between all sentences, but they are needed, for example, in this faulty series:

> Baseball is said to be the national game; I do not like it. If it is the national game, millions must enjoy watching it, or playing it. I know people who do not ever attend a game; I know people who see as many as fifty games a year. I should not make a dogmatic statement about the appeal of the sport; I have never witnessed a game.

By adding another thought and by noting that transition is often a matter of repetition of words rather than artificial and labored addition of words and phrases, you can make this paragraph more effective:

> *Although* baseball is said to be America's national game, I do not like it. *Yet* if *it* is the *national game*, thousands must enjoy playing the *game* and millions must enjoy watching *it*. I know people who see as many as 50 or 60 *games* a season and who drive many miles to see *them*; on the other hand, I know people who never attend a *game* and who wouldn't walk across the street to see *one*. *Perhaps* it is all

a matter of *sporting* taste, *and perhaps* I should not make a dogmatic statement about the appeal of *baseball. You see,* I have never seen a *game, and* I prefer a sport that I can take part in, peacefully, quietly, badly perhaps, and without "fan"-fare. *I prefer* golf.

The competent writer has a knowledge of connectives and their proper use. The following are some of the more frequently used transitional words and phrases: *also, at that point, and, again, accordingly, as a result, as I said, afterward, but, for, for example, for instance, fortunately, furthermore, hence, here, however, in like manner, indeed, in short, likewise, meanwhile, moreover, namely, now, of course, on the contrary, on the other hand, similarly, soon, temporarily, therefore, truly, thus, well, while.*

Unfinished grammatical construction.   This error occurs when a writer or speaker forgets, or fails to notice, how he began a sentence and shifts to another construction. Every statement must be related, both logically and grammatically, to the remainder of the sentence.

> *Wrong:*   Anyone who can be really happy, most people would look upon him with envy.
>
> *Correct:*   Anyone who can be really happy would be envied by most people.
>
> *or*
>
> Most people would envy anyone who can be really happy.

> *Wrong:*   The fact that he had always been a good student, he did well at medical college. (The first part of the sentence is left unfinished; the noun *fact* requires a full construction.)
>
> *Correct:*   The fact that he had always been a good student accounted for his doing well at medical college. (But since "the fact that" is a wordy expression, how about "His having always been a good student accounted for his doing well at medical college"?)

Unity. Unity means *oneness, singleness of purpose.* Sentence unity does not mean that only one object or idea should be mentioned or that the sentence must be short. A unified sentence may refer to several people, places, objects, or ideas, and may be lengthy. For example, this is a unified sentence: "Although the weather had turned warmer during the night, nevertheless Jim and I decided to pack our provisions and sharpen our skates in the hope that our guide would decide the ice was still safe for skating." The sentence is long and refers to several things and people; but it is unified because it has a singleness, a oneness, of purpose. The ideas are closely related and form a unit of thought. But a sentence could be one-fourth as long as this and refer to only one person, and yet violate the principle of unity: "Joe was a good mechanic, being the possessor of a new hat." The reader of this sentence very propery asks, "What have the two ideas in common?" The answer is, of course, "Nothing. The sentence is not unified."

(1) Introducing too many details and (2) combining unrelated ideas violate sentence unity, essential to clear writing. Avoid rambling sentences which introduce too many details.

> *Wrong:*   They offered to meet our party at Moose Junction, a little town in Minnesota which has only five hundred inhabitants, but which contains two general stores, three churches, and, since 1933, several saloons and a distillery owned by a wealthy man named Parks.
>
> *Revised:*   They offered to meet our party at Moose Junction, a little town in Minnesota which has only five hundred inhabitants, two general stores, and three churches. Since 1933 it has maintained several saloons and a distillery. The latter is owned by a wealthy man named Parks.

Avoid placing incongruous ideas in the same sentence.

> *Wrong:*   The grass was cut short, and she had bought the seed from Mrs. Thomas.
>
> The woman wore a white dress, and she had a good time at the reception.

Sometimes you can attain unity by making one idea subordinate to the other in the sentence, but ideas so unrelated as those immediately above should be placed *in separate sentences*.

Unnecessary details. The use of unnecessary details is called *prolixity*. A prolix sentence may be unified, but it is always ineffective because details obscure or weaken the point of the main idea.

> I decided to kill him at once, with a revolver which I had purchased at a low price only a few weeks ago.
>
> The town in which he formerly lived was small, it having a population of only one thousand, more than half of whom worked in the Smith and Brown Mattress Factory, Inc.

These two sentences are so verbose that whole ideas must be deleted. From the first, delete the mention of price: "I decided to kill him at once, with a revolver which I had purchased only a few weeks ago." If the matter of price is important, place it in another sentence. The second sentence contains two distinct ideas which may be placed in separate sentences or which may be combined and shortened: "He formerly lived in a town of only one thousand, more than . . ."

Upside-down subordination. Avoid putting the main idea of a sentence into a subordinate construction.

This is called "upside-down subordination." It shows that you have not evaluated the worth of your statements, and it may cause your reader to attach undue importance to a subordinate idea. However, it is sometimes difficult to determine which *is* the subordinate idea. Usually, the most dramatic incident and the effect, rather than the cause, are major ideas; preliminaries (place, time) and attendant circumstances normally are minor, that is, subordinate, ideas.

> *Inaccurate:* Our muscles were getting tired, when we decided to hail a taxicab.
>
> I saw an automobile heading straight toward me, when I was unable to move, from fear.

Improved: Since our muscles were getting tired, we decided to hail a taxicab.

Although I saw an automobile heading straight toward me, I was unable to move, from fear.

See *Subordination.*

Useless repetition. Avoid the useless repetition of an idea This fault is called *tautology.* Frequently, a writer who is not thinking carefully will repeat an idea, for no purpose, in different words. The result is a *tautological construction* (which see).

Tautological: I was very anxious for him to succeed and eager that he do so.

This absolutely new and novel innovation will please them; they will like it very much.

More concise: I was eager for him to succeed.

They will like this innovation.

See *Conciseness* and *Wordiness.*

Vague reference. In formal English, every pronoun (especially *that, these, those, it*) should refer clearly to its antecedent or should be made clear by some other statement in the sentence.

Faulty: His attitude gave me *that* sinking feeling.

Better: His attitude gave me a sinking feeling.

or

His attitude depressed me.

Faulty: In this magazine article *it* states that war is not inevitable.

Better: This magazine article states that, etc.

Faulty: *They* say that Alaska is a potentially wealthy state.

Better: It is said that Alaska is, etc.

Faulty: This book is so written that the reader may study any one section and so that *it* may be studied as a unit.

Better: This book is so written that the reader may study any one section or this section may be studied as a unit.

> *Faulty:* When a salesman hands over an article to a customer, *he* is not always certain of its worth.
>
> *Better:* A salesman is not always certain of the worth of an article when, etc.

Be precise in using such reference words as *former, latter, first, second, third, last;* make certain the reader can understand exactly the point you have in mind.

Variety. A series of sentences monotonous in structure is ineffective. We tire of reading a long succession of identical sentences, just as we tire of sameness in anything. Variety is much more than the spice of writing; it is a quality which reflects the mature processes of the writer's mind.

Revise sentences to make certain that they have *variety.* Vary their length and, occasionally, their normal word order. Vary the form of sentences (declarative, interrogative, etc.) and use periodic sentences as well as loose. Avoid a series of simple sentences and try to phrase more that are complex. Even simple sentences may be varied in structure.

Terms used in the preceding paragraph are discussed at appropriate places in this section; study them.

Verb and verbal phrases. Since a verb (expressed or implied) must appear in every well-constructed sentence, you should be able to distinguish between two major forms of this part of speech. A *verb phrase* consists of a group of words serving the function of a verb, such as an auxiliary verb with its main verb or a verb with its modifiers: You *will have been promoted* before I get even one salary increase.

A *verbal phrase* contains a participle, infinitive, or gerund. *Having finished my work* (participial); *his playing of the concerto* (gerund); *to achieve success* (infinitive) are examples of verbal phrases.

For *verb phrases* see *Tense,* above, and the same entry in Part V. For *verbal phrases,* see *Dangling modifier* and *Position of modifiers.*

Voice. When the subject of a verb is the doer of action expressed by the verb or is in the state or condition named by the verb, the verb itself is in the *active* voice. When the subject of the verb "receives" the action, the verb is *passive.* The passive is usually formed by some part of the verb *to be* and a past participle.

These different expressions of a verb offer considerable flexibility in *word order* (which see). See also V*oice* in Part V and *Passive voice* and *Shifts in subject and voice*, above.

Wordiness. A sentence may be complete and unified and still be ineffective because it is wordy. Clear, effective sentences demand accuracy of thought and conciseness of expression. This does not mean that you should use a *telegraphic style* (which see). Nor does it mean that all sentences must be brief. A sentence of one hundred words may be concise and one of twenty may be wordy. But sentences are rarely effective when they contain superfluous words or ideas.

In making sentences concise you can eliminate unnecessary words, turn clauses into phrases, and use word-saving suffixes. For example, you would not refer to "a great, big, enormous man." Probably only the last adjective would suffice. "Any typist who is qualified can become a member of the secretarial staff" may be shortened to "Any qualified typist can become a secretary." And a sentence such as "I was waiting for his telephone call until I became frantic" can be written: "I was waiting frantically for his telephone call." If such condensation violates meaning, it should not be employed. But you will effectively hold readers only when your sentences are lean and vigorous.

See *Conciseness, Deadwood in sentences, Reducing predication, Unnecessary details*, and *Useless repetition*.

Word order. An English sentence does not consist of a string of words in free relation to each other but of groups of words arranged in patterns. Words in an English sentence have meaning because of their position. That is, they have one meaning in one position, another meaning in another position, and no meaning in still another position. Some linguists maintain that the basis of English grammar is word order. Certainly the order of words and of other locutions is a fundamental part of grammar and is basic in sentence construction. In addition, word order contributes to many effects of style, especially emphasis.

In highly inflected foreign languages, the relationships of words in a sentence are shown by their endings. English is not highly inflected, and confusion will result if such functional words as prepositions and auxiliary verbs are not properly used. Even if they are, vagueness will occur in a sentence in which words are incorrectly placed. Try to keep related words together so that the reader may see their connection; try to place every modifier so that it is logically and naturally connected with the word or phrase it modifies.

See *Dangling modifier, Position of modifiers, Split construction,* and *Squinting modifier.*

They spell it Vinci and pronounce it Vinchy; foreigners always spell better than they pronounce.

MARK TWAIN, The Innocents Abroad

As felicitous an instance of futile classicism as can well be found is the conventional spelling of the English language. English orthography satisfies all the requirements of the canons of reputability under the law of conspicuous waste. It is archaic, cumbrous, and ineffective; its acquisition consumes much time and effort; failure to acquire it is easy of detection.

THORSTEIN VEBLEN, The Theory of the Leisure Class

Part III
Guide to Correct Spelling

Misspelling is not the most serious error which a writer can commit, but many of your friends, acquaintances, business associates, or employers consider it a major fault. Correct spelling is an important phase of word study.

Spelling English words *is* difficult. For centuries, many words have been spelled "without rime or reason." Through this lack of sensible method, the spelling of many words has become fixed. Many words which sound alike are spelled differently; many words are not spelled as they sound; many contain silent letters. Also, spelling by analogy is far from a safe guide.

The first and most important step in correct spelling is to have the desire to learn, really to want to become a competent speller. The second is to devote the necessary time to learn. The third is to use all available means to learn. If you are, chronically and consistently, a poor speller, you should obtain a special book which deals solely with spelling problems and which gives you many spelling exercises.*

As you study, remember these words of an experienced teacher of spelling: "All the investigations indicate that any *child* of normal intelligence can learn to spell with very little difficulty in a reasonable length of time." Other spelling authorities assert that the common causes of poor spelling are *carelessness* and *laziness*.

Most people are not, by birth and constitution, chronic misspellers, but many do have trouble with spelling. In addition to

* See Harry Shaw, *Spell It Right!* (New York: Barnes and Noble, Inc., 1961).

desire, time, and *means,* it should be easy to improve if you will habitually do these seven things:

1. Pronounce words correctly.
2. Mentally *see* words as well as hear them.
3. Use a dictionary to fix words in your memory.
4. Use memory devices (mnemonics) to help remember troublesome words.
5. Learn a few spelling rules.
6. Write words carefully in order to avoid errors due not to ignorance but to carelessness.
7. *List* and *study* the words you most frequently misspell.

These seven approaches to correct spelling have been broken into more than one hundred specific items, each separately treated in alphabetical order in this section on spelling.

APPROACHES TO SPELLING

-Able, -ible. Even excellent spellers have occasional difficulties with these endings; they can unhesitatingly spell most words having one or the other of these suffixes but sometimes they, too, must seek out their dictionaries.

With this spelling problem the best advice is "Stop and look." (It won't do any good to "listen," for pronunciation is identical.) To an efficient speller a word which should end in *-ible* doesn't "look right" when it ends in *-able.* He depends on his visual image of the correct spelling.

But for those whose visual recall is deficient, there *are* some guiding principles concerning *-able* and *-ible.* They are fairly easy to learn and involve no more exceptions than most rules for spelling. There are five group forms for *-able,* listed below, and the same number for *-ible* (which see).

-Able.

1. The ending should usually be *-able* if the base (root) is a complete word: *eat + able.*

Fortunately, many of our most familiar, most used words add *-able* to form adjectives. Note that if you drop *-able* from each of the following you are left with a complete word:

acceptable	dependable	peaceable
available	detectable	perishable
avoidable	detestable	predictable
breakable	discreditable	presentable
changeable	drinkable	profitable
comfortable	fashionable	readable
commendable	favorable	seasonable
companionable	laughable	taxable
considerable	noticeable	unthinkable
creditable	passable	workable

2. The ending should usually be *-able* if the base (root) is a complete word lacking a final *e: desire + able = desirable.*

Fortunately, this group of *-able* words is not nearly so large as the preceding one. The following words illustrate the basic principle:

believable	excitable	pleasurable
debatable	excusable	sizable
deplorable	likable	usable
desirable	lovable	valuable

3. The ending should usually be *-able* if the base (root) ends in *i* (the original word may have ended in *y*): *enviable.*

This principle of spelling makes more sense than most spelling "rules." If it were not followed, we would have a double *i* (*ii*), an unusual combination even in our weird spelling system.

appreciable	dutiable	reliable
classifiable	justifiable	sociable

4. The ending should usually be *-able* if the base (root) has other forms with the sound of long *a: demonstrate, demonstrable.*

This principle will be helpful only if you actually sound out another form (or forms) of the root word to see whether it has (or they have) the long *a* sound: *abominate, abominable; estimate, estimable,* etc.

delectable	impregnable	inseparable
durable	inflammable	intolerable
flammable	inimitable	irreparable
impenetrable	innumerable	irritable

5. The ending should usually be *-able* if the base (root) ends in hard *c* or hard *g*.

Hard *c* is sounded like the *c* in *cat*; hard *g* has the sound of *g* in *get*. The following words illustrate this principle:

amicable	explicable	irrevocable
applicable	implacable	navigable
despicable	indefatigable	practicable

These five principles cover most of the fairly common words which have endings in *-able*. But if you wish to be able to spell *all* words ending with *-able*, then study the following by some other method—rules won't help much:

affable	ineffable	palpable
arable	inevitable	portable
culpable	inscrutable	potable
equitable	insuperable	probable
formidable	malleable	unconscionable
indomitable	memorable	vulnerable

Ad-. This prefix alters its form according to the root word to which it is attached. For example, before a root beginning with *sc* or *sp*, the *d* is dropped, as in *ascent* and *aspire*. Before *c, f, g, l, n, p,* and *t*, the *d* in *ad-* is assimilated (becomes the same as the following letter): *accommodate, affix, aggression, allegation, announce, appoint, attend.*

Added vowels. Some words are misspelled because in pronouncing them an extra vowel is added. A list of them would not be long, but since many of them are frequently used they merit careful study. Mispronouncing may cause you not only to misspell them but to be looked upon as careless in speech or uneducated, or both. See *Mispronunciation.*

    Athletics (sports, games) should not be spelled ath*a*letics or ath*e*letics.

    Disastrous (causing harm, grief) should not be spelled disast*e*rous.

    Entrance (act or point of coming in) should not be spelled ent*e*rance.

    Explanation (interpretation) should not be spelled expla*i*nation.

Grievous (sad to hear, deplorable) should not be spelled grievious.

Hindrance (obstacle, impediment) should not be spelled hinderance.

Hundred (the number) should not be spelled hundered.

Laundry (washing of clothes) should not be spelled laundery or laundary.

Mischievous (prankish) should not be spelled mischievious.

Monstrous (huge, enormous) should not be spelled monsterous.

Nervous (emotionally tense) should not be spelled nerveous.

Partner (associate) should not be spelled partener.

Remembrance (souvenir, keepsake) should not be spelled rememberance.

Similar (alike) should not be spelled similiar.

Spanish (pertaining to Spain) should not be spelled Spainish.

Umbrella (a shade or screen) should not be spelled umberella.

Affixes. This is a term which embraces both *prefixes* and *suffixes*.

Prefixes are syllables added at the beginnings of words to alter or modify their meanings or, occasionally, to form entirely new words. For example, we add the prefix *de-* to the word *form* and form *deform*.

Suffixes are syllables added at the ends of words to alter their meanings, to form new words, or to show grammatical function (part of speech). Thus we add *-ly* to *like* and form *likely*.

The readiness with which prefixes and suffixes are tacked on to root words in the English language is an indication of the freedom in word formation which has characterized our language for many centuries. For example, consider the word *recession*. This is derived from a Latin word *cedere* (*cessus*) which has the general meaning of "go." To this base we add the prefix *re-*, which has a generalized meaning of "back" or "again," and the suffix *-ion*, an ending which shows that the word is a noun (name of something).

Related to *recession* are many words with still other prefixes and suffixes but all coming from a similar root, or base: *recede, recess, recessive, concession, procession, secession,* etc. The prefix *re-* of *recession* occurs in such words as *reception* and *relation*. Examples like this could be extended indefinitely.

A knowledge of the ways in which prefixes and suffixes are added to words will not only increase your vocabulary but also improve your spelling.

-Ally, -ly. Because these endings appear so often in commonly used words, they account for a large number of misspellings.

1. The suffix *-ly* is used to form an adverb from an adjective: *poor* + *ly* = *poorly*.

If the adjective ends in *l*, *ly* is tacked on to the complete root, thus producing an *lly* ending. Here is a list of frequently used, and occasionally misspelled, adverbs:

accidentally	fundamentally	personally
actually	generally	physically
annually	incidentally	practically
continually	individually	really
coolly	intentionally	skillfully
cruelly	literally	successfully
especially	logically	truthfully
exceptionally	morally	universally
finally	naturally	unusually
formally	occasionally	usually

2. The suffix *-ly* is added to basic words ending in silent *e*, the *e* being retained.

absolutely	entirely	scarcely
barely	immediately	severely
completely	infinitely	sincerely

3. If an adjective ends in *-ic*, its adverbial form ends in *-ally*.

This simple rule has only one exception: *publicly*. This word you must fix in your visual memory. Here are examples of adverbs formed from adjectives with *-ic* endings:

academically	basically	grammatically
artistically	emphatically	lyrically
automatically	fantastically	systematically

The following adverbs do not completely follow the principles just enumerated. Fix them in your visual memory:

duly	possibly	truly
only	terribly	wholly

-Ance, -ence.   The suffixes *-ance* and *-ence* are added to root words (verbs) to form nouns: *attend, attendance; prefer, preference.*

There is no uniform guiding principle to your choice of *-ance* or *-ence.* Correct pronunciation is of no help. Your only safe procedure is to consult your dictionary and try to form good visual images of *-ance* and *-ence* words.

One helpful principle, and one only, is this: if a verb ends in *r* preceded by a single vowel and is accented on the last syllable, it forms its noun with *-ence*:

abhorrence	deference	preference
coherence	deterrence	recurrence
concurrence	inference	reference
conference	occurrence	transference

Here are lists of often misspelled words ending in *-ance* and *-ence.* Study each until you have a total recall of its appearance:

Frequently Misspelled *-Ance* Words

abundance	continuance	nuisance
acceptance	contrivance	observance
acquaintance	defiance	performance
admittance	deliverance	radiance
allegiance	distance	relevance
alliance	endurance	reliance
allowance	entrance	remembrance
ambulance	furtherance	remittance
annoyance	grievance	repentance
appearance	guidance	resistance
arrogance	instance	significance
assurance	insurance	substance
attendance	irrelevance	temperance
balance	maintenance	tolerance
brilliance	malfeasance	vengeance

Frequently Misspelled *-Ence* Words

absence	difference	obedience
abstinence	eminence	patience
audience	essence	permanence
circumference	evidence	preference
coherence	excellence	presence
coincidence	existence	prominence
competence	experience	prudence
conference	impudence	reference
confidence	incidence	residence
conscience	inference	reverence
convenience	influence	sentence
correspondence	innocence	silence
deference	insistence	subsistence
dependence	interference	violence

Ante-, anti-. The first of these prefixes is of Latin origin and means "before," "prior." *Anti-* is from the Greek and means "opposite," "against." Note these different spellings:

ante-bellum (before the war)	antiaircraft
antemeridian (before noon; a.m.)	antibiotic
ante-mortem (before death)	anticlimax
anteroom (room before another room)	antifreeze
antetype (an earlier form)	antisocial

Apostrophe. An apostrophe is a sign, not a letter, and yet when one is improperly added or omitted it causes misspelling. The apostrophe has several uses, all with some influence on spelling: to indicate the possessive case, to mark omission of letters, to indicate the plurals of letters and numbers. The use of an apostrophe, which is only part of a word, influences both punctuation *and* spelling.

1. Use an apostrophe and *s* to form the possessive of a noun not ending in *s*.

    girl's, dog's, women's, doctor's, moment's

2. Use an apostrophe alone to form the possessive of a plural noun ending in *s*.

    girls', dogs', doctors', soldiers', friends'

3. Use the apostrophe alone, or the apostrophe with *s*, to form the possessive of singular nouns ending in *s*.

> Keats' or Keats's (but not Keat's) poetry
> Burns' or Burns's (but not Burn's)

4. Use an apostrophe to indicate that figures or letters have been omitted.

> don't, wasn't, o'clock, the class of '59

5. Do not confuse *its* and *it's*. The former is the possessive of *it*; the latter is the contraction for *it is*.

> What is *its* significance today?
> I think *it's* after ten o'clock.

6. Never use an apostrophe with the possessive *its*, or with *hers, his, yours, theirs, ours, whose*. The apostrophe is used in the possessive case of only indefinite pronouns: *one, none, somebody, someone, each, another, either*.

> *one's* duties, *someone's* hat, *another's* dress

7. Add the apostrophe (and *s*) to the last member of a group to indicate joint possession.

> I'll meet you in *Levy and Brown's* shoe store.
> Let's get a soda at *Billings and Stover's* drugstore.

8. The apostrophe is added to the last member of a compound:

> *somebody else's* book, his *mother-in-law's* home

9. Use an apostrophe to indicate the plural of figures, letters, and words mentioned as words.

> You make 6's which look like *c*'s.
> There are four *but*'s and seven *for*'s in the first paragraph.
> Cross your *t*'s and dot your *i*'s.
> He lost his money in the 1930's.

10. Do not use an apostrophe indiscriminately.

Especially with plurals, the apostrophe is frequently misused. In a sentence such as "The Smiths were present at the party" no apostrophe is necessary for *Smiths*, which is simply the plural form of the name.

-Ar, -er, -or. The suffixes *-ar*, *-er*, and *-or* have various origins, functions, and meanings. Their most common shared meaning denotes an actor, a doer, "one who." Many thousands of English words end in *-ar*, *-er*, and *-or*, but here again accurate pronunciation is of little help in spelling; furthermore, no principles are applicable.

Following are lists of *-ar*, *-er*, and *-or* words often misspelled. In not every word is the ending a true suffix, but correct spelling is now your objective, not a study of word origins or of word-building.

Frequently Misspelled Words Ending in -Ar

altar (*n.*)
angular
beggar
calendar
caterpillar
cedar
cellar
circular
collar
dollar
grammar
hangar
insular
liar
lunar
molar
muscular
particular
peculiar
pillar
polar
popular
regular
scholar
similar
spectacular
sugar
vehicular
vinegar
vulgar

Frequently Misspelled Words Ending in -Er

advertiser
adviser
alter (*v.*)
announcer
baker
beginner
believer
boarder
border
boulder
carrier
commissioner
condenser
consumer
defender
diameter
disaster
employer
examiner
foreigner
haberdasher
jeweler
lawyer
lecturer
manager
manufacturer
messenger
minister
murderer
observer
officer
partner
passenger
prisoner
provider
soldier
teacher
traveler
writer

Frequently Misspelled Words Ending in -*Or*

accelerator	debtor	manor
actor	dictator	minor
administrator	director	monitor
aggressor	distributor	motor
anchor	doctor	neighbor
auditor	editor	odor
author	educator	pastor
aviator	elevator	prior
bachelor	emperor	professor
behavior	escalator	protector
benefactor	executor	radiator
cantor	factor	sailor
collector	governor	sculptor
commentator	harbor	senator
competitor	humor	suitor
conqueror	inferior	supervisor
contributor	inventor	tenor
councilor	investigator	traitor
counselor	janitor	ventilator
creditor	legislator	visitor

Ary, -ery. This suffix problem is simple. Many hundreds of English words end in -*ary*. Only a half-dozen fairly common words end in -*ery*. Learn the -*ery* words by whatever device works best for you. Spell all others with -*ary*.

Here are some words you might use which end in -*ery*:

cemetery	millinery
confectionery	monastery
distillery	stationery

Now, end all other words with -*ary*. You'll be right every time unless you happen to use such a rare word as *philandery*.

You will have no spelling problems with the endings of *auxiliary, boundary, dictionary, elementary, honorary, imaginary, library, secretary,* and *voluntary,* and hundreds of other such everyday words.

Attention span. See V*ision spread.*

Auditory image. We have an auditory (hearing) image when a suggested idea summons up a memory of what the recalled idea or object sounds like. Can you "mentally hear" the sounds suggested by "the bark of a gun," "a key turning in a lock," "sizzling bacon," or "a gurgling stream"? If so, you are auditory-minded and, if also visual-minded, you will have less trouble with correct spelling than persons who are neither or only one.

Base of word. In linguistics, the base of a word is a *root*, a morpheme to which may be added prefixes, suffixes, etc. An approximate synonym for *base* and *root* in this sense is *stem*; all mean the part of a word to which suffixes and prefixes are added or in which phonetic changes are made. Thus we say that *love* is the base (stem or root) of the word *loveliness*, *form* of *reform*, etc.

Capitalization. To misspell is to violate a convention. To use capital letters wrongly is to violate a convention. Actually, the use of capitals applies closely to spelling.

1. Capitalize the first word of every sentence and the first word of every direct quotation.

> The engine needs repair.
> He asked, "Does the engine need repair?"

When only a part of a direct quotation is included within a sentence, it is usually not begun with a capital letter:

> The reporter told me that the official said he felt "fine" but thought that he should "take it easy" for a few weeks.

2. Capitalize proper nouns.

Proper nouns include:

a. Names of people and titles used for specific persons:

> George Washington, Theodore Roosevelt, the President, the Senator, the Treasurer, the General, Mr. Chairman, Father, Mother

b. Names of countries, states, regions, localities, other geographic areas, and the like:

> United States, England, Illinois, the Far East, the Dust Bowl, the Midwest, the Solid South, the Rocky Moun-

tains, the Sahara Desert, the Connecticut River, Lake Michigan

c. Names of streets:

Michigan Boulevard, Fifth Avenue, Old Mill Road

d. Names of the Deity and personal pronouns referring to Him:

God, Heavenly Father, Son of God, Jesus Christ, Saviour, His, Him, Thy, Thine

e. Names for the Bible and other sacred writings:

Bible, the Scriptures, Book of Genesis, Revelations, Koran

f. Names of religions and religious groups:

Protestantism, Roman Catholicism, Presbyterian, Jesuit, Unitarian

g. Names of the days and the months (but *not* the seasons):

Monday, Tuesday, etc.; January, February, etc.; summer, winter, autumn, fall, spring

h. Names of schools, universities, colleges:

Woodberry Forest School, Kentucky Military Institute, Davidson College, Cornell University

i. Names of historic events, eras, and holidays:

Revolutionary War, Christian Era, Middle Ages, Renaissance, Fourth of July, Labor Day

j. Names of races, organizations, and members of each:

Indian, Negro, Malay, League of Women Voters, American Academy of Science, National League, San Francisco Giants, Big Ten Conference, an Elk, a Socialist

k. Vivid personifications:

Fate, Star of Fortune, Destiny, the power of Nature, the paths of Glory, the chronicles of Time

l. Trade names:

Bon Ami, Ry-Krisp, Wheaties

m. All names similar or comparable to those in the foregoing twelve groups.

3. Capitalize the first word of every line of poetry.

> How happy is he born and taught
> That serveth not another's will;
> Whose armour is his honest thought,
> And simple truth his utmost skill!
> WOTTON

4. Capitalize each important word in the title of a book, play, magazine, musical composition, etc.

> *Romeo and Juliet, The Moonlight Sonata, Good House-keeping, The Web of Earth, The Iceman Cometh.*

Note: Do not capitalize prepositions, conjunctions, and articles except at the beginning or end of the title or unless they consist of five or more letters:

> *The Return of the Native, Caught Between Storms, Mr. Pim Passes By*

See *Capital letters* and *Unnecessary capitals* in Part IV, "Guide to Correct Punctuation and Mechanics."

Carelessness.   When writing, you concentrate on what you are trying to say and not on such matters as grammar, punctuation, and spelling. This concentration is both proper and understandable. But in your absorption you are quite likely to make errors of various sorts, including some in spelling, which result from haste or carelessness, not ignorance. When you discover a mistake of this kind, or it is pointed out to you, you may reply "Oh, I know better. I just wasn't watching" or "thinking" or "being careful" or whatever excuse you choose to make.

Isn't it fair to suggest that since many English words really are difficult to spell, we should be careful with those we actually know? And yet it is the simple, easy words nearly everyone *can* spell which cause over half the errors made. Listed below are twenty words or phrases repeatedly found misspelled. They are so easy that you're likely to look at them scornfully and say "I would never misspell any one of them." The fact is that you probably do misspell some of these words, on occasion, or other words just as simple!

a lot, *not* alot	piano, *not* panio
all right, *not* alright	radio, *not* raido
Britain, *not* Britian	research, *not* reaserch
curl, *not* crul	religion, *not* regilion
doesn't *not* does'nt	surprise, *not* supprise
forty, *not* fourty	third, *not* thrid
high school, *not* highschool	thirty, *not* thrity
in fact, *not* infact	thoroughly, *not* throughly
in spite, *not* inspite	whether, *not* wheather
ninety, *not* ninty	wouldn't, *not* would'nt

Errors of this sort are easy to make. Our pen or pencil slips; a finger hits the wrong key; our minds wander. Even excellent spellers often make such silly mistakes. Be *careful*.

Cede, -Ceed, -Sede. These suffixes cause a proportionately large number of misspellings. But the problem they present is simple because so few words are involved. Only twelve words in the language end in the sound *seed*, and not all of these are in common use.

First, only one word in English ends in *-sede: supersede*. It has this ending because of its origin; it comes from the Latin verb *sedeo*, meaning "to sit." As with many other borrowed words in English, it maintains some connection with its source.

Second, only three of the twelve words ending with the *seed* pronunciation are spelled *-ceed: exceed, proceed,* and *succeed*.

Finally, the eight remaining words end in *cede*, and of these only three or four are in everyday use:

accede	cede	intercede	recede
antecede	concede	precede	secede

It won't help with spelling the *-ceed* and *-cede* words to know their origin, but it will help in avoiding a *-sede* ending: the eleven *-ceed* and *-cede* words derive not from *sedeo* (as *supersede* does) but from Latin *cedo*, meaning "to go." Thus, *pre + cede* means "to go or come before"; *inter + cede* means "to go or come between," etc.

Common words frequently misspelled. Regardless of whether we are housewives, businessmen, clerks, secretaries, or truck drivers, we *all* use certain basic words many scores of times more often than any others in the language. Any spelling list should start with them, but, fortunately, they are *never* (or hardly ever) misspelled by anyone who can write at all. The most frequently used words in the English language are *and, the, to, you, your, in, for, of, we, is, I,* and *its.* Once past this basic list, however, selecting frequently used words becomes more difficult. *Table* is an everyday word, but a baker might use *bread* and a physician might use *temperature* more often. It is reassuring to know, however, that it is neither the most simple and common words nor the ones primarily used in a trade, profession, or industry that provide spelling difficulty. The words in between are the troublemakers. And here we do have some authoritative studies of frequency word use and frequency misspellings.

Of the five hundred words occurring most frequently in our speech and writing, only twenty ever cause anyone (except very poor spellers) any trouble whatever, Probably few, if any, of them bother you—a reassuring fact. Here is the list:

across	dollar	possible	suppose
almost	don't	quite	their
believe	friend	receive	through
brought	government	should	whether
business	laugh	supply	your

Keep in mind that these twenty words, along with 480 even more easily spelled ones, are *certain* to appear in your speech and writing many times as often as all other words in the language. The one best approach to correct spelling is to *master* everyday words that you use over and over.

Compound adjectives.   See *Compound words.*

Compound nouns, plurals of.   Such words form the plural by adding *s* or *es* to the important word in the compound. Sometimes the element considered most important comes first in the compound, sometimes at the end. The end element is usually the one pluralized if it and other elements are so closely related as to be considered a single word: *handfuls, housefuls, basketfuls.* Just to confound the pluralizing of compound words, occasionally more than one element in the same word is pluralized.

The words listed below illustrate the erratic principles stated in this paragraph:

attorneys at law	major generals
attorneys general, attorney generals	manservant,
brothers-in-law	menservants
bystanders	master sergeants
commanders in chief	pailfuls
consuls general	passers-by
fathers-in-law	sons-in-law
hangers-on	

See *Apostrophe*, Rule 8.

Compound words. The general principle of word joining derives from actual usage. When two (or more) words first become associated with a single meaning, they are written separately. As they grow, through usage, to become more of a unit in thought and writing, they are usually spelled with a hyphen. Finally, they tend to be spelled as one word. This evolution may be seen in the following, the third word in each series now being the accepted form: *base ball, base-ball, baseball; rail road, railroad, railroad.* This general principle, however, is not always in operation; many common expressions which one might think in the third stage are still in the first: *mother tongue, boy friend, Girl Scout, in fact, high school.*

The hyphen is used with several groups, or classes, of compound words:

1. Between two or more words modifying a substantive (noun, etc.) and used as a single adjective.

The hyphen is especially needed in adjectival combinations placed *before* the substantive modified. These combinations may consist of an adjective, an adverb, or a noun united with a participle; or of two adjectives, an adjective and a noun, or a prefix followed by a capitalized word:

able-bodied	bad-tempered	far-fetched
above-mentioned	bell-shaped	fast-moving
absent-minded	best-known	first-rate
Anglo-Saxon	city-wide	good-natured

Latin-American	ocean-blue	stiff-necked
light-haired	rose-red	ten-foot
long-needed	sad-looking	un-American
loose-tongued	six-room	wild-eyed
midnight-black	soft-spoken	wind-blown

2. Between parts (words) of a compound noun.

Such combinations may consist of two or more words and may have an adverb or preposition as the second element:

brother-in-law	go-between	mother-in-law
by-product	great-grandson	secretary-treasurer
court-martial	Jack-of-all-trades	son-in-law
ex-president	leveling-off	take-off
fellow-citizen	looker-on	trade-mark
forget-me-not	major-domo	watt-hour

3. Between the numerator and denominator of a fraction:

four-fifths, one-half.

If the hyphen already appears in either numerator or denominator it is omitted in writing the fraction:

twenty-one thirds, three ten-thousandths

4. General cautions in using the hyphen:

   a. All the examples cited above were checked in one good desk dictionary. If your dictionary differs, don't hesitate to "take its word."

   b. Do not use a hyphen when two adjectives preceding a noun are independent.

   She wore a *faded yellow* hat.

   c. Do not use a hyphen when an adverb modifies an adjective:

   She was a *highly trained* secretary.

   d. Do not use a hyphen between double terms denoting a single office or rank:

   Major General Jones; *Executive Director* Adams

e. Do not use a hyphen in writing a fraction which is not an adjective:

He ate *one half* of the meat quickly.

f. Do not use a hyphen with reflexive pronouns:

herself, himself, yourselves

g. Many compounds formerly spelled separately or with a hyphen are now written as single words:

almighty, hateful, inasmuch, namesake

Confusing and transposing letters. Sometimes because of ignorance but more often because of carelessness and haste, letters are confused or transposed.

Corsage (small bouquet) should not be spelled *corsarge*.

Exercise (physical activity) should not be spelled *excercise*.

Garage (storage place) should not be spelled *gararge*.

Height (distance from bottom to top) should not be spelled *heighth*.

Imagine (to form an idea) should not be spelled *imangine*.

Irrelevant (unrelated) should not be spelled *irrevelant*.

Poem (literary composition) should not be spelled *pome*.

Radio (transmission of sound waves) should not be spelled *raido*.

Research (systematic inquiry) should not be spelled *reaserch*.

Strategic (favorable or advantageous) should not be spelled *stragetic*.

Temperature (degree of heat) should not be spelled *tempreture*.

Third (#3 in a series) should not be spelled *thrid*.

Tragedy (serious drama or event) should not be spelled *tradegy*.

You don't transpose or otherwise confuse letters as is done in the list immediately above? Good. But you may have difficulty pronouncing and spelling words which have prefixes. Many prefixes were borrowed from Latin and Greek, and a few do cause some people trouble with pronunciation, and hence spelling. Here are examples of words beginning with *per-*, *pre-*, and *pro-*, the only prefixes causing this difficulty of transposed letters in pronouncing and spelling:

Perform (to act, to do) should not be spelled *preform*.

Perhaps (maybe) should not be spelled *prehaps*.

Perjury (breaking an oath) should not be spelled *prejury*.

Perspiration (sweat) should not be spelled *prespiration*.

Perversely (persisting in error or fault) should not be spelled *preversely*.

Precipitate (to cause action) should not be spelled *percipitate*.

Professor (a teacher) should not be spelled *perfessor* or *prefessor*.

Proposal (a plan, scheme) should not be spelled *porposal* or *preposal*.

Consonants dropped.   See *Dropped consonants*.

De-, dis-, dys-.   These prefixes will cause spelling problems when you don't distinguish clearly between root words beginning with *s* and the prefixes themselves. Note these spellings:

describe (write down), *de + scribe*

despoil (strip, rob), *de + spoil*

dissemble (disguise), *dis + semble*

dissimilar (unlike), *dis + similar*

Only about thirty common words begin with *diss-* but ten times as many begin with *dis-*. Only three common words (and their derivatives) begin with *dys-*: *dysentery, dyspepsia, dystrophy* (as in "muscular dystrophy").

A simple rule: when the prefixes *dis-* and *mis-* are added to a *root* word beginning with *s*, neither *s* should be omitted: *dissatisfied, misstep*. When they are added to roots not beginning with an *s*, use only one *s*: *disappear, misfortune*.

Dictionary as a spelling aid.   When you are suspicious of the spelling of any word you should check it immediately in your dictionary. "*Doubt + dictionary = good spelling*" is a reliable formula. However, it is a counsel that none of us is likely always to follow. Not only that, our sense of doubt may be so great that we spend half our writing time flipping pages rather than communicating and thus grow bored and frustrated.

Also, you may have tried to look up a word in the dictionary and been unable to find it. If your visual image of a word is weak, you can frustrate yourself even more: look for *agast* and you may give up before discovering that the word is *aghast*. You won't find *pheasant* and *photograph* among words beginning with *f*. In fact, the confusion of sound and spelling has caused more than one reputable publishing firm seriously to consider preparing a dictionary for poor spellers.

Even topnotch spellers consult a dictionary for the spelling of some words. You may not hesitate over *chiaroscuro* or *chimerical*, but you may need to look up *aficionado* or *solipsism* or *Yggdrasill*. Granting that few of us would use these words in the first place, most of us would resort to a dictionary each time. In addition, *compound words* (which see) frequently require hyphens for correct spelling; even superb spellers must look up many such words.

The dictionary is a never-failing help in time of spelling trouble. But intelligent use of a dictionary can help to *prevent* trouble, too. That is, certain approaches to the vast amount of knowledge recorded in a dictionary can fix helpful principles and patterns in our minds so that we do not have to consult it for, *at most*, more than 5 per cent of the words we use. Certain facts about word derivations, prefixes, suffixes, plurals, apostrophes, hyphens, and capitalization can be learned easily—facts which apply to large numbers and classes of words and help to improve our spelling in wholesale fashion.

Doubling final consonant. The rule for doubling final consonants is somewhat complicated, but mastering it and its parts will prevent many common misspellings. Despite its complexity, it is one of the more useful rules for spelling.

1. Words of one syllable and those of more than one accented on the last syllable, when ending in a single consonant (except *x*) preceded by a single vowel, double the consonant before a suffix beginning with a vowel (*run, running; refer, referred*).

This rule is detailed, but it will repay careful study. It is especially helpful in forming the past tense, past participle, and present participle of many frequently used verbs. It also helps in forming the comparative and superlative degrees of adjectives.

Here is a list of only a few of the thousands of words to which this principle applies:

acquit, acquitted,
  acquittal
admit, admitting,
  admittance
begin, beginning,
  beginner
clan, clannish
control, controlled,
  controller
drop, dropped,
  dropping
equip, equipped,
  equipping
forget, forgetting,
  unforgettable
man, manned, mannish

occur, occurred,
  occurrence
overlap, overlapped,
  overlapping
plan, planned, planning
prefer, preferred,
  preferring
red, redder, reddest,
  redden
refer, referred, referring
run, running, runner
swim, swimming, swimmer
tax, taxes
tin, tinny
transfer, transferred,
  transferring

2. If the accent is shifted to an earlier syllable when the ending is added, do not double the final consonant:

confer, conferring, *but* conference
defer, deferring, *but* deference
infer, inferring, *but* inference
prefer, preferring, *but* preference

3. Cautions and exceptions:

   a. Derivatives from basic words that change pronunciation from a long to short vowel follow the doubling rule:

   write, writing, *but* written
   bite, biting, *but* bitten
   inflame, inflamed, *but* inflammable

   b. Words ending in a final consonant preceded by *two* vowels do not double the final consonant:

   appear, appeared, appearing, appearance
   need, needed, needing, needy
   train, trained, training, trainee

c. Words ending in *two* consonants do not double the final consonant:

> bend, bending (*not* bendding)
> turn, turned (*not* turnned)
> insist, insisted (*not* insistted)

d. Words not accented on the final syllable do not ordinarily double the final consonant:

> happen, happened, happening
> murmur, murmured, murmuring
> benefit, benefited (*but* fit, fitted)

A helpful word in fixing this principle in your mind is *combat*. It can be pronounced with the accent on either syllable, but note the spelling:

> combat′   combatted   combatting
> com′bat   combated   combating

e. Like all spelling rules, this one for doubling has many exceptions or apparent exceptions:

cancellation	gaseous	overstepping
chagrined	handicapped	questionnaire
chancellor	humbugged	tranquillity
crystallize	legionnaire	transferable
excellence	metallurgy	transference
excellent	outfitter	zigzagged

Dropped consonants. Spelling is definite, fixed, and unyielding. Not so with pronunciation, which is constantly changing, differs from place to place, and is even varied on different occasions by the same speaker. The word *garden* is always spelled g-a-r-d-e-n, but it is pronounced in half a dozen different ways. You can drop the *r* or retain it. You can use any of three different sounds for the two vowels in the word, with or without shadings of sound. Each of these pronunciations is correct and normally is completely understood when used.

Such variation in pronouncing words sometimes causes spelling problems. If our visual memory of words is stronger than our auditory image, no harm is done. But when a letter is incorrectly omitted in pronouncing a word, we have to be on guard. The following representative list of words should be studied carefully. In each word the "offending" consonant is set in boldface; try to pronounce it fully, sounding it out as an aid to your auditory memory.

1. Mr. Avery is an old acquaintance of mine.
2. The Arctic Circle is entirely imaginary.
3. This puts me in an awkward position.
4. He is a candidate for the office.
5. The driver was convicted of drunkenness.
6. He stopped school in the eighth grade.
7. Mac grew up in a poor environment.
8. February is the shortest month in the year.
9. He is opposed to all forms of government.
10. He slipped while hurrying down the steps.
11. Karen is now a proud kindergarten pupil.
12. There are thousands of books in her library.
13. The barn was struck by lightning.
14. You are perhaps too hasty in judging me.
15. Sam is probably the best salesman in the company.
16. He purchased a large quantity of food.
17. This is a quarter, not a dime.
18. Mae did not seem to recognize me.
19. He was a good representative for the firm.
20. This statement surprised me.

In addition to these twenty illustrated words, pronounce each of the following as you ordinarily would. Your pronunciation may offer a clue to the cause of some of your misspellings. The "offending" consonants appear in boldface.

accept	empty	kept	rhythm
acquire	except	landlord	slept
and	fascinate	listen	soften
answer	fasten	nestle	swept
authentic	grandfather	often	tempt
column	handful	prompt	tentative
condemn	handle	pumpkin	trestle
contempt	hustle	recognize	used to
consumption	identical	rheumatism	wrestle

Dropped vowels. There are many different ways to misspell words: you can do so by dropping vowels as well as by adding them. (See *Added vowels.*) Educated speakers often drop vowels in pronouncing some words in the following list; even acceptable pronunciation is not always a sure guide. However, a few of these words could not be pronounced correctly from the faulty spellings shown—whole syllables would drop out. Only in uninformed or TV speech would *caramel* be pronounced *carmel.*

1. John's truck *accidentally* (not *accidently*) hit the child.
2. This is an *auxiliary* (not *auxilary*) gasoline tank.
3. The physician prescribed *beneficial* (not *benefical*) drugs.
4. The pianist gave a *brilliant* (not *brillant*) recital.
5. This harsh *criticism* (not *criticsm*) is merited.
6. He is a soldier, not a *civilian* (not *civilan*).
7. She is a *conscientious* (not *conscientous*) housewife.
8. This *convenient* (not *convenent*) room is for your use.
9. John is *deficient* (not *deficent*) in his accounts.
10. Mary is an *efficient* (not *efficent*) typist.
11. Your face is *familiar* (not *familar*).
12. I seek your *financial* (not *financal*) help.
13. King Cole was a merry, *genial* (not *genal*) soul.
14. Beethoven was a man of *genius* (not *genus*).
15. Your sentence is *grammatically* (not *grammaticly*) sound.
16. The money is only *incidentally* (not *incidently*) important.
17. The chemistry *laboratory* (not *labortory*) is large.
18. I like to read good *literature* (not *literture*).
19. *Mathematics* (not *mathmatics*) deals with numbers.
20. A child is a *miniature* (not *minature*) man.
21. Your *opinion* (not *opinon*) is valid.
22. This is an *original* (not *orignal*) idea.
23. Sir Henry is a member of *Parliament* (not *Parliment*).
24. He is *proficient* (not *proficent*) as a manager.
25. Sue has an even *temperament* (not *temperment*).

Check your pronunciation of the following words. Some people slur over the vowels which are shown in boldface; some omit them entirely; some pronounce them with considerable stress. Pronounce each word as you normally do. If the letters in boldface are silent, or lightly stressed, in your speech, you are likely to omit them from your spelling.

accompaniment	definite	liable	operate
accuracy	delivery	luxury	particular
aspirin	different	magazine	privilege
bachelor	family	mathematics	regular
boundary	frivolous	memory	scenery
casualties	history	misery	similar
considerable	ignorant	mystery	temperature
criminal	lengthening	Niagara	victory

-Efy, -ify. These two suffixes cause much spelling trouble, but the problem is simple when it is clearly looked at. Actually, only four words you are likely to use end in *-efy* (and you probably won't use them every day, either). All the remainder, without exception, end in *-ify*.

Therefore, learn by whatever method seems best these four words and spell all others with *-ify*:

liquefy (to make or become liquid)
putrefy (to make or become rotten)
rarefy (to make or become rare)
stupefy (to make or become insensible)

Also, words built on these four tend to retain the *e* spelling:

liquefy	rarefy
liquefies	rarefies
liquefied	rarefied
liquefying	rarefying
liquefaction	rarefaction
putrefy	stupefy
putrefies	stupefies
putrefied	stupefied
putrefying	stupefying
putrefaction	stupefaction

Ei, ie. One of the most frequent causes of misspelling is not knowing whether to write *ei* or *ie* in literally scores of everyday words. About one thousand fairly common words contain *ei* or *ie*. It helps to know that *ie* occurs in twice as many words as *ei*, but the problem is not thereby solved.

The basic rule may be stated in this well-known verse:

> Write *i* before *e*
> Except after *c*
> Or when sounded like *a*,
> As in *neighbor* and *weigh*.

This rule, or principle, applies only when the pronunciation of *ie* or *ei* is a long *e* (as in *he*) or the sound of the *a* in *pale*. Here's another way to summarize the rule and its reverse:

When the sound is long *e* (as in *piece*) put *i* before *e* except after *c*.

When the sound is not long *e* (as it is not in *weigh*) put *e* before *i*.

Still another way to state this principle is this: When the *e* sound is long, *e* comes first after *c*, but *i* comes first after all other consonants:

ceiling	conceited	deceit	receipt
conceit	conceive	perceive	receive

achieve	cashier	handkerchief	reprieve
aggrieve	chandelier	hygiene	retrieve
apiece	chief	mischief	shield
belief	field	piece	shriek
believe	fiend	pier	siege
besiege	frontier	pierce	thief
bier	grief	priest	wield
brief	grieve	relieve	yield

This much of the rule is fairly simple: usually you write *ie* except after the letter *c* when you write *ei*—provided the sound is always long *e*. The last two lines of the doggerel refer to words in which *ei* sounds like *a*. Fortunately, only a few everyday words fall in this group:

beige	heinous	sleigh
chow mein	neigh	surveillance
deign	neighbor	veil
feint	reign	vein
freight	rein	weigh
eight	skein	weight

A few words are exceptions to this basic *ei—ie* rule or are not fully covered by the four lines of doggerel. The best advice is to learn the following words by some method other than trying to apply the rule, which doesn't work:

caffein(e)	height	seize
codein(e)	hierarchy	seizure
either	leisure	sheik
Fahrenheit	neither	sleight
fiery	protein	stein
financier	Reid	weird

Summary:

1. Use *ie* generally when sounded as long *e* (*he*).
2. Use *ei* after *c* when sounded as long *e* (*he*).
3. Use *ei* when sounded as *a* (*eight*).
4. Watch out for exceptions.

-Ence, -ance. See *-Ance, -ence.*

-Er. See *-Ar, -er, -or.*

-Ery. See *-Ary, -ery.*

Etymology. This word, taken from the Greek, means an account of the history of a given word and, more particularly, deals with its origin and derivation. Knowing what a word "comes from" often will help you to spell it correctly. For example, the word *preparation* is derived from the Latin prefix *prae-* ("beforehand") plus *parare* (meaning "to make ready"). Knowing this fact, and accenting the first *a* in *parare*, may help you to spell the word correctly: *preparation*, not *preperation*.

Similarly, our word *dormitory* (a building containing sleeping rooms) is derived from the Latin word *dormitorium*. Noting the first *i* in this Latin word, and perhaps also knowing that the French word for sleep is *dormir*, may help you to spell *dormitory* with an *i* and not an *a*.

A study of etymology primarily will aid you in building vocabulary. But it also has its uses in spelling. Here are simplified etymological comments on a few common words which may fix this principle in your mind:

Calendar. This word is descended from the Latin word for "account book," *calendarium*. Note the *a*; we frequently misspell the word as *calender* (a perfectly good word with an entirely different meaning).

Consensus. This word comes from the same Latin root as *consent* (*con* + *sentire*, "to feel"). Note the *s* in *sentire* and you will not spell the word *concensus*, as is frequently done.

Equivalent. This frequently misspelled word may be easier for you if you remember that it means "equal in value" and is derived from the prefix *equi-* and the verb *valere*. Accent the *val* sound in *valere* and connect it with *value*.

Extravagance. This word is composed of *extra-* (beyond) and the Latin participle *vagans* (*vagari*, to wander). Extravagance is wandering beyond limits. Accent the letters *v-a-g* in the root word to insure correct spelling.

Finis. This synonym for "end" has the same origin as the words *definite* and *finite*. Accent the *i* sound and remember the two *i*'s in this word.

Optimism. This word comes to us, by way of the French word *optimisme*, from Latin *optimus*, meaning "best." Focus on the two *i*'s in *optimism*.

Privilege. From *privus* (private) and *lex, legis* (law), this word can be remembered as *privy* (private), with the *y* changed to *i*, plus *legal*, which fixes the *leg* in *privilege*.

Recommend. This word comes from the Latin *recommendare*. Think of it as *re* + *commend* and avoid that all-too-present double *c*.

Figures. See *Apostrophe*.

Final e. Hundreds of everyday English words end in *e*, and hundreds and hundreds more consist of such words plus suffixes: *hope, hopeful; come, coming; safe, safety*; etc. In our pronunciation, nearly all *e*'s at the ends of words are silent: *advice, give, live*, etc. Actually, the usual function of a final silent *e* is to make the syllable long: *rate* but *rat*; *mete* but *met*; *bite* but *bit*; *note* but *not*, etc.

With these facts in mind, we can now proceed to a rule which covers more words than any other spelling rule, common words frequently misspelled:

Final silent *e* is usually dropped before a suffix beginning with a vowel but is usually retained before a suffix beginning with a consonant.

advise, advising	care, careful,	live, livable
amuse, amusing,	careless	love, lovable
amusement	come, coming	move, movable
argue, arguing	desire, desirable	owe, owing
arrive, arrival	dine, dining	purchase, purchasing
awe, awesome	excite, exciting	safe, safety
bare, barely,	extreme, extremely	sincere, sincerely
bareness	hate, hateful	sure, surety
believe,	ice, icy	use, usable, useless
believable	judge, judging	value, valuable
bite, biting	like, likable	whole, wholesome

This basic rule is clear enough, but it does not cover all words ending in silent *e*. Here are additions and exceptions to the general principle:

1. Silent *e* is retained when -*ing* is added to certain words, largely to prevent them from being confused with other words:

    dye, dyeing, to contrast with *die, dying*
    singe, singeing, to contrast with *sing, singing*
    tinge, tingeing, to contrast with *ting, tinging*

2. Silent *e* is retained in still other words before a suffix beginning with a vowel. Sometimes this is done for the sake of pronunciation, sometimes for no logical reason at all:

acre, acreage	line, lineage
cage, cagey	mile, mileage
here, herein	shoe, shoeing
hoe, hoeing	there, therein

Final y. Forming the plural of nouns ending in *y* is discussed under *Plurals*. But the problem applies also to words other than nouns. The basic principle is this:

1. Words ending in *y* preceded by a consonant usually change *y* to *i* before any suffix except one beginning with *i*:

angry, angrily	lovely, lovelier, loveliness
beauty, beautiful	lucky, luckier, luckily
busy, busily, business	marry, married, marriage
carry, carries, carrying	merry, merrily, merriment
dignify, dignified,	pity, pitiful, pitying
dignifying	pretty, prettier, prettiness
easy, easier, easily	study, studied, studious
empty, emptier, emptiness	try, tried, trying
happy, happier, happiness	worry, worried, worrying

2. Words ending in *y* preceded by a vowel do not change *y* to *i* before suffixes or other endings:

annoy, annoyed, annoyance	employ, employer
betray, betrayal, betraying	pay, payable
buy, buyer, buying	stay, stayed, staying

To the two parts of this "final *y*" rule are so many exceptions that some experts feel the rule is not helpful. However, the exceptions among commonly used words are not numerous and can easily be mastered. Here are some everyday words which follow neither part of the "final *y*" principle:

baby, babyhood	pay, paid
busy, busyness (state of being busy)	say, said
day, daily	shy, shyly, shyness
lady, ladyship	slay, slain
lay, laid	wry, wryly, wryness

Foreign plurals. Certain nouns of foreign origin retain the plural of the language from which they were borrowed. Some borrowed words have gradually assumed plurals with the usual English *s* or *es* endings. Finally, some words have more than one plural form. Here is a brief list of fairly common nouns to fix in your mind:

agendum, agenda

alumna, alumnae

alumnus, alumni

analysis, analyses

appendix, appendixes,
   appendices

axis, axes

bacterium, bacteria

basis, bases

cherub, cherubs,
   cherubim

crisis, crises

criterion, criteria,
   criterions

datum, data

erratum, errata

focus, foci, focuses

formula, formulas, formulae

genus, genera, genuses

hypothesis, hypotheses

index, indexes, indices

larva, larvae

memorandum, memorandums,
   memoranda

parenthesis, parentheses

phenomenon, phenomena

radius, radii, radiuses

stimulus, stimuli

thesis, theses

vertebra, vertebrae, vertebras

Fractions.   See *Compound words*, Rules 3 and 4e.

Homographs.   A *homograph* is a word with the same spelling as another but with a different meaning and origin. The words *bow* in "bow and arrow" and *bow* in "to bow one's head" have identical spellings, but they differ in pronunciation, meaning, and origin. *Fair* meaning "market" and *fair* meaning "beautiful" are also homographs.

Homonyms.   A *homonym* is a word having the same pronunciation as another but differing from it in meaning, origin, and often in spelling. *Bear* and *bare*, *bore* and *boar*, *meet* and *meat*, *steal* and *steel* are illustrations. Homonyms are a constant source of spelling difficulty; watch them carefully.

Hyphen as a mark of spelling.   See *Compound words*.

-Ible.   For comment on the problem of *-able* or *-ible*, see *-Able*.

1.   The ending should usually be *-ible* if the base (root) is *not* a complete word.

Contrast this principle with Rule 1 under *-Able*: If the base is a complete word, add *-able*: *mail* + *able* = *mailable*. If the base is not a complete word, we add *-ible*: *ris* + *ible* = *risible*, and *poss* + *ible* = *possible*.

audible	divisible	indelible	ostensible
combustible	edible	infallible	plausible
compatible	feasible	intelligible	tangible
credible	horrible	irascible	terrible
dirigible	incorrigible	negligible	visible

2. The ending should usually be *-ible* if the base (root) ends in *ns: respons + ible = responsible*.

These words illustrate this spelling principle:

comprehensible	indefensible	ostensible
defensible	insensible	responsible
incomprehensible	irresponsible	sensible

3. The ending should usually be *-ible* if the base (root) ends in *miss*.

Comparatively few words belong in this category. Here are several examples:

admissible	omissible	remissible
dismissible	permissible	transmissible

With roots not ending in *-miss*, but closely related, are such words with *-ible* endings as *accessible, compressible, irrepressible,* and *possible* (which also fits under Group 1, above).

4. The ending should usually be *-ible* if *-ion* can be added to the base (root) without intervening letters: *collect, collection, collectible.*

A number of words (roots) form noun forms by the immediate (nothing coming between) addition of *-ion*. All such words form adjectives ending in *-ible*; here are a few samples:

accessible	contractible	inexhaustible
affectible	convertible	perfectible
collectible	corruptible	reversible
connectible	digestible	suggestible

You should note that this "rule" is tricky: if *-ion* cannot be added to the root *immediately* (without intervening letters), the *able* ending is more likely, as in *present, presentation, presentable.*

5. The ending should usually be *-ible* if the base (root) ends in soft *c* or soft *g*.

This principle should be compared with Rule 5 under *-Able*. A soft *c* sounds like an *s* (*force*); a soft *g* sound like a *j* (*tangent*). The following words contain a soft *c* or a soft *g*. Also note that, with few exceptions, the roots are not complete words.

conducible	illegible	irascible
convincible	incorrigible	legible
deducible	intangible	negligible
eligible	intelligible	producible
forcible	invincible	seducible

Just as there are a few exceptions to the rules for *-able* endings, so are there for words ending in *-ible*. The commonly used words which are exceptions are not numerous. Among those words which, by "rule," should end in *-able* but do not are the following:

collapsible	discernible	inflexible
contemptible	gullible	irresistible

Ie, ei.   See *Ei, ie.*.

-Ify.   See *-Efy, -ify*.

Inserted k.   The letter *k* is usually added to words ending in *c* before a suffix beginning with *e, i,* or *y*. This is done in order to prevent mispronunciation; note the different pronunciations, for example, of *picnicking* and *icing*. Only a few common words are involved in this rule, but they are frequently misspelled.

colic, colicky	picnic, picnicked, picnicker
frolic, frolicked, frolicking	politic, politicking
mimic, mimicked, mimicking	shellac, shellacked, shellacking
panic, panicky	traffic, trafficked, trafficking

This rule must be applied carefully. Note, for examples, the words *frolicsome* and *mimicry*. There is no reason to add *k*, since the *c* remains hard.

Inter-. This prefix, meaning "between," is frequently confused with *intra-*, which means "inside," "within."

intercollegiate (between colleges)   intramural (within the walls)

interfere (come, carry between)   intrastate (within a state)

interstate (between, among states)   intravenous (within a vein or veins)

Irregular plurals. Here is a representative list of words with irregular or nonsensical plurals which follow none of the principles stated under *Plurals*:

alkali, alkalies, alkalis	goose, geese	scissors, scissors
bison, bison	grouse, grouse	series, series
brother, brothers, brethren	louse, lice	sheep, sheep
	madame, mesdames	species, species
child, children	man, men	swine, swine
deer, deer	moose, moose	tooth, teeth
foot, feet	mouse, mice	woman, women
	ox, oxen	

-Ise, -ize, -yze. Some five hundred fairly common words in our language end in *-ise*, *-ize*, or *-yze*. How can one master all these spellings, especially since correct pronunciation provides no help at all?

The best approach is to isolate the comparatively few words with *-yze* and *-ise* and to remember that *-ize* is by far the most common suffix and that the chances of its being correct are mathematically excellent.

These are the only four fairly common words in English ending in *-yze*, and of them you will normally use only two:

analyze, catalyze, electrolyze, paralyze

There are no clear "rules" for choosing between *-ise* and *-ize* endings. But although well over four hundred words end in *-ize*, there are only one-tenth as many with an *-ise* suffix. (If you lived in Great Britain, you would have to cope with a larger number; a number of words that the English spell with *-ise*, Americans spell with *-ize*.)

The comparatively few words which end in -*ise* can be grouped as follows:

1. Combinations with -*cise*:
   circumcise, excise, exercise, exorcise, incise

These *cise* words are so spelled because they derive from a Latin word meaning "to cut," *incisus*.

2. Combinations with *guise*:
   guise, disguise

3. Words ending in -*mise*:
   compromise, demise, premise, surmise

4. Combinations with -*prise*:
   apprise, comprise, emprise, enterprise, reprise, surprise

5. Combinations with *rise*:
   rise, arise, moonrise, sunrise, uprise

6. Combinations with -*vise*:
   advise, devise, improvise, revise, supervise

These *vise* words (except for *devise*) are derived from the Latin *visus*, "to see," and hence retain a *v* and *s*.

7. Words ending in -*wise*:
   contrariwise, lengthwise, likewise, otherwise, sidewise, wise

8. Miscellaneous combinations with -*ise*:
   advertise, chastise, despise, franchise, merchandise

This makes a total of less than forty common words ending in -*yze* and -*ise*. All others with this suffix pronunciation end in -*ize*. Here are a few of the hundreds of words with this ending (in American spelling):

agonize	colonize	generalize
apologize	criticize	harmonize
authorize	crystallize	humanize
baptize	demoralize	jeopardize
brutalize	economize	legalize
cauterize	equalize	liberalize
characterize	familiarize	localize
civilize	fertilize	modernize

monopolize	pasteurize	scrutinize
moralize	patronize	solemnize
nationalize	plagiarize	specialize
naturalize	pulverize	subsidize
neutralize	realize	symbolize
organize	recognize	tantalize
ostracize	reorganize	utilize
particularize	scandalize	vocalize

K inserted. See *Inserted k.*

Lightly stressed syllables. See *Unstressed vowels.*

Listing troublesome words. Learning to spell is an individual, highly personal matter. One attack on correct spelling will work for one person but not for another. Also, the words whose spelling gives you trouble may not be the words which bother any of your friends and acquaintances. Perhaps it would be more precise to say that although certain words cause trouble for a majority of people, any list of commonly misspelled words will contain some that give you no difficulty and omit others that do. The best list of words for you to study is the one you prepare yourself to meet your own needs and shortcomings. Start making *your* list now.

-Ly. See *-Ally, -ly.*

Memory devices. See *Mnemonics.*

Mentally seeing words. An important method of improving your spelling is to look at, or repeat, a word until you can really *see* it. Actually, the mental process most helpful in word study, and particularly in spelling, is that of forming mental images of the words concerned. These images are of several kinds. See *Auditory image, Motor image, Visual-mindedness.*

Mispronunciation. Actually mispronouncing words causes more trouble than does a difference between the spelling and sound of a correctly pronounced word. In other words, correct pronunciation is sometimes of little help in spelling, but *mispronouncing* often adds an additional hazard. It is probably improper pronunciation which would make you spell *Calvary* when you mean *cavalry*. *Affect* and *effect* look somewhat alike, but they do have different pronunciations as well as different meanings. A *dairy* is one thing; a *diary* is another and will be so indicated by correct pronunciation. There is some reason why, from the sound of the word, you might spell *crowd* as "croud" or *benign* as "benine." But there may be no reason except poor pronunciation for spelling *shudder* as "shutter," *propose* as "porpose," or *marrying* as "marring."

Spelling consciousness, an *awareness* of words, depends in part on correct pronunciation. Properly pronouncing the following words will help some persons to spell them correctly. Mispronouncing them will cause *nearly everyone* spelling trouble. Look at each word until you are fully aware of it. Pronounce each word correctly, consulting your dictionary often and carefully. The list is merely suggestive; many people mispronounce so many words in so many different ways that no list can be complete.

caliber	concur	gesture	relic
caliper	conquer	jester	relict
carton	dinghy	gig	sink
cartoon	dingy	jig	zinc
casualty	elicit	impostor	specie
causality	illicit	imposture	species
celery	errand	minister	tenet
salary	errant	minster	tenant
cemetery	faucet	pastor	veracity
symmetry	forceps	pasture	voracity
color	finally	plaintiff	way
collar	finely	plaintive	whey

Mnemonics.   One kind of memory device has the rather imposing name of *mnemonics*. The word is pronounced nee-MON-iks and comes from a Greek word meaning "to remember." (Mnemosyne was the goddess of memory and mother of the Muses in Grecian mythology.) A *mnemonic* is a special aid to memory, a memory "trick" based on what psychologists refer to as "association of ideas," remembering something by associating it with something else. You have been using mnemonics most of your life. The term applies to a basic characteristic of the human mind.

Any mnemonic is a sort of crutch, something we use until we can automatically spell a given word "without even thinking." But so is a rule a "crutch," and, in a different sense, a dictionary is, too. In time, we can throw away our spelling crutches except on rare occasions; until then we can use them to avoid staggering and falling.

A mnemonic will be most helpful when you base it upon some happening or some person meaningful in your life. That is, you must invent, or use, only mnemonics that have a *personal* association of ideas.

Here are a few examples of mnemonics. They may not help you because they have no personal association, but they will provide ideas for the manufacture of your own:

> *all right.* Two words. Associate with *all correct* or *all wrong.*
> *compliment.* A compliment is what *I* like to get.
> *piece.* Have a *piece* of *pie.*
> *together.* To + get + her.
> *vaccine.* Vaccine is measured in cubic centimeters (*cc's*).

Motor image. Related to the *auditory image* and *visual-mindedness* (both of which, see) is the *motor image*. Motor images are connected with different muscles of the body and the impulses which our brains direct toward them. Have you ever said of a word, "That may not be the correct spelling. Wait until I write it"? If so, you were calling upon a motor image (hand-motor memory) to aid your visual memory. Some people actually feel the motions called into play by writing. Can you close your eyes and, without "conscious" thought, write your signature? If so, you proceed by means of a motor image.

Omission of letters, figures. See *Apostrophe.*

"One-plus-one" rule. When a prefix ends in the same letter with which the main part of the word begins, be sure that both letters are included.

When the main part of a word ends in the same consonant with which a suffix begins, be sure that both consonants are included.

When two words are combined, the first ending with the same letter with which the second begins, be sure that both letters are included.

accidentally	glowworm	really
bathhouse	illiterate	roommate
bookkeeping	interrelation	soulless
brownness	irresponsible	suddenness
cleanness	meanness	transshipment
coolly	misspelling	underrate
cruelly	occasionally	unnecessary
dissatisfied	overrated	unneeded
dissimilar	override	unnoticed
drunkenness	overrun	withholding

The only important exception to this rule is *eighteen*, which, of course, is not spelled *eightteen*. Also, keep in mind that three of the same consonant are never written solidly together: *cross-stitch*, not *crossstitch*; *still life* or *still-life*, not *stilllife*. See *Compound words*.

-Or. See *-Ar, -er, -or*.

Origin of words. See *Etymology*.

Plurals. Many people find it fairly easy to spell the singular of a word (meaning "one") but have trouble forming and correctly spelling plurals (meaning "more than one"). This is quite understandable, since many English words form plurals in unusual ways. You can "look it up" in a dictionary when you are puzzled, but a few principles of plural-forming can easily be mastered. See *Compound nouns, plurals of; Foreign plurals; Irregular plurals; Pronoun plurals;* and *Verb plurals*.

1. The plural of most nouns is formed by adding *s* to the singular:

bed, beds	cracker, crackers	hat, hats
book, books	dog, dogs	sheet, sheets
chair, chairs	food, foods	table, tables

2. Nouns ending with a sibilant or *s* sound (*ch, sh, s, x, z*) form their plurals by adding *es*:

arch, arches   buzz, buzzes   mass, masses
box, boxes   church, churches   tax, taxes
bush, bushes   loss, losses   watch, watches

3. Nouns ending in *y* preceded by a consonant usually change *y* to *i* before adding *es*:

activity, activities   fly, flies   quantity, quantities
city, cities   forty, forties   sky, skies
community, com-   library, libraries   strawberry, straw-
    munities   berries

4. Nouns ending in *y* preceded by a vowel usually add *s* without changing the final *y*:

alley, alleys   key, keys   toy, toys
attorney, attorneys   money, moneys   turkey, turkeys
chimney, chimneys   monkey, monkeys   valley, valleys

5. Nouns ending in *o* preceded by a vowel add *s* to form their plurals:

cameo, cameos   radio, radios
folio, folios   rodeo, rodeos

6. Nouns ending in *o* preceded by a consonant often add *es* to form the plural:

buffalo, buffaloes   mosquito, mosquitoes
cargo, cargoes   Negro, Negroes
echo, echoes   potato, potatoes
embargo, embargoes   tomato, tomatoes
fresco, frescoes   tornado, tornadoes
hero, heroes   volcano, volcanoes

7. Some nouns ending in *o* preceded by a consonant, including most musical terms, add *s* to form their plurals:

alto, altos   memento, mementos
banjo, banjos   piano, pianos
basso, bassos   quarto, quartos
canto, cantos   silo, silos
concerto, concertos   solo, solos
contralto, contraltos   soprano, sopranos
dynamo, dynamos   zero, zeros

8. Nouns ending in *f* form their plurals in such variable ways that you should *always* consult your dictionary when in doubt. Nouns ending in *ff* usually add *s*. Most nouns ending in *fe* change *fe* to *ve* and add *s*. The following examples will be sufficient to make you remember the formula: doubt + dictionary = correct spelling.

belief, beliefs	leaf, leaves	sheriff, sheriffs
chief, chiefs	life, lives	staff, staves (or
grief, griefs	loaf, loaves	staffs)
half, halfs	mischief, mischiefs	tariff, tariffs
(or halves)	roof, roofs	thief, thieves
handkerchief,	scarf, scarves	wife, wives
–chiefs	self, selves	wolf, wolves

Possessives.   See *Apostrophe.*

Prefixes.   A *prefix* is an *affix* (see *Affixes*) which is put before a word, stem, or word element to add to or qualify its meaning. Here is a brief list of prefixes which appear in a large number of misspelled words; approximate meanings are added as an aid to spelling and vocabulary improvement. See, also, specific comments on prefixes given elsewhere in this list: *ad-, de-, dis,-* etc.; and see *Confusing and transposing letters.*

a-, ab- (from, away) as in *avert, absent*
ad- (toward, to) as in *adhere, adverb*
ante- (before) as in *antecedent, antedate*
anti- (against, opposite) as in *antidote, antitoxin*
com-, con- (with) as in *commit, confide*
de- (away, down) as in *decline, depressed*
di-, dis- (separation, reversal, apart) as in *divert, disappoint*
e-, ex- (out of, former) as in *elect, exclude, ex-president*
hyper- (over, above) as in *hyperacidity, hypercritical*
in- (not) as in *inexact, invalid*
inter- (between) as in *intercede, intervene*
mis- (wrong, bad) as in *misconduct, mistake*
non- (not, not one) as in *non-American, nonresident*
ob- (against) as in *object, obloquy*
poly- (many) as in *polygamy, polytechnic*
pre- (before) as in *predict, prenatal*

pro- (forward) as in *proceed, propel*
re- (again, back) as in *repay, restore*
sub- (under) as in *subscribe, submarine*
trans- (across) as in *transfer, transport*
ultra- (beyond) as in *ultramodern, ultraviolet*
un- (not) as in *unhappy, untruth*

Pronoun plurals. Pronouns have plurals just as do nouns. It is doubtful, however, that misspelling of pronouns is due to their number. If you misspell *their*, a plural pronoun, you are probably confusing *their* and *there*, rather than having trouble with a plural. *We, they, our, us, them*, all pronouns, are easy to spell.

Pronunciation. Our system of pronunciation makes spelling difficult more than does any other cause. In fact, pronunciation is *the* prime reason for the perplexity, confusion, paradox, and contradiction which prevail in the spelling of words in the English language.

A system which tolerates, for example, *cough* and *through* is far from perfect. A frequently cited illustration is that if you spell the sound of *f* as in *enough*, of *i* as the *o* in *women*, and of *sh* as the *ti* of *fiction*, you can spell *fish* as *ghoti*. For another example of confusion confounded, consider the sound of *ain*, the sound we have in *pain*. It can be, and is, represented by these entirely different spellings: *complain, pane, reign, vein, campaign, champagne*. In fact, pronunciation is so unreliable a guide to spelling that you can quite logically spell *coffee* as *kauphy*—with not a single corresponding letter in the two words. See *Mispronunciation*.

Proofreading. When we read we usually see only the outlines, or shells, of words. Only poor readers need to see individual letters as such; most of us comprehend words and even groups of words at a glance. As our eyes move along a line we neither see nor recognize individual letters, and this, of course, is as it should be.

But have you ever noticed how much easier it is for you to detect spelling errors in someone else's writing than in your own? This may be due to the fact that in reading someone else's writing you are *looking* for mistakes. Or it may be that you look more carefully at the writing of someone else than at your own because you are unfamiliar with it and have to focus more sharply in order to comprehend.

Whatever the reason for closer scrutiny, we narrow the range of our vision and thereby pick up mistakes hitherto unnoticed by the writer. In short, we detect careless errors in spelling not by reading but by *proofreading*.

It is indeed naïve for any of us to think that we can write rapidly without misspelling some words, even though we are good spellers. Only careful proofreading will uncover spelling errors in our own writing or, indeed, in anyone else's.

This kind of reading requires that we see words and phrases not as such but that we actually see every letter they contain. When each letter stands out distinctly, it is simple to detect errors in spelling. See *Vision spread*.

Proper nouns. See *Capitalization*.

Root. See *Base of word*.

Rules for spelling. If you happen carefully to study a number of words which have similar characteristics, you can make some generalizations about their spelling. In fact, observers have been doing just this for more than a century with the result that nearly *fifty* spelling rules have been formulated.

Generalizations about the groupings of letters which form classes of words definitely help some people to spell more correctly. Those people with good visual or motor memories will not need them. Other writers apparently have a "psychological block" against spelling rules. But experience has shown that rules—or at least a few of the more basic ones—do help some people to spell correctly certain classes of words.

Six rules are stated and fully explained in this section: those concerning *ei* and *ie*; final *e*; final *y*; inserted *k*; doubling final consonant; and the "one-plus-one" rule. See each of these in its proper alphabetical position.

Schwa. See *Unstressed vowels*.

Sight spread. See *Vision spread*.

Silent letters. Some spelling authorities believe that the single greatest cause of misspelling connected with pronunciation is the silent letter. Sounds have been dropping out of our language for many centuries, but their disappearance has affected pronunciation much more than spelling. Actually, many letters no longer pronounced in certain words persist in our spelling "without rime or reason." For example, the *l* in such words as *could*, *would*, and *should* has been silent for hundreds of years but it hangs on in spelling.

The problem is compounded when we realize that the majority of the letters of our alphabet appear as silent letters in one word or another:

A is silent in *dead*.	L is silent in *salmon*.
B is silent in *doubt*.	M is silent in *mnemonics*.
C is silent in *scene*.	N is silent in *column*.
D is silent in *handsome*.	O is silent in *too*.
E is silent in *come*.	P is silent in *raspberry*.
F is silent in *off*.	T is silent in *often*.
G is silent in *sign*.	U is silent in *guess*.
H is silent in *honest*.	W is silent in *answer*.
I is silent in *weird*.	ch is silent in *yacht*.
K is silent in *knife*.	gh is silent in *bough*.

Most silent letters cause little difficulty in spelling. If you are "visual-minded," you will automatically put a *k* in *knee* or a *g* in *gnat*. But some letters which are silent, or are so lightly sounded as to be almost unheard, do cause trouble. Here is a list of some common words which, in the pronunciation of most educated people, contain silent letters:

align	ghastly	knit	psychology
benign	ghost	knob	through
bomb	gnash	knock	thumb
comb	gnat	knot	tomb
condemn	gnaw	know	womb
crumb	hymn	knuckle	wrap
daughter	indebted	plumber	wreck
dough	knack	pneumatic	wrench
dumb	knave	pneumonia	wretch
eight	knee	prompt	wring
fourth	kneel	psalm	write

Speech sounds. Scholars are agreed that the total number of speech sounds used by those who speak English is about fifty.

To express these sounds we have only 26 letters in our alphabet and they appear in about 250 spelling combinations. For example, there are eleven ways of spelling the sound of long *e*, the sound we have in *equal*:

1. eve
2. seed
3. read
4. receive
5. people
6. key
7. quay
8. police
9. piece
10. amoeba
11. Caesar

This is entirely illogical, isn't it? Of course. But the situation is not hopeless.

Actually, some relationship often exists between sound and spelling; a large number of words are spelled exactly as they sound, and many others have sounds and spellings almost alike. The words *bat, red*, and *top* are spelled as they sound to most people. Many longer words are also spelled as they sound, especially if you break them into syllables: *lone-li-ness, mem-o-ry; part-ner*, for example.

Moreover, many words which differ most greatly in sound and spelling are those which you rarely use. Like almost everyone else, including good spellers, you look up such words in a dictionary before attempting to write them; they do not have to be learned. Few people can spell, on demand, such a word as *phthisic*. They consult a dictionary. So should you.

Stem.   See *Base of word*.

Suffixes.   A *suffix* is an *affix* (see *Affixes*) which follows the element to which it is added, as in *swift, swiftly*.

It would be possible to make a list of suffixes, but doing so would not in itself be of much help in spelling. For one thing, the list would have to be very lengthy; for another, many suffixes have several different meanings, and others have vague or general meanings.

There are only eight suffix groups which cause major spelling problems. Within each group are many words which give trouble, some of the most often misspelled words in the language. Each of these eight groups is separately discussed in this section: *-Able, -ible; -Ally, -ly*; etc.

Syllabication as an aid to spelling. *Syllabication* (also spelled *syllabification*) means the "formation of, or division into, syllables." *Syllables* are words or parts of words pronounced with a single, uninterrupted sounding of the voice. Syllabication helps in the pronunciation of words, which in turn helps in spelling. One good way to learn the correct spelling of a word is to separate it into syllables and focus on each syllable in turn. See *Proofreading* and *Vision spread.*

Transposing letters. See *Confusing and transposing letters.*

Un-. When this prefix is added to a root word beginning with *n*, neither *n* is omitted (see *"One-plus-one" rule*):

unnamed	unnegotiable	unnoticeable
unnatural	unneighborly	unnoticed
unnecessary	unnerved	unnumbered
unneeded	unnoted	unnurtured

Unnecessary capitals. See this entry in Part IV, "Guide to Correct Punctuation and Mechanics."

Unstressed vowels. No words in English are more often misspelled than those which contain unstressed (or lightly stressed) vowels. An unstressed vowel, like the *a* in *dollar*, is uttered with little force; its sound is faint, indistinct, blurred.

A technical name, *schwa* (ə), is used to indicate this sound of unstressed vowels. It resembles a kind of "uh," a quiet sound much less vigorous than the stronger "uh" sound found in such words as *flood* and *rush.*

This unstressed vowel sound may be represented in spelling by any one of the vowels: *a, e, i, o, u.*

a
   grammar, sofa, above, ago, along
e
   corner, model, establish, system
i
   nadir, peril, origin, sanity
o
   professor, sponsor, occur, gallon
u
   murmur, sulfur, luxury, focus, circus

The letter *y* is sometimes a vowel also. Its unstressed sound is illustrated in the word *martyr*.

Although the schwa sound ("uh") is the most frequent unstressed vowel sound, it is not the only one. An unstressed *i* sound appears in such words as *solid* but is not always spelled as *i*. Note, for example, such words as *private*, *women*, and *busy*. Still other unstressed vowel sounds occur in American speech but isolating them is not helpful in learning to spell.

Unless both your auditory and visual memory are excellent, you must be suspicious of words containing lightly stressed syllables. It may help to exaggerate the "trouble spots" when you pronounce such words. Doing so may result in strained or even incorrect pronunciation, but you will increase your auditory image of words which, by sound alone, could be spelled in various ways. If the word *separate*, for example, causes you trouble, pronounce it sep-A-rate until you have its spelling firmly fixed in your visual, auditory, and motor images. Here is a representative list of everyday words often misspelled because of the unstressed vowels they contain:

academy	dilute	medicine
accident	discipline	monastery
actor	distress	optimism
applicant	dollar	politics
arithmetic	ecstasy	possible
benefit	excellent	private
busy	existence	privilege
calendar	grammar	propaganda
category	hangar	repetition
clamor	humorous	respectable
comparative	hunger	ridiculous
competitive	hypocrisy	separate
democracy	loafer	solid
describe	maintenance	swindler
despair	martyr	terror
develop	mathematics	vulgar

Verb plurals. The plurals of verbs are simple to spell. Main verbs have the same form for both singular and plural except in the third person singular, present tense: he *sees*, he *moves*, he *thinks,* he *does.* That is, most verbs add an *s* (or *es*) in the third person to form a singular. It's easy to remember this: most nouns and verbs form their plurals in directly opposite ways.

Vision spread.   An important method of detecting errors in your spelling is *proofreading.* (See this term above.) Much of the effectiveness of proofreading depends upon the spread of your vision.

This triangle will show you how wide your vision (your sight spread) is. Look at the top of the triangle and then down. How far down can you go and still identify each letter in each line with a *single* glance? Your central vision is as wide as the line above the one where you cannot identify each letter *without moving your eyes at all:*

<pre>
            a
          a r
         a r d
        a r d c
       a r d c f
      a r d c f g
     a r d c f g x
    a r d c f g x y
   a r d c f g x y z
  a r d c f g x y z p
 a r d c f g x y z p w
</pre>

People differ in their range of vision as they do in nearly everything else. But most people have difficulty in identifying more than six letters at a single glance. Some have a span of vision embracing only three or four letters. Whatever your span, you should not try to exceed it when you are carefully checking for spelling errors. If you do, you are reading—perhaps with excellent understanding—but you are not *proofreading.* And only proofreading will enable you to eliminate spelling errors due not to ignorance or stupidity but to carelessness.

Visual-mindedness.   Each of us can form a *visual* image when a suggested idea calls up in our minds a picture of some sort. When the word *tree* is mentioned to you, you can immediately "see in your mind" a vision, or representation, of some kind or shape of tree. Almost any object—*train, bus, church, child,* *cashier, rain*—will summon up a visual image. If you are "visual-minded," you can readily call up such images. And if you *are* visual-minded, you are probably an above-average speller. When you need to spell any word, try to see it "in your mind's eye."

Vowels added.   See *Added vowels.*

Vowels dropped.   See *Dropped vowels.*

Vowels unstressed.   See *Unstressed vowels.*

Yze.   See *-Ise, -ize, -yze.*

Part IV

Guide to Correct
Punctuation and Mechanics

An experienced writer means a point as definitely as he means a word.

Arlo Bates

Punctuation marks are useful because the signals they give are based on familiar custom and expectations. A writer who keeps within the not very narrow limits of accepted usage can make his meaning clear; if he transgresses these limits, his writing is likely to appear eccentric or incompetent even when the meaning can be guessed.

George Summey, Jr.

Part IV
Guide to Correct
Punctuation and Mechanics

Correct, clear, effective writing is impossible without proper punctuation. Our thoughts—and the relationships of our thoughts—are in considerable part dependent upon punctuation for their clear and orderly transmission to readers. Actually, punctuation originally developed because, without it, written language was unable to indicate or reproduce certain definite and clear qualities of speech. We can always tell, for example, from a person's voice whether he is making a statement or asking a question. But in writing we would not know which sentence made a statement and which asked a question unless we saw a period at the end of one and a question mark terminating the other. We also know that a pause, or a rising inflection, means something in speech.

These and other meanings and qualities in speech are reproduced in writing by certain marks of punctuation. In addition, since English is not a highly inflected language, the essential meaning of a sentence and the relationships of its parts are revealed only by word order. But word order is flexible, and punctuation is required to show or to suggest the grouping of words and phrases in a sentence which conveys meaning.

Punctuation is not entirely arbitrary and mechanical; it is truly an integral (or organic) part of writing. You cannot indiscriminately sprinkle your writing with punctuation marks and expect it to be fully understood. To be sure, punctuation usage varies with individual writers, but certain basic principles remain steadfast. These principles may be called "descriptive rules," since they have been formulated from hundreds and thousands of examples of punctuation as applied by reputable authors and, much more importantly, by professional editors and printers. When we have enough examples of one use of a certain mark of punctuation, we state this as a general principle or rule, beginning it thus: "Use the . . ." or "*Always* use the . . ." When most of our examples agree: "The mark is *usually* used . . ."; when examples are insufficient to make a generalization: "The mark is *occasionally* used . . ." Correct punctuation permits individuality only to the extent that communication of thought from writer to reader is aided, not impeded.

What is usually considered correct punctuation is about as fixed in usage as is correct spelling, and for a similar reason. Our punctuation usage is based upon the practice of editors and printers who normally follow one or more of a group of standardized books of rules; spelling practices, too, are made rigid by the same professional groups relying upon standard guide books and dictionaries.

The most important marks of punctuation are:

.	Period	,	Comma
?	Question mark	;	Semicolon
!	Exclamation point	:	Colon
—	Dash	" "	Double quotation marks
-	Hyphen	' '	Single quotation marks
'	Apostrophe	( )	Parentheses

Less commonly used marks:

[ ]	Brackets	^	Caret
. . .	Ellipsis periods	"	Ditto marks
***	Asterisks	^, ˘, ‥, ¯, ˜, ´, `	Diacritical and accent marks
/	Bar	¶	Paragraph

These important marks serve to *end*, to *introduce*, to *separate*, and to *enclose*. These purposes of punctuation, as well as scores of specific sentence situations requiring punctuation and mechanical marks, are mentioned and discussed in the glossary of applied punctuation presented at the appropriate places in this part of the book.

PROPER USE OF PUNCTUATION

Abbreviations. Use a period after a standard abbreviation. See *Period*, Rule 3.

Absolute phrase. This term is also referred to as a "nominative absolute." Use commas. See *Commas to enclose*, C3.

Accent marks. These are marks used with a letter or group of letters to indicate the nature and place of the spoken accent or, especially in French words adopted into English, the quality of sound of the letter marked. Accent marks are used in formal writing and in most formal publications except for newspapers. In everyday usage, the word *cafe* is usually written without an acute accent (*café*); *role* instead of *rôle*; etc. For further comment on accent and diacritical marks see *Acute accent; Cedilla, Circumflex accent, Grave accent, Macron, Tilde*.

Act—scene. Separate by a colon. See *Colon*, Rule 4.

Acute accent. This is a mark (´) used to indicate stressed or accented syllables, the quality or quantity of a vowel or consonant sound: *refer'*; *passé*; *idée*; *résumé*; *fiancé* and *fiancée* (feminine); *attaché*.

Adjective clauses. See *Clauses, dependent*.

Adjectives. Separate by commas two or more adjectives modifying the same noun or pronoun. See *Commas to separate*, B3.

Adverbial clauses. See *Clauses, dependent*.

Although. Never preceded by a semicolon, unless other conditions warrant. See *Conjunctions, subordinating*.

Ampersand. This is a mechanical mark (&) meaning *and*. It represents the *e* of the Latin word for "and," *et*. Primarily designed and used to save space, it appears often in business writing, reference works, and company names. Except in these connections, its use is considered substandard in formal writing.

Apostrophe. This is a sign (') rather than a letter, but since it influences spelling more than the mechanics of writing it is fully discussed elsewhere; see this entry in Part III, "Guide to Correct Spelling."

Apposition. Use commas. For long or emphatic appositional phrases, use dashes. See *Commas to enclose,* C4, and *Dash,* Rule 3.

Asterisk. This mechanical sign is a starlike device (*) used largely in reference works to indicate omissions and footnotes. It is occasionally employed to indicate omissions in general writing, although *ellipsis periods* (which see) are considered better form. It is a conspicuous mark which normally attracts undue attention; use it sparingly, if at all.

Bar. In the meaning of "a short slanting stroke between two words," *bar* does not appear in most dictionaries. The preferred term is *virgule,* a pedantic word from Latin *virgula,* a rod. Whatever it is called—and printers call it a *bar*—it is a mark of punctuation showing that either of two words may be used in interpreting the sense of expressions such as *and/or*. It also appears at the ends of lines of poetry when they are written solid rather than as separate verses (lines).

Because. Never preceded by a semicolon, unless other conditions warrant. See *Conjunctions, subordinating.*

Brace. A mechanical device ({) used in printing and some writing to indicate that two or more words or lines are to be taken together.

Brackets. These are marks, always used in pairs, for setting off inserted matter remotely related, or only incidental, to the context. Such additions are usually editorial interpolations and comments not by the author of the text itself. That is, brackets are used to enclose the writer's additions to *quoted* material, whereas parentheses are used to enclose the author's own words.

Use brackets to enclose a comment of the writer interpolated in a quoted passage.

> "Next came the Queen of the Mardi Gras [Miss Florence Mueller] dressed in white satin."
> "The youth of today [1775] are a froward and unruly lot."

Break or shift in thought. Use a dash. See *Dash,* Rule 1.

Business letters, punctuation in. The business letter is largely utilitarian: its object is to convey information by precise wording. Therefore, it is concerned with both *content* and *presentation*. Quality of paper, neatness, and arrangement of letter parts are almost as important to the total effect of business letters as is content. The mechanics of business letter writing deserve careful study: margins; indented and block systems of typing; open and closed systems of punctuation; formalities concerning the heading, inside address, salutation, complimentary close, and signature. For adequate comment on the punctuation and mechanics of business letters you should consult a full-length manual dealing with the subject.

Cancellation.   Do not use parenthesis marks to cancel. Erase or draw a line through the material to be deleted. See *Parentheses*, Rule 4.

Capital letters.   Any letter written or printed in a form larger than, and often different from, that of a corresponding small (i.e., lower case) letter is a capital: A, B, C as contrasted with *a, b, c*. Capitalization is more a matter of spelling convention than of mechanics. Therefore, see *Capitalization*, in Part III, "Guide to Correct Spelling," for comment on sentence capitals, proper names, titles, etc. See also *Unnecessary capitals*.

Caret.   This is a mark (⌃) used to show that something interlined or placed in a margin belongs in the space indicated. Place the caret below the line at the place of omission and write the inserted letter or expression directly above or in the margin.

Cedilla.   This is a hooked mark put under the letter *c* when it is to be pronounced as a voiceless *s: façade; garçon.*

Circumflex accent.   A mark used to show the quality or tone of pronunciation: *hôtel de ville; tête à tête, crêpe de chine.*

Clauses.   For a definition of this term, see listings in Part V. Also, as you read the suggestions listed below, see the appropriate entries for marks of punctuation mentioned.

Independent clauses. (1) Joined by pure co-ordinating conjunction, use a comma. If the clauses are long with complicated internal punctuation, use a semicolon. (2) Not joined by any conjunction, use a semicolon. (3) Joined by a conjunctive adverb, use a semicolon. (4) Used parenthetically, enclose in dashes or parentheses. (5) Between contrasting independent clauses, use a comma.

Dependent clauses. (1) Adverbial clause preceding independent clause, use a comma. (2) Adverbial clause following independent clause: if restrictive, use no punctuation; otherwise, use commas if adverbial clause is nonrestrictive or fairly long. (3) Adjective clause: if nonrestrictive, use commas; if restrictive, omit punctuation. (4) Noun clauses: used as subject or object or complement, no punctuation. (5) Dependent contrasting clauses, use a comma.

Colon. The colon was originally used as a form of semicolon, but the two now have different uses. The semicolon is a mark for *co-ordinating* sentence elements; the colon is primarily a mark for *introducing* lists, series, and quotations.

1. Use the colon after an introductory statement which reveals that something is to follow: an enumeration, tabulation, list, or explanation.

> There were three reasons for his success: integrity, industry, a good personality.
>
> I am positive there is one appeal which you cannot overlook: money.

Do not overwork this introductory function of the colon. There is no justification for its use in such a sentence as "The three cities are: New Orleans, New York, and San Francisco." No punctuation is needed after *are*.

2. Use the colon to separate introductory words from a quotation which follows, if the quotation is formal, long, or paragraphed separately.

> Robert E. Lee is reputed to have said: "Duty is the sublimest word in the English language."
>
> The actor then stated: "I would rather be able adequately to play the part of Hamlet than to perform a miraculous operation, deliver a great lecture, or build a magnificent skyscraper."

3. Use the colon after the formal salutation of a letter.

> Dear Mr. Brown:
> Gentlemen:

The usual practice is to place a colon after the salutation of a formal or business letter and either a colon or a comma after the salutation of an informal, friendly letter.

4. Use a colon to separate hour and minute figures in writing time, the act from the scene of a play, the title of a book from the subtitle.

> 7:35
> *Hamlet* I:2
> *Principles of Photography: A Complete Manual*

Comma. The correct use of the comma (more than that of any of the other marks) depends upon a complete understanding of the exact meaning which you wish to convey. Thus it presupposes a knowledge of syntax (the grammatical relationships between words in sentences). All punctuation, and especially comma usage, depends primarily on your *understanding* of what you are writing. You must be able to distinguish main ideas from those which are of minor importance. You must be able to distinguish phrases, clauses (both main and dependent), and the various parts of speech. In short, you must think carefully and understand basic grammatical principles. See, in Part V, definitions and explanations of terms used in discussing the comma.

The comma has varied and distinct purposes and is both the most frequently used and most troublesome of all marks of punctuation. Since use of the comma is detailed and involved, you might consider first these five broad principles dealing with comma use:

1. Use a comma to separate long independent clauses of compound sentences. See *Commas to separate, B1.*

2. Use a comma to set off long introductory subordinate elements, usually adverbial or participial. See *Commas to separate, B2.*

3. Use commas to divide elements in series. See *Commas to separate, B3.*

4. Use commas to set off parenthetical word groups, including nonrestrictive elements (words, phrases, clauses). See *Commas to enclose, C1, C2, C3, C4.*

5. Use commas in setting off or enclosing dates, initials, numbers, etc. See *Commas to enclose*, C6.

Mastering use of the comma in these five situations will not fully solve the problem but will cover at least three-fourths of it.

Comma fault (splice).   This common and serious error is so important that it is also discussed in Part II, "Guide to Correct Sentence Structure." The *comma fault*, which is also called "comma blunder" and "comma splice," is the joining of two separate, complete statements by a comma. This punctuation is confusing and misleading. It constitutes what is perhaps the most frequent and flagrant misuse of punctuation possible to the writer.

Commas to introduce.

A1.   Use a comma to introduce a word, phrase, or clause.

> My purpose in coming here is simple, to collect the money.
> He needs only two things, rest and attention.

This principle of the introducing comma applies to asking a mental question or musing aloud:

> I pondered, should I tell my employer?
> The next question is, where do we go now?

A2.   Use a comma to introduce, or separate, a short quotation.

> Pearson asked, "Are you coming now?"
> "I can't believe you," he said.

This rule refers not to dialogue but to occasional quotations of speech which may be no more than a single sentence.

Make a careful distinction between quotations which are really quotations and quoted material which is the subject, object, or complement of a verb. Study the punctuation of the following:

> All I can say is "May the best man win."
> "Make haste slowly" came to my mind at once.

Use a colon before a long or formal quotation. See *Colon*.

Commas to separate.

B1. Use a comma to separate independent clauses joined by the co-ordinating conjunctions *and, but, for, nor, or, neither, yet.*

> You understand the use of the comma, and your reader is overjoyed.
> You do not understand the use of the comma, but that is not your reader's fault.
> You understand the use of the comma, for you have learned the laws of syntax.

If the clauses are short, the comma may be omitted. This statement, however, immediately brings up the question "How short is short?" If the independent clauses consist of only subject and verb, then they are obviously short and the comma may be omitted. Examples:

> John studied and Mary played. I laughed and I cried.

Sometimes, lack of punctuation between short clauses may cause momentary misreading:

> We ate *bacon and the girls* ate eggs.

Fairly long clauses are sometimes written without a comma between them if their connection in thought is particularly close.

> His health had improved over the past few months and he was looking forward to complete recovery.

If the subject of two separated verbs is the same, the comma is frequently omitted.

> She spoke clearly and made a favorable impression upon the audience.

Always use commas between clauses to which you wish to give special emphasis.

Long independent clauses which contain internal punctuation should be separated by semicolons.

B2. Use a comma to set off an introductory dependent clause or lengthy phrase.

An introductory phrase or clause should be set off from the remainder of the sentence when vagueness or misunderstanding would result from lack of punctuation. There is no formula to indicate when an introductory phrase or clause is sufficiently long to require separation; the degree of closeness in meaning between the introduction and what follows should determine. ("If I go I shall make an early start" requires no comma.) Ordinarily, introductory *adverbial* clauses containing a participle, a gerund, or an infinitive are followed by a comma. Be especially careful not to separate from the predicate an introductory noun clause acting as the subject.

> If you had not gone, the plan would have been successful.
> You should not make such statements; although they are correct, they will do no good.
> Because of some half-formed fear, I felt that I could not trust him.
> To win fame, he gave up his friends and left home.

B3. Use commas to separate words, phrases, or clauses in a series.

> John picked up his books, coat, hat, and gloves.
> He is a large, wizened, ungainly man.
> He looked behind the door, under the table, beneath the chair.
> He walked, he trotted, and finally he ran.

Punctuation of a series may be represented by A, B, and C. Some writers use A, B and C. Greater clarity is obtained by use of the comma before the conjunction.

A semicolon is sometimes used to separate the elements in a series if any one of them contains commas.

> I bought an old, dilapidated chair; a Sheraton table which was in beautiful condition; and a new, ugly, white and blue rug.

Writers often have difficulty in punctuating co-ordinate adjectives (adjectives in a series, modifying a noun). The following examples clarify the difficulty:

> He was an old, wizened, ungainly, pitiful man.
> He was a wizened, ungainly, pitiful old man.

Notice that a comma is *never* used to separate the last adjective from the noun—that in the second sentence the last two adjectives are not separated by commas. When we say "old man," "old woman," etc., we think of the two words as one; we consider the adjective a part of the noun. One way of testing is to say that a comma is used when "and" could be put naturally between the words.

B4. Use a comma to separate words which might be misread.

In certain constructions, punctuation is necessary to prevent misunderstanding.

> Outside a group of boys were waiting. (Supply comma after *outside*.)
> Beyond the door could be seen, half-open. (Supply comma after *beyond*.)
> What he means is is it true? (Supply comma after the first *is*.)

Constructions in which commas are needed to prevent misreading are usually faulty. If possible, rephrase such sentences to eliminate awkwardness of construction.

B5. Use a comma to separate contrasted co-ordinate elements.

> My name is John, not Henry.
> Punctuation is organic, not mechanical.
> This medicine is effective, yet safe.
> He struck forcefully, but wildly.

B6. Use a comma to separate thousands, millions, etc. (that is, numbers of four or more digits).

> The population was 1,857 in that census.
> The deficit totaled $3,115,486 last year.

Digits used in representing years, telephone numbers, and house numbers are *not* separated by commas:

> Her telephone number is Clearwater 6514.
> They are now living at 3650 Avondale Avenue, having moved there in 1959.

Commas to enclose.

C1. Use commas to enclose *nonrestrictive* clauses and phrases within the sentence.

Clauses and phrases are nonrestrictive when they do not restrict or limit the meaning of the sentence. Study these examples:

> The *Queen Mary*, which is a large ship, was built in Scotland.

> The ship which arrived yesterday is named the *Queen Mary*.

In the first sentence, the omission of *which is a large ship* does not materially change the meaning of the sentence. In the second, the clause *which arrived yesterday* is necessary for the full expression of the idea. That is, it tells which ship *is* the *Queen Mary*. The first clause is nonrestrictive and is thus separated by commas from the remainder of the sentence; the second is restrictive; it is not set off (or enclosed).

> Chapter Ten, *which tells of the rescue*, is well written. (Nonrestrictive clause.)
> The chapter *which tells of the rescue* is well written. (Restrictive clause.)
> The book, *dog-eared and dirty*, had been soaked in the rain. (Nonrestrictive phrase.)
> The book *on the table* is dog-eared and dirty. (Restrictive phrase.)

Restrictive phrases and clauses may be further explained as ones which are necessary to identify the word they modify. They answer the questions Who? Which one? Example:

> John Mackay, *who is our postman*, is a former aviator.
> The man *who is our postman* is a former aviator.

In the first of these sentences, "who is our postman" is nonrestrictive; in the second, the clause actually identifies the word it modifies, *man*; it answers the question, "Which man?"

The *context* sometimes determines whether a clause or phrase is restrictive or nonrestrictive. Example:

> The man who mended our tire was a Cuban.
> We had a flat tire just opposite a gate on which a man was sitting; the man, who later mended our tire, was a Cuban.

In the first sentence, *who mended our tire* is restrictive. But in the second sentence, the main point is the man's nationality and not the aid which he gave in mending the tire. Thus the clause *who later mended our tire* is nonrestrictive.

C2. Use commas to enclose parenthetical words, phrases, or clauses.

Note that if the expression is really parenthetical, it may be omitted without materially affecting the meaning of the sentence.

> *However,* your statement is correct.
> You are, *however,* entirely correct in your statement.
> John's answer, *on the other hand,* was entirely incorrect.
> The moral, *if there is a moral,* is that one should live honestly.

Inserted sentence elements such as emphatic, suspended, or transposed expressions are somewhat similar to parenthetical words, phrases, and clauses and are also set off by commas. Such inserted expressions are frequently more essential to the thought of the sentence than purely parenthetical material, but they are nonrestrictive in function. Examples:

> He did not make that statement, *as you will see if you read more carefully,* and I am certain that he did not mean it.
> This is a good novel, *not only because it contains plenty of action,* but because it fully develops three characters.

C3. Use commas to enclose absolute phrases.

An absolute phrase is a group of words that has no syntactical relation to any word in the sentence.

> *The job being done,* we left as soon as possible.
> He stepped on the platform, *notes in his hand,* and started to talk.

C4. Use commas to enclose words in apposition.

> Jones, *an Englishman,* was an excellent sailor.
> My task, *to write a long club paper,* seemed endless.

Omit the commas when the appositive is restrictive or part of a proper name:

> The novel *Hard Times* was written by Charles Dickens.
> The river Mississippi is beloved of song writers.

The old proverb "A watched pot never boils" is little comfort on a cold morning in camp.

Richard the Lion-Hearted was an English king.

C5. Use commas to enclose vocatives (direct address).

John, have you gone insane?

I like you, *Mr. Martin*, but you are too sarcastic.

Please write to her at once, *Mrs. Wallace*.

Never doubt, *my friend*, that you will be punished.

C6. Use commas to enclose dates, places, and initials or titles.

John left on July 6, *1960*, to go to Chicago.

Dover, *Delaware*, is a beautiful town.

Jackson, *E. T.*, and Wharton, *F.*, are on the list.

James Norman, *D.D.*, and Frank Hale, *M.D.*, are the owners.

The items concerned above are parenthetical. Therefore, a *pair* of commas must be used.

Commas unnecessary. See *Unnecessary commas*.

Complex sentence. See this entry in Part V.

Compound predicate. With two members only, usually no commas; with three or more, commas. See *Series*.

Compound sentence. See this entry in Part V.

Compound words. Usually separate the parts by a hyphen or hyphens. See *Compound words* in Part III, "Guide to Correct Spelling."

Conjunctions, co-ordinating. (1) Pure conjunctions joining independent clauses, use a comma before, but not after. (2) Pure conjunctions joining two words or two phrases, no punctuation; joining three or more, commas. (3) Conjunctive adverb (see *Conjunctive adverb*). (4) Correlative conjunctions: apply same principle as for pure conjunctions.

Conjunctions, subordinating. Never place a comma or a semicolon after, unless for other reasons; place a comma before if the clause is adverbial. is nonrestrictive, and follows the independent clause.

Conjunctive adverb.   Use a semicolon before when placed between two independent clauses. Use a comma or no mark after, depending upon parenthetic strength.

Contraction.   Use an apostrophe. See *Apostrophe*, Rule 4, in Part III, "Guide to Correct Spelling."

Contrasted co-ordinate elements.   Use a comma. See *Comma to separate*, B5.

Co-ordinate adjectives.   See *Adjectives*.

Correlative conjunctions.   See *Conjunctions, co-ordinating*.

Curves.   See *Parentheses*.

Dash.   The dash is a mark of punctuation most characteristically used to denote a sudden break or shift in thought. It has been described as "the interruption, the mark of abruptness, the sob, the stammer, and the mark of ignorance." The last epithet probably refers to the fact that although the dash is useful, too frequent use of it reveals ignorance of the correct use of other marks of punctuation and makes for a choppy, incoherent style. A dash is approximately equivalent to a comma (both may be used in pairs or alone, and between expressions of co-ordinate or unequal rank). Logically, some other mark can always be substituted for the dash, but its occasional use provides emphasis or surprise.

The dash is the only common mark of punctuation not on the standard keyboard. To type a dash, use two hyphens; no space precedes or follows the hyphens. Only in typing is the dash equal to two hyphens; the printed hyphen is smaller than half a dash.

1. Use the dash to indicate a break or shift in thought.

   Here is a fuller explanation—but perhaps you are not interested.
   "I was on the point of—" and then the speaker flushed, and sat down.
   Do we—can we—propose such action to the management?

2. Omit the period when a statement ends with a dash.

   Well, if that is how you feel—
   George began, "May I ask—"

3. Use the dash to set off sharply distinguished matter, to secure emphasis or suspense.

> I am unalterably opposed—unalterably, I repeat—to this suggestion.
>
> She was aware—she must have known—that the proposal was hopeless.
>
> I was pleased—delighted, I should say—to hear your excellent news.

When the parenthetical material set off by dashes requires an exclamation point or question mark, such punctuation should precede the second dash:

> If you should miss the train—Heaven forbid!—please telephone me.

4. Use the dash to indicate the omission of words or letters.

> The Civil War was fought in 1861—1865.
> Gen. B— was an excellent soldier.
> Please study pages 3—14.
> What the d— could he have meant?

5. Use the dash sparingly.

The dash is legitimately used in the instances cited, but other marks of punctuation have their functions, too. Frequent use of the dash detracts from its special quality and effectiveness.

Dates and places.   Enclose in commas when they explain preceding dates and places. See *Commas to enclose*, C6.

Decimal.   See *Period*, Rule 4.

Declarative sentence.   See *Sentence*.

Dependent clause.   See *Clauses*.

Dialogue.   Use quotation marks and commas.   See *Comma to introduce*, A2, and *Quotation marks*.

Diction.   For provincialisms, slang expressions, misnomers, and unusual technical terms, use *quotation marks*, which see. Better yet, don't use such terms at all.

Dieresis.   This mark (also spelled *diaeresis*) is a sign placed over the second of two adjacent vowels to indicate separate pronunciation: *coöperate* (pronounced *co-operate*). There is a growing tendency not to use this sign with such words as *coöperate*, *coördinate*, *aërate*, and *zoölogy*. It is useful, however, in words like *reënforce* and *naïve* to prevent momentary confusion or mispronunciation.

Direct address (vocative).   Use commas. See *Commas to enclose*, C5.

Ditto marks.   The word ditto means "the same" or "a duplicate." Ditto marks (") are used in itemized lists and tables to show that a word, figure, or passage above is to be repeated. (In typewritten manuscript use quotation marks to represent ditto marks.) Ditto marks are less used than formerly and are advised against in standard ordinary writing.

Division of words.   See *Hyphen* and *Word division*.

Dollars and cents.   Use a period between. See *Period*, Rule 4.

Doubt or uncertainty.   Use a question mark in parentheses. See *Question mark*, Rule 3.

Ellipsis periods.   Use ellipsis periods (three) to indicate an omission from a sentence or quotation.

This device is especially helpful when only part of a sentence or line of poetry is quoted. Thus:

". . . nothing walks with aimless feet."
TENNYSON

"Your eyes smile peace . . ."
ROSSETTI

Notes: 1. A question mark or exclamation point may follow ellipsis periods. When ellipsis periods follow a complete sentence, the end-of-sentence period is also used.
2. Do not use ellipsis periods instead of the dash.
3. Do not use ellipsis periods purely as a stylistic device. Writers occasionally use them to indicate that much more could be said. Probably they have nothing in mind.

Emphasis. See *Italics*, Rule 4, and *Surprise, strong emotion.*

Enclosing punctuation. See *Purposes of punctuation.*

End-stop. This is a mark of punctuation used at the end of a sentence. An end-stop is usually a period, question mark, or exclamation point but occasionally may be a dash or ellipsis periods. When two end-stops would fall together (for example, a question within a sentence) use only the one mark more emphatic or more necessary to convey meaning. See *Purposes of punctuation* and *Sentence.*

Exclamation point. Like the period and the question mark, the exclamation point is usually a mark of termination.

1. Use the exclamation point to express surprise, command, emphasis, or strong emotion.

   Help! Help!
   What! Are you certain?
   Go at once!

2. An exclamation point may be used after a phrase or sentence to express irony. In this use it is often put in parentheses.

   Are we to be the slaves of the sales manager!
   She said that she might possibly condescend (!) to write.

   Do not overuse the exclamation point. The emotion must be strong, the surprise genuine, the command really imperative to call for the use of this punctuation. Too frequent use of the exclamation point weakens its effectiveness. A comma, not an exclamation point, should be used after the mild interjection *oh.*

Exclamatory sentence. See *Sentence.*

Figure-and-letter combinations. See *Numbers.*

Figures. With four or more figures, use commas in front of each three. See *Comma to separate, B6,* and *Numbers.*

For. As a conjunction, use a comma preceding. As a preposition, use no punctuation.

Foreign words, phrases. See *Italics,* Rule 2.

For example, for instance, namely, etc.   Used parenthetically, enclose in commas, unless they are followed by an independent clause; then use a colon or semicolon before, a comma after.

Fractions.   Use a hyphen between the numerator and the denominator. See *Compound words*, Rule 3, in Part III, "Guide to Correct Spelling."

Grave accent.   A mark used to show the quality of a vowel as in the French *chère* and *à la mode*; the full pronunciation of a syllable normally elided or slurred over: *lovèd*.

Hour—minute.   Separate by a colon. See *Colon*, Rule 4.

Hyphen.   The hyphen is more a mark of spelling than of punctuation. (See *Compound words* in Part III, "Guide to Correct Spelling.") But the hyphen is a mechanical device necessary for correct, clear writing as well as for spelling. It should be sharply distinguished from the *dash* (which see).

1. Use a hyphen to indicate the division of a word broken at the end of a line.

   The rambling old house, it is true, would have looked considerably better if it had been freshly painted.

   Do not divide a word at the end of a line if you can avoid it. Place the hyphen at the end of the first line, never at the beginning of the second.

2. Never divide a monosyllable.

   Such words as *curse, through, though, ground, death, grace, quick, asked,* and *breadth* cannot be divided. Write them in their entirety on the first line; if that is not possible, leave a blank space and carry the whole word over to the next line.

3. Consult your dictionary to determine the correct syllabication of words.

   It is easier to approach an authority than to learn the various rules for dividing words. These simple suggestions may be helpful, however:

Prefixes and suffixes may be written separately.
Compound words are divided between their main parts.
Two consonants are usually divided.

Imperative sentence.   See *Sentence.*

Independent clause.   See *Clauses.*

Indirect question.   Use a period, not a question mark. See *Question mark*, Rule 2.

Indirect quotation.   Use neither commas nor question marks. See *Quotation marks*, Rule 8, and *Unnecessary commas*, Rule 6.

Initials.   See *Period.*

Inserted material.   (1) Inserted sentence elements, use comma or commas. See *Commas to enclose*, C2. (2) Omitted material inserted later, indicate by a caret (⌃). See *Caret.*

Interjections.   Mild, use a comma; strong or fairly strong, use an exclamation point. See *Exclamation point.*

Interpolated material.   Use *brackets*, which see.

Interrogative sentence.   See *Sentence.*

Interruption in dialogue.   Use a *dash*, which see.

Introducing punctuation.   See *Purposes of punctuation.*

Introduction.   Before a word, phrase, or clause being introduced, use a comma, colon, or dash.

Irony.   Occasionally, indicate by an exclamation point within parentheses. See *Exclamation point*, Rule 2.

Italics.   Indicate italicized words (words in different type) either by underlining or by enclosing them in quotation marks. Underlining is generally preferable. Except in printing, distinction in the use of italics and quotation marks for emphasizing or defining certain expressions, indicating titles, etc., is probably unimportant, because fountain pens cannot yet be made to write in italics.

1. Use italics (underlining) to indicate titles of magazines, newspapers, books, long poems, plays, and the names of ships, trains, and airplanes.

From the library of the <u>Queen Elizabeth</u> he borrowed a copy of <u>Life</u>, the <u>New York Times</u>, and Roberts' Cornflakes and Beaujolais.

Titles of magazine articles, short stories, and short poems are usually put in *quotation marks* (which see) rather than italics. When both the title of an article (or story or poem) and the magazine in which it appears are given, in order to distinguish them use quotation marks to indicate the former and underline the latter.

Cartwright, Wilburn, "The Motorist Girds for War," <u>Harper's Magazine</u>.

2. Use italics (underlining) to indicate foreign words and phrases.

Your dictionary is the best guide to words still considered distinctly foreign and those which have been naturalized.

A scheme such as that has no <u>raison d'être</u>.
She has a <u>je ne sais quoi</u> personality.
The accident occurred on the <u>Autobahn</u> near Munich.

3. Use italics (underlining) to refer to a word, letter, or number spoken of as such.

Please dot your <u>i</u>'s and cross your <u>t</u>'s.
You wrote <u>steal</u> but you must have meant <u>steel</u>.
You make a <u>6</u> which looks like a <u>9</u>.

4. Use italics (underlining) to emphasize a word or phrase.

You must <u>always</u> be on time for work.
You must <u>never, under any conditions,</u> be late for work.

Italics for emphasis are occasionally effective. Overused, they become monotonous, lose effectiveness, and exhibit "school-girl style."

Lower case letters. See *Capital letters*.

Macron. A short, straight, horizontal mark placed over vowels to denote their long quality: ā as in *dāme*, ō as in *ōld*, etc.

Marks of parenthesis.   See *Parentheses*.

Misreading.   Between words and elements that may be misread, use a comma, or recast. See *Commas to separate*, B4.

Namely.   See *For example*.

Names of ships, trains, airplanes.   Use quotation marks or italics. See *Italics*, Rule 1.

Nominative absolute.   See *Absolute phrase*.

Nonrestrictive clause.   See *Clauses*.

Nonrestrictive phrase.   See *Phrases*.

Noun clause.   See *Clauses*.

Numbers.   The practice of writing words for numbers or of using figures is more a matter of convention and custom than of correctness. However, representing numbers *is* a matter of mechanics, and a troublesome one at that. See *Figures*.

1. Use words to represent numbers in special uses:

   A. Isolated numbers less than 10.

      At least three men should be nominated for secretary.
      We can choose one of six magazines to read.

   B. Indefinite expressions or round numbers. (Figures are also acceptable, however.)

      This theater will seat two or three thousand persons.
      or
      This theater will seat 2 or 3,000 persons.

      The mid-fifties will probably be known as the atomic fifties.
      or
      The mid-50's will probably be known as the atomic 50's.

      Right now I could use a hundred dollars.
      or
      Right now I could use $100.

      We have some forty cows and about six hundred chickens on our farm.
      or
      We have some 40 cows and about 600 chickens on our farm.

C. One number or related numbers at the beginning of a sentence.

> Three of our officers are from Syracuse.
> Twenty to thirty employees will be absent on an inspection trip to Detroit.

D. Numbers preceding a compound modifier containing a figure.

> To line this wall we need twelve ½-inch pieces of plywood.
> Our tent is supported by two 8-foot poles.

E. Fractions standing alone.
> Be sure that the plywood is one-half inch thick.
> I live about one-fourth of a mile from the highway.

2. Use figures to represent numbers in special uses:

A. Isolated numbers of 10 or more.

> Only 35 parents attended the meeting at the school.
> The amount is 12 times what it was in 1960.

B. Dates, including the day or the day and the year.

> Please report for duty by July 1.
> They were married on June 26, 1957.
> I worked there from May 1 to October 15, 1960.

C. House, room, telephone, and postal zone numbers.

> She lives at 472 Old Mill Road; her telephone number is Capital 6143.
> She was in Room 2145 at the Ansonia Hotel, Columbia 6, North Dakota.

D. Highway and comparable numbers.

> We were driving on Route 46.
> The best programs will be found on Channel 20.

E. Measurements.

> Standard typewriter paper is 8½ by 11 inches in size.
> The package weighed 6 pounds 4 ounces.
> 5-foot pole   ¼-inch wire   2-inch margin

F. Time.

> 9:00 P.M.   2:35 A.M.   half past 5
> 11:00 o'clock (not: 11 o'clock a.m. or 11 a.m. in the morning)
> 5 hours 8 minutes 12 seconds; 6 years 3 months 21 days

G. Percentage.

> 8 per cent   one-half of 1 per cent   5¼ per cent return
> You waste 5 to 10 per cent of your lunch hour.

H. Money.

> $5.60 $0.60   60 cents $4 per dozen   28¢ apiece

I. Chapters and page numbers.

> Chapter 7   See p. 121   pp. 15—30

3. Use figure-and-letter combinations appropriately.

Occasionally, you will need to write figures and letters in combination, especially in expressing ordinal numbers (first, 1st; second, 2nd; etc.) Such combinations are correctly used in tables, sometimes in numbering items in a list, sometimes in dates—but not when the year immediately follows, and usually in expressing a numbered street from 10th on.

> Your April 15th request (or: your request of April 15) has been noted.
> Your request of April 15, 1960, has been noted.
> 472 Old Mill Road; corner of 10th Street and Fifth Avenue; 105 Fifth Avenue; North 210th Street

4. With four or more figures, use a comma before each three numbers.

> 2,956; 46,795; 195,679; 1,683,295

Also, see *Comma to separate*, B6.

Numerals. Use a hyphen between the parts (from twenty-one through ninety-nine). See *Compound words* in Part III, "Guide to Correct Spelling."

Numerals, Roman. See *Roman numerals*.

Object.   Use no comma between a verb and its object or a preposition and its object (except for additional reasons). See *Unnecessary commas*, Rule 1.

Oh.   As a mild interjection, use a comma following; as a strong interjection, use an *exclamation point*, which see.

Omission of letters.   In a word, use a dash. In a contraction, use an apostrophe. See *Dash*, Rule 4, above, and *Apostrophe*, Rule 4, in Part III, "Guide to Correct Spelling."

Omission of words.   Use *ellipsis periods* or *asterisks*, which see.

Paragraph mechanics.   A paragraph is a group of sentences dealing with one phase of a longer piece of writing. A few mechanical matters are involved:

Indent the first line of every paragraph one-half inch, or more. Use indentations of equal length for all the paragraphs in the same document. Make no exception for *numbered* paragraphs.

Avoid excessive use of the marks "¶" and "no ¶," meaning, respectively, "a new paragraph intended" and "not a new paragraph." If possible, you should recopy the entire page, correcting the indentations (also spelled *indentions*).

Do not leave part of a line blank unless a new paragraph begins on the next line.

Keep the margins to the left and right as symmetrical as possible. A line left partly blank causes a jagged appearance.

In writing dialogue or in quoting conversation, paragraph each speech separately.

Note the correct form of both the actual speeches and the accompanying introductory and explanatory words in the following:

> The play had moved me so deeply that I could not sleep. I got up and walked into John's room.
>
> "Why aren't you asleep?" he asked. He was seated at his desk, studying French.
>
> "I kept thinking about that TV show and couldn't sleep," I answered. "It seems to me that the young doctor made a terrible mistake."
>
> "How can you tell?" asked John, getting up from the

desk. "You can't really know until you are a scientist yourself."

Parentheses. Sometimes called "curves," sometimes "marks of parenthesis," *parentheses* are marks of enclosure.

1. Use parentheses to enclose parenthetical material only remotely connected with the context.

> This proposal (I am convinced it is important) should be carefully studied.
>
> If you find any holly berries (surely they must be numerous now) please bring me some.

In such constructions the parenthetical material merely amplifies the thought. Thus you may prefer dashes to parentheses. The marks may be used interchangeably, although parentheses are more commonly used when the parenthetical material is a complete sentence.

2. Use parentheses to enclose references and directions.

> You should not attempt it for three reasons: (1) your health is poor; (2) your father needs your aid; (3) the distance is too great.

3. Use parentheses to enclose figures repeated to insure accuracy.

> He paid ten dollars ($10.00) for the shoes.
> There were thirty (30) claims for damages.

You may have an idea that a number written out *must* be followed by numerals. Apart from commercial writing, words alone are sufficient.

4. Do not use parentheses to cancel parts of your writing. Erase or draw lines through the words you wish to delete.

Parenthetic words, phrases, clauses. If these are weak, use no punctuation; if fairly strong, use commas; if strong and emphatic, use dashes or parentheses. See *Commas to enclose, C2; Dash*, Rule 3; *Parentheses*, Rule 1.

Period. The period is usually a mark of terminal punctuation, although it has a special use for abbreviations, and, in a series, a particular use to indicate separation.

1. Use a period at the end of every complete declarative sentence.

> It was a cold, dismal day.
> Although his health was poor, he decided to leave at once.
> You go ahead with your proposed trip; I shall remain at home.

2. Periods are used after mildly imperative sentences; exclamation marks after vigorously imperative sentences.

> Look before you leap.
> Leave the house at once!

3. Use a period after a standard abbreviation.

> James Smith, Esq.
> Henry Jones, D.D. (b. 1900; d. 1960)
> Dec. 10; bbl.; N.B.; *seq.*; *q.v.*; Gen.

If a declarative sentence ends with an abbreviation, one period only is used. If the sentence is interrogative or exclamatory, a question mark or exclamation point follows the abbreviation period. Inside the sentence, the period is followed by any logical punctuation which would have been used regardless of the period. Note the semicolons in the third line of examples above.

4. Use a period before a decimal, to separate dollars and cents, to precede cents written alone.

> 3.75 per cent $4.52 $.75

Phrases. (1) An introductory modifying phrase containing a verb form, use a comma; not containing a verb form, use no punctuation, unless fairly long and then use a comma. See *Commas to separate,* B2. (2) Nonrestrictive phrases, use commas; restrictive phrases, use no punctuation. See *Commas to enclose,* C1.

Places. See *Dates and places.*

Plurals. Formed by adding s, es, or by change in form. *Never* use an apostrophe, except to form the plurals of words as words, of letters, and of figures. See *Apostrophe* and *Plurals* in Part III, "Guide to Correct Spelling."

Possessive case. Use the apostrophe in forming the possessive case of nouns and indefinite pronouns. Do *not* use the apostrophe in forming the possessive case of other classes of pronouns. See *Apostrophe* in Part III, "Guide to Correct Spelling."

Predicate. See *Compound predicate.*

Preposition and object. Use no comma between. See *Unnecessary commas.*

Provincialisms. See *Diction.*

Pure conjunctions. See *Conjunctions, co-ordinating.*

Purposes of punctuation. Ordinarily you will apply a principle or specific "rule" of punctuation to a particular instance or sentence element. But you may be helped in such application by remembering that punctuation usually serves one of four purposes:

1. To *end* or *terminate* a statement (use period, question mark, or exclamation point).

   Little progress was reported.
   Are you going home?
   What an occasion!

2. To *introduce* (use comma, colon, or dash).

   Only one quality is needed, perseverance.
   My purpose is simple: to succeed in life.
   My goal in life is simple—success.

3. To *separate* parts of a sentence or word (use comma, semicolon, dash, hyphen, or apostrophe).

   If you have any influence at all, try to have me released.
   Some people prefer dinner at noon; others prefer it in the evening.
   Commas, periods, semicolons, and colons—these are common marks of punctuation.
   Mr. Brown was elected secretary-treasurer.
   It isn't nine o'clock yet.

4. To *enclose* parts of a sentence or a whole sentence (use commas, dashes, quotation marks, single quotation marks, parentheses, brackets).

Enclosure marks are used in pairs, except when the capital letter at the beginning of a sentence takes the place of the first or when a terminating mark at the end takes the place of the second.

> You are, my dear Henry, the first one I've asked.
> My dear Henry, you are the first one I've asked.
> You are not—and everyone knows this—a careful driver.
> You are not a careful driver—and everyone knows this.
> "The word 'lousy' is not in reputable use as a term in literary criticism," said the lecturer.
> You are referred to the United States Constitution (see especially Article VIII).

Different marks to indicate these four principal purposes are, obviously, not necessarily interchangeable. The comma and the dash, for example, can serve three of the purposes. In applying to your writing general and specific principles of punctuation and mechanics, answer these questions when you have a problem:

1. What is it here which requires punctuation? That is, what kinds of sentences? What kinds of elements within sentences? What kinds of relations between elements?

2. What purpose do I wish my punctuation to serve? Termination? Introduction? Separation? Enclosure? What kind of punctuation or mechanics will be correct? Will make for clearness? Add effectiveness?

3. What mark or marks of punctuation or mechanics will best accomplish that purpose?

Queries, series of. Use question marks. See *Question mark*, Rule 4.

Question mark. The question mark, like the period and the exclamation point, is usually employed as a terminal mark of punctuation.

1. Use a question mark at the end of every direct question.

> Do you really know?
> You really do know?

2. Do *not* use the question mark after an indirect question.

> *Wrong:*   I was asked if I wanted to go?
> *Right:*   I was asked if I wanted to go.

3. Use a question mark, enclosed in parentheses, to express doubt or uncertainty.

> This is a genuine (?) leather bag.
> Richardson was born in 1930 (?), in Selma.

Do not overuse the question mark for this purpose. If it is impossible for you to find the exact information needed, you may use the question mark. But do not use it as a lazy substitute for research.

The use of question marks in parentheses to indicate ironical or humorous meanings is rarely allowable. You can nearly always find some other way to phrase the sentence.

4. Use question marks to indicate a series of queries in the same sentence.

> Will you be there? on time? properly dressed?
> Can you come? or your brother? or your parents?

Quotation marks.   These are solely marks of enclosure for words, phrases, clauses, sentences, and paragraphs. The word *quotation* means repeating what someone has said or written, but the marks themselves have several specialized uses.

1. Use quotation marks to enclose every direct quotation.

> He asked, "Did that hat cost only five dollars?"
> "That's all," I answered. "I bought it at Johnston's Haberdashery. It was on sale."

2. Use quotation marks to enclose technical terms in nontechnical writing.

> This is a heavily "watered" issue of stock.
> The pilot made a "three-point" landing.

3. In formal writing use quotation marks to enclose words which suggest a different level of usage.

If a word is appropriate, no quotation marks should be used as a form of apology. If it is not appropriate, the expression can usually be altered. In some instances, however, you may wish to shift to a different level of usage in order to communicate meaning exactly or emphatically:

> The prevailing opinion is that President Black informed Secretary White that the recommendation of Congress was "cockeyed."
>
> The symphony was conducted by a "stuffed shirt."

4. If a direct quotation extends for several paragraphs, put quotation marks at the beginning of each paragraph, but at the end of only the last paragraph.

5. In dialogue, every change of speaker requires a separate paragraph.

> "We really should stay here today and work," said Milton weakly.
>
> "Yes, but I want to go see the game," replied Jack.
>
> "If we do go, we'll be behind tomorrow, and Simonson is sure to cause trouble."
>
> "I suppose you're right. Let's work."

6. Place quotation marks correctly with reference to other marks.

The comma and the period come *inside* the quotation marks.

> "I understand perfectly now," he said. "I wasn't listening at first."

Every question mark, exclamation point, and dash comes *outside* the quotation marks unless it is part of the quotation.

> Did she say, "I have enough money"?
>
> She asked, "Have I enough money?"
>
> "Have I enough money?" she asked.

Semicolon and colon come outside the quotation marks.

> Read E. B. White's "Walden"; it is, I think, his best essay.
>
> "Give me liberty or give me death"; this was Patrick Henry's most famous utterance.

7. Quotation marks *always go in pairs.* Be careful to indicate both the beginning and the end of a quotation.

Wrong: "I like bowling better than baseball, he said. And I like tennis better than any other sport."

Right: "I like bowling better than baseball," he said. "And I like tennis better than any other sport."

8. Do *not* put quotation marks around an indirect quotation.

Wrong: The conductor asked "how many had their return tickets."

Right: The conductor asked how many had their return tickets.

or

The conductor asked, "How many of you have return tickets?"

See *Single quotation marks.*

Quotation marks with other marks of punctuation. See *Quotation marks,* Rule 6.

Quotation running more than one paragraph. Use quotation marks at the beginning of each paragraph, but at the end of only the last paragraph.

Quotation within a quotation. Use *single quotation marks,* which see.

References and directions. When these amplify, enclose in parentheses. See *Parentheses,* Rule 2.

Restrictive clause. See *Clauses.*

Restrictive phrase. See *Phrases.*

Roman numerals. Our present figures (1, 2, 3, 4, etc.) came to us from the Arabs and are called Arabic numerals. Although these are generally preferable, Roman numerals still find occasional use in current writing: numbering the preliminary pages of a book, marking year dates, and frequently indicating acts of plays, volume numbers of books and magazines, and chapter numbers of books.

The preliminary pages in this book are numbered from v through xi.

George I, George II, and George III reigned in the 18th century, George V and George VI in the 20th.

Prince Hal and Falstaff first appear in Act I, Scene 2, of Shakespeare's *Henry IV, Part I.*

This imposing building bears the date when it was constructed—MDCCCLXXIV.

Notice how Roman numerals are formed: a repeated letter repeats its value; a letter placed after one of greater value adds to it; a letter placed before one of greater value subtracts from it; a dashline over a letter denotes multiplied by 1,000.

ROMAN NUMERALS

I	1	XXV	25	CD	400
II	2	XXX	30	D	500
III	3	XL	40	DC	600
IV	4	L	50	DCC	700
V	5	LXXXV	85	DCCC	800
VI	6	LXXXIX	89	CM	900
VII	7	XC	90	M	1,000
VIII	8	XCV	95	MD	1,500
IX	9	XCIX	99	MM	2,000
X	10	C	100	MMM	3,000
XV	15	CL	150	MMMM	4,000
XIX	19	CC	200	$\overline{V}$	5,000
XX	20	CCC	300	$\overline{M}$	1,000,000

Salutation.   In a business letter, use a colon after the salutation; in a friendly letter, use a colon or a comma. See *Colon*, Rule 3.

Semicolon.   The semicolon is a "stronger" mark of punctuation than the comma; it signifies a greater break or a longer pause between sentence elements. It is not, however, so forceful as terminal marks of punctuation. The semicolon has definitely established uses which are not difficult to master. Remember: the semicolon is used only between elements of equal rank; it is entirely a mark of *co-ordination.*

1. Use the semicolon to separate co-ordinate clauses *not* joined by a simple conjunction.

   Please close the window; the room is too cold.

My companion and I walked down the street; he saw only shop windows; I saw only people's faces.

2. Use the semicolon to separate co-ordinate clauses joined by a conjunction if the clauses are lengthy or contain internal punctuation.

It has been a long, long time since I was last in Joplin; and yet, the sights are so familiar, it seems only yesterday that I was there.

Success in life, so some maintain, requires intelligence, industry, and honesty; but others, fewer in number, assert that only personality is important.

3. Use semicolons to separate phrases of great length, as well as clauses, and series of words in which extreme clearness is desired.

Nominations for the presidency included the names of Mrs. G. B. Jones, member of the Garden Club; Mrs. Alton Pesky, local librarian; and Miss Sonia Block, official of the League of Women Voters.

4. Use the semicolon to separate co-ordinate clauses joined by a conjunctive adverb (*besides, however, nevertheless, therefore, thus, so, consequently, hence, in addition, likewise, furthermore, still, also, then, moreover,* etc.).

He took great care with his work; *therefore,* he was very successful.

Your sentences seem to be well phrased; *however,* there are a few minor errors.

He did not wish to go; *besides,* it was a cold, damp day.

Distinguish between a conjunctive adverb and a simple conjunction. A conjunctive adverb has an adverbial function which no simple conjunction possesses; conversely, the connecting force of a conjunctive adverb is relatively weak. *Because, whereas, inasmuch as* are subordinating conjunctions, not conjunctive adverbs.

Sentence. (1) After a declarative sentence, use a period. (2) After a mildly imperative sentence, use a period; if it is vigorous, an exclamation point. (3) After an interrogative sentence, use a question mark. (4) After an exclamatory sentence, use an exclamation point.

Separating punctuation. See *Purposes of punctuation.*

Series. Three or more words or phrases or clauses, separate by commas, including one before but not after the conjunction. When the conjunction joins each two members of the series, use no punctuation. But see *Clauses* and *Commas to separate,* B3.

Sign of the paragraph (¶). See *Paragraph mechanics.*

Single quotation marks. In England, single quotation marks are often used where double marks would be used in the United States. In this country, single quotation marks are experiments in typography or a kind of affectation—with one exception.

Use single quotation marks (often called *quotes*) to enclose a quotation within a quotation.

> "Tell me," she asked after the ceremony, "whether the groom really answered 'I guess so.'"

On the rare occasions when you have to punctuate a quotation within a quotation, the order is double marks, single marks, double marks. See *Quotation marks.*

Slang. See *Diction.*

Slant line. See *Bar.*

Strength of punctuation. Some marks of punctuation are more forceful than others. For example, the comma is always used within a sentence and therefore differs from terminal marks (period, question mark, exclamation point) in *degree*. It shows a brief pause, less complete separation than full stops.

The period, the semicolon, and the comma form a series in which members have a relative strength. The *period* is the strongest mark of the three; it points out the most important division of thought, the sentence; it also indicates the greatest remoteness in thought. The *semicolon* is used between longer and more important groups *within a sentence* or between those which have a comparatively remote connection in thought. The *comma* is the weakest mark of the three; it separates short groups within the sentence and indicates comparatively close connection. See *Purposes of punctuation.*

Subject—predicate. Use no comma to separate. See *Unnecessary commas.*

Subordinating conjunctions. See *Conjunctions, subordinating.*

Such as. Use a comma or no punctuation preceding; use no punctuation following. See *Colon,* Rule 1.

Summarizing final clause. Use a dash preceding.

Surprise, strong emotion. Use an exclamation point.

Suspended elements. Use commas, usually. See *Commas to enclose,* C2.

Syllabication. See *Hyphen,* above, and *Syllabication as an aid to spelling,* in Part III, "Guide to Correct Spelling."

Technical words. See *Diction.*

Terminal punctuation. See *End-stop* and *Purposes of punctuation.*

Tilde. A mark (~) which appears over the letter *n* as in Spanish *cañon.*

Title—subtitle. Separate by a colon. See *Colon,* Rule 4.

Titles. (1) Titles of books, magazines, newspapers, motion pictures, use italics, or, less preferably, quotation marks. (2) Titles at the beginning of a report or paper or chapter, use neither quotation marks around nor a period following. (3) Titles (personal) and initials following a name, use comma preceding.

Transposed elements. Use commas, usually. See *Commas to enclose,* C2.

Uncertainty. See *Question mark,* Rule 3.

Underlining. See *Italics.*

Unfinished statement or word. Use a dash. See *Dash,* Rule 1.

Unnecessary capitals. Capitalization is a mechanical and somewhat conventional device. For a discussion of proper uses of capitals, see *Capitalization*, in Part III, "Guide to Correct Spelling."

Capitals are often overused or wrongly used. It is as great a mistake to use a capital letter when it is not called for as to fail to use one when it is needed.

Avoid unnecessary and careless use of capitals.

1. If the reference is to *any one* of a class of persons or things rather than a specific person or thing, do not capitalize the noun or the adjective:

   He is a general. His name is General John Jones.
   I am going to a theater. I am going to the Bijou Theater.
   He is a vice-president of this company. This is Vice-president (or Vice-President) Samuel Jones.
   I attended high school. I attended Henry Hudson High School.

2. Do not carelessly make small (lower case) letters so large that they resemble capitals (upper case letters).

3. Do not capitalize names of points of the compass unless they refer to a specific section.

   Correct: He lives in the West.
   He walked south along the avenue.

4. Do not capitalize nouns such as *father* and *mother* if they are preceded by a possessive.

   Correct: My father is a tall man.
   I love Mother very much.
   Your sister thinks I am quiet, but Grandma says I talk entirely too much.

Unnecessary commas. Comma usage varies with different writers, but every comma used must be needed for sense construction. Modern punctuation usage omits more commas than formerly; therefore, be able to account for each comma you use. Above all, do not needlessly separate closely related sentence elements.

1. Do *not* separate a verb and its complement or a subject and its verb. (Remember that noun phrases and clauses act as

the subjects and objects of verbs and should not be separated
by commas.)

> *Wrong:* I asked, for the book.
>
> The clerk standing thère, is named John Gregg.
>
> There is no doubt in the mind of anybody who
> knows anything about it, that he will be a
> successful lawyer.
>
> To ride in a motor boat, is enjoyable.

2. Do *not* use a comma indiscriminately to replace a word
omitted.

> *Wrong:* He said, he would come. (The comma is incor-
> rectly substituted for the word *that*.)

3. Do *not* use a comma to separate two words or two phrases
joined by a co-ordinating conjunction.

> *Wrong:* He has dignity, and integrity.
>
> The leader has strength of body, and firmness of
> purpose.

4. Do *not* use a comma indiscriminately after a conjunction.
Commas should follow conjunctions only when the intention
of the writer is to *stress* the idea implied by the conjunction.
Ordinarily, such stress is supplied by a conjunctive adverb
(*besides, moreover,* etc.) and not by a simple conjunction.

> *Wrong:* And, there were no eggs in the basket.
>
> But, I do not agree with President Adams when
> he says that a stock option increases incentive.

5. Do *not* use a comma before the first or after the last member
of a series.

> *Wrong:* You write the, first, second, and fourth paragraphs.
>
> He bought her a lovely, expensive, coat.

6. Do *not* use a comma before an indirect quotation.

> *Wrong:* One of my friends said the other day, that he
> wanted to go to Spain.

l. Do *not* use a comma before a title in italics.

> *Wrong:*   Last month I read Maugham's, *Of Human Bond-age.*

Verb—object, verb—complement.   Use no comma to separate. See *Unnecessary commas.*

Virgule.   A slanting stroke between two words. See *Bar.*

Vocative.   See *Direct address.*

Word division.   Use a hyphen at the end of the line, between syllables, when the word is continued on the next line. Never use a hyphen at the beginning of a line. See *Hyphen.*

Part V

Guide to Grammar and Composition:
A Dictionary of Terms

The best reason for studying grammar is that grammar is interesting.

PAUL ROBERTS, *Understanding Grammar*

Good grammar is not merely grammar which is free from unconventionalities, or even from the immoralities. It is the triumph of the communication process, the use of words which create in the reader's mind the thing as the writer conceived it. . . .

JANET AIKEN, *Commonsense Grammar*

Real education must ultimately be limited to men who insist on knowing; the rest is mere sheep-herding.

EZRA POUND, *A.B.C. of Reading*

Dictionaries are like watches; the worst is better than none, and the best cannot be expected to go quite true.

DR. SAMUEL JOHNSON, Mrs. Piozzi:
Anecdotes of the Late Samuel Johnson

Part V
Guide to Grammar and Composition:
A Dictionary of Terms

This section provides a quick-reference dictionary of useful terms commonly encountered in a study of English grammar and composition of all kinds. In your everyday activities as housewife, businessman, employee, student, or whatever you may be, you will find that an understanding of these terms will help you to avoid errors and improve your use of spoken and written language.

GRAMMATICAL TERMS

Grammar is that science which deals with words, forms of words, and word combinations. Broadly speaking, grammar is a descriptive statement of the way language works. What we usually call "good English" is the use of words and word forms in combinations appropriate to English as it is spoken and written by thoughtful people. Recognizing and avoiding common errors in English requires a working knowledge of English sounds, words, and the formation and arrangement of words.

This basic knowledge is not difficult to acquire. Like any science, grammar becomes difficult and involved once first principles are out of the way, but your purpose now is not to become a linguist but to learn how to use English which is appropriate for you in different situations.

Actually, grammar has nothing to do with "correctness" as such. It *describes* but does not *prescribe*. Even so, in order to speak and write without making what are generally considered minor mistakes or outright blunders, you need some knowledge of the English way of saying and writing things. Such knowledge you may have resisted for many years because you always thought that grammar is "dull," "lifeless," "not worth studying." These attitudes toward basic grammatical principles are commonly held. Nevertheless, they are both thoughtless and incorrect.

Grammar is "dull" and "dry" only when it is studied for its own sake, not when it is properly considered as only a means to an end. A minimum knowledge of fundamental grammar is a powerful aid in effective writing on all levels.

Nor can grammar be thought of as "lifeless," because it is a kind of organism, filled with life and constantly developing and changing. The primary purpose of grammar is to describe change and development. Language is not based on grammar, for the latter is a controlled study and record of speech habits. Again, grammar is not a rigid set of do's and don't's; it is not something imposed by authorities. Grammar truly is a series of scientifically recorded observations about language and is subject to frequent and drastic change. Nothing can be more alive than grammar because nothing is more human.

Grammatical principles may seem to you to be fixed and definite, but because both language and the grammar based upon language are progressing day by day and year by year, the language used and the grammar studied by our children and grandchildren will differ at least somewhat from practices of today.

Also, grammar is "worth studying" because, properly understood, it can help us to express our ideas clearly and effectively in both speech and writing. Weakness in writing—particularly incorrectness of sentence structure—is often due to insufficient understanding of grammar. And yet this knowledge does not have to be memorized or consciously applied. Many skilled speakers and writers are more concerned with what they have to say than with grammar, as such; they have mastered basic grammatical principles and apply them as instinctively or unconsciously as you and I might drive an automobile or run a sewing machine. If you do not know what a phrase and a clause are, you might find it difficult to apply a suggestion that you "reduce predication." But you will need little knowledge of grammar to change the sentence "Infantile paralysis, which used to be a deadly illness, is now rare" to "Infantile paralysis, once a deadly illness, is now rare." The second version is shorter and more direct—made so by the application of a grammatical principle involving changing a clause into a phrase. Every speaker and every writer should have at least a minimum working knowledge of words and their ways.

Many writers have partly or completely forgotten the grammar they learned in school, or so they think. Actually, some "unconscious" knowledge remains, because otherwise they could not make their meaning clear to other people. It is true, however, that definitions of certain grammatical terms may have been forgotten. This is unfortunate only when a lack of knowledge of the meanings of terms (as above with phrases and clauses) results in awkward or obscure phrasing. In the glossary of grammatical terms appearing in this book you will find definitions or brief discussions of items and grammatical situations which will constantly confront you in speaking and writing. You don't need to memorize definitions of these elements of grammar, but you will need to refer to them constantly if your study of sentence structure, punctuation and mechanics, diction, and even spelling is to be meaningful and rewarding.

GENERAL TERMS

Avoiding common errors in speaking and writing is no simple task. For example, you can deliberately concentrate on correct spelling with good results but continue to make glaring errors in sentence structure and punctuation. Or you can strive for mastery of the sentence and continue to misspell or make mistakes in grammar. The problem of correct English is somewhat like that of repairing a worn automobile tire: you repair one leak only to have air escape through several additional holes. Mastering good English is not an impossible assignment by any means, but it is surely an exasperating and complex one.

Similarly, it is not easy to pigeonhole mistakes in English usage. A flaw in sentence structure may involve fundamental grammatical principles or spelling or faulty punctuation, or all three. A mistake in diction may involve pronunciation or mechanics or grammar or sentence structure, or even all four simultaneously. In the several sections of this book, basic errors are listed alphabetically, described, discussed, and corrected. But it is quite true that many of these errors involve more than one principle of correct usage.

Therefore, a list of *General Terms* is included. This list will enable you to secure quick understanding of terms used elsewhere in the book and will suggest further study at appropriate places. Additionally, the list contains brief definitions of terms which you are likely to encounter in your daily reading of newspapers and magazines and on TV and radio programs. Frankly, it is a sort of catchall, included to provide mention of terms not logically belonging to any particular segment of correct English usage but nevertheless important in an over-all approach to the subject. Also, you may refer to it frequently while you are studying other sections of the book in order to form meaningful impressions of terms which might be strange or generally unclear. Please remember, however, that definitions provided in this glossary of general terms are purposely brief and are intended for only casual use. Be certain always to refer to the full discussions contained elsewhere in this book or to your dictionary. In short, use this section as need arises, but don't be fully content with what you find.

DEFINITIONS OF TERMS

Abbreviation. A shortened form of a word or phrase, such as *Mr.* for *Mister* and *S.C.* for *South Carolina*. Abbreviations, except the most common ones, are normally unacceptable in standard writing and should never be overused. Also, periods are required with most of them.

Ablative case. A Latin case form not used in English. Its functions are performed by prepositional phrases: *at home, from the town.*

Absolute expression. An "absolute" expression (also called *nominative absolute*) is one which has a thought relationship, but no grammatical relationship, with the remainder of the sentence in which it occurs. An absolute expression is usually composed of a noun or pronoun and a participle:

> *The tire being flat*, we decided to pump it up.
> *Two hours having elapsed*, we again set forward.

Abstract. A word or phrase is *abstract* when it is not concrete (definite and specific) in meaning. It applies to a quality thought of as being apart from any material object; *honor* and *beauty* are abstract words.

As a noun, *abstract* means a brief statement of the essential contents of an article, speech, book, etc. (See *Summary* and *Synopsis*.)

Abstract noun. The name of a thing not evident to one of the senses, such as a quality or condition: *honor, duty, happiness*.

Accent. This word has several meanings, two of which apply particularly to English speech or writing. We may say that someone has an *accent*, by which we mean his distinguishing regional or national manner of pronouncing or the tone of his voice (a Southern *accent*). *Accent* also means the emphasis (by pitch or stress or both) given to a particular syllable or word when speaking it. Thus we say "Please *accent* that word more clearly" or "The *accent* in the word *refer* is on the second syllable." As a noun, the first syllable of *accent* is stressed; as a verb either syllable may be stressed, according to the use of the word.

Accent mark. A mark used to distinguish between various sounds of the same letter. Thus we add a stroke above the letter *a* to show that it has a long sound as in the word *fāme*. Certain words in English require an acute accent, or grave accent, or circumflex accent, etc. An accent mark is related to *Diacritical mark*, which see, below, and *Accent mark*, Part IV, "Guide to Correct Punctuation and Mechanics."

Accusative case. A case name meaning the same as the *objective*, which see. The word is uncommon in English usage.

Active voice. The form of an action-expressing verb which tells that the subject of the verb performs or does the action. See *Voice*.

Adjective. An *adjective* modifies a noun or pronoun by describing, limiting, or in some other closely related way making meaning more exact. An adjective may indicate quality or quantity, may identify or set limits. Consequently, adjectives are of three general types: descriptive (a *black* dress, an *easy* lesson, a *smashed* thumb); limiting (the *sixth* period, her *former* home, *several* times); proper (an *American* play, a *Colorado* melon).

Some adjectives—indeed, most—have endings which mark them as adjectives. The more important of these include:

   y: muddy, stony, funny, dreamy, seedy
-*ful:* beautiful, faithful, hurtful, sinful
-*less:* faithless, timeless, lawless, guiltless
-*en:* rotten, golden, wooden, silken
-*able* (-*ible*): payable, desirable, permissible
-*ive:* permissive, constructive, excessive, decisive
-*ous:* vigorous, nervous, horrendous, marvelous
-*ish:* mannish, selfish, Danish, one-thirty-ish
-*al:* cordial, promotional, optional, deviational
-*ic:* metric, carbonic, Byronic, artistic
-*ary:* elementary, visionary, contrary, secondary
-*some:* lonesome, tiresome, handsome, bothersome

An adjective may modify a noun directly ("this *yellow* light thrown upon the color of his ambitions") or indirectly ("the survivors, *tired, hungry,* and *emaciated,* moved feebly toward the ship"). In sentences such as "The water felt *warm*" and "The corn is *green,*" each adjective is related to the subject, the word it modifies, by a linking verb. (A linking verb has little meaning of its own; it functions primarily as a connection between subject and predicate noun or predicate adjective.) In the sentences above, *warm* and *green* are called *predicate adjectives* or *complements,* both of which see. Also see *Attributive.*

Adjective clause. In the following examples each dependent clause is used as an adjective; each italicized group of words functions precisely as would a single adjective:

> The price *which he paid* was too much. (Clause modifies *price.*)
> People *who rarely think* should say little. (Clause modifies *people.*)
> You are the very person *whom I saw.* (Clause modifies *person.*)
> He is a man *I never admired.* (Clause modifies *man.*)

Adjective phrase. A phrase may modify a noun or pronoun, may function, that is, exactly as a single adjective functions; such a phrase is called an *adjective* (or *adjectival*) *phrase.*

> The farmers *in the West* need rain.

Here the phrase describes *farmers;* in its place the writer might have used a single adjective: "The *western* farmers need rain."

Adverb.   An *adverb* modifies a verb, an adjective, or another adverb. In "A distant bugle sang *faintly*," the adverb modifies the verb *sang*. In "We were *almost* ready to start," the adverb modifies the adjective *ready*. And in "Open this jar *very* slowly," the adverb modifies the adverb *slowly* (which, in turn, modifies the verb *open*).

Adverbs have the following characteristics:

1. Adverbs are commonly distinguished from corresponding adjectives by the suffix *-ly*: *bad, badly*; *sure, surely*; *easy, easily*.

2. Certain adverbs are distinguished from corresponding nouns by the suffixes *-wise* and *-ways*: *sideways, lengthwise*.

3. Certain adverbs are distinguished from corresponding prepositions in not being connected to a following noun:

   Adverb: He came *up*.
   Preposition: He came *up* the street.

4. Like adjectives, but unlike nouns and verbs, adverbs may be preceded by words of the *very* group (intensifiers):

   The *very beautifully* dressed girl. . . .
   He went *right* by.

Adverbial clause.   Dependent clauses function as *adverbs* in these sentences:

   I shall pay the bill *when you send it*. (Clause modifies the verb *shall pay*.)
   We are working harder *than you are*. (Clause modifies the adverb *harder*.)
   He was braver *than the other soldiers were*. (Clause modifies the adjective *braver*.)

   See *Adverbial clause* . . . , Part II, "Guide to Correct Sentence Structure."

Adverbial phrase. An adverbial phrase modifies a verb, an adjective, or an adverb and may function exactly like a single adverb.

> The woman fell *on the sidewalk.*

Here the phrase states *where* the woman fell; it modifies *fell* even as a single adverb would.

Adverbs and adjectives, use of. Ordinarily, it is not difficult to determine when an adjective or adverb should be used. An *adjective* modifies only a noun or pronoun; an *adverb* modifies only a verb, adjective, or another adverb. This rule is simple enough, and yet misuse of adjective and adverb is frequent. A part of the confusion is caused by the fact that idiomatic usage permits constant violation of this fundamental precept.

Still more confusion comes from the fact that the form of a word does not always reveal whether it is an adjective or adverb; most words ending in *-ly* are adverbs, but *womanly* and *holy*, for example, are not. Again, some adjectives and adverbs have identical forms (*quick, little, early*), but these cause no trouble until you are called on to tell which is which. Finally, a few adverbs have two forms which differ in meaning (*sharp, sharply; late, lately,* etc.)

In formal writing, remember that if the term about which you are in doubt primarily modifies a noun or pronoun, the chances are that it should be an adjective. But if the term modifies or even loosely applies to a verb, it should be an adverb.

1. Do not use an adjective to modify a verb.

> *Wrong:* He talks too *rapid.* (*Rapidly* should modify the verb *talks.*)
> *Wrong:* He takes himself too *serious.* (Use *seriously.*)
> She dresses *neat* when he comes. (Use *neatly.*)

2. Do not use an adjective to modify another adjective.

> *Wrong:* He is a *real* good carpenter. (Use *really.*)
> That is a *strong* made box. (Use *strongly.*)

3. After such verbs as *appear, be, become, feel, look, seem, smell, taste,* etc., the modifier should be an adjective if it refers to the subject, an adverb if it describes or defines the verb.

Correct: The cake tastes *good.* (Adjective)

The girl looked *beautiful.* (Adjective)

She looked at him *angrily.* (Adverb)

She feels *strongly* that she was cheated. (Adverb)

The first two italicized modifiers are adjectives because they refer to the *subjects* of the sentences. The last two are adverbs because they modify *verbs.*

He looks *careful.* (Adjective: he appears to be a person who is careful.)

He looks *carefully.* (Adverb: descriptive of the verb *looks.*)

4. Be accurate in the use of words that may be either adjectives or adverbs and of adjectives that end in *-ly. Cheap, deep, far, fast, wrong,* etc., are both adjectives and adverbs. In addition, *cheap, deep,* and *wrong* also have *-ly* forms. Words such as *lovely, timely, manly, kindly, goodly,* etc., are adjectives. Consult a dictionary when in doubt.

Correct: This is a *fast* color. (Adjective)

He ran *fast.* (Adverb)

Wrong: He acted *manly.*

Correct: He acted *in a manly fashion.*

Affectation. Artificial behavior or manners intended to impress others. An *affectation* is a mannerism for effect which involves show or pretense. In language, it is most evident in pronunciation and in the use of words or expressions not customary for the speaker or writer employing them. For most people, "aren't I" is an affectation; so is the pronunciation of *been* as *bēn* (bean). Increasing the vigor and effectiveness of one's speech and writing is laudable, but deliberately trying to be different usually results in misunderstanding or confusion.

Agreement. This word means "being in unison or concord." It involves correspondence, or sameness, in number, gender, and person. Thus, when a subject agrees with its verb, they are alike in having the same *person* (first, second, or third) and *number* (singular or plural). Pronouns agree not only in person and number but also in gender (masculine, feminine, etc.). For extended discussion, see the two following entries.

Agreement of pronoun and antecedent. A pronoun does not always agree with its antecedent in case, but it should agree in *gender, number,* and *person.*

> The *woman* put on *her* hat. (Feminine, singular, third)
> The *women* put on *their* hats. (Feminine, plural, third)
> The *boy* misplaced *his* tickets. (Masculine, singular, third)
> The *boys* misplaced *their* tickets. (Masculine, plural, third)

1. Singular pronouns refer to singular antecedents.

> Each person present will please raise *his* hand.
> Everybody is expected to contribute *his* share.

In the sentence immediately above, *everybody* may refer to men and women. Only in colloquial English could you say "Everybody is expected to contribute *their* share." You may write "Everybody is expected to contribute his or her share," although this construction sounds somewhat artificial, even awkward. In grammar—and in few other situations and places—men are more important than women.

2. A pronoun agrees with the nearer of two antecedents.

> He loves anything and everybody *who* is connected with his work.
> He loves anybody and anything *which* is connected with his work.
> Either the plant or the flowers will lose *their* freshness.

3. A collective noun used as an antecedent takes either a singular or plural pronoun, depending upon the sense of the sentence.

> The crowd of men took off *their* hats. (The crowd acted as individuals.)
> The crowd of men was cheering *its* loudest. (The group acted as a unit.)

Agreement of subject and predicate (verb). Few problems of agreement between subject and predicate arise because English verbs (except *to be*) have one form for singular and plural and for all persons except the third person singular present. But the errors which do occur are important. Usually they appear when a writer or speaker is confused over the *number* of the subject because of other words or when he uses a verb to agree not with the grammatical form of a subject but with its meaning. In short, you need to know what the subject is and whether it is singular or plural.

1. A verb must agree with its subject in person and number.

> The *men speak* too rapidly. (*Men* and *speak* are in the third person and are plural in number.)
> *I agree* to your proposal. (*I* and *agree* are in the first person and are singular in number.)
> *He agrees* to your proposal. (*He* and *agrees* are in the third person and are singular in number.)

The statement above covers the general rule; however, study the following subsections to avoid errors.

2. A verb should not agree with a noun which intervenes between it and the subject.

> *Correct:* The *cause* for all the requests and demands *was* not apparent.
>
> *I*, the delegate, *am* the one to determine that.
>
> *I*, together with John and Mary, *am* going.
>
> The *boy*, as well as all the members of his family, *was* determined to stay.

3. Singular pronouns require singular verbs. These pronouns are singular: *each, everyone, everybody, anyone, anybody, someone, somebody, no one, nobody, one, many a one, another, anything, either, neither.*

> Each *has* his own money.
> Someone *is* speaking now.
> One of you *has* made a mistake.
> No one *sews* better than Peggy.

None (literally *no one*) may be followed by either a singular or a plural verb. Studies of the use of *none* by good writers and speakers have revealed that it is as frequently followed by a plural verb as by one in the singular, especially when the phrase which modifies *none* contains a plural noun (*none of the men*).

The "standard" rule, however, is that *none* requires a singular verb.

Agreement based on meaning and agreement based on grammatical form sometimes conflict. In this sentence, "*Each* of the boys in this group *is* sixteen years old," *each* and *is* are in grammatical agreement. But in "*Each* of the boys in this group *are* sixteen years old," *are* is plural because the meaning of "each of the boys" is construed to be "all of the boys." The same principle may be illustrated thus: "Everyone in the apartment house tuned *his* TV (*their* TV's) to that station." Careful speakers and writers follow grammatical agreement in such sentences; agreement based on meaning is widely employed but most appropriately in only informal speech and writing.

4. For nouns plural in form but singular in meaning, use a singular verb.

Authorities differ in their opinions about the number of many such nouns. A good rule, according to usage, is: When in doubt, use a singular verb. The following are nearly always used with singular verbs: *physics, economics, mathematics, news, politics, whereabouts, mechanics, ethics, mumps,* and *stamina.*

> Physics, they were told, *is* the study of heat, light, sound, mechanics, and electricity.

5. Subjects plural in form, which indicate a quantity or number, require a singular verb when the subject is regarded as a unit.

> Ten miles *is* too far to walk.
> Two from five *leaves* three.

6. Use a plural verb with two or more subjects joined by *and*.

> Both the house and the automobile *were* painted green.
> Behind the wall *stand* a house and a garden.

When the two subjects form a single thought or have a very closely related meaning, a singular verb is frequently used by good writers.

> My comrade and friend *was* present.
> The sum and substance of his remarks *is* clear.

7. Two or more singular subjects joined by *or* or *nor* require a singular verb.

   Neither John nor Henry *was* able to leave.
   Either Mark or Peter *is* certain to be there.

8. If the subjects differ in number or person, the verb agrees with the nearer.

   Neither Jack nor the other men *know*.
   Either they or I *am* at fault.

9. Relative pronouns referring to plural antecedents require plural verbs.

   Each of those who *are* there should listen carefully.
   He is one of the most able men who *have* ever been in the Senate.

10. If *only* or some similar qualifying word precedes *one*, the verb in the subordinate clause is singular.

    He is the *only one* of those present who *listens* carefully.

11. A verb does not agree with a predicate noun.

    The best part of the meal *is* the coffee and cigars.
    Coffee and cigars *are* the best part of the meal.

   Note that after the expletive *there* the verb is singular or plural according to the number of the subject that follows. Always use a singular verb after the expletive *it*.

    Fortunately, there *exist* (not *exists*) forces which can help us.
    There *were* (not *was*) baseball, tennis, and swimming.
    In the meadow there *stands* (not *stand*) a towering tree.
    It *is* (not *are*) the women who must decide.

12. A collective noun takes a singular verb when the group is regarded as a unit, a plural verb when the individuals of the group are regarded separately.

    The crew *has asked* him to appear at the meeting.
    The crew *are coming* on board in a few hours.
    The family *was named* Brown.
    The family *were seated* on the lawn.

Allegory. An *allegory* is a figurative treatment of one subject under the guise of another. Most often, allegory involves the presentation of an abstract or spiritual meaning under concrete or material forms. When you read an allegory you should get not only the apparent, or "front," meaning but also the hidden truth or tale which lurks behind it. Special forms of allegory are *fables* and *parables*, which see.

Alliteration. Repetition of an initial sound in two or more words of a phrase, sentence, or line of poetry: "Ada ambled across the avenue." In poetry, alliteration is often effective; in prose, it is usually considered an *affectation*, which see.

Ambiguity. An ambiguity is a word or other expression whose meaning is doubtful, uncertain, capable of being misunderstood or of being understood in more than one sense. Ambiguous expressions occur often in speech and writing; getting rid of them is one of the prime objects of all writers who wish to be effective. An antonym of ambiguity is *clearness* (clarity).

Americanism. This term means a word or phrase peculiar to the English language as developed in the United States. Americans use *er* in words such as *theater* and *center*; the English are much more likely to write *theatre* and *centre*. Americans double fewer consonants (*wagon, traveler*) than the English (*waggon, traveller*). In the United States we refer to an *elevator*, in England reference is to a *lift*.

Many minor differences exist between the language generally used in England and in the United States. Several learned books have pointed out these distinctions (A *Dictionary of Americanisms, The Dictionary of American English*). For Americans to adopt British methods of pronunciation, British spelling, and British vocabulary is generally an affectation. See *Briticism*.

Analogy. This word suggests "partial resemblance" and implies similarity in some respects between things otherwise unlike. In linguistics, *analogy* is the process by which new or less familiar words, constructions, or pronunciations conform with older ones. Thus, we form *energize* from *energy* by analogy with *apologize* from *apology*.

Reasoning by analogy can cause serious blunders in logic.

Trying to spell by analogy is hopeless: for example, *smile* and *aisle* rhyme but their spelling is quite dissimilar.

Analysis of a sentence.   Theoretically, you should be able to analyze a sentence both by words and groups of words—*if you know grammar.*

Consider the following sentence:

> The little old lady across the street is carefully knitting a sweater for her grandson, who is a newsboy.

A grammatical analysis of this sentence is as follows:

The is a definite article modifying the noun *lady*. *Little* and *old* are adjectives modifying the noun *lady*. *Lady* is a noun used as *subject of the sentence*. *The little old lady* is the *complete subject* of *is knitting*.

Across is a preposition introducing the prepositional phrase; *the*, a definite article modifying the noun *street*; *street*, a noun used as object of the preposition *across*. The entire prepositional phrase, *across the street*, is used as an adjective modifying *lady*.

Is is an auxiliary verb which with the present participle *knitting* forms the present progressive tense, active voice, and is the *predicate of the sentence*.

Carefully is an adverb modifying the verb phrase *is knitting*.

A is an indefinite article modifying *sweater*, which is a noun used as direct object of the verb phrase *is knitting*.

For is a preposition; *her*, the possessive pronoun, third person singular feminine, refers to *lady* and modifies *grandson*; *grandson*, a noun, is the object of the preposition *for*. The entire prepositional phrase, *for her grandson*, is used as an adverb, modifying *is knitting*, if we think of the phrase as being closely associated with and tied to the verb phrase *is knitting*; if, however, we think of *for her grandson* as closely associated with *sweater*, then both by logic and common sense we can call it a prepositional phrase used as an adjective modifying *sweater*.

Who is a relative pronoun, nominative case, referring to *grandson* and used as the subject of *is*; *is* is a linking verb; *a* is an indefinite article modifying *newsboy*; and *newsboy* is a predicate noun after a linking verb. The group of words, *who is a newsboy*, is an adjective clause modifying *grandson*.

The entire sentence is *complex* in its grammatical structure.

Anglicizing foreign words. English has been borrowing words and word roots from other languages for centuries. The process by which they are assimilated into English is called *Anglicizing*, that is, bringing them into some sort of conformity with English usage. Many borrowed words retain their foreign form and pronunciation (*hors d'oeuvre*); others are in a transitional stage (*maneuver, manoeuvre*); still others are so useful that they have almost replaced their English equivalent: *ersatz* for *substitute*.

Antecedent. *Antecedent* means literally "going before." The substantive (noun or pronoun) to which a pronoun refers is its antecedent.

> The *girl* has lost *her* gloves. (*Girl* is the antecedent of *her*.)
> *Men* were willing to stake *their* lives on the issue. (*Men* is the antecedent of *their*.)
> Remember that *pronouns* agree with *their* antecedents in gender, number, and person. (*Pronouns* is the antecedent of *their*.)

See *Agreement*.

Anticlimax. This word implies a sudden drop, a descent. The fall may be from the dignified and important to the trivial, from something sublime to something ridiculous, etc. In drama, it involves action which is in disappointing contrast to a previous moment of intense interest. In sentence structure, it involves arrangement of a series in order of descending importance or interest. See *Climax*.

Antonym. A word which is opposite in meaning to that of another word: *sad* is the antonym of *happy*; *small* and *little* are antonyms of *large*. See *Synonym*.

Apocrypha. The term *apocrypha* is specifically applied to fourteen books of the Bible which appeared in early Greek versions of the Old Testament but which were rejected later by Protestant reformers on the grounds that they were unauthentic and uninspired. The word is now applied to any works of doubtful authenticity or authorship. For example, some forty plays attributed at one time or another to Shakespeare are now considered a part of the "Shakespeare Apocrypha."

Appositive. A substantive added to another substantive to identify or explain it. The appositive signifies the same thing and is said to be "in apposition."

> One important product, *rubber*, this country had to import. (*Rubber* is in apposition with *product*.)
>
> More hardy than wheat are these grains—*rye*, *oats*, and *barley*. (*Rye*, *oats*, and *barley* are in apposition with *grains*.)

An appositive agrees with its substantive in number and case; it is set off by commas if its relationship is loose (nonrestrictive) and is used without punctuation if the relationship is close (restrictive). See *Restrictive and nonrestrictive clauses, phrases*, below, and *Commas to enclose*, C1, in Part IV, "Guide to Correct Punctuation and Mechanics."

Appropriateness. This term implies using words and constructions which are fit, suitable, proper. The appropriateness of language is determined by the subject being discussed, the situation or medium for discussion, the reader or listener, the writer or speaker. For further discussion, see *Levels of usage, Standard English*.

Archaism. The use of words and constructions once common in the language but now antiquated, old-fashioned. Examples: *enow* for *enough*; *gramercy* for *thank you*.

Argument. A reason or reasons offered for or against something. Argument refers to a discussion in which there is disagreement and suggests the use of logic and a statement of facts to refute or support a position or point. *Argument* is one of the *forms of discourse*, the others being *narration*, *exposition*, and *description*, all of which see.

Articles. The articles (*a, an, the*) may be classed as adjectives because they possess limiting or specifying functions. A and *an* are indefinite articles; *the* is the definite article: *a* phonograph, *an* error, *the* physician. The initial sound of the following word determines the choice of *a* or *an*: *an* is used before words beginning with a vowel sound (including silent *h*); *a* is used before consonant sounds (except silent *h*) and before initial vowels that have both consonant and vowel sounds.

> an apple   an hour   a hero   a European visitor

Asserting word. The *verb* is the only asserting word among the parts of speech. See V*erb.*

Assonance. A partial or approximate similarity of sound. *Assonance* occurs in words like *fate* and *make,* in which partial rhyme is achieved because the stressed vowel sounds are alike but consonant sounds are different.

Attributive. An adjective which stands next to the substantive which it modifies is called *attributive*: an *old* hat, a hat *old* and *crushed.* An attributive is contrasted with a *predicate adjective* which is related to its substantive by a linking verb: "The hat is *old.*" (See *Predicate adjective* and *Complement.*) Also, a noun modifying another noun is an attributive: *race* horse, *cube* root.

Autobiography. An account of a person's life written by himself is an *autobiography.* Carefully distinguish this term from *biography,* which see.

Auxiliary verb. This is a verb used to "help" another verb in the formation of tenses, voice, mood, and certain precise ideas. Examples: *be* (*am, is, are, was, were, been*); *have* (*has, had*); *do* (*does*); *can, could, may, might, shall, should, will, would, must, ought, let, need, dare.*

Frequently, auxiliary (helping) verbs add particular shades of meaning—usually of time or voice—to the main verb. Such combinations are usually called *verb phrases* (which see).

> On one of the lawns in the outskirts of the village a woman *was cutting* the grass with a motorized lawn mower.
> The man of the soil *has been pushed* more and more out of the American economy.
> A careful analysis of the oxygen content *should have been made* at the time.

Awkwardness. A general term of disapproval which implies clumsiness, ungainliness, lack of grace and smoothness. Unfortunately, it applies to far too many phrases and sentences.

Balanced sentence. A sentence so written that certain thoughts or ideas have similar phrasing for purposes of comparison, contrast, or emphasis. See *Sentence, arrangement of content,* below, and *Position and arrangement of words,* Part II, "Guide to Correct Sentence Structure."

Ballad. A simple narrative poem composed in short stanzas and adapted for singing. The term is often loosely applied to sentimental or romantic songs sung by "crooners" and popular TV personalities.

Barbarism. A word or expression not standard in a language as, for example, *youse* for *you.* See *Illiteracies.*

Belles-lettres. This term refers to the higher or finer forms of literature. In the broadest sense, the term *literature* includes any type of writing on any subject: e.g., the literature of botany. Usually, however, *literature* is used to refer to artistic writings of a country or period characterized by beauty of expression and form and by universal appeal. *Belles-lettres* is the term applied to such writing.

Bibliography. A list of sources of information on a given subject or of literary works of an author. Do not confuse this word with *biography,* which see.

Big words. These are polysyllabic or learned expressions unsuitable for most writing. Use direct and simple words wherever possible: *home* for *domicile, barbershop* for *tonsorial parlor,* etc.

Biography. An account of a person's life described by someone else. It means "life story" and should not be confused with *bibliography,* which see. *Autobiography* means "memoirs of one's life written by oneself."

Blend. This refers to a mixing, fusing, or mingling of elements or varieties, as a *blend of tea.* In language, it means a word or construction formed by fusing two or more words: *motel* from *motor hotel, radioration* from *radio oration.* Some blends have been accepted in standard English; others have not. See *Portmanteau word.*

Boner. A slang term for "a stupid mistake," "a silly blunder." The person who referred to the "plastic" in his socks committed a blunder by not writing "elastic."

Book review. A critical discussion of a book, especially of a newly published one, is a *book review*. Such a review usually contains some indication of the contents of the book being discussed and some comment on the author's purpose, style, and accomplishment.

Briticism. A word, phrase, or construction peculiar to British English, as *petrol* for *gasoline* (motor fuel). See *Americanism*.

Bromide. An unusually dull *platitude*, which see.

Burlesque. A *burlesque* is a literary or dramatic composition which vulgarizes lofty material or treats ordinary material with mock dignity. That is, *burlesque* is a ludicrous take-off or debasing caricature. In the United States, the term is applied to a theatrical entertainment displaying coarse and often crude dancing and comedy.

Business English. The forms, conventions, idioms, and customs peculiar to communication in trade and industry. It is, or should be, merely standard English applied to the specific needs of industry and trade. However, its mechanical forms are so fixed and standardized that reference to a book on the subject is required for thorough knowledge.

Cacophony. A harsh, jarring sound. Generally considered discordant are words like *flak* and *clack*, *hiss*, *wrangle*, *gutter*, and *gaseous*. The antonym of *cacophony* is *euphony*, which see.

Cant. Originally the whining speech and secret slang of beggars, *cant* has been extended to mean the special words used by those in any particular occupation, sect, etc. A synonym is *shoptalk*, which see. *Cant* also means "insincere or meaningless talk."

Case. *Case* is one of the forms that a noun (or pronoun) takes to indicate its relation to other words in the sentence. There are only three cases in English: nominative (subjective); genitive (possessive); and objective (accusative).

A noun or pronoun is in the *nominative* case (subject of a sentence) when it indicates the person or thing acting; in the *possessive* case when it denotes the person or thing owning or possessing; in the *objective* case when it indicates the person or thing acted upon. There is no change in the *form* of a noun to denote the nominative and objective cases. Word order in the sentence provides the only clue:

> The child rode his tricycle. (*Child* is in the nominative case, *tricycle* in the objective.)
> The tricycle was ridden by the child. (*Tricycle* is in the nominative case, *child* in the objective.)

The possessive case does involve a change in the form of a noun. See *Genitive (possessive) case*.

Also, see *Nominative case* and *Objective case*. The distinction between these two cases affects only pronouns, since nouns have a *common* case (both nominative and objective).

Character.   This is a term commonly applied to a person represented in a play, novel, short story, or other literary composition. In drama, it may refer specifically to a particular part or role.

Circumlocution.   A lengthy, indirect, roundabout way of expressing something. An effective and clear synonym for this term is *deadwood*; a pedantic synonym is *periphrasis*. See both terms. Vigorous and emphatic sentences are lean and direct; they contain no wordy expressions. "The sort of lightweight metal they employ in the making of kitchen utensils" can be more directly expressed by the single word *aluminum*.

Citation.   The act of quoting is called *citation*. The term also means "a reference to an authority or a precedent." A *footnote* (which see) is usually a citation.

Classicism.   This term is applied to literature and other arts when they are characterized by simplicity, regularity, restraint, balance, proportion, and controlled emotion—as opposed to the freedom and enthusiasm of *romanticism*, which see.

Clause.   A *clause* is a group of words which has both subject and predicate. Clauses are of two kinds: *independent* (or *main*, or *principal*) and *dependent* (or *subordinate*).

See *Adjective clause* and *Adverbial clause*, *Dependent clause*, *Independent clause*, *Noun clause*, and *Restrictive and nonrestrictive clauses*.

Clearness.   Freedom from haziness and muddiness; intelligible, easily grasped, not capable of misinterpretation. *Clearness* is the single most important quality of good writing because it, more than any other characteristic of language, aids in communicating thought from writer and speaker to reader and listener. Clarity is the result of many positive language constructions and the avoidance of many faults. Perhaps in this order, your writing and speaking should be *clear, effective,* and *correct.* See *Ambiguity* and *Coherence.*

Cliché.   An expression or idea which has become trite, hackneyed, weak through constant repetition.

The origins of the words *triteness, hackneyed,* and *cliché* are illuminating: the first comes from the Latin word *tritus,* the past participle of *terere,* which means "to rub, to wear out"; *hackneyed* is derived from the idea of a horse, or carriage, let out for hire, devoted to common use, and thus worn out in service; *cliché* comes from the French word *clicher,* meaning "to stereotype."

Thus clichés resemble slang because both are rubber stamps, "stereotyped plates" of thought and expression. They may be tags from common speech, or overworked quotations, or outworn phrases from newspapers. They save the writer the task of thinking exactly what he means, but their use results in writing both stale and ineffective. Such words and phrases may seem humorous; they are, indeed, often used for humor or irony. Used seriously, they suggest that the speaker, or writer, is naive.

Familiarity with trite words and expressions is likely to cause them to occur to us more readily than others which are more effective. Look suspiciously upon each word or phrase which leaps to mind until you can be certain that the expression is exact and unhackneyed. Words and phrases which do not seem trite to us may be clichés to any reader or listener more familiar than we with overworked expressions.

Climax.   A series of ideas or events arranged or occurring progressively so that the most forceful comes last. In plays, *climax* means the turning point of the action. In sentence construction, *climax* means the arrangement of a series of words, phrases, clauses, or even sentences in an order of increasing value or force. See, also, *Anticlimax.*

Cognate.   This word means "related by family," "having the same ancestor." Thus we say that English *apple* and German *Apfel* are cognates, or cognate words.

Coherence. The order and consistency of thought or of statements. *Coherence* means "holding together." Writing is coherent when its parts (words, phrases, clauses, sentences, paragraphs) have been so carefully woven together that a reader is never confused about the relationship of ideas. Like *clearness* (which see), coherence is a fundamental but somewhat elusive quality of good writing.

Coinage. Anything made, invented, or fabricated. In language, the word means an expression created to express a particular shade of meaning or a different concept or object. For example, *Kodak, Wheaties, honk, snafu, beatnik, handyma'am, marketize, slanguage, brunch,* are coinages. All recent coinages are called *neologisms* (which see); many coinages are slang words not acceptable in standard English.

Collective noun. The name of a group of individuals considered as a unit: *audience, class, jury.* See *Agreement of pronoun and antecedent,* Rule 3, and *Agreement of subject and predicate (verb),* Rule 12.

Colloquialism. A colloquialism is a conventional expression which is permissible in, and frequently indispensable to, an easy, informal style of writing and speaking. If it is used only in familiar talk and informal writing, there is no objection. Colloquialisms are necessarily used even in the formal writing of dialogue to aid in developing the characteristics of speakers.

Dictionaries mark words as colloquial (*Colloq.*) when in the judgment of the editors they are more common in speech than in writing or more appropriate in informal than formal discourse. Because editors differ in the interpretations of their findings and because formal English has a far wider range than formerly, this label may apply to many kinds of words.

The best test for the use of colloquialisms is *appropriateness* (which see). No objective test or exact rule will enable you to determine when colloquialisms may be used. Certainly it is better to employ them than to avoid them if there is no other way to keep from seeming artificial and awkward. But in formal, well-planned writing they should be avoided unless they are deliberately used to achieve some stylistic effect. Consult the dictionary to determine what words are considered colloquial.

Some words are colloquial in all their meanings; others are colloquial only in one or more of various meanings.

Examples (avoiding as do dictionaries and linguists any attempt to indicate their comparative ranking):

> *angel* (financial backer), *brass* (impudence), *freeze* (stand motionless), *jinx, enthuse, phone, ad, gumption, cute, hasn't got any, brass tacks* (facts), *show up, try and, take a try at, alongside of, flabbergast*

Common case. See *Case.*

Common noun. A noun referring to a member, or members, of a general group: *automobile, coat, hat, street.*

Comparative degree. See *Comparison.*

Comparison. The change in the form of an adjective or adverb to indicate greater or smaller degrees of quantity, quality, or manner. The change is commonly indicated by the endings *-er* and *-est* or by the use of adverbial modifiers: *more, most, less, least.* The three degrees of comparison are *positive, comparative,* and *superlative.*

large	larger	largest
slow	slower	slowest
slowly	less slowly	least slowly
wise	wiser	wisest
wisely	more wisely	most wisely

Some comparisons are irregular: *good, better, best; little, less, least.*

Some adjectives are logically incapable of comparison because their meaning is absolute: *perpendicular, unique, excellent,* etc. Only in informal speech and writing can something be *more impossible* or *more final* or *more fatal* or *more round.*

Comparative degree is used to show relationship between two persons, objects, or ideas:

> Fred is *taller* than I.
> This box is *less full* than the other one.

Superlative degree is used to show relationships among three or more:

Alan is the *smartest* one in his family.
The sewing kit is the *most attractive* of the six available.

Complement. A word or expression used to *complete* the idea indicated or implied by a verb. A *predicate complement* (sometimes called *subjective complement*) may be a noun, a pronoun, or an adjective which follows a linking verb and describes or identifies the subject of the linking verb.

This book is *a novel*.
The leaves of this tree are *red*.

An *object complement* may be a noun or adjective which follows the direct object of a verb and completes the necessary meaning:

We are painting our house *gray*.
Our neighbors named their baby *Maryann*.
The bowling team elected Schmidt *captain*.

Complex sentence. A sentence containing one independent clause and one or more dependent clauses. See *Sentence, grammatical structure of*.

Composition. A *composition* is a literary, musical, or artistic product which usually reveals care in its formulation and plan. It may refer to any piece of writing with a definite *theme* (which see) and may be an *esssay, short story, book review*, etc., all of which see.

Compound-complex sentence. A sentence containing two or more independent clauses and one or more dependent clauses. See *Sentence, grammatical structure of*.

Compound object. See *Object*.

Compound predicate. See *Predicate*.

Compound sentence. A sentence containing two or more independent clauses. See *Sentence, grammatical structure of*.

Compound subject. See *Subject*.

Conciseness. This term refers to the quality of brevity, terseness. Writing is *concise* when it expresses much thought in **few** words. Succinct writing is both brief and comprehensive. **The**

word *concise* comes from Latin *concisus*, which means to "cut off." Since all of us write somewhat wordily, we must edit (cut) our writing to make it concise.

Concreteness. Concrete words, in contrast to abstract terms, are those that name objects or persons which can be seen, touched, etc.—*train, filing clerk, store, apple.* Each of these words has at least a slightly different meaning for each of us, but they have a "core" of reality which is readily understood. And yet your idea and mine of such abstract words as *goodness, duty,* and *sophistication* may differ widely. For this reason, concrete words are more exact than abstract ones, and concreteness is a highly valued quality in writing.

Concrete noun. A noun referring to an object evident to one of the senses of sight, hearing, taste, etc.: *trousers, hymn, tea,* etc. This is contrasted with an *abstract noun,* which see.

Conjugation. The changes in the form and uses of a verb to show *tense, mood, voice, number,* and *person.* See these five terms in this section.

Conjunction. A *conjunction* is a linking word used to connect words or groups of words in a sentence. Conjunctions are of two main kinds: *co-ordinating,* which join words or groups of words of equal rank, such as *and, but, for, or, nor, either, neither, yet; subordinating,* which join dependent clauses to main clauses, such as *if, since, because, as, while, so that, although, unless,* etc.

Certain co-ordinating conjunctions used in pairs are called *correlative* conjunctions. Most frequently used of these are *both . . . and; either . . . or; neither . . . nor; so . . . as; whether . . . or; not only . . . but also.*

Another kind of conjunction is the *conjunctive adverb,* an adverb used as a connective. Examples are *accordingly, anyhow, indeed.*

Conjunctions, particularly those which are to join clauses, must be chosen with care, for they always show logical relationships of ideas. Often a careless writer will use *and* where the relationship of clauses needs to be more accurately expressed, probably by use of subordination. Compare emphasis and meaning in these sentences:

The search for the chemical formula has been rewarding, *and* further investigation will make the rewards even greater.

Although the search for the chemical formula has been rewarding, further investigation will make the rewards even greater.

Conjunctive adverb. A certain kind of *adverb* (which see) that can also be used as a conjunction co-ordinating two independent clauses: *also, thus, furthermore, nevertheless, however, besides, therefore, so, consequently, hence, likewise, still, then, moreover,* etc. See *Conjunction.*

Connective. A word used to connect (join) words, phrases, clauses and sentences, such as conjunctions and prepositions.

Connotation. This word applies to the overtones of words— values and meanings which are suggested rather than specifically expressed in a dictionary definition. For example, San Francisco is "a seaport city in northern California," but the name itself has such connotations as "Golden Gate," "Chinatown," "Barbary Coast," "Gateway to the Orient," and "Earthquake of 1906." Connotative words have implied, suggestive, associated meanings, in contrast to *denotative* words. See *Denotation.*

Consonant. In *phonetics* (which see) a *consonant* has a sound in which the breath is somewhat restricted or even stopped. Consonant sounds may be contrasted with *vowel* sounds, which are made with less friction and fuller resonance. The vowels in our alphabet are *a, e, i, o, u,* and sometimes *y.* All the other letters are consonants: *b, c, d, f,* etc. See *Vowel.*

Contents. This word means "that which is contained." When we speak of the *contents* of a book, for example, we mean the sum total of its message and meaning. The phrase *table of contents* means a tabulated, condensed summary; a systematic outline of the contents of a book. The phrase *table of contents* is often confused with *index,* which see.

Context. This word means the parts of a piece of writing or of speech which precede or follow a given word or passage with which they are directly connected. If we say that such and such a passage in a novel is obscene but that in its *context* it is essential and not shocking, we mean that what comes before or follows provides meaning that is important, even essential, to understanding and judgment.

Contraction. A shortened form of a word, such as *can't* for *cannot*, *I'll* for *I shall* or *I will*. Most contractions seem out of place in standard English except when used to convey the actual tone and flavor of dialogue.

Co-ordinating conjunction. A conjunction (which see) relating words or phrases or clauses of equal grammatical value or importance.

Co-ordination. This word means "harmonious combination," "due ordering or proper relation." In grammar, it involves the relationship between two or more elements of the same grammatical rank. See *Co-ordinating conjunction*.

Copula. See *Linking verb*.

Correlative conjunction. Common correlative conjunctions (co-ordinating conjunctions used in pairs) are *either . . . or, both . . . and, neither . . . nor, not only . . . but also*. Each member of the pair should be followed by the same grammatical phrasing.

> Both Joy *and* Tommy are natives of Massachusetts. (Nouns are co-related.)
>
> My work tools were *neither* at home *nor* at the plant. (Prepositional phrases are co-related.)

Counter word. This expression, itself a *coinage* (which see), means a term which is used in a vague sense of approval or disapproval but without any exact meaning. Many counter words are slang and all are trite (see *Triteness*). Examples: *swell, lousy, nice, terrible, ghastly, cool*. *Counter words* are prevalent in advertising and colloquial speech but are not suitable for standard writing.

Criticism. The act or art of passing judgment is called *criticism*. The word comes from a base meaning "skilled in judging," and, contrary to popular opinion, does not mean only fault-finding. *Criticism* is evaluation and may be favorable or unfavorable. A **form of** criticism is the *book review*, which see.

Dative case. In some inflected languages, this case has as its main function that of representing the indirect object of a verb. There is no dative case, as such, in English. Normally, we show the dative case (indirect object) by means of a preposition (*for, on, to*) followed by the common case form for nouns and the objective (accusative) case for pronouns.

Deadwood. This word actually means, of course, dead wood on trees and, by extension, has come to mean anything which is useless or burdensome. In writing, it is a convenient label for wordiness and is applied to words and phrases which add little or nothing to the sentence in which they appear:

> *This is a topic that* may be written *This topic*
> *The fact that I came* may be written *My coming*
> *In the year of 1960* may be written *In 1960*

Declarative sentence. A sentence which states a fact, a possibility, a condition. See *Sentence, meaning and purpose of.*

Declension. The changes in the form or use of a noun or pronoun to indicate case, number, and person. *To decline* means to give these grammatical changes.

	SINGULAR		PLURAL		
Nominative:	man	I	who	men	we	who
Possessive:	man's	my, mine	whose	men's	our, ours	whose
Objective:	man	me	whom	men	us	whom

Deductive reasoning. This term comes from the word *deduction*, which means "the process of drawing a conclusion from something assumed or known." *Deductive reasoning* and *inductive reasoning* (which see) are alike in that they both refer to processes of reasoning, but they are quite different in meaning.

In deductive reasoning, an accepted general statement, which may be true or false, is applied to a particular situation or case. For example: "All horses are animals; this is a horse; therefore, this is an animal." In inductive reasoning, a set of individual particulars is studied experimentally and, from observations made, a general principle is drawn or formed. Example: "Every horse I have seen has four legs; therefore, I can expect all horses to have four legs."

Deductive and inductive order describe methods of organizing mental processes used in developing an idea.

Definite article. See *Articles*.

Degree. See *Comparison*.

Demonstrative pronoun. A *demonstrative* pronoun points out and identifies. It is declined (that is, inflected) for number but not for gender or case. The most important demonstrative pronouns are *this, that, these, those, such*.

> *This* is the way to clean a window.
> *That* is my new television set.
> *These* are your books; *those* on the desk are mine.

Denotation. The exact, literal meaning of a word as contrasted with its *connotation*, or suggestive meaning. Thus, *home* has a denotative meaning of "house," "apartment," "fixed dwelling place." Its connotation might be "refuge," "place of peace," "retreat," "haven of rest," etc. See *Connotation*.

Dependent clause. A *dependent clause* is not capable of standing alone; it depends upon the remainder of the sentence for its meaning; it is subordinate. Dependent clauses function as *nouns, adjectives,* or *adverbs*. Like an independent clause, a dependent clause contains a complete predication (subject and verb), but it shows its dependence by the linking word which joins it to the independent clause.

Description. Representation by written or spoken words. To *describe* someone or something is to convey an impression or image which reveals the appearance, nature, and attributes of the person or thing described. *Description* is one of the four *forms of discourse*, which see.

Determiner. English has an indefinite number of small word classes which are called *determiners*: words which "pattern" with nouns and signal that a noun is to appear. Such words as *his, the, that, my, one*, etc., are determiners.

Diacritical mark. A diacritical mark, point, or sign is attached to a letter or character to distinguish it from another of the same form or to give it a particular phonetic value, indicate stress, etc. For example, diacritical marks are used to show the sound of *a* as in *cär* and *a* as in *āble*. Every good dictionary employs diacritical marks: study those in your dictionary until you are thoroughly familiar with them.

Diagraming. This is a mechanical device by which you are aided in identifying words as parts of speech, in identifying phrases and clauses, and in indicating the uses or functions in a sentence of these words, phrases, and clauses. These purposes are accomplished through the use of lines: horizontal, perpendicular, slanting, etc. The practice of diagraming was once the principal method of studying sentence structure. For a detailed discussion, see Appendix, "Sentence Diagraming." Also see *Analysis of a sentence*, p. 275.

Dialect, dialectal. A *dialect* is the speech customs (pronunciation, vocabulary, grammatical habits, etc.) characteristic of a region. Thus we might refer to Scotch (Scots) dialect or mountaineer dialect, etc.

Dialectal is an adjective which applies to dialect words. An expression is dialectal when it attracts no notice in the region where it is used but seems out of place elsewhere. *Localisms* and *provincialisms* (which see) are dialectal words.

Dialogue. Conversation, talking together. *Dialogue* (also spelled *dialog*) refers to the passages of talk in a story, novel, play, etc. Fixed rules apply to the paragraphing and punctuation of dialogue; see appropriate entries in Part IV, "Guide to Correct Punctuation and Mechanics."

Diction. The choice and use of words for the expression of ideas. *Diction* comes from Latin *dictio*, meaning "saying," "word." You are familiar with this root word; it appears in *dictionary*, *dictate*, *dictator*, and *dictaphone*.

Because there are many words to choose from, because many ideas require expression in different shades of meaning and emphasis, and because errors must be avoided, diction is troublesome for most writers and speakers. And yet all good writing and speaking depend upon good diction. Just as a sound builder carefully selects materials for the construction of a house, so must the writer make a real effort to choose carefully the words, the basic materials, which he uses. Effective communication, the primary aim of all writing and speaking, is impossible without effective choice and use of words.

Dictionary. A book containing a selection of words, usually arranged alphabetically, concerning which information about meanings and a wealth of other material is given. A dictionary is not an arbiter of what we should say or write; it is a *record* of the language and is indispensable to both writer and speaker.

Suitable dictionaries are what economists refer to as "durable goods." When you purchase a good dictionary, you should expect to keep and use it for many years. It is unwise to buy a "cheap" dictionary when an excellent one can be purchased for only a few dollars and its price can be amortized over a long period. A pocket dictionary is almost worthless, except as a flimsy guide to spelling and pronunciation. Equip yourself with a sufficiently large dictionary (approximately 100,000 entries) published by a reliable firm. Examples of such dictionaries are

The American College Dictionary
Webster's Seventh New Collegiate Dictionary
Webster's New World Dictionary
The Concise Oxford Dictionary
Funk & Wagnalls Standard College Dictionary
The Random House Dictionary of the English Language, College Edition
The American Heritage Dictionary of the English Language

Excellent larger dictionaries are preferable to those mentioned above except that they are more expensive and difficult to carry.

Digest. A *digest* is an abridgment of an article, book, etc., or an organized arrangement of topics under heads and subheads, as "a magazine containing *digests* of articles" and "a *digest* of criminal law." This term is related to *abstract* (as a noun), *summary*, and *synopsis*, all of which see.

Digraph. A group of two letters representing a single speech sound: *ea* in *meat*, *th* in *then*, etc.

Diphthong. A speech sound of the vowel class made up of two sounds gliding from one to the other; the sound ends so differently from its beginning that two letters are needed for adequate representation: *ou* representing *ä* + *oo*.

Direct address.   In this construction, also called the *vocative*, the noun or pronoun shows to whom speech is addressed:

> *Paul*, where are you?
> When we finish rolling the court, *Fred*, we'll still have time for two sets of tennis.

Direct quotation.   A quotation which reproduces the exact words written or spoken by someone.

> Father wrote, "I'll be there on Friday."
> "Please use your dictionary more often," the office manager said.

Dissertation.   This is a formal discourse, a written *essay* (which see) developing a *thesis* (which see). It is usually characterized by rigid form and is especially used to refer to the type of research paper prepared by candidates for the degree of Doctor of Philosophy.

Division of words.   This phrase means the marking off, or separation, of the parts of a word. These parts are *syllables* (which see), a letter or group of letters constituting the smallest possible portion of speech and writing. Definite rules exist for the breaking of words at the ends of lines; this division is more a printing problem than one in writing.

Drama.   A *composition* in *verse* or *prose* presenting in *dialogue* or *pantomime* a story involving conflict or contrast of character. Such a composition is usually designed for presentation on a stage and is called "a play." See in this glossary the five words italicized in the foregoing definition.

Economy.   In writing, this term involves the clear transmission of thoughts and ideas from writer to reader with the fewest possible hindrances to understanding. Frugality in the use of words and prodigality in thought itself are the ideal. Unnecessary words, complicated constructions, and idiomatically unacceptable expressions all thwart economy. See *Deadwood*.

Editorial "we."   The use of "we" instead of "I" by a columnist or reporter. Its use is a convention of journalism but somewhat of an *affectation* (which see) and does not appear so often as it once did.

Effectiveness. That quality in writing which enables a writer to produce results intended or expected. The primary aim of all writing is clear communication from writer to reader. Writing is most effective which most nearly meets this ideal.

Elegant variation. Unwillingness to repeat words already used. It is a form of *jargon* (which see). A famed writer once cited Lord Byron as "that great but unequal poet," "the gloomy master of Newstead," "the meteoric darling of society," etc. Nearly all of us were once accustomed to reading of Joe Louis, the former prize fighter, as "The Brown Bomber," "The Detroit Menace," "The Tan Terror," etc. Such variation looks affected; it should be avoided.

Elegy. A mournful, melancholy, plaintive funeral song or poem is called an *elegy*, "a lament for the dead."

Ellipsis. The omission from a sentence of a word or words which would fulfill or strengthen meaning. To show such omission, *ellipsis periods* (. . .) are normally used; asterisks may also be used for this purpose, but ellipsis periods are preferred. Dashes may be used to indicate omitted words, but in special situations only. Apostrophes indicate omitted letters in contractions.

Elliptical clause. From *ellipsis*, a clause from which a word or words have been omitted; the omitted element is not needed because it is understood from other words or from context. An elliptical clause is occasionally an independent clause; usually it is a dependent clause with its subject and part of its predicate omitted, since these are clearly understood from the main clause. In the following examples, the words shown in brackets are often omitted in speaking and writing.

> Some of the patriots carried guns, others [carried] swords, still others [carried] clubs and sticks.
> While [we were] drifting downstream, we grounded on a sand bar.
> He was 40 years of age, his brother [was] 44 [years of age].
> Although [he is] in New York frequently, Father rarely goes to the theater.

Emphasis. Force of thought, feeling, action, or expression. In writing, emphasis depends less upon force than upon careful diction, position and arrangement of words, effective repetition, and the use of intensives. Emphasis is one of the most desired of all qualities in writing and speaking and one of the most difficult to define or obtain.

Emphatic verb form. Present or past tenses using the auxiliary verb forms, *do, does, did,* for emphasis.

> Though I *did* work and still *do* work, I make no progress.

English, standards of. The tens of millions of people who daily use English differ widely in every conceivable way. Obviously, then, their methods of communication must be on many levels. In order to be understood generally, English words must be in *present-day use* on a *national* (not merely local) basis and must be *reputable* (not socially frowned upon, faulty, obscene, etc.). Other than this, no standards of English can be absolute and final. Our language usage must often be modified by considerations of time, of place, of situation. See *Appropriateness*.

Our word choice is not inflexibly "good," "standard," or "substandard." English, like women's hats, is influenced by many changes of taste; with diction as with hats, appropriateness is the only worth-while test. See *Levels of usage, Standard English*.

Epic. An *epic* is a long, dignified narrative poem celebrating the deeds of a central hero. Loosely and inexactly, we refer to almost any imposing or grandiose motion picture or TV spectacular as "an epic."

Epigram. A witty, ingenious, pointed saying, tersely expressed. An example from Mark Twain: "The calm confidence of a Christian with four aces."

Epilogue. An *epilogue* is a concluding part added to a literary work. Usually it is employed to refer to a speech delivered by one of the actors at the conclusion of a play. See *Prologue*.

Epitaph. Brief writing on a tomb or mortuary monument. The most famous commemorative inscription in all literature may well be Stevenson's "Requiem," the last two lines of which are engraved on his tomb in Samoa:

> *Home is the sailor, home from sea,*
> *And the hunter home from the hill.*

Epithet. A descriptive name or title applied to a person or group; a word or phrase expressing a characteristic: *Khrushchev the Cruel*; a *black-hearted* bus conductor.

Essay. A short literary composition on a particular subject is called an *essay*. Originally the word "essay" meant "a weighing" or "an attempt." Consequently, an *essay* is an attempt to throw light on a subject or to reveal facts and show facets of it. If the mood and purpose of the essayist are light and personal, we call the result an "informal essay." If his purpose is more rigid and his style and form more fixed, his composition is called a "formal essay."

Etymology. The origin and development of a word; tracing a word back as far as possible by means of comparative *linguistics*, which see.

Eulogy. A speech or writing in praise of a person or thing, especially an oration in praise of a deceased person. The term always involves high praise and commendation.

Euphemism. The substitution of a mild, bland, inoffensive expression for a blunt or harsh one. "To depart this life" is a *euphemism* for "to die."

Euphony. Agreeableness of sound; a speech sound pleasing to the ear. *Euphony* is largely a negative quality in English prose; it consists of avoiding unpleasant sounds such as sibilants, guttural expressions, and the like. Euphonious words selected by some writers: *vermilion, melody, nevermore, cuspidor, cellar door, moonlight*. See *Cacophony*.

Euphuism. An affected style, artificial and high-flown, named after the title of a work by a sixteenth-century English writer, John Lyly. See *Affectation*.

Exact word. The precise and only expression called for in a given situation. For each idea there is a word or phrase which will more nearly express precise meaning than any other. Finding this exact word takes time, causes trouble, defeats many.

Exaggeration. The act of unduly magnifying, overstating, going beyond limits of truth. In writing, *exaggeration* is used not so much to deceive as to intensify or strengthen meaning: "starved" or "famished" for "hungry"; "a million thanks"; "abject adoration." See *Hyperbole*.

Exclamatory sentence. A sentence expressing strong feeling or surprise. See *Sentence, meaning and purpose of*.

Expletive. An expletive is a word or phrase added either to fill out a sentence or to provide emphasis. This latter function is performed by expressions which are exclamatory or profane. The more frequently employed function of the expletive is complementary, however; in this sense, *surely, indeed, why, yes*, etc., may be considered expletives. *It* and *there* are commonly used as expletives:

> *It* was Alice sitting there.
> *It* is a truism that men love freedom.
> *There* are four hundred people present.

Some grammarians further classify *it*. For example, Professor Paul Roberts (in *Understanding Grammar*) discusses "impersonal *it*," "situation *it*," and "expletive *it*," illustrating each as follows:

> *Impersonal:* It is raining.
> It is Wednesday.
> It snowed last night.
> *Situation:* It was Borg who started the trouble.
> It's Lois and the children.
> Was it the cat?
> *Expletive:* It is hard to believe that Clinton is sixteen.
> It is true that we were once great friends.

Exposition. A *form of discourse* (which see) that defines, explains, and interprets. As contrasted with other basic forms of discourse, *exposition* is all writing which does not primarily describe an object, tell a story, or maintain a position. It includes much of what we read: magazine articles, newspaper editorials, textbooks, etc.

Fable. A *fable* is a short tale or incident designed to teach a moral or stress an example. Animals or inanimate objects are usually involved as characters (the fox and the grapes, the tortoise and the hare). A *fable* is a form of *allegory*, which see.

Fallacy. A deceptive, misleading, or false notion or belief. In logic, *fallacy* refers to any of various types of erroneous reasoning which make argument unsound. See *Deductive reasoning* and *Inductive reasoning.*

In literature, especially poetry, the term *pathetic fallacy* is applied to "the attachment of human traits and feelings to inanimate objects or to nature": "angry sea," "a stubborn window."

Fiction. Works of imaginative narration are called *fiction.* The word "fiction" comes from a Latin word meaning "a feigning," "a fashioning" and implies a story invented to entertain, to instruct, or to deceive. *Novels, short stories,* and *drama* are dominant forms of fiction; see these terms in this glossary.

Figure of speech. A method of expression in which words are used out of their literal sense, or out of ordinary locutions, to suggest a picture or image: "She is an angel"; "eating like a pig." Among figures of speech are *hyperbole, irony, litotes, metaphor, metonymy, personification, simile,* and *synecdoche,* which see.

Fine writing. "Fine writing" is writing which is mistakenly thought to be free from all impurities because it has been brought to perfection; actually, it is affected or overcareful writing. It results from using pompous or polysyllabic words rather than direct, simple ones; from *euphemisms,* which see; from overuse of modifiers; from overuse of *foreign words* and *Anglicisms,* which see.

Finite verb. A verb form or phrase which serves as a predicate; it has number and person. Contrasted is the *nonfinite* verb form which cannot serve as a predicate. Such nonfinite forms are participles, gerunds, and infinitives. See *Verbals.*

Foot. A group of syllables constituting a metrical unit of a *verse,* which see. A "foot" may consist of from one to three syllables; a line of poetry (that is, a verse) may consist of from one to eight feet.

Footnote. A note or comment at the foot of a page, referring to a specific part of the text on the page. Regulations and mechanics for footnotes are fairly well established; consult a full-length manual if you have occasion to use them.

Foreign words in English. Our language has been borrowing words and expressions from other tongues for many centuries. Most borrowed words are now so much a part of our language that they can hardly be told from native expressions. Those not yet assimilated cause some trouble—in spelling, pronunciation, forming of plurals, etc. Words still considered to be foreign are so marked in dictionaries. Find out what system your dictionary employs for making this distinction. See *Foreign plurals*, Part III, "Guide to Correct Spelling."

Foreword. An introductory statement in a book. The words *introduction, preface,* and *foreword* each refer to material given at the front of a book to explain or introduce the book to the reader. An *introduction* is a formal preliminary statement or guide to the book; a *foreword* is usually more informal than an *introduction. Preface* and *foreword* have the same meaning, but the latter is more often used in the United States because of a partiality for native terms.

Formal English. The language and speech of formal occasions. Its grammar and sentence structure are correct; diction and pronunciation are careful, precise, proper. See *Levels of usage, Standard English.*

Forms of discourse. It is conventional to divide writing into four forms of discourse (communication of thought by words). The forms—*description, exposition, narration,* and *argument*—are rarely found in a pure or unmixed state; even a novel, which is basically narrative, usually contains much description and some exposition and argument. Each of the four forms is discussed at an appropriate place in this section.

Function words. This is a rather vague and general term applied to words which indicate relationships or point out grammatical functions but do not themselves contribute much to the meaning of a statement. Prepositions and conjunctions are the principal function words; also included are auxiliary verbs, some adjectives and adverbs, and relative pronouns.

Future perfect tense. The time of the action of a verb beginning in the present and ending at some time in the future. (By tomorrow I *shall have been* here one month.) See *Tense.*

Future tense. The time of a verb expressing "after now" or "after the present." (I *shall* go tomorrow.) See *Tense*.

Gallicism. French idiom or expression used in another language; a French linguistic peculiarity. Example: "I have hunger" (from French *J'ai faim*) or "It gives one furiously to think." See *Idiom*.

Gender. The gender of nouns and pronouns is determined by sex. A noun or pronoun denoting the male sex is called *masculine: man, boy, lord, executor, he*. A noun or pronoun indicating the female sex is called *feminine: woman, girl, lady, executrix, she*. Nouns which denote no sex are referred to as *neuter: house, book, tree, desk, lamp, courage*. Some nouns and pronouns may refer either to masculine or feminine and are said to have *common* gender: *child, individual, friend, doctor, visitor, it*.

Genitive (possessive) case. A noun or pronoun linked with a gerund should preferably be in the genitive case.

> He resents *your* having more than he.
> Joe sent the money without *my* asking him.
> She objected to the *manager's* being there.

This rule is not invariably followed by all good speakers and writers. The *best* usage requires the genitive case with a gerund, however, because it is always clear, whereas the objective is not. When the use of a possessive with a gerund causes awkwardness, recast the sentence.

Do not confuse the possessive-with-gerund and noun-with-participle constructions.

> I heard the manager's *appealing* for more spirit. (Gerund)
> I heard the manager *appealing* for more spirit. (Participle)

Do not attribute possession to an inanimate object; use an *of*-phrase.

> *Awkward:*   The *house's* roof was on fire.
> *Better:*   The roof *of the house* was on fire.

Do not follow this last rule implicitly if it violates good idiomatic usage. Such expressions as these are permissible and even preferable: *a day's work; an hour's time; a dollar's worth; at his wit's end; the law's delay; tomorrow's weather report.* See *Case*.

Gerund. The *gerund* is a verbal noun ending in *-ing* (*speaking, singing*). Because the gerund has the same form as the present participle, note the difference in their functions: the participle is a *verbal adjective;* the gerund is a *verbal noun.* A gerund can take an object and be modified by an adverb, and, as a noun, it can be the subject or object of a verb or the object of a preposition.

> *Playing* tennis is good exercise.
> All the campers enjoy *swimming.*

Glossary. A list of terms is sometimes called a *glossary.* The word is often used to denote a list of technical, dialectal, or difficult words in a subject or field of study; frequently the terms in a glossary are defined or illustrated, or both.

Gobbledygook. A colloquial or slangy expression characterizing language that is pompous, wordy, involved, and often unintelligible. Also spelled *gobbledegook,* the word is attributed to a former congressman grown weary of involved and circumlocutory governmental reports, etc.

Grammar. The science which deals with words and their relationships to each other. *Rhetoric* deals with the art of expressive speech and writing—with the laws of clear, effective writing; *grammar* is concerned with a consideration and account of the features of a language and with speech and writing according to various standards of usage but *not* according to *correctness,* as such.

Hackneyed language. Words and expressions made common, stale, and trite from repeated use. See full discussion under *Cliché.*

Historical present. The present tense used in narrating a past event as if it were happening at the time of narration. Not recommended for extended use; it soon grows wearisome.

Homograph. Two words which have the same spelling but different meanings, origins, and perhaps pronunciations: *air* (atmosphere) and *air* (melody).

Homonyms. Two words which have close or identical pronunciation but different meanings, origins, and frequently spellings: *pale* and *pail*; *sew* and *so*; *steal* and *steel*.

Humanism. This term characterizes any manner or system of thought in which human interests dominate. Emphasis is laid upon the importance of human concerns in this life rather than, as in the teachings of the Middle Ages, upon life in the here-after. *Humanism* should be compared with *naturalism* and *realism*, which see.

Hyperbole. An extravagant expression not intended to be taken literally, an obvious and deliberate exaggeration: "as old as time." See *Exaggeration*.

Idiom. The forms or variety of expression of a language, the characteristic way in which it is put together. In speaking of French idiom, for example, we refer to such a distinct usage as putting the adjective after its noun or the fact that an adjective in French has forms for singular and plural and for masculine and feminine gender.

An *idiom*, as distinct from *idiom*, is a structural form peculiar to a language. Normally, an idiom is an accepted word or phrase which violates grammar, or logic, or both.

Idiom is always familiar and deep-rooted. Many idioms defy grammatical analysis but, because they are sanctioned by current usage, are looked upon as correct. "How do you do?" is an accepted idiom, although an exact answer to the question would, of course, be ridiculous.

Not English alone but every language has its idioms, its peculiarities. French and German and Spanish idioms are difficult for us to understand and master, and many foreign expressions cannot be translated literally. In literal translation, the French say "Here one speaks French" and "We have come from eating"; the English equivalent is "French is spoken here" and "We have just eaten."

Likewise, idiomatic English is difficult not only for foreigners but for all who have not listened closely to the talk of acceptable speakers. For example, foreigners may have trouble with *the*, using it where English-speaking people omit it, and omitting it where we use it, as "When I came to the America, thing that impressed me most was vast distance between the New York and the San Francisco." Or we may tell a foreigner not to misuse number or concord by saying "many man," "many man is," "a salesmen," "ten foot," and then confuse him by saying, correctly, "many a man is," "a few salesmen," and "a ten-foot pole."

Despite the fact that idiom cannot be explained scientifically, idiomatic expressions are necessary short cuts in our language and make writing vigorous and picturesque. In fact, idioms are the essential material of which language is made: the widespread, everyday usage of people.

Idiomatic usage. The manner of expression characteristic of a language. See *Preposition*.

Illiteracies. Words and phrases not normally accepted in either colloquial or standard usage. Also called *barbarisms* and *vulgarisms* (which see), *illiteracies* are characteristic of uneducated speech, to be avoided in writing unless put into the mouths of people being characterized. Illiteracies are not necessarily coarse, are frequently effective, but should not be used without specific purpose.

Dictionary-makers apply different restrictive labels to "illiterate" or "vulgar" English. What may be marked *illiterate* in one dictionary may be termed *colloquial* in another. And because most dictionaries primarily record "standard" usage, many illiteracies are not listed at all.

The following words and phrases should be avoided: *ain't, to burgle, boughten, borned, losted, drownded, mistakened, disremember, irregardless, scairt, anywheres, nohow, nowheres, hisself, concertize, vacationize, kepted, hadn't ought, this here, couldn't of, being as, being as how, dassent, snuck* (past of *sneak*), *acrossed, fellers, ourn, brung, them there, them's* (those are), *drug* (past of *drag*).

Image, imagery. These words have several meanings, but in writing and speech they refer to words or groups of words used to make a reader or hearer form mental pictures or conceptions. *Images* may consist of *descriptions* and *figures of speech* (which see) and appeal primarily to the senses· "Time had some score of small voices in that shop, some stately and slow as was becoming to their great age, others garrulous and hurried. All these told out the seconds in an intricate chorus of tickings." From this imagery created by Stevenson we can hear and even feel clocks. See *Symbolism*.

Imperative.   The mood (mode) of a verb expressing a command or a request. See *Mood*.

Imperative sentence.   A sentence expressing a command or a request. See *Sentence, meaning and purpose of*.

Impersonal construction.   A method of phrasing in which neither a personal pronoun nor a person as noun is stated as the actor. The passive voice is used, or words like *it* or *there*.

> I have three reasons for my choice. (Personal)
> There are three reasons for this choice. (Impersonal)
>
> We must consider three proposals. (Personal)
> It is necessary to consider three proposals. (Impersonal)
> *or*
> There are three proposals to be considered.
> *or*
> Three proposals must be considered.

Impressionism.   *Impressionism* is a term used to describe the theory and approach in both literature and painting based upon the concept that objects should not be represented in detail but rather as they have *impressed* the writer or artist at the time of observation.

Improprieties.   Improprieties are recognized English words misused in function or meaning. The word constituting an impropriety is acceptable; its misuse causes an error.

A word may be transferred from one part of speech to another, but it should not be employed in its new function until sanctioned by good use. Examples of improprieties in function:

> Verbs used as nouns: *eats, an invite, a fix, a think, a combine* (combination)
> Nouns used as verbs: *to suspicion, to suicide, to author*
> Adjectives used as adverbs: *real* pretty, *sure*, *some* tall, etc.

A second class of improprieties includes words similar or somewhat similar to other words and used inexactly or wrongly for them: *hour, our*. Such words include *homonyms* and *homographs*, which see.

Indefinite article. See *Articles*.

Indefinite pronoun. *Indefinite* pronouns are somewhat less exact in meaning than other pronouns. Among the more frequently used indefinite pronouns are *another, any, anyone, anything, everybody, everyone, everything, few, many, nobody, none, one, several, some, someone*, and *something*. Compound forms built upon the pronoun *one* or the element *-body* take the possessive form (*anyone's, everybody's*).

Indention or **indentation.** Setting in, or setting back, as is done with the first line of a paragraph. See *Paragraph*.

Independent clause. An *independent clause* makes a complete statement and may stand alone; that is, it makes reasonable sense if the remainder of the sentence is omitted.

> *I watched* TV.
> Although I should have been working last night, *I watched* TV.

Sometimes there may be more than one independent clause in a sentence.

> *John worked*, but *I watched* TV.

Index. An *index* is a detailed alphabetical key to topics, names, and places in a book with reference to their page location. An *index* always appears at the end of a book and should not be confused with *table of contents*, which see.

Indicative. The mood (or mode) of a verb expressing a fact or what seems to be a fact. See *Mood*.

Indirect object. A noun or pronoun which precedes the direct object of a verb and before which the word *to* or *for* is understood. When an indirect object follows the direct object, a preposition (*to, for*) is actually used. See *Dative case*.

> Yesterday I bought *him* a coat.
> Yesterday I bought a coat for *him*.

Indirect question. Restatement by one person of a direct question asked by another.

> *Direct:* When will you pay me?
> *Indirect:* Joe asked when I would pay him.

Inductive reasoning. Drawing a general conclusion or principle from a group of individual particulars or observations. See *Deductive reasoning*.

Infinitive. An *infinitive* is a word which has the function of both verb and noun and which also may be employed as an adjectival or adverbial modifier. The infinitive is usually introduced by the sign *to* (*to* speak, *to* sing).

Like a *gerund* (which see), an infinitive can take an object and be modified by an adverb. Also like a gerund, an infinitive, in its function as a noun, can be the subject or object of a verb and the object of a preposition.

> I must *work* tonight. (Infinitive as part of predicate)
> *To succeed* in my job is my first aim. (Infinitive as noun)
> The person *to see* is the manager. (Infinitive as adjective)
> She is going *to tell* us of her recent trip. (Infinitive as adverb)

Infinitive phrase. A phrase introduced by an infinitive: *to work in the garden.* See *Infinitive*.

Inflection. A change in the form of a word to show a change in use or meaning. *Comparison* (which see) is the inflection of adjectives and adverbs. *Declension* (which see) is the inflection of nouns and pronouns. *Conjugation* (which see) is the inflection of verbs.

Informal essay. This term applies to *essays* (which see) that are usually whimsical, humorous, or satiric. The informal essay, also called "personal" essay and "familiar" or "light" essay, has no set form or length and may reflect any of numerous moods and feelings. The type is not so prevalent as it once was but still appears in magazines and newspaper columns.

Intensifiers. Adverbs such as *very, much,* and *too* sometimes intensify (strengthen) meaning; they are called *intensifiers*. The superlative of adjectives and adverbs also may be classed as intensifiers. See *Comparison.*

Intensive. A word or element used to strengthen, increase, or enforce meaning. For example, *certainly* and *tremendously* are adverbs used as intensives.

Intensive pronoun. A pronoun having the same form as the *reflexive pronoun,* which see.

Interior monologue. The extended thoughts, feelings, and reactions of a person as revealed through his subconscious or subliminal mind. *Interior monologue* is a synonym of *stream of consciousness,* which see.

Interjection. The eighth part of speech, the *interjection,* has two distinguishing qualities: (1) it has no grammatical connection with the remainder of the sentence; (2) it expresses emotion—surprise, dismay, disapproval, anger, fear, etc. Grammarians distinguish two kinds of interjections. First are those forms used only as interjections, never occurring otherwise in speech: *oh, ouch, tsk-tsk, psst, whew, alas,* etc. Some of these contain sounds not used otherwise in English and consequently difficult to represent in writing: *tsk-tsk* is an inadequate representation of the clucking sound made to indicate disapproval. Next are forms that occur sometimes as interjections and sometimes as other parts of speech: *goodness, well, my,* etc. The two groups are hard to separate, since many words now used only as interjections originate from other parts of speech: *alas,* for example, has its root in a word meaning "wretched."

Interlude. This term generally means an intervening episode, period, or space. Specifically, it is used to refer to entertainment between the acts of a play or, in music, to an instrumental passage beween the parts of a church service or drama.

Interrogative adverb. Adverbs used in asking a question: *where, when, how, why, whence,* and *whither.*

> *Where* is the nearest restaurant?
> *When* did you arrive?

Interrogative pronoun. An *interrogative* pronoun (*who, which, what,* occasionally *whoever, whichever, whatever*) introduces a question.

Who shall demand that a pardon be granted?
Which is the route we should take from Hammond?
What do you have in mind?

Interrogative sentence. A sentence asking a question and followed by a question mark. See *Sentence, meaning and purpose of.*

Intransitive verb. See *Transitive verb.*

Introduction. A preliminary statement; for fuller discussion, see *Foreword.*

Inversion. Reversal of the usual or natural order of words. The most common inversion is placing the verb before the subject:

"Came the depression and we . . ."

Irony. A figure of speech in which the literal (denotative) meaning of a word or expression is the opposite of that actually intended. *Irony, sarcasm,* and *satire* agree in indicating derision of someone or something. In *irony,* emphasis is upon contradiction: one thing is said but another is meant. "Lovely day, isn't it?" is an ironical remark when uttered during a blizzard. In *sarcasm,* emphasis is upon the harsh or cutting quality of what is said: "You couldn't catch a ball in a bushel basket." *Satire* essentially exposes or attacks vices and follies in a malicious or playful spirit: making a *satirical* comment on drivers who ignore traffic regulations. See *Sarcasm* and *Satire.*

Irregular verbs. Irregular verbs, sometimes called *strong* verbs, do not follow a regular pattern in forming their principal parts. Principal parts of irregular verbs are usually formed by vowel change: *see—saw—seen; drive—drove—driven; choose—chose—chosen.* Let the dictionary be your guide. See *Regular verbs.*

Jargon. Unintelligible or meaningless talk or writing; gibberish. Essentially, jargon violates the principle that we should use simple, understandable English. Some writers succeed in hiding what they really mean under a mass of pseudo-technical gobbledygook and tortuous phrases and sentence construction. Remember the comment which describes this fallacy: "the belief that nothing can be profound unless it is also obscure."

Joining words. The joining words among the parts of speech are *prepositions* and *conjunctions,* both of which see.

Journalese. A style of writing supposed to characterize newspaper usage. Good newspaper writing is terse, accurate, complete, and frequently employs relatively short sentences. Faults of some *journalese* are triteness, forced humor, neologisms, and occasional resort to polysyllabication. Some newspaper writing is wordy and lazy, but much is vigorous and effective, remarkably so since prepared under pressure of time.

Kinds of sentences. Sentences may be classified and named in several ways: periodic, loose, and balanced; simple, compound, complex, and compound-complex; declarative, interrogative, imperative, and exclamatory. See *Sentence, arrangement of content; Sentence, grammatical structure of; Sentence, meaning and purpose of.*

Levels of usage. Each of us employs a different level of usage depending upon whether we are speaking or writing, upon who are our audience and readers, upon the kind of occasion, etc. As Professor John S. Kenyon has pointed out, what are commonly grouped together in one class as different levels of language are false combinations of two categories: cultural levels and functional varieties.

Among *cultural levels* may be included narrowly local dialect, ungrammatical speech, illiterate speech, slovenly vocabulary and construction, exceptional pronunciation, excessive and unskillful use of slang, etc. On a higher level is the language used generally by cultured people over wide areas; it is both clear and grammatically "correct." These two cultural levels are *substandard* and *standard.*

Among *functional varieties* not depending upon cultural levels, Professor Kenyon mentions colloquial language (itself existing in differing degrees of formality or familiarity as in familiar conversation, private correspondence, formal conversation, familiar public address, formal platform or pulpit speech, public worship, legal writing, etc.). Functional varieties may be grouped in two classes: *familiar* and *formal* speaking or writing.

The term *level* does not properly apply to functional varieties:

colloquial, familiar, formal, legal, scientific, etc. As Professor Kenyon suggests, these varieties are equally suitable for their respective functions and do not depend on the cultural status of the users. See *Appropriateness* and *Standard English*.

Linguistics.   The science of language. English linguistics is a study of the structure and development of the English language and its relationship to other languages. Involved in linguistics are *etymology, morphology, phonetics, semantics,* and *syntax,* all of which see.

Linking verb.   Such a verb (also called a *copula, copulative verb, coupling verb,* and *joining verb*) does not express action but only a state of being or a static condition.

The *linking* verb is like other verbs in all respects except that the linking verb can stand between a noun and an adjective ("The man *looks* sick") and other verbs cannot. In present-day English there are scores of forms which may occur as linking verbs; among these are *be, feel, look, seem, taste, smell, become, appear, sound, get, remain, turn.* Other linking verbs occur only in a limited number of contexts: e.g., *slam* in "slam shut," *ring* in "ring true."

> The price *seems* high.
> He *feels* happy today.
> This *is* my desk.

Litotes.   A figure of speech in which something is expressed by denying the contrary: "not a few" means "many"; "not bad at all" means "good."

Localism.   A way of speaking (or acting) peculiar to one locality; a word, meaning, or expression in local use, as opposed to national acceptance. See *Provincialism*.

Loose sentence.   A sentence with its parts arranged so that its meaning is clear before the end of the sentence. See *Sentence, arrangement of content*.

Lyric.   Colloquially, the term *lyrics* is used to refer to the words of a song. More exactly, the word *lyric* refers to poetry having the form and musical quality of a song or characterized by strong feeling and emotion. *Lyric expression* is always subjective and highly emotional.

Magazine. *Magazine* comes from a base word meaning "storehouse." It means a publication normally appearing at stated periods (see *Periodical*) and containing miscellaneous articles or pieces in prose and verse.

Malapropism. Ridiculous misuse of words, usually resulting from confusion of words similar in sound but different in meaning: *progeny* for *prodigy*; fighting a *dual* (*duel*). The word comes from the name of a character in Sheridan's *The Rivals*—Mrs. Malaprop consistently misapplied words. See *Boner*.

Mannerism. Marked or excessive reliance upon, or addiction to, an unusual custom or trick; for example, using foreign words in English prose or using archaic words to achieve humorous effects. See *Affectation*.

Manuscript. Literally, a letter, report, document, book, etc. written by hand (from Latin words for "hand" and "writing"). *Manuscript* is now used to mean composition prepared by hand or on the typewriter, as contrasted with type.

Mechanics. The technical aspect of something as, in writing, the mechanical aspects of paragraphing, capitalization, use of italics, figures for numbers, etc.

Melodrama. A play or other dramatic spectacle which employs sensational or startling action. The language used in a melodrama is lurid, exaggerated, and highly emotional; intended effect upon the listener is one of horror or pity and sorrow.

Metaphor. A figure of speech in which a term or phrase is applied to something to which it is not literally applicable. This is done in order to suggest a resemblance: "She is a perfect lamb." *Metaphor* and *simile* are allied in meaning; a *simile* expresses resemblance directly but does so by using *as, as if, like*: "She is as sweet as a flower."

Unfortunately, most metaphors are either strained or trite. Many figures of speech are often "mixed"; standard advice is to sustain one figure and not suddenly shift to another: "We had the crankcase drained and thus nipped our trouble in the bud." See *Figures of speech*, *Mixed metaphor*, and *Simile*.

Meter. A poetic measure is called *meter*. It involves the arrangement of words in regularly patterned (metered) lines or verses.

Metonymy.   The use of the name of one thing for that of another to which it has some relation: "The White House" for "office of the Presidency," "bottle" for "milk" or "strong drink."

Middle English.   This term refers to the language spoken and written during the period from approximately 1100 to 1500 A.D. It differs markedly in pronunciation, spelling, and grammar from *Modern English* (our language since about 1500).

Mixed metaphor.   An incongruous assemblage of ideas, as "Pushing her along is the powerful magnet of advertising with its fangs of generalities." See *Figures of speech, Metaphor.*

Mode.   A term meaning the same as *Mood,* which see.

Modify.   To limit or describe or qualify a meaning in some other specific and closely related way, adjectives are used with nouns and pronouns and adverbs are used with verbs, adjectives, and other adverbs. Limiting: *five* acres, the *only* meal. Descriptive: *blue* skies, *large* houses.

Monologue.   Talk or discourse by a single speaker is called a *monologue.* For example, an entire poem may consist of the thoughts (speech) of one person; in a play, an actor may speak alone for a protracted period. See *Dialogue* and *Interior monologue.*

Monosyllable.   A word of one sylable, such as *yes, no, through.* See *Polysyllable* and *Syllable.*

Mood.   The mood (or *mode*) of a verb indicates the manner in which a statement is made. Thus, if we wish merely to express a fact or ask a question of fact, we use the *indicative* mood.

> The maple tree *is* tall. (Statement of fact)
> *Is* the maple tree tall? (Question)

If we wish to express a condition contrary to fact, or a desire, we use the *subjunctive* mood.

> If I *were* rich, I should give you the money. (Contrary to fact)
> Oh, how I wish I *were* rich! (Desire)

If we wish to give a command, we use the *imperative* mood.

Close the door, please.

The indicative and imperative moods are not troublesome, and the use of the subjunctive has largely disappeared. However, careful speakers and writers employ the subjunctive to express the precise manner in which they make their statements, when the indicative would not serve. *Were* and *be* are the only distinct subjunctive forms now in general use. Our speech still retains numerous subjunctive forms, however, in sayings handed down from times when this mood was more widely used: Heaven *forbid*, if need *be*, *suffice* it to say, *come* what may, etc.

1. As indicated above, use the subjunctive mood, not the indicative, to express a condition contrary to fact.

   If I *were* a king, I would have you decorated.
   If you *were* I, would you do it?

The subjunctive is used in expressions of *supposition* and to indicate that a condition is *highly improbable* even though not completely contrary to fact.

   He worked as if he *were* never going to have another chance.
   Suppose he *were* to ask you a question!
   If I *should be* too talkative, let me know.

2. Use the subjunctive in clauses introduced by *as though* or *as if* to express doubt or uncertainty.

   He talks as if he *were* the only intelligent person in the house.
   As though he *were* any smarter himself!

3. Use the subjunctive in *that*-clauses expressing necessity or a parliamentary motion.

   It is essential that he *appear* at the meeting of the committee.
   She insisted that I *come* to her office.
   I move that the chairman *be authorized* to proceed with the work.

4. Use the subjunctive mood to express a desire. (Wish, volition.)

She wishes that she *were* a man.
I desire that you *be* rewarded.

5. In parallel constructions do not shift the mood of verbs.

Wrong: If I *were* in your position and *was* not prevented, I should certainly go. (Change *was* to *were*.)

Differences between the indicative and subjunctive may be illustrated thus:

INDICATIVE	SUBJUNCTIVE
I take (am taken)	(if) I take (be taken)
you take (are taken)	(if) you take (be taken)
he, she, it takes (is taken)	(if) he, she, it take (be taken)
we take (are taken)	(if) we take (be taken)
I took (was taken)	(if) I took (were taken)
I am we are	(if) I be we be
you are you are	(if) you be you be
he is they are	(if) he be they be
I was we were	(if) I were we were

Morpheme. Any word or part of a word not further divisible into smaller meaningful elements: *boy*; *-ish* in "boyish"; *ad-* in "advice."

Morphology. The patterns of word formation in a language, including derivation and inflection. *Morphology* and *syntax* (which see) together form a basic division of grammar.

Mysticism. This is a term for somewhat obscure thought or speculation. It is applied to the beliefs and ideas of those who attempt to communicate directly with the Divinity or any other assumed supernatural power. Those who believe in a direct and intimate union of the soul with other-world or transcendent forces are called "mystics."

Naming words. The parts of speech which are *naming words* include *nouns* and *pronouns*.

Narration. That one of the *forms of discourse* (which see) which relates or recounts events; novels, short stories, plays, etc. are narration.

Naturalism. This term is applied to the attempt of an artist to represent objects in their everyday, natural form. This attempt to imitate nature is sometimes called *realism* (which see), but *naturalism* is more correctly used to refer to slavish efforts at reproducing details from life without any selection whatever ("photographic realism").

Neologism. A new word or phrase or a known word or phrase employed in a new meaning. See *Coinage.*

Newspaper English. Language thought to be characteristic of journalistic writing. See *Journalese.*

Nominative absolute. See *Absolute expression.*

Nominative case. The subject of a finite verb is in the nominative case.

> *I* should like to accompany you.
> *She* is an excellent cook.

A predicate complement is in the nominative case.

> It was *they*. (Not *them*.)
> Is it *she* who is going?
> That is *he*.

It is me and *it's me* are acceptable in colloquial speech and highly informal writing. *It is I* (*it's I*) is employed by careful speakers and writers.

Also, see *Case.*

Nominative or objective case, use of. Many errors arise from misunderstanding the *function* of the pronoun, particularly with *who* or *whom* and with *whoever* or *whomever*. In the following sentences, *who* and *whoever*, nominative forms, are correct because they act as subjects of the verbs in the dependent clauses.

> I demand membership for *whoever* wishes it.
> The question of *who* can ask for membership should not arise.

In the first sentence, *whoever* is a part of the dependent clause; it functions as the subject of the finite verb *wishes*. The whole clause is the object of the preposition *for*. Similarly, in the second sentence, *who* is the subject of the finite verb *can ask.*

These sentences illustrate proper use of *whom* and *whomever,* *objective* forms.

> This is the same man *whom* I saw at Oak Bluffs last summer.
> The first person *whom* I met was Martin Henderson.
> He asked *whomever* he knew.
> He told the same old story to *whomever* he met.

In these four sentences, the pronouns function in the dependent clauses as objects of the verbs. In the last sentence, notice that the whole clause is the object of the preposition *to.*

The nominative and objective cases are frequently confused because of intervening words. The case of a pronoun must not be influenced by words which come between the pronoun and its antecedent.

> He asked me *who* I thought would be chosen.
> *Who* do you suppose drew up these plans?
> She asked the question of the one student in the whole class *who* had not prepared the assignment.

An appositive should be in the same case as its antecedent.

> We, *you* and *I*, must leave at once. (Nominative)
> The man laughed at us, *you* and *me.* (Objective)

An elliptical clause of comparison, preceded by *than* or *as,* requires the case called for by the expanded construction.

> He is much taller than *I* (am). (Nominative)
> He is as strong as *I* (am). (Nominative)
> He terrified her as well as (he terrified) *me.* (Objective)
> The clown amused her as much as (he amused) *me.* (Objective)

Also, see *Case.*

Nonfinite verb.   See *Finite verb* and *Verbals.*

Nonrestrictive.   A modifier which does not limit but does describe or add information. See *Restrictive and nonrestrictive clauses, phrases.*

Noun.   A *noun* names a person, place, or thing, a quality, idea, or action. Common nouns name all members of a common group: *man, officer, city, building, state*. Proper nouns name particular members of a group: *Mr. Ward, Jefferson Davis, Dallas, Parthenon, Ohio*. Some common nouns are concrete: *book, candy, hammer, sweater*—names of objects which can be perceived by the senses of touch, sight, taste, hearing, or smell. Some are abstract nouns: *honesty, intelligence, grace, strength*—names of things which cannot be perceived by the senses. Some are collective nouns: *crew, family, assembly, union*—names used for groups considered as units.

Nouns have the following characteristics:

1. Nouns can be, and usually are, preceded by such words as *the, a, my, his, this, some, each* (determiners).

2. Most nouns can express the meaning "more than one" by various formal devices, the regular one being the addition of "s" (in speech, *-s, -z,* or *-iz*): *caps, cabs, edges.*

3. Certain groups of nouns have typical endings—like *-tion, -ness, -ment, -ure*—which distinguish them from corresponding verbs (e.g., *determination, determine*) or from corresponding adjectives (e.g., *goodness, good*).

4. Many nouns are distinguished from corresponding verbs by stress: *sub'ject, subject'.*

5. Nouns are also marked as such by their occurrence in a complicated but well-ordered set of positions: e.g., before the verb in statements; after prepositions; etc. Proper nouns are marked as nouns by position only. All other nouns are, or may be, marked by one of the other formal characteristics.

Nouns have *number*, singular or plural; *gender*, masculine, feminine, neuter, common; *person*, first, second, third; and *case*, a common form (for both nominative and objective) and a possessive form (genitive).

Noun clause.   In the sentence, "*What you paid* was too much," the dependent clause in italics is used as a noun, the subject of the verb *was*. The writer could have used a single noun instead of the clause to make the same statement: "The *price* was too much."

He promised *that he would lend me the money*. (Noun clause used as the object of *promised*)

I am fearful of *what he has in mind*. (Noun clause used as the object of the preposition *of*)

His remark *that he hated animals* surprised me. (Noun clause used as an appositive)

His remarks usually were *whatever came to mind first*. (Noun clause used as a predicate complement)

Noun phrase. A phrase can be used in a sentence as a noun is used—as subject, object, etc.

> *Playing on top of the automobile* was his special delight.

Used as a noun, the phrase is called a noun phrase. It functions in the sentence exactly as a single noun functions. In the example quoted, the noun phrase "playing on top of the automobile" serves as a name—a name for the particular activity which is a "special delight." It acts as the subject of *was*.

Novel. A novel is a narrative, usually in prose, which portrays characters, actions, and settings involved in action which is more or less representative of real life. A novel is always somewhat fictitious (see *Fiction*) and runs to considerable length, as distinguished from a *short story* or *novella*, which see.

Novella. This word borrowed from the Italian is applied to stories somewhat shorter than novels. A *novella* contains a compact plot but usually places little emphasis upon characters or setting. A *short story* (which see) running more than 10,000 words is usually called a *novella*; a *novel* normally extends to a minimum of 30,000 word.

Number. The change in the form of a noun, pronoun, or verb to show whether one or more than one is indicated. See *Plurals* and *Verb plurals* in Part III, "Guide to Correct Spelling."

Object. The noun, pronoun, or noun clause following a transitive verb or a preposition.

> Your hat is on the *floor*. (Object of preposition)
> She struck *him* with a newspaper. (Object of verb)
> I see *what you have in mind*. (Object of verb)

A *simple object* is the substantive alone. A *complete object* is a simple object together with its modifiers. A *compound object* consists of two or more substantives.

> The Duanes built the large green *house* on the hill. (Simple)
> The Duanes built *the large green house on the hill.* (Complete)
> The Duanes built *the house and the barn.* (Compound)

Object complement. A word, usually a noun or adjective, used after the direct object of certain verbs and intended to complete meaning.

> We have chosen Sue *leader.*
> Let me make this problem *simple.*

Objective case. The object of a verb or preposition is in the objective case.

> The foreman blamed *her.*
> *Whom* did she see?
> This was bad news for *them.*
> A group of *us* protested the decision.

The subject, object, or object complement of an infinitive is in the objective case.

> *Whom* did you take *her* to be? (*Her* is the subject of *to be; whom* is an object complement.)
> George made *him* do that. (Subject of [to] *do*)
> His desire to please *her* was great. (Object)
> Did you think her to be *me?* (Object complement)

Also, see *Case.*

Obsolete expression. An obsolete word is one which has completely passed out of use; an *obsolescent* word is one which is becoming *obsolete.* Examples: *infortune* for *misfortune; bene* for *prayer; dole* for *grief; permit* for *commit; prevent* for *precede* or *anticipate.* Obsolete words and obsolete meanings of words are so marked in good dictionaries.

Old English. This is the English of periods prior to 1100 A.D. Often called *Anglo-Saxon,* it is as foreign to the native speaker and writer of Modern English as German or Latin.

Onomatopoeia. The formation of a word by imitating sound associated with the object or action named: *tinkle, buzz, whir, chickadee.*

Orthography. A ten-dollar word for "correct spelling."

Outline. An *outline* is a general sketch or report suggesting the main features of an object. In writing, an *outline* is a sort of blueprint for ordering the parts of a *composition* (which see) or a recipe naming ingredients and offering instructions for using them.

Pantheism. The theological belief that God is everything in the universe and is everywhere. This belief involves a denial of God's personality and tends to identify nature and God.

Pantomime. A form of dramatic art in which the performers express themselves by mute gestures. In general, the term means "significant actions without speech."

Parable. A brief story or tale in which characters are used to teach a moral or preach a doctrine or belief. The term *parable* is sometimes employed in referring to a saying or piece of writing which confers its meaning by comparison: the *parable* of the Good Samaritan. See *Allegory*.

Paragraph. A *paragraph* is a group, or bundle, of sentences developing either one single topic or idea or a specific part of a larger topic. The purpose of the paragraph is to aid in communicating thought by setting off the single topic which it develops or by providing clear distinctions between the separate parts of a longer piece of writing.

Every paragraph should be indented (see *Indention*). Dialogue and quoted conversations require separate paragraphing.

Parallelism. *Parallel*, a word from the field of mathematics, means two or more lines (in the same plane) extending in the same direction and at the same distance apart at every point. In grammar, the word has come to mean "close resemblance," "similarity." When two or more ideas in a sentence are related and serve a similar purpose, they can be phrased in the same grammatical form. The simplest form of parallellism consists of two or more words in a series: the *little, old* man. For an extended discussion see Part II, "Guide to Correct Sentence Structure."

Paraphrase.   A *paraphrase* is a statement of the sense of a passage (piece of writing or speech) in other words. A free rendering or translation, the *paraphrase* is designed to foster clearness.

Parenthetical statement.   A word, phrase, clause, or sentence, by way of explanation, which is inserted in or added to a statement grammatically complete without it. Such a statement is usually enclosed by marks of parenthesis, commas, or dashes.

Parody.   A work in which the style or subject matter of another work or author is imitated, usually for purposes of ridicule.

Parsing.   *Parsing* is naming and describing the grammatical forms and functions of words in a sentence. It is concerned with parts of speech, inflectional forms, syntactic relationships, etc. See *Analysis of a sentence.*

Participial phrase.   A phrase introduced by a *participle* (which see) or an adverbial modifier combined with a participle.

> *Working steadily,* I soon finished the task.
> *Carefully watching the lights,* we made our way home safely.

Participle.   A *participle* is a word which has the function of both verb and adjective. The *present participle* always ends in *-ing* (*speaking, singing*). The *past participle* has various forms (*spoken, sung, walked, set*); it is regularly in the passive voice. The *perfect participle* consists of *having* or *having been* plus the past participle (*having spoken, having been sung*); it is either active or passive in voice.

The participle, since it is a form of the verb as well as an adjective, can take an object and can be modified by an adverb. The participle resembles the adjective in that it can be modified by an adverb and can itself modify a noun or pronoun.

> The ball *kicked* by the player went into the stands.
> The boy expertly *riding* the horse is named John.
> The tree *swaying* in the breeze is lovely.

Parts of speech.   Words are classified according to their use in larger units of thought, that is, sentences. This functional division results in the so-called parts of speech; every word in the English language belongs to one or more of these parts of speech. There are eight such parts:

Noun	Adverb
Pronoun	Conjunction
Verb	Preposition
Adjective	Interjection

Many words are always used in a certain way, as a particular part of speech. But since our language is constantly changing, the functions of words reflect that change. *Chair,* for example, is almost always a noun, yet it has been used as a verb; the poet A. E. Housman tells of carrying a victorious athlete "shoulder-high" in a parade through his home town:

> The time you won your town the race
> We *chaired* you through the market-place.

Noun, verb, adjective, adverb name the four large form classes in English. They have the best title to the collective term "parts of speech."

1. The main parts of speech are large groups, each of them incorporating thousands of words in the average vocabulary.

2. The membership of the main parts of speech is unstable and shifting. New nouns are constantly being formed, new prepositions seldom.

3. The native speaker of English recognizes important parts of speech *as parts of speech* by formal signals in the sentence; he recognizes other groups by remembering each individual word as belonging to some particular group (i.e., having a particular pattern of occurrence). This is shown by our ability to identify nonsense words as parts of speech:

> A *grobically stoused blemen* had been *dorking* a rather *drengful whacktort.*

This sentence is structurally clear (i.e., we know it's a statement, know what the action is and who the performer is, etc.) because the parts of speech are identifiable. But if we retain real words for the main parts of speech and substitute nonsense words elsewhere, we get no structural clarity:

Gru beautifully dressed lady *gorb neel* watching *slobe nanto* happy child.

Words *name, assert, modify,* and *join.* To determine what part of speech a given word is, see how the word is used in the sentence of which it is a part.

Passive voice.   The form of an action-expressing verb which tells that the subject of the verb does not perform or act but is acted upon. That is, the subject is *passive.* See *Voice.*

Past participle.   The third principal part of a verb, used as an adjective or as part of a predicate. See *Participle* and *Principal parts of verbs.*

Past perfect tense.   The time of the action of a verb beginning at a point in the past and ending at a later point in the past. (She *had been planning* to leave before you arrived.) See *Tense.*

Past tense.   This is the second principal part of a verb and also represents the time of a verb which expresses a before-now action. (He *left* yesterday.) Also, see *Tense.*

Pathetic fallacy.   Defined and illustrated under *Fallacy.*

Perfect infinitive.   An infinitive formed by the auxiliary *to have* plus the past participle: *to have worked.*

Perfect participle.   A participle formed by the auxiliary verb *having* followed by the past participle: *having worked.*

Periodical.   A publication (usually a *magazine,* which see) issued at regular intervals of more than one day.

Periodic sentence.   A sentence with its parts arranged so that its meaning is not clear or complete until the end is reached or nearly reached. See *Sentence, arrangement of content.*

Periphrasis.   A roundabout way of writing or speaking. See *Circumlocution.* (Both *periphrasis* and *circumlocution* are pedantic and polysyllabic words; why not use *deadwood* or *wordiness?*)

Person.   The change in the form of a pronoun or verb—sometimes, merely a change in use as with verbs—to indicate whether the "person" used is the person speaking (*first person*), the person spoken to (*second person*), or the person or thing spoken about (*third person*).

I, Steve, testify that this is a true story. (First person)
Please, *Steve,* try to tell the truth. (Second person)
It is difficult for *him* (*Steve*) to tell the truth. (Third person)
I see, *you* see, *he* sees, *she* sees, *it* sees, *we* see, *you* see, *they* see

Personal pronoun.   A *personal* pronoun is a direct substitute for a noun as subject or object: "Where did *you* buy it?" Like a noun, it has number, gender, person, and case as is shown by the following table:

SINGULAR

	Nominative	*Possessive*	*Objective*
1st person:	I	my, mine	me
2nd person:	you	your, yours	you
3rd person:			
Masculine:	he	his	him
Feminine:	she	her, hers	her
Neuter:	it	its	it

PLURAL

1st person:	we	our, ours	us
2nd person:	you	your, yours	you
3rd person:	they	their, theirs	them

Grammatical problems frequently arise from the fact that, unlike nouns, both personal and relative pronouns have distinct forms for the nominative and objective cases.

Personal pronouns vary to show a change in person; other classes of pronouns do not. For example, *I* and *we*, representing a speaker, are in the first person. *You*, the person spoken to, is in the second person. Those spoken of (*she, he, it, they*) are in the third person.

Personal pronouns in the third person singular change to indicate gender. *He* is masculine, *she* is feminine, *it* is neuter. See *Person*.

Personification.   A figure of speech in which human attributes are given to an animal or to an inanimate object, or the representation of an idea or quality in the form of a person: the paths of Glory, a comptometer performing like a mathematician, a dog with a soul.

Phoneme. A class, or family, of closely related sounds regarded as a single sound. (These speech sounds are called *phones*.) For example, by contrast of the phoneme *p* with other phonemes, *nip* differs from *pip*, *tip*, etc.

Phonetics. The science of speech sounds and their production.

Phrase. A *phrase* is a group of related words which does not contain both a subject and a predicate. A phrase is used as a part of speech, the equivalent of a noun, adjective, or adverb. See *Adjective phrase*, *Adverb phrase*, *Noun phrase*, and *Restrictive and nonrestrictive phrases*.

Platitude. A platitude is a trite, commonplace remark or idea, especially one uttered as if it were important or novel. An informal synonym of *platitude* is *bromide*, referring to a particularly dull and tiresome expression. See *Cliché*.

Pleonasm. Redundancy; the use of more words than necessary for the expression of an idea. See *Deadwood*.

Plural. A classification of nouns and pronouns (and also subjects and predicates) to indicate two or more units or members.

Most nouns and verbs form their plurals in directly opposite ways. Except for special groups, nouns form their *plurals* by adding *-s*, *-es*, *-ies*: desk, desks; glass, glasses; lady, ladies. (See *Plurals* in Part III, "Guide to Correct Spelling.") Most verbs add an *-s* in the third person *singular*: he walks, they walk; she speaks, the men speak.

Remember that for most nouns and verbs, the procedure is vice versa.

Poetry. Literary work in metrical form. *Poetry* and *verse* both refer to the work of a poet, but they differ in substance and form. *Poetry* is lofty thought or impassioned feeling expressed in imaginative language; *verse* is any work which conforms to metrical rules and structure. Strictly speaking, *a verse* is a single metrical line.

Polysyllable. Having many, or more than three, *syllables* (which see). A *monosyllable* is a word of only one syllable. Good writing requires words of varying length, but "big words" should never be used merely to make an impression. See *Affectation, Fine writing*.

Portmanteau word. A word made by telescoping or blending two or more words: *brunch* from "breakfast and lunch," *dandle* from "dance and handle," *aquabelle* from "girl swimmer," *aristobrat* from "aristocrat and brat." See *Blend* and *Coinage*.

Positive degree. The simple form of an adjective or adverb in which no comparison is expressed: *red, tall, rapid, beautiful, swiftly*. See *Comparison*.

Possessive. The case form of nouns and pronouns indicating, usually, ownership or some idiomatic use like extent of time or space: *the woman's coat, my job, the people's choice, a week's vacation*. See *Genitive (possessive) case*.

Predicate. The verb or verb phrase in a sentence which makes a statement—an assertion, an action, a condition, a state of being —about the subject. A *simple predicate* is a verb or a verb phrase alone, without an object or modifiers; a *complete predicate* consists of the verb with its object and all its modifiers; a *compound predicate* consists of two or more verbs or verb phrases.

> Mr. Tyler drove the ball nearly two hundred yards.
> (*Drove* is the simple predicate; *drove the ball nearly two hundred yards* is the complete predicate.)
> I *wrote* the letter last night *and mailed* it this morning.
> (Compound predicate)

Predicate adjective. An adjective used in the predicate after a linking or joining or coupling verb; this adjective modifies or qualifies the subject. See *Complement*.

> This task is *difficult*.
> Today seems *colder* than yesterday.

Predicate complement (also called subjective complement). A *predicate noun* or *pronoun*, or a *predicate adjective*. See these terms in this glossary. Also, see *Complement*.

Predicate noun or pronoun. A noun or pronoun used in the predicate after a linking or joining or coupling verb and identifying the subject. See *Complement*.

> She was *the best friend* I ever had.
> This is *he* speaking.

Preface. A preliminary statement; see *Foreword*.

Prefix. A syllable, group of syllables, or word joined to the beginning of another word to alter its meaning or to create a new meaning. Thus, the prefix *pre-* added to *heat* forms *preheat*.

Preposition. A *preposition* is a linking word used to show the relationship of a noun or pronoun to some other word in the sentence. Prepositions show position or direction (*at, with, to, from*) or indicate cause or possession (*because of, of*).

The preposition is always followed by a noun or pronoun (or the equivalent), with which it forms a unit. The only apparent exception is the use of prepositions in certain structures with *who* (*whom*), *which*, and *what*: "Whom are you going with?" "What's it made of?"

Forms in common use are *against, ahead of, along, alongside, amid, among, apart from, apropos, around, as far as, as to, at, back of, because of, before, behind, below, beneath, beside, besides, between, beyond, by, concerning, contrary to, despite, down, due to, during, for, from, in, in place of, inside, in spite of, into, in view of, like, near, of, off, on account of, onto, out of, over, owing to, past, per, round, since, through, throughout, till, to, toward, under, until, upon, up to, via, with, within.*

In common usage, certain prepositions are used with certain other parts of speech, forming idiomatic combinations (see *Idiom*):

comply with	entertain at dinner
independent of	plan to go
blame you for	different from
adapted to	differences between (two)
angry with	differences among (three)
fond of	take a dislike to
fondness for	analogous to
as regards	listen to
with regard to	at home

Prepositional phrase. A phrase introduced by a preposition. For examples, see *Preposition*. Sometimes the preposition *follows* its object: *Which car* did you ride *in?*

Present participle. A verb form (verbal) ending in *-ing* and used as part of the predicate or as an adjective. See *Participle*.

> I am *working* every afternoon. (Part of predicate)
> This restaurant does a *thriving* business. (Adjective use)

Present perfect tense. The time of the action or state of being of a verb, beginning in the past and just ending or still going on in the present. (I *have had* a splendid trip.) See *Tense*.

Present tense. This tense shows the "now" time of a verb. (She *plays* bridge carefully.) It includes the *simple present*, the *progressive present*, and the *emphatic present*. See these terms in this section and, also, *Tense*.

Primary source. The word *source* means "any thing or place from which something comes or is obtained." *Primary* means "immediate or direct, not involving any intermediate agency." Therefore, *primary source*, or *primary source material*, may be defined as original, authoritative materials used in research and study: diaries, manuscripts, authentic documents, etc.

Primitivism. A belief or theory that the qualities of early cultures are superior to those of contemporary civilization. In philosophy, sociology, and literature, *primitivism* is a theory that human virtue had its highest manifestation in the "noble savage" uncorrupted by contact with civilized society.

Principal parts of verbs. The principal parts of an English verb are the *present tense* (present infinitive), the *past tense*, and the *past participle* (*see—saw—seen*). An excellent way to recall these parts of a verb is to put the verb in these expressions:

> I *see* today.
> I *saw* yesterday.
> I *have seen* every day this week.

1. Do not misuse the past tense and past participle.

> *Wrong:* I *swum* the lake yesterday. (I *swam* . . .)
> He *drunk* the whole cup. (He *drank* . . .)
> The rain has *fell* all day. (. . . has *fallen* . . .)

2. Do not confuse a strong verb with a weak verb.

Verbs which form the past tense and past participle by adding *-ed*, *-d*, or *-t* to the infinitive are called *weak*; those which form these parts by a vowel change without any addition are called *strong* verbs.

> Wrong: He *drawed* a bucket of water from the well. (He *drew* . . .)
>
> The cloth has *shrinked* too much. (. . . has *shrunk* . . .)

The following verbs are troublesome. Study them carefully; put them into the three expressions mentioned above.

arise	arose	arisen
bear	bore	borne (born—given birth to)
begin	began	begun
bid	bid	bid (as in an auction)
bid	bade	bidden (as in a command)
bite	bit	bitten (bit)
blow	blew	blown
break	broke	broken
burst	burst	burst
catch	caught	caught
choose	chose	chosen
come	came	come
deal	dealt	dealt
dig	dug	dug
dive	dived	dived
do	did	done
drag	dragged	dragged
draw	drew	drawn
drink	drank	drunk
drown	drowned	drowned
eat	ate	eaten
fall	fell	fallen
flow	flowed	flowed
fly	flew	flown
forget	forgot	forgotten (forgot)
freeze	froze	frozen
get	got	got (gotten)

go	went	gone
hang	hung	hung (object)
hang	hanged	hanged (person)
know	knew	known
lay	laid	laid
lead	led	led
lend	lent	lent
lie	lay	lain (recline)
lie	lied	lied (falsehood)
loose	loosed	loosed
lose	lost	lost
pay	paid	paid
prove	proved	proved
raise	raised	raised
ride	rode	ridden
rise	rose	risen
run	ran	run
set	set	set
sing	sang	sung
sit	sat	sat
speak	spoke	spoken
swim	swam	swum
take	took	taken
tear	tore	torn
wake	waked (woke)	waked (woke)
wear	wore	worn
wring	wrung	wrung
write	wrote	written

Progressive verb form. A statement of continuing action or state of being within a tense, formed by the proper forms of the auxiliary *to be* followed by the present participle.

> We *are writing* our reports today.
> John *was playing* golf when I arrived.
> *Are* you *coming* early? We *shall be leaving* before six o'clock.

Prolixity. The state or quality of being tedious, long, or wordy; speaking or writing at great length. See *Circumlocution, Conciseness, Deadwood, Economy, Redundancy,* and *Tautology.*

Prologue. A *prologue* is a preface to, or introductory part of, a novel, play, poem, or discourse of any kind. In drama, *prologue* refers to an introductory speech, often in verse, calling attention to the theme of a play or recounting action which occurred prior to the time of action of the play itself.

Pronoun.   A *pronoun* substitutes for a noun or a noun-equivalent. Every pronoun refers directly or by clear implication to a noun or a noun-equivalent (called the *antecedent* of the pronoun) and agrees with that antecedent in person, number, and gender (but not necessarily in case): "Each boy present will please raise *his* hand."

Pronouns in common use are *I, me, mine, you, yours, he, him, his, she, her, hers, it, its, we, us, ours, they, them, theirs; myself, yourself, yourselves, himself, herself, ourselves, themselves; each other, one another; this, that, these, those, such; each, either, both, some, few, many, much, none, several, all, any, most, anybody, anyone, anything, somebody* (etc.), *everybody* (etc.), *nobody, nothing, one, two, three* (etc.).

Pronouns, which are used in all the grammatical functions of nouns (as object, subject, etc.), are of several kinds: *personal, relative, demonstrative, interrogative, reflexive* (*intensive*), *indefinite*, and *reciprocal*.

Pronoun agreement.   See *Agreement of pronoun and antecedent*.

Pronunciation.   The act, or result, of producing the sounds of speech. *Pronunciation* is complex and many-faceted; it involves, among other things, levels of pronunciation, dialect, provincialisms, and spelling. Concerning pronunciation, the single best piece of advice is this: acquire a good dictionary and study its pronunciation key thoroughly.

Proper name.   The name of a particular person, thing, or event: President Kennedy, California, Christmas. Proper names are always capitalized.

Proper noun.   A noun naming a particular or individual member of a group: William, Mrs. Jane Wilson, Canada, Presbyterian.

Properties of verb.   Properties of the verb are *voice* (active and passive), *mood* (indicative, subjunctive, imperative), *tense, number*, and *person*. The last two of these properties are more concerned with the subject than with the verb itself.

Proportion. The comparative relation between things or magnitudes as to size, quantity, number, emphasis, etc. In writing, proportion usually refers to the relationship between length and emphasis of paragraphs or to the amounts of space given development of different ideas in a letter, report, etc.

Prose. Ordinary written or spoken language, without metrical structure, is called *prose*. Each of us has been speaking, reading, and writing *prose* since childhood. See *Poetry*.

Provincialism. A provincialism, or localism, is a word or phrase used and understood in only a particular section or region of the country. Such words are difficult to detect because a writer or speaker may have come to accept them as reputable and to assume that they are nationally understood since he himself has known them from childhood. The northeastern (New England), southern, and western parts of the United States, among others, are especially rich in colorful localisms which add flavor to speech but which may not be immediately understood in other areas.

Such provincialisms are appropriate in informal writing and conversation but should be avoided in standard writing. Examples: *chunk* and *chuck* for *to throw*; *tote* for *carry*; *tote* (noun) for *a load*; *poke* for a *bag* or *sack*; *fatback* for *bacon*; *bunk into* for *bump into*; *reckon* for *think* or *suppose*; *choose* for *wish*; *heft* for *lift*; *trunk* for *tap*; *draw* for *gully*; *chuck wagon* for a *supply wagon*; *rustler* for *cattle thief*; *selectman* for a *town official*; *to home* for *at home*; *loco* for *crazy*.

Linguists differ among themselves over which of such expressions are provincialisms and which are merely colloquial. See *Localism*.

Pure conjunction. A short or simple and commonly used co-ordinating conjunction: *and, but, or, nor, neither*, etc. See *Conjunction*.

Purist. One who observes, and insists upon, scrupulous and excessive respect for the refinements of style and precise usage in language. A purist seems to feel that man was made for language and refuses to acknowledge that language was not only made for man but that it is determined and shaped by his use—and nothing else.

Realism. This term is somewhat loosely used in criticism of literature and art to denote or classify works which depict life "as it is" or as the artist saw it. It involves treating subjects with fidelity to nature or to real life and should be contrasted with *romanticism, sentimentalism, naturalism,* and *classicism,* which see.

Reciprocal pronoun. A *reciprocal* pronoun indicates an interchange of actions suggested by the verb. This interchange may be seen in the following sentences involving the only two reciprocal pronouns in English:

> The blonde and the brunette complemented *each other.*
> The members of the group shouted at *one another.*

Redundancy. An excess; too many words to express ideas; superabundance; superfluity. See *Prolixity* and the entries there listed.

Reflexive pronoun. A *reflexive* (intensive) pronoun is used for simple reference to the subject. It is composed of one of the personal pronouns plus *-self* or *-selves.* Called *reflexive* because action of the verb is directed toward the subject, such a pronoun is construed as an adjective when it is used *intensively,* that is, when it emphasizes an antecedent. Most frequently employed reflexive (intensive) pronouns are *myself, yourself, himself, herself, itself, ourselves, yourselves, themselves.*

> His laboratory assistant burned *himself.* (Reflexive use)
> They appointed *themselves* as law enforcement officers. (Reflexive use)
> The nurse *herself* was at fault. (Intensive use)
> We employees *ourselves* are wholly responsible. (Intensive use)

Regular verbs. Also called *weak verbs,* regular verbs usually form their past tense and past participle by adding *-d, -ed,* or *-t* to the present infinitive form: *help, helped, helped.* See *Irregular verbs.*

Relative pronoun. A *relative* pronoun relates or connects a clause to its antecedent. It does have case but no forms distinctive of gender or number. However, the choice of a relative pronoun is determined in part by its antecedent: *who* (or *whom*) is used to refer only to persons; *which* is used in reference to things (inanimate objects, animals) and may be used for a group of persons considered as a group; *that* may refer to either things or persons.

> The flyer *who* served in World War II is now an airline official.
>
> Radar equipment *which* is to be used for ships must be installed carefully.
>
> The team *which* collected the most money was awarded a prize.
>
> The hat *that* I bought last summer is now out of fashion.
>
> The man *that* I saw was named Hugh Riddleberger.

Who, which, and *that* are the most frequently used relative pronouns. *Whoever, whichever,* and *whatever* are less frequently employed compound forms; *whosoever, whichsoever,* and *whatsoever* have gone almost entirely out of current use.

Relative pronouns show the following changes:

> *Nominative case:*   who, that, which
> *Possessive case:*   whose
> *Objective case:*   whom, that, which

Repetition.   Act of saying or writing again. In writing and speaking, some repetition is a genuine aid in achieving effectiveness; some is merely *deadwood*. Discovering which is which is a large part of the process of learning to write.

Report.   An account presented, or a statement made, as the result of investigation or observation. A *report* may contain the results of research in office, field, or laboratory, or it may be a recommendation for action or decision. Basically, it is an orderly presentation of data, carefully arranged for a specific purpose. Ease of reference and clearness should be its distinguishing characteristics.

Restrictive and nonrestrictive clauses.   If a dependent clause is essential in order to explain or identify the word to which it refers, the clause is called *restrictive*. If the dependent clause is not necessary, if it is in the nature of a parenthetical remark which could be removed from the sentence, leaving the essential meaning intact, it is called *nonrestrictive*. Nonrestrictive clauses are always set off from the remainder of the sentence by commas

The man *who spoke at our Forum* is a member of the Securities and Exchange Commission.

The dependent clause is here restrictive, for it is necessary as a means of identifying the particular man. But in the following sentence the clause is nonrestrictive; the identification is made by the use of the proper name.

Captain Stiles, *who spoke at our Forum,* is a member of the Securities and Exchange Commission.

See *Commas to enclose, C1,* in Part IV, "Guide to Correct Punctuation and Mechanics."

Restrictive and nonrestrictive phrases. If a phrase is essential in order to explain or identify the word to which it refers, the phrase is called *restrictive.* If the phrase is not absolutely necessary, it is called *nonrestrictive.* Nonrestrictive phrases are always set off by commas from the remainder of the sentence.

The citizens' committee gains *in political stature.*

In this example, the adverbial phrase is *restrictive* because it tells the particular way in which the committee gains.

The citizens' committee, *gaining in political stature,* began to demand reforms within the city government.

Here the adjective phrase is *nonrestrictive* because it is not essential to the writer's purpose in telling what the committee began to demand. See *Commas to enclose,* in Part IV, "Guide to Correct Punctuation and Mechanics."

Résumé. A summing up. See *Summary.*

Rhetoric. The art or science of literary uses of language. *Rhetoric* is concerned with the effectiveness and general appeal of communication and with methods of achieving literary quality and vigor. In no way is it connected with "correctness" or with specific details of mechanics, spelling, grammar, etc., as such. See *Grammar.*

Rhetorical question. A query designed to produce an effect and not to draw an answer. It is used to introduce a topic or emphasize a point; no answer is expected.

Rhyme. Words or verses which agree in their terminal (end) sounds. Rhyme occurs when, for example, the accented vowels of two words and all succeeding sounds in the words are identical: rain, stain.

Rhythm. Uniform recurrence of a beat or accent. In English prose, rhythm is marked by variety of movement. Reading aloud is the best method of detecting the rise and fall of prose and its repetition of stresses. Good prose writers achieve rhythmic patterns, but not, of course, to the degree which poets do. Among many contributors to rhythm in prose: balanced sentences; variety in sentence length and structure; transitional devices; euphony; effective beginnings and endings of sentences.

Romanticism. As opposed to *realism*, *romanticism* refers to the style in art or litererature which represents "life as it is not" by means of distortion or escape. *Romanticism* also differs from *classicism* because the romanticist tends to express his individuality in defiance of established artistic rules. In general, *romanticism* in literature involves subordination of form to matter, freedom of treatment, picturesqueness, and imagination.

Saga. A *saga* is a narrative, or legend, of heroic exploits. The term *saga* is loosely applied to many motion pictures and TV spectaculars undeserving of the name.

Sarcasm. Harsh or bitter derision. For further discussion, see *Irony*.

Satire. The use of ridicule, invective, or humor to expose or deride vice, folly, or stupidity. See *Irony*.

Schoolgirl style. A rather unchivalrous and unkind term for a manner of writing characterized by gushiness, exaggeration, and an overuse of intensives. Counter words, triple underlinings, exclamation points, and dashes are used generously. As indicated, maturity is at a premium. Mechanical forms of emphasis are always self-defeating.

Secondary source. A source which is somewhat removed from primary, or original, material. See *Primary source*.

Semantics. The study of word meaning and changes of meaning. As the science of meanings, *semantics* is contrasted with *phonetics*, the science of sounds. The word itself is derived from Greek *semainein*, "to mean," "to signify," but it is concerned less with "dictionary" definitions of words than with verbal and non-verbal meanings and their importance in our private lives and public affairs. In short, semantics is concerned not alone with word meanings but with a study of human beings and what words mean to them at different times and under different circumstances.

Sentence.   A *sentence* is a group of words containing a complete, independent thought or a group of closely related thoughts. It may also be defined as a group of words (or even one word) conveying to reader or listener a sense of complete meaning. A sentence must contain a *subject* and a *predicate*, expressed or understood. The subject is the name of the person or thing about which the verb makes a statement. The predicate is what is said of the subject; it must contain a verb which can make a complete, independent statement. Such a verb is called a *finite* verb; participles, infinitives, and gerunds are *nonfinite* verb forms.

Sentence, arrangement of content.   Sentences may be classified according to the *arrangement* of their content.

A sentence in which the words are so set down that the meaning is not completed until the end or near the end is called *periodic*.

A sentence so constructed that the thought may be completed before the end is *loose*.

Our conversation and informal writing contain many more loose sentences than periodic. Yet a periodic sentence does provide suspense and variety; it holds the attention of reader or listener and contributes to stylistic effectiveness. Although a natural form of expression, the periodic sentence tends to become monotonous and forced and should not be overused.

> Act quickly, or you will be too late to secure the bargain you want. (Loose)
> He liked to play bridge and tennis but more than either he enjoyed dancing and ice-skating. (Loose)
> If you do not wish to go, please say so. (Periodic)

According to a former college president, to be at home in all lands and ages; to count Nature a familiar acquaintance and Art a familiar friend; to gain a standard for the appreciation of other men's work and the criticism of one's own; to make friends among men and women of one's own age who are to be the leaders in all walks of life; to lose one's self in generous enthusiasm and to co-operate with others for common ends; to learn manners from students who are gentlemen and gentlewomen; and to form character under professors who are dedicated— these are the returns of a college for the best four years of one's life. (Periodic)

A *balanced sentence* is so constructed that similar or opposing thoughts have similar structure. Such a sentence is sometimes used to make a statement especially emphatic and for comparisons and contrasts.

Time is money; money is important.
You can take a man out of the country; you can't take the "country" out of a man.
You may call him the man who invented sin, but I would say he is the man whom sin invented.

See *Periodic sentence* and *Variety* in Part II, "Guide to Correct Sentence Structure."

Sentence, grammatical structure of. Sentences may be classified according to grammatical structure as *simple, compound, complex,* or *compound-complex.*

A *simple sentence* contains only one subject and one predicate and expresses only one thought.

The street is paved.
The boy and the girl talked and danced.

A *compound sentence* contains two or more independent clauses. The clauses of a compound sentence are grammatically capable of standing alone, but they are closely related parts of one main idea.

The days are warm but the nights are cool.
She read and I wrote letters.

A *complex sentence* contains one independent clause and one or more dependent (subordinate) clauses.

> The woman said that she had walked for over an hour.
> He is an athlete whose muscles are unusually supple.

A *compound-complex sentence* contains two or more independent clauses and one or more dependent clauses.

> Since the day was unpleasant, we stayed indoors; Ned studied, and I worked on my stamp collection.

Sentence, meaning and purpose of. Sentences may be classified according to *meaning* and *purpose*.

A *declarative sentence* states a fact or makes an assertion.

> The house has twelve windows.

An *interrogative sentence* asks a question.

> Does the house have twelve windows?

An *imperative sentence* expresses an entreaty or command.

> Please come as soon as possible.

An *exclamatory sentence* expresses strong feeling.

> Oh, if he were only here!
> Thank goodness, you are here at last!

Sentence fragment. A word, or group of words, not expressing completeness of meaning. Some sentence fragments—such as exclamatory sentences, answers to questions, and broken conversation—are justifiable. All other fragments are not. See *Fragmentary sentence* in Part II, "Guide to Correct Sentence Structure."

Sentimentalism. Weak emotionalism, predominance of sentiment over reason. *Sentiment* is a sincere and refined feeling of emotion; *sentimentalism* (sentimentality) implies affected, excessive, even mawkish feeling.

Sequence of tenses. The tense of the verb in a subordinate clause depends on the tense of the verb in the main clause.

1. The present tense is used in a dependent clause to express a general truth.

> Some people did not believe that the earth *is* a planet.

The present tense is used alone to express a "timeless" truth.

> Water *is* wet.
> Thought *makes* the whole dignity of man.

Do not allow the tense of a verb to be attracted into the past when it should be present: "Last summer, I visited a small town in Utah; the houses *were* old and picturesque." (It is conceivable that the town has been wiped out, but is that what is meant?)

Passages in some short stories and novels are written in the present tense although the action occurred in time which is past. This use of what is called the *historical present* sometimes makes narrative more vivid, but it quickly becomes monotonous.

2. Use a present infinitive except when the infinitive represents action completed before the time of the governing verb.

> I intended *to see* (not *to have seen*) you about it.

3. A present participle indicates action at the time expressed by the verb; a past participle indicates action before that of the verb.

> *Being* wealthy, he *is* able to satisfy his whims.
> *Having been* a good worker, he *was* able to get many letters of recommendation.

4. When the narration in the past tense is interrupted for reference to a preceding event, use the past perfect tense.

> In April they *repaired* the streets which *had been damaged* by cold weather.
> The book which he *was reading had been published* in Philadelphia.

Summary:

These two formulas for the sequence of tenses may help:

1. PAST ⟵——————— PRESENT ———⟶ FUTURE
2. PAST PERFECT ⟵—— PAST ————⟶ FUTURE

Explanation: The present or the past is the principal tense. Each becomes the norm, as it were, for other tenses, as is indicated above. Thus:

1. He *tells* me that he *was* here yesterday and that he *will be* here tomorrow.
2. He *told* me that he *had been* here yesterday and that he *would be* here tomorrow.

Also, see *Tense.*

Shifts. This is a term applied to *shifted constructions* and refers to elements which have the same relationship to the statement being made but not the same grammatical structure. Adjectives should be paralleled by adjectives, nouns by nouns, etc.; shifting from one form to another may confuse a reader. See *Parallelism.*

Shoptalk. The specialized or technical vocabulary and idioms of those in the same work, same way of life, etc. That is, *shoptalk* is the colloquial language people use in discussing their particular line of work. To "talk shop" is the verb form of this expression. See *Cant.*

Short story. Many definitions of a *short story* are possible, none of them fully satisfactory. Here's an adequate definition: A short story is a relatively short narrative which is designed to produce a single dominant effect and which contains the elements of drama. The short story differs from both the *novel* and *drama* (which see) in its adherence to one primary effect upon the reader.

Sign of the infinitive. The word *to* accompanying the infinitive form of the verb: *to* go, *to* read, *to* sell. See *Infinitive.*

Simile. A simile is a figure of speech by which are compared two things essentially different but thought to be alike in one or more respects. The point of resemblance is expressed by *like, as, as if:* "as sweet as candy." See *Metaphor.*

Simple sentence. A sentence containing one subject (simple or compound) and one predicate (simple or compound). See *Sentence, grammatical structure of.*

Simple verb form. Usually a statement of a "snapshot" or instantaneous action of a verb. (He *talks*.) Compare with *Emphatic verb form* and *Progressive verb form*.

Singular. The number classification of nouns, pronouns, subjects, and predicates to indicate *one*: *girl, boy, tree, he, is, has, pays*.

Slang. A particular kind of colloquialism or illiteracy. Formerly the term was applied to the *cant* (which see) of gypsies, beggars, and thieves, or to the *jargon* (which see) of any particular class of society. Now, *slang* is defined as language which consists of widely current terms having a forced or fantastic meaning, or displaying eccentricity. It is markedly colloquial language below the range of standard or cultivated speech.

Slang is popular, but it has little place in standard English. There are sound reasons for avoiding it.

First, many slang words and expressions are ephemeral; they last for a brief period of time and then pass out of use, becoming unintelligible and violating the principle that words must be in current use. Who today uses such formerly popular expressions as "23 skiddoo" and "Ishkabibble"? How many people would understand them if they were used? Numerous currently popular slang expressions will be outmoded in a short time.

Second, the use of slang expressions prevents searching for exact words to express meaning. Many slang expressions are only rubber stamps; to refer to a person as a "jerk" hardly expresses exactly or fully any critical judgment or intelligent description. To argue that such a word conveys precisely the intended meaning is to reveal a poverty of vocabulary, or careless thinking, or laziness. The most serious charge against slang is that it becomes a substitute for thinking.

Finally, slang is not appropriate in most standard writing because it is not in keeping with the context. Words should be appropriate to the audience, the occasion, and the subject matter.

Note these typical slang expressions: *to get away (by) with it, C-note, bang-up, beatnik, a bum hunch, to put it across, so what?, goof off, took the count, going some, put on the dog, have a heart, attaboy, mooch, cut no ice, fall for it, hard-boiled, get the goods on him, talk through your hat, cool, cool cat, goofy, wacky, to crab, let it ride, stow the gab, jitterbug, what's cooking?, you said it, in the groove, a smooth number, square, to get hep, cooking with gas, to dig, sharp, a rat race, on the beam, sourpuss, cockeyed, good egg, mike, croak* (meaning "die" or "kill"), *slob, stuffed shirt, brass hat, brass* (high officials), *screwball, payola, psyched up,* VIP or V.I.P.

Several of these expressions are unfamiliar to you? Quite likely. Many slang words have short lives; only a few prove permanently useful.

There are good arguments in favor of slang and places where it should be used. Slang does express feeling, although explosively and sometimes grotesquely. It also makes effective short cuts in expression and often prevents artificiality in writing. Furthermore, it should be used in reporting dialogue to give the flavor of the speech actually used. Avoid *excessive* or *injudicious* use of slang.

Solecism. An error, inconsistency, or *impropriety*, which see. *Solecism* is a somewhat general term applied to almost any fault in writing but especially to errors in the choice and use of words. An example of such an intrusion of substandard speech or writing: "They was."

Soliloquy. The act of talking when alone or as if alone is called *soliloquy*. In literary art, especially in drama, *a soliloquy* is the solitary oral expression of one speaker.

Source. The place of origin (book, person, statement) supplying information is known as a *source*. See *Primary source, Secondary source*.

Split construction. When closely related parts of a sentence are separated from each other, a split construction results. Since English is not a highly inflected language and, as a result, both clarity and effectiveness depend upon word order, it is advisable not to split the verbs in a verb phrase, subject and predicate, verb and object, preposition and object, etc.

Spoonerism. A slip of the tongue whereby initial or other sounds of words are transposed as, "It is kistomary to cuss the bride." The term derives from the name of an Oxford don famed for such transpositions.

Standard English. Language used in the conduct of public affairs, in various types of literature, in letters and documents carefully prepared, in magazines, speeches, and books. It is not necessarily overprecise and pedantic nor does it rule out all colloquialisms and everyday expressions.

No standards of diction can be absolute, but it is safe to say that standard English is that which is used by reputable speakers and writers. Such usage is never fixed but changes constantly as the product of custom or of appropriateness of words to context. For a writer's vocabulary is the *number* of words he can command; a writer's diction is the *kind* of words he uses. Words once considered not acceptable are now sanctioned, and vice versa. Diction ranges from philosophical abstractness to racy slang, from lofty Shakespearian utterances to the dialect of *Huckleberry Finn*. No single word, *in itself,* is "standard" or "substandard," for a word perfect in one context may be inappropriate in another. But general principles applying to standard usage have remained constant and may serve as guides: Words should be in *present* use, in *national* use, and in *reputable* use. See *Appropriateness, Levels of usage.*

Stanza. A *stanza* is a group of lines of verse arranged and repeated according to a fixed plan. Thus we speak of the *stanzas* of a song, hymn, or poem when referring to divisions, or parts.

Stream of consciousness. This term refers to thoughts regarded as a succession of states constantly moving onward in time. A *stream-of-consciousness* novel is a narrative in which the action is reported through, or along with, the thoughts of one or several characters. In such a novel (Joyce's *Ulysses,* for example) the outer world of action is relatively unimportant; the inner world of several of the characters is essential.

Strong verb. See *Irregular verbs.*

Style. This term has been defined in many ways but never satisfactorily, since every writer and speaker has his own notion of the term. In general, *style* is a "manner or mode of expression in language, a way of putting thoughts into words." It also refers to a specific or characteristic manner of expression or construction. An author's or speaker's style is the impress (influence) of his personality upon his subject matter.

Subject. The person or thing (noun, pronoun, noun phrase, noun clause) about which a statement or assertion is made in a sentence or clause. A *simple subject* is the noun or pronoun alone. A *complete subject* is a simple subject together with its modifiers. A *compound subject* consists of two or more nouns, pronouns, noun phrases, noun clauses.

> The green *house* is for sale. (Simple subject)
> *The green house on the hill* is for sale. (Complete subject)
> *The green house and two acres of land* are for sale. (Compound subject)
> *What you say and what you do* are no concern of mine. (Compound subject)

Subjective complement. See *Predicate complement*.

Subjunctive. The mood (or mode) of a verb expressing possibility, desire, or a condition contrary to fact. See Mood.

Subordinate clause. Another name for *dependent clause*, which see.

Subordinating conjunction. A conjunction joining a dependent clause (noun or adverbial) to its independent clause: *when, if, since, because,* etc. See *Conjunction*.

Substantive. An inclusive term for noun, pronoun, verbal noun (gerund, infinitive), or a phrase or a clause used like a noun. The practical value of the word *substantive* is that it saves repeating all the words included in this definition. The following italicized words are examples of substantives:

> My *dog* is three years old. (Noun)
> *They* will arrive tomorrow; in fact *everyone* is arriving tomorrow. (Pronouns)
> Your *coming* is looked forward to. (Gerund)
> *To improve* myself is my *aim*. (Infinitive, noun)
> *From Chicago to San Francisco* is a long distance. (Noun phrase)
> *What you say* is *no concern of mine*. (Noun clause, noun phrase)
> Do *you* know *that he was here yesterday?* (Pronoun, noun clause)

Suffix. A sound, syllable, or syllables added at the end of a word or word base to change its meaning, give it grammatical function, or form a new word: *-er* in *smaller*, *-ness* in *smoothness*.

Summary. A brief but comprehensive presentation of facts or statements. A *summary* is a terse restatement of main points, as a *summary* of a chapter. It is related in meaning to *digest* and *résumé*, which see. *Summary* is used more often in connection with nonfiction than with fiction; *synopsis* (which see) usually is employed to refer to a compressed statement of the plot of a play, novel, etc. Also see *Abstract*.

Superlative degree. The form of an adjective or adverb comparing three or more objects, persons, etc. See *Comparison*.

> Of the three brothers, Albert is the *tallest*.
> In our family, Mother is the one who drives *most cautiously*.

Syllable. In phonetics, a *syllable* is a segment of speech uttered with one impulse of air pressure from the lungs. In writing, *syllable* refers to a character or set of characters (letters of the alphabet) representing one sound. In general, *syllable* refers to the smallest amount or least portion of speech or writing.

Symbolism. Something used or regarded as standing for or representing something else. It may be a material object representing something either immaterial or quite general: a figure, token, or sign. The dove is the *symbol* of peace. The *symbol* of Christianity is the cross. *Symbolism* is closely related to *image*, which see.

Synecdoche. A figure of speech in which a part or an individual is used for a whole or a class, or the reverse of this: "bread" for "food," "a Croesus" for "a rich man," "the navy" for "a sailor."

Synonym. A word having the same meaning as another, or nearly the same meaning: *cold, chill, chilling, chilly; hotel, inn, tavern; prevent, forestall, preclude, obviate, avert.* See *Antonym*.

Synopsis. A statement giving a brief, general review or condensation. It is most frequently used in connection with retelling the plot of a story, novel, or play. See *Summary* and *Abstract*.

Syntax. The arrangement of words in a sentence to show their relationship. It is a rather vague and general term, but one for which our language has no adequate substitute. Although *syntax* is a branch of *grammar*, the latter term is more useful in referring to word order, parts of speech, and the like.

Table of contents. A tabulated list of topics covered by a book or other document; see *Contents* and *Index*.

Tale. A *tale* is a narrative relating events in the life of some real or imagined person. It is a synonym of *story* but often lacks the structured orderliness and insistence upon a single effect which characterize the *short story*.

Tautology. Needless repetition of an idea in a different word, phrase, clause, or sentence. See *Deadwood*.

Technical terms. Terms which have special meanings for people in particular fields, occupations, or professions. Special subject labels are attached by dictionaries to such words in the fields of astronomy, engineering, psychology, etc. Technical terms should be used sparingly in writing for the general public and, when so employed, should be enclosed in quotation marks and usually should be defined.

Telegraphic style. The clipped, abbreviated style employed in telegrams to save on words. [Your] *letter* [has been] *received*. [I am] *answering immediately*. [Please accept my warm] *regards*.

Tense. This term indicates the *time* of the action or state expressed by a verb. The three divisions of time—past, present, and future—are shown by six tenses in English.

The three primary, or simple, tenses are the *present tense*, the *past tense*, and the *future tense*. The other three are secondary, or compound, tenses: the *present perfect*, the *past perfect*, and the *future perfect*.

English, unlike a highly inflected language such as German, has few tense *forms*. Verbs reveal change in tense only by inflection or by the addition of auxiliary words.

The following tables and comments on each tense should be carefully studied:

ACTIVE VOICE

Present: I see (am seeing)
Past: I saw (was seeing)
Future: I shall see (shall be seeing)
Present perfect: I have seen (have been seeing)
Past perfect: I had seen (had been seeing)
Future perfect: I shall have seen (shall have been seeing)

PASSIVE VOICE

Present: I am seen (am being seen)
Past: I was seen (was being seen)
Future: I shall be seen
Present perfect: I have been seen
Past perfect: I had been seen
Future perfect: I shall have been seen

VERBALS (NONFINITE VERB FORMS)

Present infinitive: to see
Perfect infinitive: to have seen
Present participle: seeing
Past participle: seen
Perfect participle: having seen

1. *Present tense.* This tense indicates that the action or condition is going on or exists *now.*

   He *hits* the ball.
   The truth *is* known.

2. *Past tense.* This tense indicates that an action or condition took place or existed at some definite time in the past.

   I *saw* the man yesterday.
   The winter of 1955 *was* cold.

3. *Future tense.* This tense indicates that an action will take place, or that a certain condition will exist, in the future.

   He *will go* with you tomorrow.
   I *shall be* better prepared at that time.

The future may be stated by the present tense accompanied by an adverb (or adverbial phrase) of time. Such constructions as the following are common:

> He arrives soon.
> I am going to Ruston soon.
> This Thursday the plane leaves for Decatur.

4. *Present perfect tense.* This tense indicates that an action or condition was begun in the past and is completed at the present time. The time is past but it is connected with the present, and the action or condition may possibly still be going on. The present perfect tense presupposes something in the present.

> You *have been* very ill.
> The ice *has been* too thin for skating.
> I *have* long *been* a Gilbert and Sullivan addict.

5. *Past perfect tense.* This tense indicates that an action or condition was completed at a time now past. It indicates action "two steps back." That is, the past perfect tense presupposes some action or condition expressed in the past tense, to which it is related.

> The roads were impassable because the snow *had fallen* fast.
> He lived in High Street. He *had been* there for over a year.

6. *Future perfect tense.* This tense indicates that an action or condition will be completed at a future time.

> I *shall have gone* by that time.
> The snow *will have melted* before you arrive.

The three secondary, or compound, tenses always indicate *completed* action, whether it be in the present (present perfect tense), in the past (past perfect tense), or in the future (future perfect tense).

Terminology. The names, or terms, forming a system is known as *terminology.* Thus we speak of the "*terminology* of accounting" when we mean the set of terms employed especially in that profession.

Theme. This word means "a topic," "a subject." When, for example, we speak of the *theme* of a play or a musical composition we mean its controlling idea, its central subject matter and content. Also, a short, informal essay, such as a school composition, is known as a *theme*.

Thesaurus. Any book containing a store of words, such as a dictionary, but more especially a book of classified *synonyms* and *antonyms*, which see.

Thesis. A proposition stated or laid down and intended to be discussed, defended, and proved is known as a *thesis*. *Thesis* is also a somewhat loose synonym for *theme* in the sense of "subject" or "content."

Tone. This word has many meanings, several of which apply to writing, as when we refer to the *tone* (meaning quality or appeal or point of view) of a novel, speech, play, etc. More particularly, *tone* distinguishes a characteristic of tenses of verbs, indicating within any one tense *emphasis* or *progress* or *simple* time: I still *do* work; I *was leaving* when you telephoned; I *mailed* the letter. See *Emphatic verb form*, *Progressive verb form*, and *Simple verb form*.

Transition. Passage from one position, state, stage, etc., to another. In writing and speaking, the term refers to methods by which writer and speaker bridge gaps between what has been covered and that which is to come.

Transitive verb. Verbs are classified as either transitive or intransitive. A *transitive* verb is regularly accompanied by a direct object; this direct object completes the meaning of the verb: "They *accepted* his resignation." An *intransitive* verb requires no direct object: "He *will obey*." Whether a verb is transitive or intransitive depends upon meaning, upon the idea which the writer wishes to show: *will obey* in "He *will obey* our orders" is transitive.

Triteness. State of being worn out, overused, hackneyed by constant repetition. See *Cliché*.

Understatement. A comment or statement representing an idea or opinion less strongly than the truth will bear. This term is the antonym of *exaggeration* and *hyperbole*, which see.

Unity. A term meaning "oneness." In writing and speaking, it refers to sentences and paragraphs which stick to their subjects and permit no extraneous material to filter in. *Unity* is a by-product of clear, careful thinking.

Verb. A verb asserts, or says, something. It may make a statement, give a command, or ask a question. A verb expresses action or a state of being. This definition may not be particularly helpful, but you can see that, according to this definition, italicized words in the following sentences are verbs: the first says something; the second asks a question; the third gives a command.

> They *bought* a new tire.
> *Is* dinner ready?
> *Get* there on time.

Verbals. In English, verbs are finite and nonfinite, depending on whether they are so formed and accompanied by another word as to make complete predications. Nonfinite verb forms (words incapable of standing alone and making complete predications) are called verbals. The verbals are *participles, infinitives,* and *gerunds.*

Understanding the differences in form and function between finite verbs and verbals will insure avoiding the most serious error in sentence construction, the half-sentence or fragment. Verbals cannot stand alone; if a group of words contains a verbal, it must also include a finite verb in order to be a complete sentence.

Verb phrase. A verb together with an auxiliary or auxiliaries, or with its object or its modifiers: *is seeking, was finished, shall have seen, will have been spent, builds daydreams for herself.* Be certain that you can distinguish between a *verb phrase* and a *verbal* (participle, infinitive, gerund): *has been singing, to sing.*

Vernacular. Native or originating in the place of its occurrence. *Vernacular* refers primarily to the common, everyday language of ordinary people in a particular locality. See *Provincialism.*

Verse. Any writing which contains a succession of metrical feet or a rhythmic pattern. See *Poetry.*

Vocative. See *Direct address.*

Voice. Verbs are classified as to *voice—active* or *passive*. A verb is *active* when the subject is the performer of the action or is in the state or condition named.

> The engineers *threw* a bridge across the river.
> A bridge *was thrown* across the river by the engineers.

> The lookout *sighted* the ship on the horizon.
> The ship on the horizon *was sighted* by the lookout.

> Tom *laid* the book on the table.
> The book *was laid* on the table by Tom.

> We *rested* on the beach.

In the first three examples above, the point of view and the emphasis are quite different. The verbs which are *active* stress the doers of the action—engineers, lookout, and Tom; the verbs which are *passive* stress the recipients of the action—bridge, ship, and book.

Choice of active or passive voice depends upon context, upon relative importance of the doer and the recipient of the action. Since intransitive verbs rarely fulfill the conditions which make verbs active or passive, only transitive verbs can have a passive voice.

In the last example above, *rested* is in the active voice because the subject, "we," is in the state or condition named.

Vowel. In phonetics, a speech sound articulated so that there is a clear channel for the voice through the middle of the mouth. In spelling and grammar, a letter representing such a sound: *a, e, i, o, u.* See *Consonant.*

Vulgarism. A term derived from Latin *vulgus,* "the common people." It means a word or expression occurring only in common colloquial usage or in coarse speech. See *Illiteracies.*

Weak verb. See *Regular verbs.*

Who, whom. See *Nominative or objective case, use of,* and *Relative pronoun.*

Word. The word is the smallest grammatical element which can stand alone as an utterance.

Part VI

Guide to Pronunciation

The right rule is to speak as our neighbours do, not better.
H. W. FOWLER, *A Dictionary of Modern English Usage*

Demosthenes overcame and rendered more distinct his inarticulate and stammering pronunciation by speaking with pebbles in his mouth.

PLUTARCH, *Lives*

Say now *Shibboleth*: and he said *Sibboleth*, for he could not frame to pronounce it right.

The Book of Judges, 12:6

Speak the speech, I pray you, as I have pronounced it to you, trippingly on the tongue; but if you mouth it, as many of your players do, I had as lief the town-crier spoke my lines.

SHAKESPEARE, *Hamlet*, Act 3, Scene 2

Part VI
Guide to Pronunciation

Everyone learned to speak before he learned to write. Each of us continues to speak many times more often than we write. For each of us, words actually *live* in oral rather than in printed or handwritten form. Consequently, pronunciation is a more direct, immediate, and constant concern than sentence structure, word usage, spelling, punctuation, grammar, or any other aspect of communication.

Pronunciation, as defined on page 331, is the act, or result, of producing the sounds of speech. More simply, pronunciation is the way words sound when we speak them, the way in which words and phrases as they come from our lips strike our ears and those of our hearers. Pronunciation is "making speech sounds," but the act involved is complex and involves problems not generally understood. This section deals with those phases of pronunciation that directly touch upon success or failure in communicating with those who hear the sounds we utter.

WHAT PRONUNCIATION IS ALL ABOUT

The life of everyone is surrounded by sounds, most of them those which he makes or that enter his ears as they issue from the lips of others. People engage in speaking and listening more than in any other single pursuit of their lives. Surely this everyday, widespread activity should be freed from the misconceptions that have become associated with it.

Everyone Speaks His Own Language

First, none of us speaks "*the* English language" or even that variety known as "American English." That is, no one speaks *language* at all but rather a *particular* language. Each of us makes sounds with speech characteristics peculiar to a specific locality and social group. Everyone learns and tends to retain certain speech patterns that are uniquely his own; to a trained ear, the speech sounds of no two persons are identical.

In addition, no two people ordinarily use the same words or even the same syntax in voicing a given idea or opinion. Despite apparent conformity to group or social usage, everyone has his own *idiolect*, the language (speech pattern) peculiar to him at a particular period of his life. It should be kept in mind that no such thing as total conformity in pronunciation is possible, since every speaker of a given language (English, French, Spanish, German, or whatnot) employs *his own dialect* (the precise meaning of the term idiolect). One should also remember that no stigma attaches to the word *dialect*, a term for a variety of language distinguished from other varieties by features of sound, grammar, and word choice.

With many millions of idiolects for the English language in use, no one dialect flatly may be termed "better than" or "preferable to" another except to the extent of its success in communicating meaning with ease, naturalness, appropriateness, and effectiveness in the specific speech situation in which it is used.

In the United States, No Single Standard Exists

American English (like "English" English, "Canadian" English, "Australian" English, etc.) is made up of numerous local and regional types of speech. In recent years, scholars have painstakingly identified several major speech areas in the United States. For example, in the eastern part of the country and in Canada, three areas have been isolated: Northern, Middle Atlantic, and Southern. These sections, in turn, embrace distinct subareas, such as Eastern New England, Western New England, New York City, etc.

As one travels west, he discovers that lines separating speech areas from each other become less distinct, but evidence exists to identify such regional divisions as Central Midland (extending from Ohio to the Rocky Mountain states of Colorado, Utah, and Wyoming), North Central (east of the Great Lakes to the Dakotas), Northwest (Washington, Oregon, Montana, Idaho), and Pacific and Southwestern (California, Nevada, Arizona). Experts claim that many subareas of speech thrive within each of these regions and in others not named here.

The distinctive speech patterns of sections of the United States, however, involve flavor more than substance, so that communication between speakers of different dialects constitutes no major problem. As a result, these distinctive patterns remain firmly established. No single, accepted pronunciation has developed; no regional dialect has gained ascendancy.

What, Then, Is Correct Pronunciation?

In judging what speech patterns are acceptable, experts frequently use the terms *standard* and *nonstandard*. To those varieties of speech used by the cultivated, or educated, people of any given community or region is applied the word *standard*. To departures from this speech pattern is given the designation *nonstandard*.

Since most Americans pronounce most words in about the same way, these labels are not applied to some 90 percent of the total vocabulary. To a question concerning the remaining 10 percent, "What is the *correct* pronunciation?" the only accurate answer is that the pronunciation of any word or phrase is "reputable" and therefore "correct" if it is one employed by a majority of educated speakers under a similar set of circumstances in a particular major speech area. In short, "cultivated" and "correct" speech is used in every part of the United States.

Such an answer lacks the "final authority" often being sought, but it is the only truly informed and honest response that can be made. This answer also suggests an obvious truth: every person, on occasion, uses different styles of speech. The most commonly identified of these are *formal* and *informal*. For instance, one who customarily employs "cultivated" speech would pronounce words in a *cultivated, formal* style when making a speech or giving a carefully prepared report. In what might be called "business suit" or "black tie" situations, such a speaker would use the same standard of pronunciation in conversation. At other times and in other places, the same speaker might use *cultivated, informal* speech that could be careless, slurred, casual, and filled with language shortcuts (such as contractions), slang, shoptalk, grammatical inaccuracies, and even vulgarities, obscenities, and profanity. Instead of asking "What pronunciation is correct?" one should rather inquire "What pronunciation is correct under what circumstances and on what occasion?"

Cultivated, informal pronunciation often verges on nonstandard usage but is the result of deliberate casualness rather than ignorance. For example, an educated, cultivated speaker might occasionally use the word "ain't" (pronounced with a long "a" sound as in *able*) in a folksy, or relaxed, or humorous, or self-conscious situation. He would not employ the expression in "normal" speech because he knows that the word is nonstandard and that its use might cause hearers to judge him illiterate. It is, however, more important for everyone to avoid nonstandard pronunciation than the informal, relaxed usage of educated speakers.

In summary, correct pronunciation is the pronunciation of careful, educated speakers of the general region in which they have formed their speech habits. A person whose language background lies along the northern Atlantic coast may reasonably be expected to use what linguists refer to as "eastern speech." One who has formed his speech patterns in, say, Minnesota, normally uses what is termed "north central" speech.

So far as a standard may be said to exist, the standard of pronunciation is that usage which prevails among cultured, educated people to whom the language is native. Nevertheless, since different pronunciations are used by cultivated, educated people in different regions, uniformity of expression is nonexistent in the English-speaking world and *correctness* is a flexible, relative term.

Isn't a Dictionary an Authority on Pronunciation?

The term "correct pronunciation" is often employed, but those who use it would have difficulty in explaining the exact meaning of the phrase. Correctness implies a standard of measurement—*one* standard, not a large number such as exist in several large speech areas in the United States. No one standard may be said to apply to pronunciation when the criterion is that a given pronunciation is correct because it is used by a sufficient number of cultivated, educated speakers. How does one determine what is meant by a "sufficient number"? And who judges the degree of "cultivation" and "education" of speakers who set a standard?

The makers of dictionaries—highly skilled persons known as *lexicographers*—weigh the differences in pronunciations of words and phrases in various areas and also the historical development of these speech patterns. With as much freedom from local prejudice and as much breadth of view as possible, lexicographers record the most widespread pronunciations prevailing in what they consider the "most reputable" present usage. It is a basic principle of all lexicographers that the one and only criterion of correctness is *educated usage*. Of little or no significance in determining standard pronunciations are tradition, rules, word derivation, or spelling.

No reliable dictionary attempts to dictate what correct usage should be. Only to the degree that any dictionary is acknowledged as an accurate and unbiased recorder and interpreter of usage may it be considered an "authority." Remember: a "good" dictionary strives to provide an objective description of pronunciation; it will not flatly assert that this pronunciation is "right" and that that pronunciation is "wrong."

The current attitude of dictionary makers is summarized in this statement by Dr. Daniel Jones, eminent former professor of phonetics and author of an authoritative book, *The Pronunciation of English:*

> It is useful that descriptions of existing pronunciation should be recorded, but I no longer feel disposed to recommend any particular forms of pronunciation . . . or to condemn others. It must, in my view, be left to individual English-speaking persons to decide whether they should speak in the manner that comes to them naturally or whether they should alter their speech in any way.

Why Study Pronunciation At All?

If there is no one correct standard of pronunciation in the United States, and if even experts are apparently inclined to think that everyone might as well talk in ways that come to him naturally, why then all the fuss? If it is incorrect to assume that the dictionary, any dictionary, is a never-failing guide in determining what specific pronunciation is acceptable at a given time, what or whom is one to consult? What *is* a *final* authority?

If you wish to argue that one pronunciation is "as good" as another so long as it is understood, experts will agree, provided that you accept a restricted meaning of the phrase "as good." The situation is similar to that of a writer who might be justified in saying that his grammar is good (by which he means practical or effective) if his readers understand what he means when he writes, for example, "She don't want none." For another illustration, a letter filled with inaccurate punctuation and misspelled words somehow may convey meaning and therefore be considered effective—translated "good."

Good and *effective* are relative terms. Any method of getting food in one's mouth is effective as a step toward nourishment, but nearly everyone agrees that table manners are usually judged by standards of taste, appearance, and social acceptability. Almost any kind of clothing will prevent one from arrest for indecent exposure, but who will claim that no standards exist for suitable apparel in differing situations and on differing occasions? In pronunciation, too, standards of what is "good" and "effective" are flexible and constantly changing, but they do exist. The careful and improving speaker will ignore them to his embarrassment, discomfort, and social or business peril.

Nine out of ten words in the English language that you are likely to use either (1) cause no difficulty in pronouncing or (2) have only one contemporary and reputable pronunciation. Words in the remaining 10 percent either (1) present pronunciation difficulties or (2) are pronounced somewhat differently by educated groups of users. It is this 10 percent that merits study. Pronouncing words from this group in accordance with standard usage will result in benefits and advantages comparable to those deriving from effective sentence structure, correct spelling, accurate diction, suitably applied punctuation, or, for that matter, from acceptable dress, approved table manners, and agreeable behavior in general.

In addition, pronunciation has a direct relationship to several other important items discussed in this book: punctuation, spelling, and the use of a dictionary.

Pronunciation and Punctuation

When we talk, we do not depend upon words alone to tell a listener what we mean. The tone and stress of one's voice influence the meanings of the words he utters. On occasion, each of us whispers or shouts. We speak angrily or calmly. We lower or raise our voices at the end of a statement or a question. (Rising inflection in one's voice when asking a question suggests precisely what a question mark does at the end of a written sentence.) A strongly emotional tone in speaking conveys a suggestion of determination or anger or command, such as would be indicated by an exclamation point in writing. Strongly accenting a given word in a spoken sentence (similar to underlining a word in writing) can and does convey one meaning, whereas emphasizing another word provides a different idea. Notice the varying meanings produced by accenting the sounds of each italicized word in these sentences:

> *Priscilla* has finally found happiness.
> Priscilla *has* finally found happiness.
> Priscilla has *finally* found happiness.
> Priscilla has finally *found* happiness.
> Priscilla has finally found *happiness.*

Furthermore, bodily and facial gestures and expressions add meaning to spoken words. We stamp a foot, wiggle a finger, raise an eyebrow, clasp hands, bend forward or backward, shrug a shoulder, grin or grimace, nod or shake the head. Again, meaning in talk is affected by pauses and halts that are often as significant as words themselves. Nearly everyone has seen a skilled actor or actress convey ideas and moods without using any words at all. The pauses, inflections, and stresses that occur in speech are a part of pronunciation in that they help to make clear to listeners the meanings of words themselves. In this sense, pronunciation bears a relationship to speaking similar to that of punctuation in writing. Pronunciation involves more than standard and substandard ways of uttering words and phrases as isolated items.

Pronunciation and Spelling

As is suggested on pages 203 and 209, mispronouncing words can cause spelling problems—an additional reason for studying pronunciation. (Many people consider mispronouncing words as serious a social and business error as misspelling them.) Properly pronouncing certain words will positively assist in spelling them because there *is* some relationship between sound and spelling. For instance, if you learn to pronounce *cartoon* (drawing, sketch) and *carton* (box, receptacle), you will not mistakenly misspell one for the other.

In Part III, look up and study the entries for *Added vowels, Confusing and transposing letters, Dropped consonants, Dropped vowels, Silent letters, Speech sounds,* and *Unstressed vowels.* Pronunciation and spelling have a loose, uneasy, but often genuine relationship to each other.

PRONUNCIATION AND A DICTIONARY

With a somewhat fuller idea of what pronunciation involves and perhaps a clearer concept of what is meant by standard and nonstandard ways of saying words, we can now take a look at the role dictionaries play in this important aspect of "errors in English." As is mentioned on page 292, a reliable dictionary is a valuable tool for every user of the language. A dictionary as an aid in spelling is discussed on pages 186–187. A good dictionary is also indispensable as an aid in, and guide to, the pronunciation of words and phrases.

First, we should thoroughly understand what a dictionary does *not* supply as a guide to pronunciation.

It hardly seems necessary further to reiterate that a dictionary is not a supreme authority on pronunciation and that it does not attempt to be. A good dictionary, however, is the best guide available; it will unfailingly assist you in making a choice of pronunciations suitable for specific occasions. As your mentor, the dictionary will reveal what its makers think to be the most general pronunciations employed by educated people in the significant speech areas in the United States. The style of pronunciation set forth will be that of *formal, educated* speech. Methods of pronouncing words and phrases on informal levels are rarely provided, although their omission does not necessarily imply that such pronunciations are incorrect in every situation. Further, the omission of less "precise" pronunciations does not indicate that dictionary makers are unaware of them or that they do not exist.

Another limitation of a dictionary as a guide to pronunciation is that its compilers understandably have been unable to record the "correct" pronunciation of words as they occur in *connected* speech. We pronounce many words in one way when we say them alone and in quite a different way when we use them in conversation. No dictionary can indicate the rising or falling pitch of one's voice. No dictionary can even suggest the emphasis that might be given to a word in a spoken sentence, because this emphasis depends upon the speaker's exact meaning. In ordinary conversation, vowels in unaccented syllables become indistinct in the speech of even educated, careful speakers. Cultivated persons whose pronunciation is standard often slur certain consonants in speaking and sometimes drop out entire syllables. For example, it is possible to say "ham and eggs" with emphasis on each word. In normal speech, however, the phrase sounds like "ham 'n' eggs" or even "hamneggs." In saying "bread and butter" one can accent each word, but in formal and informal and standard and nonstandard speech the phrase sounds more like "breadnbutter." In everyday speech, even educated and cultivated speakers may pronounce "it's all right" as "sawright." Other locutions that constantly appear in rapid speech but that are nowhere noted in any dictionary are these: "smothertam" for "some other time"; "whachusay" for "what you say"; "gonna" for "going to"; "wanna" for "want to"; and "y'know" for "you know." Experts disagree whether the following pronunciations result from informality or ignorance, but they appear often in the speech of many people: "innerference" for "interference"; "gennelmen" for "gentlemen"; "congradulate" for "congratulate"; "inny" for "any"; "wunnerful" for "wonderful"; and "izda" for "is the." No dictionary records such speech usage if for no other reason than that such speech cannot accurately be noted, at least not in a dictionary.

We all know that, in speech, words frequently flow together without the pauses which, in writing, are shown by spaces. If one were to say, for example, "The person who can do this well deserves a reward," we would need to interrupt the flow of sound after either *this* or *well* in order to be fully understood. (The sentence has two distinct meanings, depending upon where the speaker pauses.) The "sound boundary" of a word or phrase, known to linguists as *juncture*, is nowhere indicated in any dictionary.

Finally, reliable dictionaries do not always agree on which of several acceptable pronunciations of a given word is "best," that is, in widest use by cultivated speakers. For instance, most dictionaries of quality give three standard pronunciations for the word *advertisement*. One excellent dictionary provides only two pronunciations of the word; one lists five. All reputable dictionaries offer only pronunciations that are popular and current, but dictionary makers differ in their judgments. It is rare that one, and only one, acceptable pronunciation can arbitrarily be preferred to all other favored choices. Of course, where pronunciation usage is not divided—as it is not in most instances—this difficulty does not arise.

Using Your Dictionary as a Guide to Pronunciation

Despite the limitations and shortcomings of any dictionary as a guide to correct pronunciation, it is your only unbiased, reliable, and always available mentor and counselor. You should acquire a dictionary (see page 292) and, having done so, learn how to use it. You should unfailingly consult it whenever a problem with pronunciation comes up. Such questions *will* arise and arise often.

Pronunciation depends upon the sound given to alphabetical letters or letter combinations and upon accent or emphasized syllables.

Accent. The matter of accent, or stress, is far less complicated than the pronunciation of sounds but is nonetheless important. Carefully study the method your particular dictionary employs for indicating accents. Some dictionaries include accent marks and syllabication dots (periods) in the entry word; other dictionaries carry only dots to indicate syllabication in the entry word and use accent marks in the *pronunciation word* that follows. Learn the method your dictionary has adopted for indicating heavy (or primary) stress and less heavy (secondary) stress. Whatever devices your dictionary uses, the system will be made fully clear in an introductory article at the front of the book and will be uniformly applied in all entries.

Pronunciation of sounds. Because only twenty-six alphabetical letters can be used in some 250 common spellings of sounds in the English language, makers of dictionaries have had to resort to carefully devised systems for the representation of sounds. The best-known set of symbols for providing a consistent system of transcribing the sounds of language is the International Phonetic

Alphabet (IPA). This arrangement is popular with linguists and students of phonetics. But since it is applicable to the sounds of all languages, not just English, it is somewhat more complicated and extensive than the average speaker needs or can readily understand. The IPA, however, is the most accurate system yet devised for the transcription of the sounds of speech.

Every modern American dictionary presents its own system of pronunciation symbols designed to represent major sound distinctions. Each dictionary compiler selects anywhere from forty to sixty symbols that are adequate, in his judgment, for explaining all practical problems in pronunciation. The procedure of most dictionaries is to include a *pronunciation word* in parentheses immediately after the entry word. It is a respelling of the word, giving the sounds of vowels and consonants, by syllables, according to the *pronouncing key* that the dictionary has adopted. Every user of a dictionary should become thoroughly familiar with the key that his particular dictionary has chosen. An abbreviated form of the key usually appears at the bottom of each page, or each alternate page, of the dictionary. A full key is included inside the front or back cover, or both, of every modern dictionary. One can get by with use of the abbreviated key only, but the serious, accomplished dictionary-user will master the expanded key as well.

As an indication of the kinds of information appearing in an abbreviated pronunciation key, find out how the dictionary you are using represents sounds of the letter *a*. Probably you will find that *a* is indicated by these symbols:

> a—as in *act, apple, bat, fact,* etc.
> ā—as in *able, age, inflation, pay,* etc.
> à—as in *air, care, dare, rarely,* etc.
> ä—as in *art, far, father, tar,* etc.

Study the key in your dictionary to find out the varied sounds of other vowels, of consonants, and of several letter combinations (*th, ng,* etc.). Practice saying aloud the illustrative sample words until you have a particular sound clearly in mind and clearly in your ear.

Multiple pronunciations. When two or more pronunciations of a word are provided, the one more commonly used (that is, more nearly standard) may or may not be shown first. One important dictionary lists first the pronunciations its makers consider most prevalent in Eastern speech (along the northern Atlantic seaboard); another gives first what its compilers judge to be that pronunciation most widespread in "general American" usage. Every pronunciation listed is correct, although some dictionaries make a distinction by preceding a given pronunciation with the word "also." You should note that some pronunciations are labeled *British*, or *Brit.*, *Chiefly British*, etc., indicating that such pronunciations are more common in Great Britain than in the United States. (Generally speaking, for an American to adopt British pronunciation is a kind of affectation. Overly careful, precise, and labored pronunciation is an affectation, as is mentioned on page 269).

Diacritical marks. Each of the symbols and signs appearing with words in a pronunciation key is a kind of diacritical mark. (The word *diacritical* comes from a Greek term meaning "distinctive," "capable of distinguishing.") Still other signs or points may be added to letters to indicate a particular sound value or to indicate some form of stress (accent). Among these are the *circumflex* (∧), the *cedilla* (ᶜ), the *tilde* (∼), and *umlaut* (··). Because such marks distinctly influence pronunciation, you should carefully note their appearance in such words and phrases as *bête noire, raison d'être, hôtel de ville; façade, garçon, Français, soupçon; cañon, mañana, señor; Die Walküre, Tannhäuser, schön.* Some dictionaries will not employ such diacritical marks with each of these words. Others will provide a separate "foreign sounds" key for words adapted from another language.

Makers of American dictionaries are aware that different languages have different patterns of stress and that no series of accent marks or other visual symbols can adequately substitute for first-hand knowledge of a foreign language. The situation applies in reverse, of course: few native speakers of other languages than English can pronounce "American talk" with exactly the same intonations and inflections as a native of this country. (It is reasonable to suggest that every cultivated speaker should *try* to reproduce as accurately as possible the sounds of a language foreign to him. Few of us have earned the right to be as indifferent, or arrogant, as the late Winston Churchill, who is reported to have pronounced all foreign words as though they were some sort of inferior English.)

Diacritical marks are inexact methods for suggesting the reproduction of sounds, but their use is an additional example of the lengths to which dictionary compilers have gone in trying faithfully to provide a record of the sounds of spoken language.

When to Use Your Dictionary as a Guide to Pronunciation

No one can be expected to spell correctly every word in the language. Neither can anyone be prepared to pronounce, on demand, every sound in the vast inventory of English words. Fortunately, we use comparatively few words in ordinary speech, and the overwhelming majority of these cause no problems whatever in pronunciation.

The dozen most often employed words in speech and writing are *a, and, he, I, in, it, is, of, that, the, to,* and *was.* It may be surprising, but comforting, to learn that these twelve simple words account for about one-fourth of everything spoken and written in English. These dozen words and thirty-eight more (a total of only fifty words) comprise half of the running total in all American (and English) speech and writing. Increase the number to the one thousand most common words and you will have accounted for some 80 percent of all the words *everyone* uses in speaking or writing and come across in reading. These statements may be difficult to accept, but they are vouched for by the authoritative word count contained in *The Teacher's Word Book of 30,000 Words,* prepared under the direction of two eminent scholars, Edward L. Thorndike and Irving Lorge.

Well, you may say, if only one thousand words are involved in 80 percent of all the expressions that I read, write, and say, it should be easy to learn to pronounce this limited number. The problem is even simpler than that. Few of the thousand words occurring most often present much greater difficulties than do the dozen most common—*a, and, he,* etc.

The first word, alphabetically, in this list of one thousand that could conceivably cause difficulty is *across.* A careless or uninformed person might say *acrost* (acrossed), but no one reading this book is likely to make such an error. To see just how simple pronunciation problems are with 80 percent of all the words you will ever use or encounter through listening or reading, look at the following list of fifty words which might possibly cause difficulty in pronunciation for some persons. They are given in alphabetical order with the pronunciation of each word indicated in a slightly inexact, highly simplified form. The first twenty-five words appear in the list of the five hundred most frequently occurring words; the second twenty-five in the five hundred words appearing next most frequently.

across	uh KRAWS, uh KROS
answer	AN suhr, AHN suhr
business	BIZ nes, BIZ nis
company	KUHM puh ni
different	DIF uhr uhnt
either	EE thuhr, AI thuhr
evening	EEV ning
figure	FIG yuhr
government	GUHV uhrn muhnt
human	HYOO muhn
hundred	HUHN druhd
interest	IN tuhr est, IN tuhr ist
laugh	lahf, laf
money	MUHN i
national	NASH uhn uhl, NASH uhn 'l
perhaps	puhr HAPS, puhr APS
picture	PIK chuhr, PIK tyuhr
question	KWES chuhn
suppose	suh POHZ
through	throo
water	WAW tuhr, WAH tuhr, WOT uhr
whether	HWETH uhr
window	WIN doh
woman	WOOM uhn
would	wood
accept	ak SEPT
beautiful	BYOO tuh fool, BYOO ti fool, BYOO tuh f'l
century	SEN choo ri, SEN chuh ri, SEN tyoo ri
certainly	SUHR tin li, SUHR t'n li

daughter	DAW tuhr
escape	es KAYP, e SKAYP, is KAYP
experience	eks PIER i uhns, ek SPIER i uhns, eks PEER i uhns
fellow	FEL oh
foreign	FOR in, FAWR in
future	FYOO chuhr, FYOO tyuhr
gentleman	JEN t'l muhn
judge	juhj
listen	LIS 'n
million	MIL yuhn
necessary	NES uh ser i, NES i ser i
neither	NEE thuhr, NAI thuhr
probably	PROB uh bli
purpose	PUHR puhs
rule	rool
soldier	SOHL juhr
strength	strength, strengkth
surprise	suhr PRAIZ, suh PRAIZ
usually	YOO zhoo uhl i
view	vyoo
yellow	YEL oh

You may feel that all, or almost all, of these words are ridiculously easy to pronounce and that none could cause you trouble. That is perhaps true. You may also question the accuracy of the Thorndike-Lorge list from which these fifty words were selected—although experts do not. It is possible that some other words than those chosen from the one thousand appearing most frequently might cause greater difficulty, although the selections were carefully made. But regardless of your reaction, what pronunciation problems are presented seem minor if not well-nigh nonexistent.

Further simplifying the matter of pronunciation is that only nine thousand additional words (the next most frequently occurring ones) account for 18 percent of *all* words read or spoken. Thus only ten thousand words comprise 98 percent of all expressions regularly used in speaking, writing, and reading. It is true that after the first ten thousand words, problems in pronunciation (and in spelling) multiply. And yet, words in the 10,001–

20,000 frequency group occur less than one-twelfth as often as those in the group from 1,001–10,000. Those in the group from 20,001 to 30,000 appear on an average only one two-hundredths as often as words in the most common ten thousand. In short, pronunciation errors do occur, but they appear infrequently because of rare use and because a relatively small number of words is involved.

Now that the matter has been narrowed to its proper proportions, what is the best method of tackling the problems that do remain? First, do not bother with the pronunciation of any word until you read it, hear it, or anticipate the need for it in your own speech. "Swallowing the dictionary" is a silly procedure in its application to pronunciation just as it is with word meanings and spelling. Little is to be gained, and much effort lost, from trying to become expert in the handling of words without *use* value to you. Concentrate on words that you actually do employ or might conceivably do so; even in simplified and lessened form, the task will be difficult enough.

Second, if you have a sensitive ear and spend considerable time listening to speakers on radio and television or in person, you can learn the pronunciation of numerous difficult words. This method has several weaknesses, however, among which two are major: (1) in any particular broadcast, conversation, or speech, it is unlikely that you will hear those specific words that you need to learn to pronounce in your own speaking and (2) not every effective speaker, including broadcasters and telecasters, is infallible in his use of standard pronunciation. (Leading networks have their pronunciation guides and manuals, but speakers do not always follow them.)

The most economical and efficient way to learn to avoid errors in pronunciation is to consult your dictionary *when the need arises*. These encounters and needs will supply you with enough words to keep you busy for the remainder of your life.

Precisely what these words will be must vary from person to person. No two persons have the same vocabulary; no two persons make the same demands on language if only because no two can have the same audience or the same material to present. Consequently, no complete and authoritative master list can be provided. However, from various lists you can select words that do give you pronunciation trouble and that you might need to know how to pronounce in some speaking situation. Single out these words and study them carefully; others on the list you can either overlook or put aside until further need arises. Keep reminding yourself that it is a waste of time to try to learn the pronunciation of words that have *no use value to you personally*.

Here, for a starter, is a list of sixty words beginning with the letter *a*. All of them have raised pronunciation problems for some persons. From the list, select those that you wish to learn; to these words apply the principles of dictionary study set forth in preceding pages. Say each word aloud until you have mastered its sound according to standard usage. In most instances, you will be pleased to discover that your pronunciation is close to that standard or those standards recommended by your dictionary.

abdomen	alternate (verb, noun, adj.)
abject	aluminum
absorb	amateur
absurd	amenable
accidentally	amour
acclimate	anchovy
acumen	anemone
adage	annihilate
address (verb and noun)	antarctic
adieu	apartheid
adult	apparatus
advertisement	appendicitis
aegis	applicable
aerate	appreciative
aerial	apricot
affidavit	apropos
agate	archives
agile	aria
aisle	arraign
albino	asexual
albumen	asparagus
alias	asthma
ally (noun and verb)	athlete
almond	athletics
alms	attaché

attacked
atypical
august (adjective)
aura
automation

automaton
auxiliary
aviation
awkward
azure

Careful study of whatever words you select from this list will introduce you to every important diacritical mark and indication of accent that you are likely to come across, no matter what word you later look up. Gaining this familiarity, and that alone, is the purpose of providing this list. As a conscientious student of pronunciation, you will necessarily make your own lists of pronunciation trouble spots and study them until you have mastered them thoroughly.

Swallowing the dictionary letter-by-letter is wasteful, and you are again urged not to attempt to improve your pronunciation by any such arbitrary method. Looking up words as you need to, however, and entering them after a period of time in your own word-book by letters of the alphabet is not a bad way to record findings. Here, for instance, is the record of one careful reader who found that over a period of two months he had encountered the following words beginning with *b,* the pronunciation of which caused him momentary difficulty.

bacilli
bade
bairn
barrage
bases (plural of *basis*)
bayou
benign
bestial
bicycle
bison

bosom
boudoir
bouillon
bourbon
bourgeoisie
bravado
brooch
buffet
bureaucracy
Byzantine

Any list of *b*-words that you make probably would differ markedly, because some of the words noted may give you no trouble or may be words for which you have no present or foreseeable need. The point is, however, that you should look up the words you *do* need, study them carefully, and perhaps note their pronunciations in a notebook of your own in which you record correct spelling, standard pronunciation(s), and varied meanings.

To gain some idea of where you stand in the matter of pronunciation and how long a road you have to travel toward mastery, check through the list that follows. The words were encountered in haphazard fashion in reading, in listening, and in personal use but are here listed alphabetically to facilitate your looking them up. The list consists of three hundred words, about each of which the following statements may be made: (1) it has caused numerous persons to mispronounce it; (2) it is a potentially useful word for a large number of people; (3) it usually has more than one acceptable ("standard") pronunciation. It will be interesting for you to match your pronunciation of each word with those provided in the dictionary you are using.

cabal	cognac
cache	combatant
cairn	concerto
camouflage	concord
candidate	conduit
caoutchouc	conifer
caramel	conjure
carburetor	consommé
cavalry	contemplative
cayenne	corps
centrifugal	corpse
cerebral	corsage
chaise	coterie
chary	coup
chassis	crescendo
chauffeur	curator
chiaroscuro	data
chic	debris
chiffon	debut
chocolate	debutante
clique	decadent
coadjutor	decedent
cobra	décolleté
cocoon	decorous

decorum
deign
demesne
demolition
depot
desert (noun and verb)
despicable
desultory
devotee
dexterous
diapason
diocesan
diphtheria
diphthong
disastrous
disputable
disputant
divan
dour
drama
drought
duplicate (noun and verb)
eccentric
economic
edict
effete
egregious
egress
elm
emendation
ensign
epicurean
epoch
equable
err
excise (noun and verb)
exemplary
exigency
exquisite

extrapolation
exude
eyrie
facade
facet
faucet
fetid
finance
financier
flaccid
flimsy
florid
flue
fogy
foible
forehead
forte
foulard
fourteen
fuchsia
fungicide
fusillade
futurism
gala
garish
genie
genuine
gibberish
giblet
gladioli
gratis
guinea
gunwale
halcyon
harass
heinous
hemoglobin
herculean
hiatus

hindrance

holocaust

hussar

hussy

ibis

imbroglio

imperturbable

impotent

impugn

indisputable

intestate

inveigle

irreparable

isolate

January

jewelry

jocose

jowl

juvenile

khaki

kiln

kilometer

kindergarten

knoll

laboratory

lamentable

leeward

legate

legume

leprechaun

lever

leverage

lewd

lichen

lingerie

liter

lithe

longevity

long-lived

machination

magi

malign

marquis

marquise

material

matériel

mauve

medicinal

menu

mien

minutiae

mischievous

mobile

municipal

naiad

naïve

naphtha

nauseous

necromancy

news

niche

nomenclature

nonpareil

noose

oasis

obdurate

obloquy

obsequies

occult (noun and adjective)

often

omega

onyx

orchid

orgy

padre

paean

panorama

papyrus

parabola
parliament
parvenu
pasteurize
pecan
penalize
phlegm
phthisic
pianist
piazza
piquant
poignant
porpoise
poultry
premier
premiere
presage
primer
process
prodigy
promulgate
protein
provost
psalm
ptomaine
pueblo
quaff
qualm
quasi
quay
quinine
rabies
ragout
rancid
ration
recess (noun and verb)
recitative
recondite
repertoire
research
respite

résumé
rigmarole
rodeo
rout
route
sachem
sachet
sacrilegious
saga
salmon
salve
scenic
schism
scythe
seine
seraglio
servile
silhouette
sinecure
slake
slough
soiree
solecism
squalor
status
suave
suit
suite
sycophant
syrup
taciturn
telepathy
testate
thyme
tomato
tout
travail
truculent
truths
turbine
umbrage

unctuous	vase
unguent	vaudeville
unison	waistcoat
usury	wassail
vagaries	wharf
valet	whelp
variegated	women

SUMMARY

The book you now hold in your hands deals with many topics, but it is possible that you think of it as a "grammar" book. The term *grammar*, however, covers a great deal. It is sometimes said to consist of three parts: *syntax, morphology,* and *phonology.* These big words need not frighten you. Syntax refers to the *structure of sentences,* the general subject matter of Part II of this volume. Morphology shows how roots, prefixes, suffixes, and inflections are put together to form the *shapes of words,* matters dealt with in Parts I, III, and V. Phonology is the subject matter of the section just treated, *the sound system* of our language. This section has tried to show how we use sound resources to give spoken form to words and sentences. In short, phonology deals with the grammar of speech.

Handling the grammar of speech is important. As has been indicated, it is possibly more important than any other division of grammar simply because it is a concern of nearly everyone during nearly every waking hour of every day. The only systematic way to tackle the problem is through careful use of a dictionary. The word *careful* involves all that you have just been reading: thorough study, knowledge of diacritical and accent marks, awareness of multiplicity of *standard* pronunciations of many words and phrases, and a use restricted to *individual* needs.

One thing you should never forget: the so-called authority of a dictionary is based solely upon the actual speech and writing of a community of what have been called "effective" citizens. As Professor Cabell Greet, a recognized authority, once wrote:

Without seeking to impair any citizen's right to be his own professor of English, we [the makers of dictionaries] look for what is national, contemporary, and reputable. This is our standard of correctness. . . .

EXERCISES

The exercises that follow are an inadequate substitute for methods of study suggested in preceding pages, but you may have become deeply interested in pronunciation. If you wish to become skilled in using a dictionary as a means of thorough understanding of pronunciation, doing the drills that follow will develop considerable expertise and possibly provide some entertainment.

1. Each of the following words has two or more pronunciations. What does each pronunciation indicate about the meaning of the word and its part(s) of speech?

address   object

appropriate   present

compound   produce

contest   progress

contrast   protest

increase   rebel

insert   record

insult   refuse

minute   subject

moderate   transfer

2. Here is a list of "pronouncing words." What is the correct spelling of each? (The *schwa* (ə), a phonetic symbol to represent an indeterminate sound in some unstressed syllables, is used here. Your dictionary may use the schwa or some other symbol to represent, for example, the sound of *a* in *alone* or *sofa*; the sound of *u* in *circus*, etc. You should become familiar with this phonetic symbol, however, because nearly all modern dictionaries employ it.)

ak′ wē es   rōō mə tiz′ əm

bēr   sī kol′ə jē

klōz   târ

doś əl   hə bich′ ōō əl

fik′ əl   in′ tə mə sē

jí ənt   nī

kwôr′ tər   noś tik

kwik   ō pak′

paś ij   rīt
vegí tə bəl   məshē′ nərē

3. What is a standard pronunciation(s) of each of the following
geographical terms?

Addis Ababa	Guantanamo
Aleutian	Honolulu
Arkansas	Kilimanjaro
Assisi	Laos
Attu	Marseilles
Auckland	Monaco
Austerlitz	Oahu
Beaufort	Pompeii
Bucharest	Rio de Janiero
Cannes	Riviera
Cappadocia	Saigon
Caribbean	San Juan
Cheyenne	Sault Ste. Marie
Chihuahua	Sverdlovsk
Cinque Ports	Thames
Dolomites	Thermopylae
Dunsinane	Ticonderoga
Ecuador	Tientsin
Eire	Vietnam
Gibraltar	Worcester

4. What is the acceptable pronunciation (or pronunciations) of
each of the following proper names? (While you are working
with your dictionary, why not learn something else about each
individual named?)

Amundsen	Chou En-lai
Aquinas	Cortes
Audubon	Daguerre
Benes	Euripides
Botticelli	Galileo
Brueghel	Garibaldi
Charlemagne	Ho Chi Minh

Ingres
Kenyatta
Khrushchev
Kierkegaard
Liszt
Mao Tse-tung
Michelangelo
Oglethorpe
Paracelsus
Phyfe
Plautus
Puccini
Renoir

Rilke
Robespierre
Rousseau
Rubens
Socrates
Tacitus
Tagore
Tecumseh
Thant
Thucydides
Tschaikovsky
Van Gogh
Velazquez

5. Some of the following words and phrases have been "naturalized" into English and some have not. What is a standard pronunciation of each?

ad infinitum
agenda
à la carte
amigo
annus mirabilis
argot
au courant
au naturel
bona fide
chaise longue
chef d'oeuvre
coup de grace
cul de sac
de jure
dolce far niente
ersatz
ex officio
faux pas
habeas corpus
imprimatur

laissez faire
noblesse oblige
non sequitur
par excellence
parfait
pièce de résistance
prima facie
raison d'être
savoir faire
sine die
sine qua non
sotto voce
status quo
table d'hôte
vice versa
visa
Wanderlust
Weltpolitik
Weltschmerz
Zeitgeist

Appendix

Sentence Diagraming

Appendix
Sentence Diagraming

The analysis of a sentence is given on page 275. To reinforce your knowledge of grammar and sentence structure, you may wish to resort to the visual device known as diagraming. This is a mechanical method of identifying words as parts of speech, of identifying phrases and clauses, and of indicating the uses of these elements in a sentence. Diagraming is merely a form of sentence analysis, a graphic means involving the use of lines: horizontal, perpendicular, slanting, curved, and dotted.

Please remember that diagraming is a *means*, not an end in itself. Some authorities feel that it is of little value, but its graphic form may be of value to some students. What follows is a brief introduction to a system once widely used in learning the structure of the English sentence.

The parts of a sentence are put on lines in the positions indicated in the following skeleton diagram. The three most important parts of the sentence (subject, predicate, object) are usually put on a horizontal line; any modifiers are appropriately placed on lines underneath.

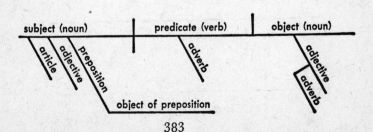

Filled in, such a diagramed sentence might read:

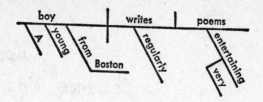

The simple subject, the simple predicate, the direct object, the object complement, the predicate noun (or pronoun), and the predicate adjective are written on the main horizontal line. (If you have forgotten the meaning of these terms, look up each one at its appropriate alphabetical position in the preceding pages of this book.) Subject and predicate are separated by a perpendicular line intersecting the horizontal line. The direct object is separated from the verb by a short perpendicular line extending up from the horizontal line. The object complement, the predicate noun or pronoun, or the predicate adjective is set off by a short slanting line extending to the left from the horizontal line. The following diagrams illustrate the principles just stated and show how simple sentences are diagramed:

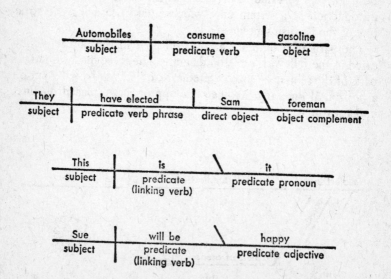

When conjunctions are used, dashes or dotted lines (usually perpendicular) are used to join, and the conjunction is written along or across such a line. Here is one method of diagraming a simple sentence with a compound subject, compound predicate, and compound object:

Boys and girls read or write newspapers and magazines.

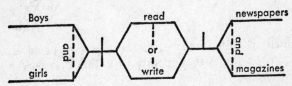

Slanting lines below the horizontal line are used for adverbial and adjectival modifiers. Each adverb and adjective is placed on a separate line:

The old woman slowly and painfully removed her shoes.

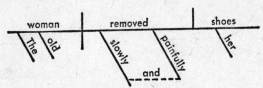

An adverb modifying an adjective or another adverb is written on an additional slanting line (or a stair-step line):

The unusually feeble man moved very slowly.

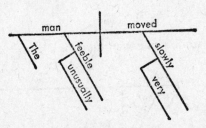

Prepositional phrases are attached below the words they modify by a slanting line for the preposition and a horizontal line for the object of the preposition:

A teammate of my brother gave her the ball with the battered cover.

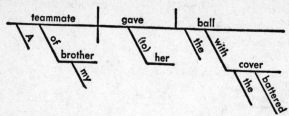

Participial and infinitive phrases (as adjectives or adverbs) are attached to the words they modify by a line that curves into a horizontal one:

The boy wearing the dark suit is the boy to be nominated for secretary.

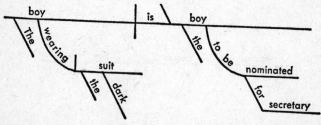

A gerund phrase or an infinitive phrase used as a noun is placed on a horizontal line supported by a vertical line. This vertical line is placed to indicate whether the phrase is used as a subject, object, etc. A noun clause or an infinitive "clause" is similarly supported.

Gerund phrase as subject:

Occasionally earning an honest dollar is a worthy aim.

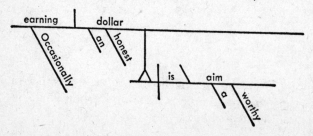

Infinitive phrase as predicate noun:

A goal worthy to be sought by everyone is gladly to forgive your enemies.

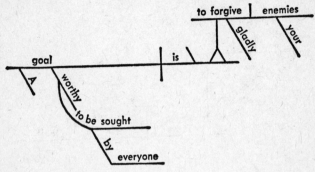

Infinitive "clause":

Bill asked me to lend him my car.

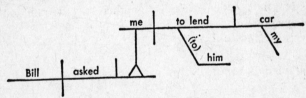

Noun clause as (1) subject and (2) object:

1. *What you paid has appalled me.*
2. *Henry stated that he had paid his obligations promptly*

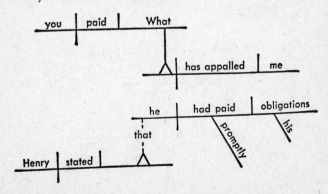

Absolute phrases are similarly placed on a vertically supported line. Such phrases, however, are usually enclosed in brackets to reveal the fact that they have no actual close relationship to any other part of the sentence:

Our meal being finished, we left the table.

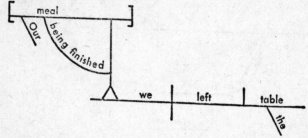

A vertical dotted line may be used to link an adjective clause to the noun (substantive) modified. Vertical lines are also used to relate adverbial clauses to the proper word in the main clause and to link one independent clause to another. Any conjunction used is written across the dotted line.

Adjective clause:

I met a man whom I dislike.

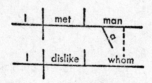

Adverbial clause:

We lost the order because we had the poorer product.

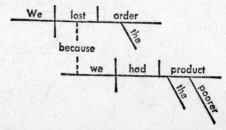

A compound sentence is diagramed much as are two or more simple sentences:

I like books but Janet prefers movie magazines.

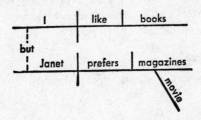

Various other situations can, and do, arise in sentence structure. However, the examples given above cover the principal kinds of sentence structure and word order, and variations of the material given can be adapted to fit unusual situations—such as inverted or transposed word order, nouns in direct address, and the like. After all, diagraming is only a mechanical device, a sort of game. Don't take it seriously unless it really helps you to a mastery of the sentence.

Perhaps this method of showing relationships in *linear* fashion does not appeal to you. If you wish to diagram in some other way, you can place each word in a sentence in a box—that is, surrounded by lines—and come up with a set of boxes, each enclosed in another box except the last, which encloses the entire sentence.

Still another method of diagraming is done by using lines that branch like the limbs of a tree. In "tree" diagraming, the first branching is from the sentence (S) to the subject (noun or noun phrase, N or NP) and the predicate (verb or verb phrase, V or VP). Further branchings reveal as many levels and kinds of structural relationships as the sentence to be diagramed involves.

The simplest tree diagram is of such a two-word sentence as "Dogs bark." Here is how it would be diagramed in tree form:

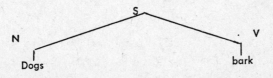

If the sentence were "The small black dogs bark loudly," then the label N (for noun) would become NP (noun phrase) and would represent "The small black dogs." Similarly, V (for verb) would become VP (for verb phrase) and would represent "bark loudly." The words are written out in their usual order below each final branch; their grammatical construction (or part of speech) is labeled at the point at which branching occurs. This point is called a *node*.

In tree diagraming, the sentence on page 384, "They have elected Sam foreman," would appear like this:

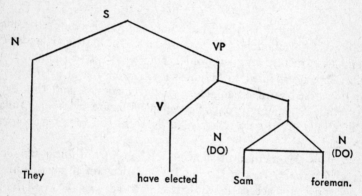

In this diagram, the sentence consists of a noun (N)—really a pronoun—and a verb phrase (VP). The latter contains both a direct object (DO) and an object complement (also DO), both referring to the same person. Thus the two are joined by a horizontal line.

Whether you diagram with lines, boxes, or trees, remember that "fun and games" are less important than learning to write with clearness, effectiveness, and appropriateness.

Index